FOR ORGANS, PIANOS & ELECTRONIC KEYBOARDS

E•Z PLAY® TODAY

263

THE GREAT IRISH SONGBOOK

ISBN-13: 978-1-4234-2644-8
ISBN-10: 1-4234-2644-4

HAL•LEONARD® CORPORATION

7777 W. BLUEMOUND RD. P.O. BOX 13819 MILWAUKEE, WI 53213

In Australia Contact:
Hal Leonard Australia Pty. Ltd.
4 Lentara Court
Cheltenham, Victoria, 3192 Australia
Email: ausadmin@halleonard.com

Visit Hal Leonard Online at
www.halleonard.com

Arthur McBride

Registration 1
Rhythm: Waltz

Traditional Irish Folk Song

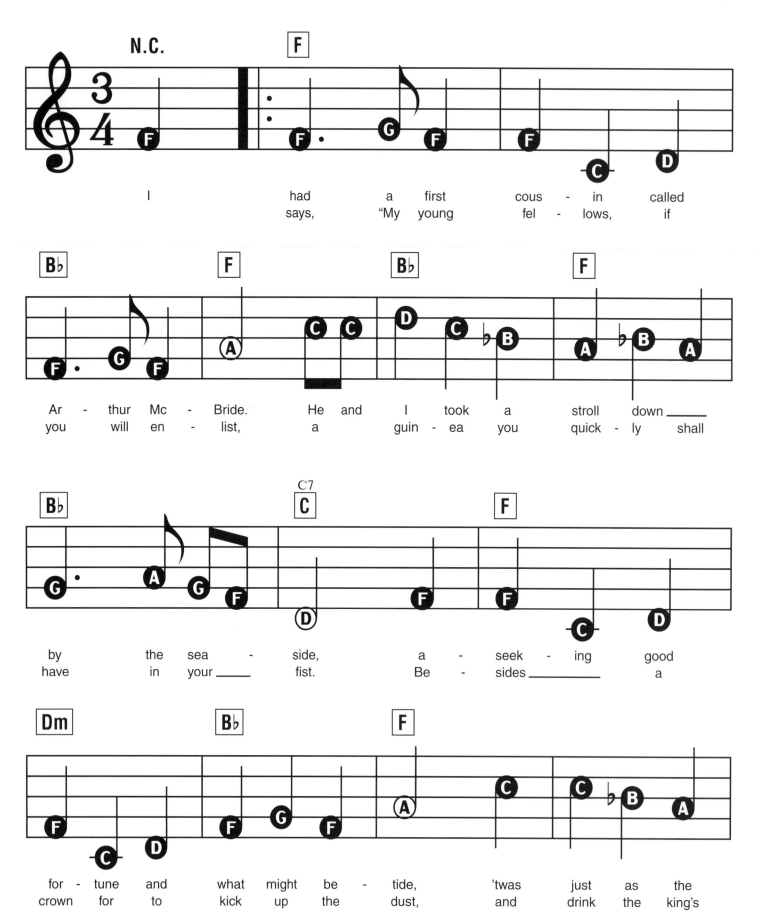

5

Avondale

Registration 2
Rhythm: Ballad or Fox Trot

Traditional Irish Folk Song

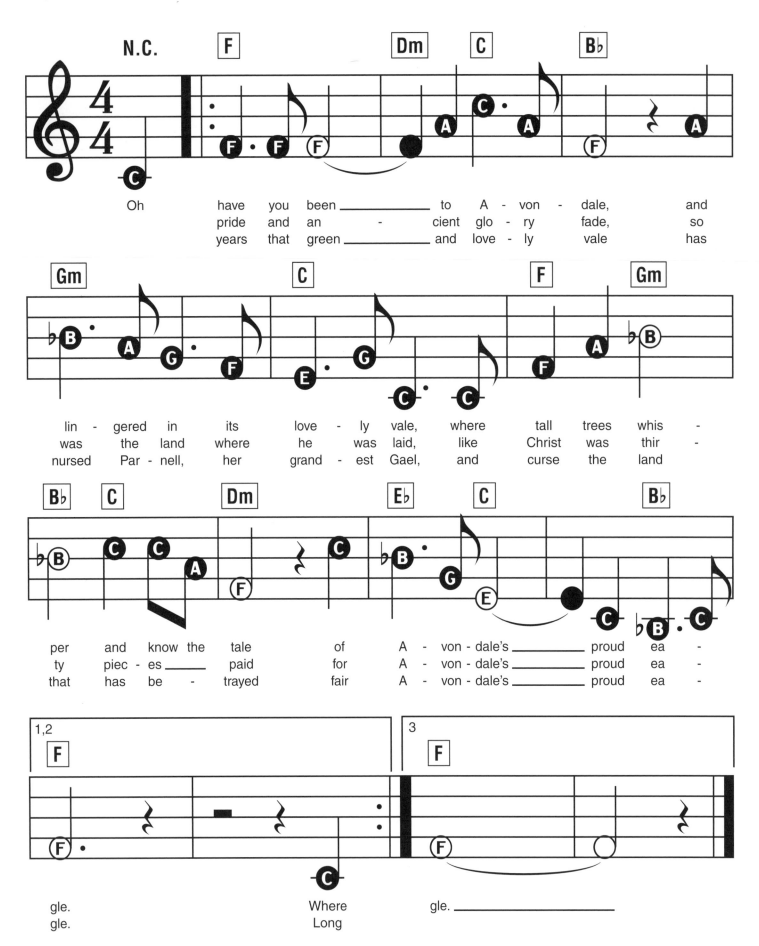

The Banks of My Own Lovely Lee

Registration 1
Rhythm Waltz

Traditional Irish Folk Song

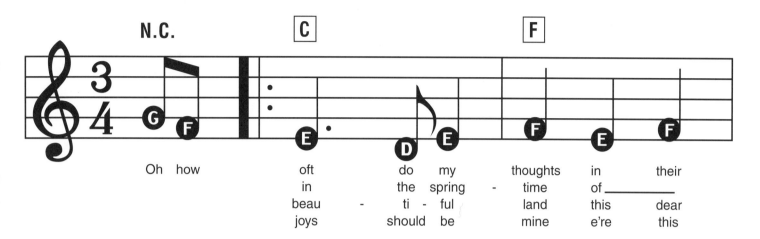

Oh how   oft   do my   thoughts   in   their
in   the spring - time   of _____
beau - ti - ful   land   this   dear
joys   should be   mine   e're   this

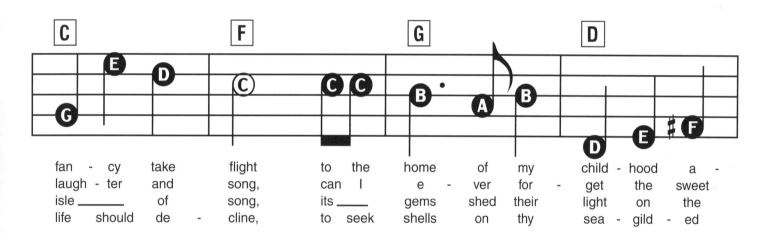

fan - cy   take   flight   to the   home   of   my   child - hood   a -
laugh - ter   and   song,   can I   e - ver   for - get   the   sweet
isle _____ of   song,   its _____ gems   shed   their   light   on   the
life   should de - cline,   to seek   shells   on   thy   sea - gild - ed

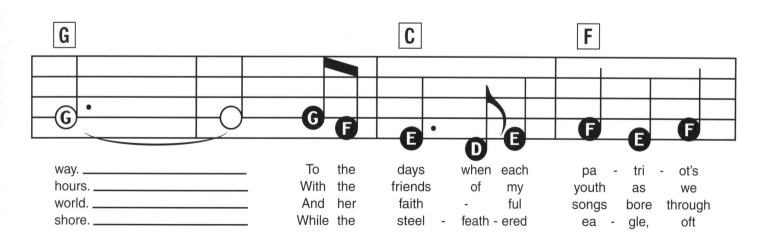

way. _____ To the   days   when each   pa - tri - ot's
hours. _____ With the   friends   of   my   youth   as   we
world. _____ And her   faith - ful   songs   bore   through
shore. _____ While the   steel - feath - ered   ea - gle,   oft

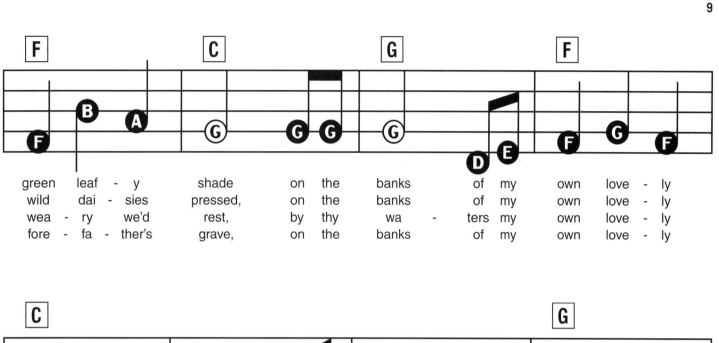

green leaf - y   shade   on   the   banks   of   my   own   love - ly
wild   dai - sies   pressed,   on   the   banks   of   my   own   love - ly
wea - ry   we'd   rest,   by   thy   wa - ters   my   own   love - ly
fore - fa - ther's grave,   on   the   banks   of   my   own   love - ly

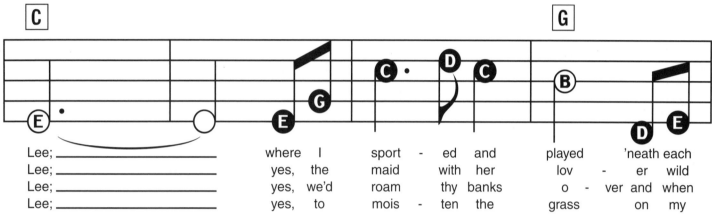

Lee; _____   where I   sport - ed and   played   'neath each
Lee; _____   yes, the   maid   with her   lov - er   wild
Lee; _____   yes, we'd roam   thy banks o - ver and when
Lee; _____   yes, to   mois - ten the   grass   on my

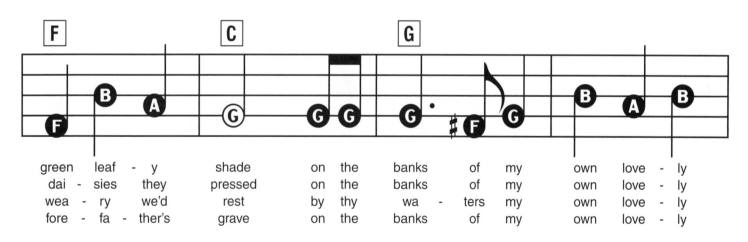

green leaf - y   shade   on   the   banks   of   my   own   love - ly
dai - sies   they   pressed   on   the   banks   of   my   own   love - ly
wea - ry   we'd   rest   by   thy   wa - ters my   own   love - ly
fore - fa - ther's grave   on   the   banks   of   my   own   love - ly

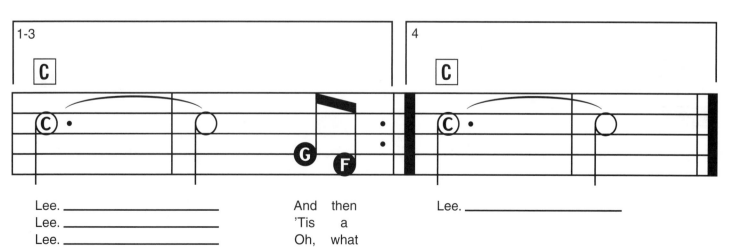

Lee. _____   And then   Lee. _____
Lee. _____   'Tis a
Lee. _____   Oh, what

The Banks of Claudy

Registration 8
Rhythm: Waltz

Traditional Irish Folk Song

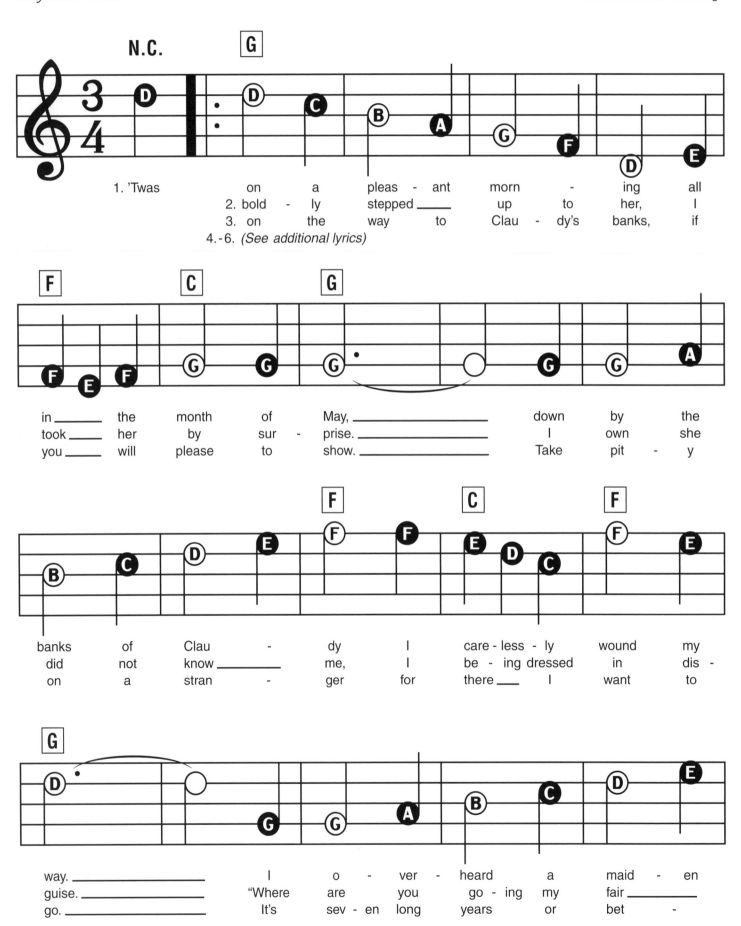

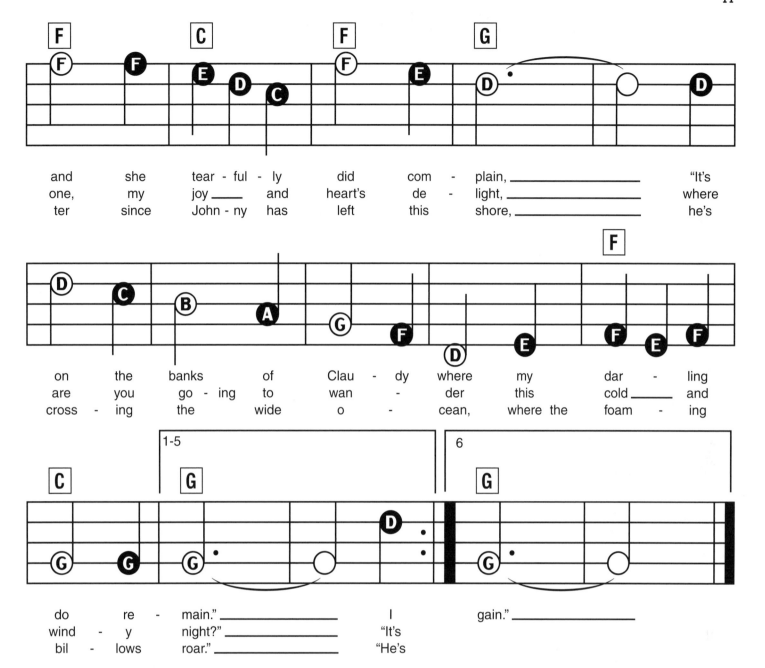

and   she   tear - ful - ly   did   com - plain, _____   "It's
one,   my   joy ___ and   heart's   de - light, _____   where
ter   since   John - ny has   left   this   shore, _____   he's

on   the   banks   of   Clau - dy where   my   dar - ling
are   you   go - ing   to   wan -   der   this   cold ___ and
cross - ing   the   wide   o -   cean,   where the foam - ing

do   re - main." _____   I   gain." _____
wind -   y   night?" _____   "It's
bil -   lows   roar." _____   "He's

Additional Lyrics

4. "He's crossing the wide ocean for honour and for fame
   His ship's been wrecked so I've been told down on the Spanish Main."
   "It's on the banks of Claudy fair maiden whereon you stand
   Now don't you believe young Johnny, for he's a false young man."

5. Now when she heard this dreadful news she fell into despair
   For the wringing of her tender hands and the tearing of her hair,
   "If Johnny be drowned no man alive I'll take
   Through lonesome glens and valleys I'll wander for his sake."

6. Now when he saw her loyalty no longer could he stand
   He fell into her arms saying, "Betsy, I'm the man."
   Saying, "Betsy, I'm the young man who caused you all the pain
   And since we've met on Claudy's banks we'll never part again."

Banna Strand

Registration 8
Rhythm: Waltz

Traditional Irish Folk Song

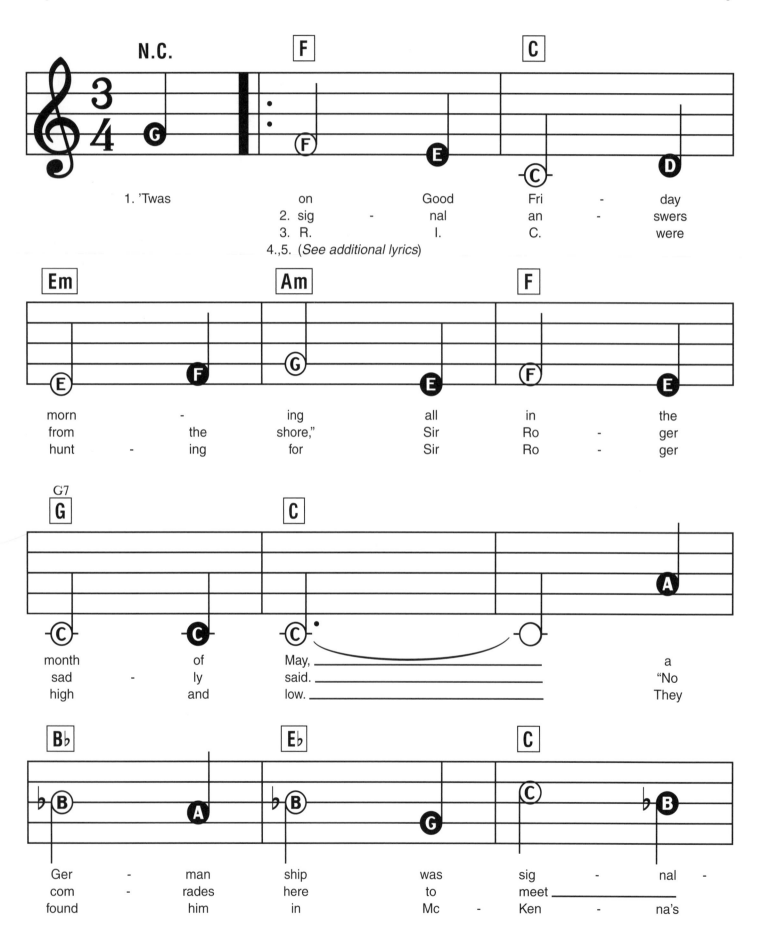

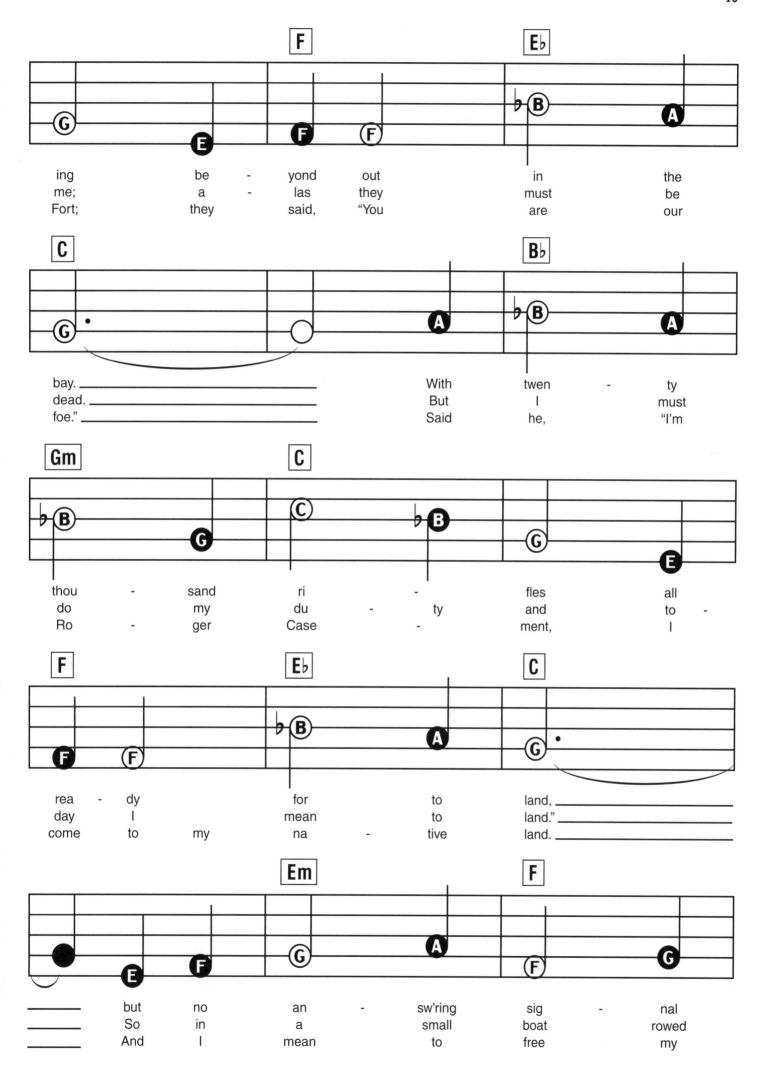

14

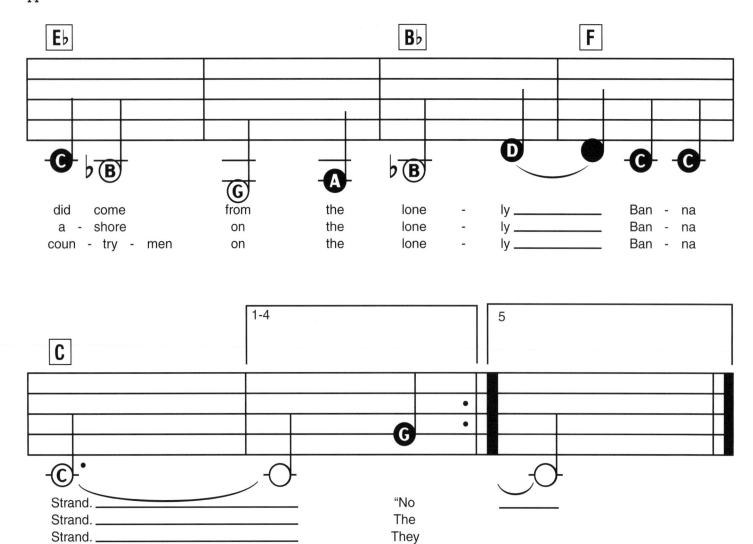

did   come   from   the   lone - ly _____ Ban - na
a - shore   on   the   lone - ly _____ Ban - na
coun - try - men   on   the   lone - ly _____ Ban - na

Strand. _____ "No
Strand. _____ The
Strand. _____ They

Additional Lyrics

4. They took Sir Roger prisoner and sailed to London Town,
   And in the Tower they locked him up; a traitor to the Crown.
   Said he, "I am no traitor," but on trial he had to stand,
   For bringing German rifles to the lonely Banna Strand.

5. 'Twas in an English prison that they led him to his death.
   "I'm dying for my country," he said with his last breath.
   They buried him in British soil far from his native land,
   And the wild waves sang his requiem on the Banna Strand.

Bold Fenian Men

Registration 4
Rhythm: Fox Trot

Traditional Irish Melody
Words by M. Scanlan

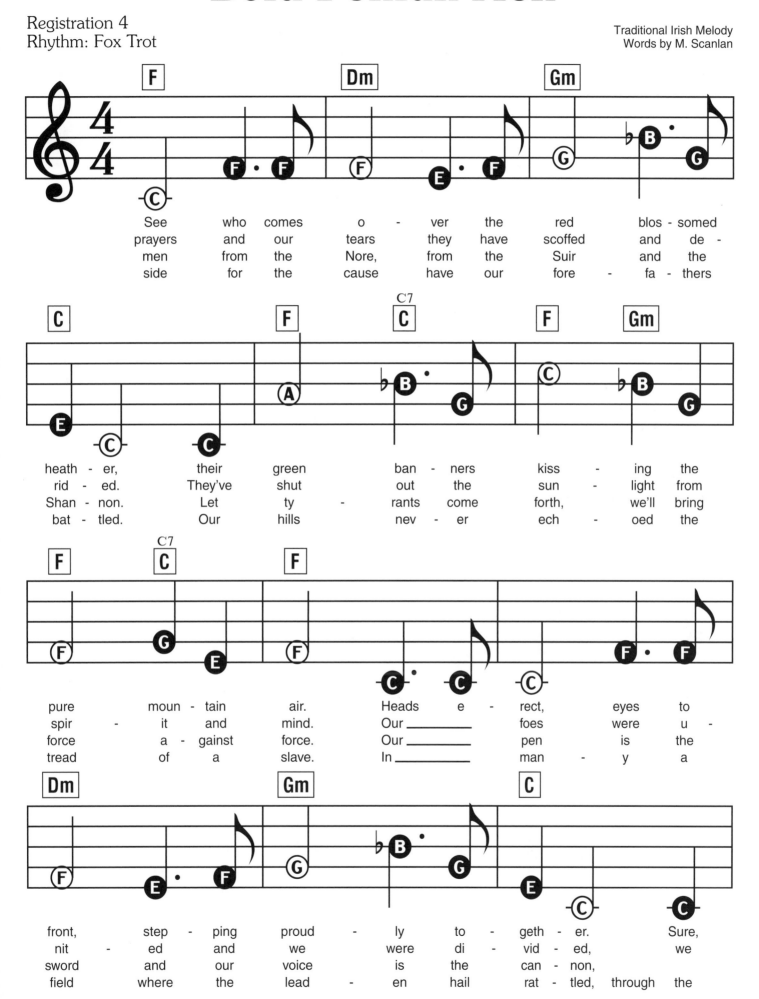

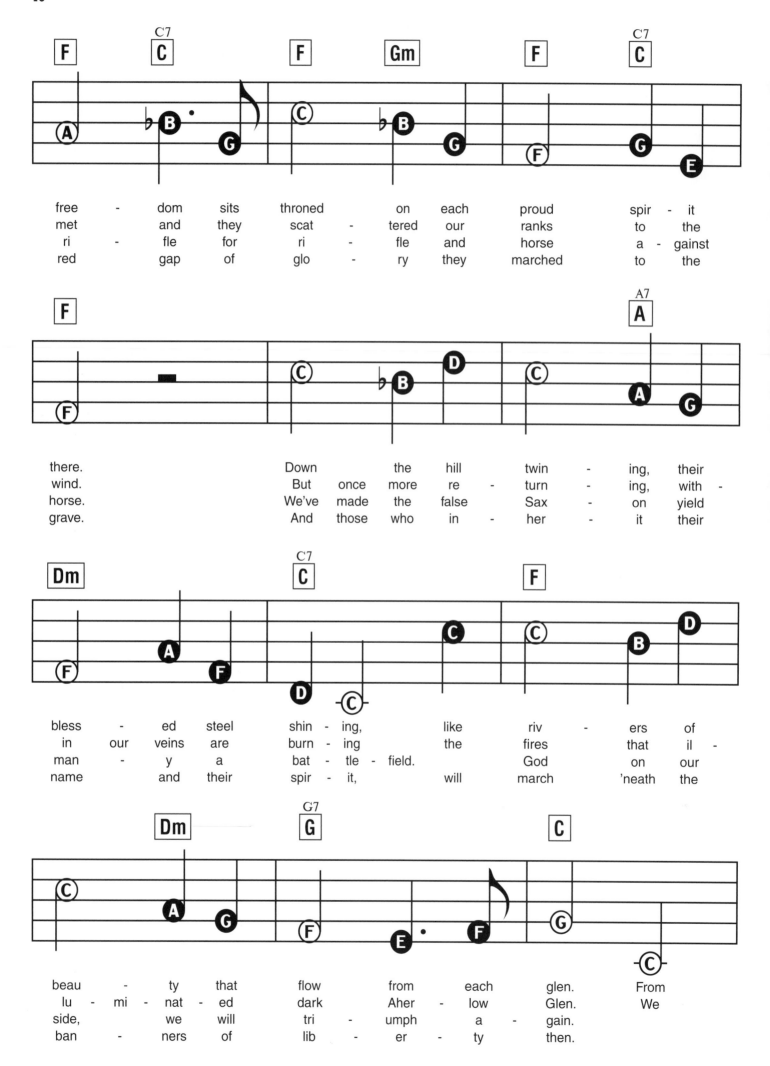

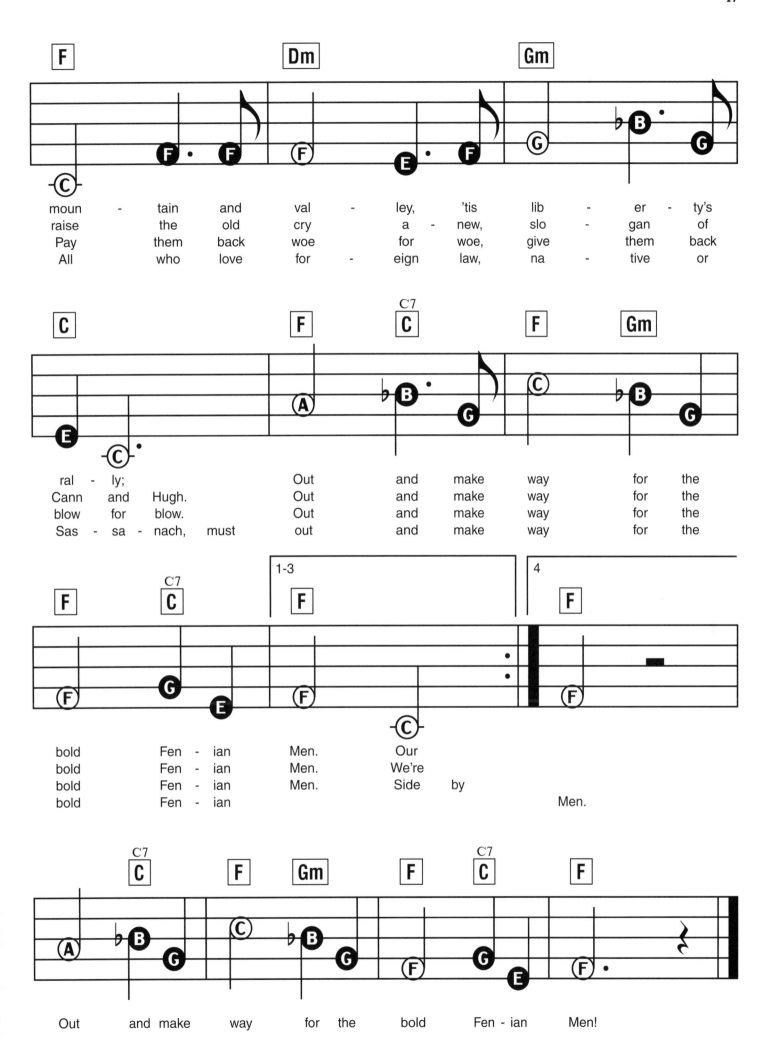

The Bard of Armagh

Registration 1
Rhythm: Waltz

Traditional Irish Folk Song

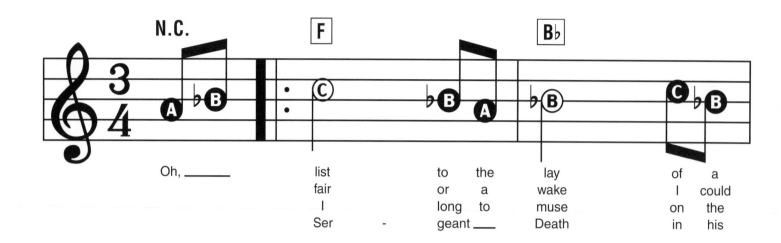

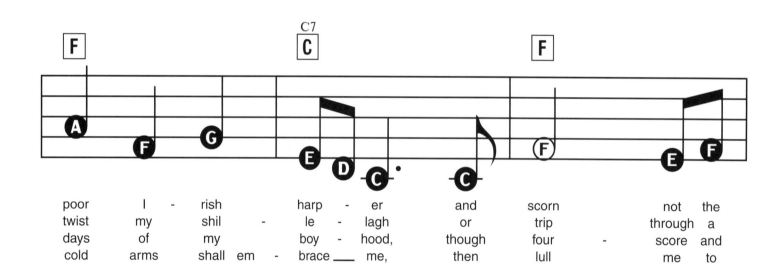

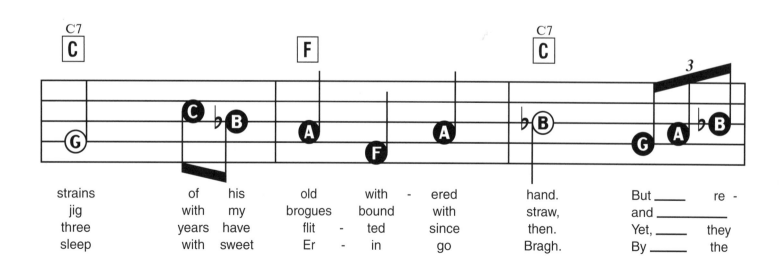

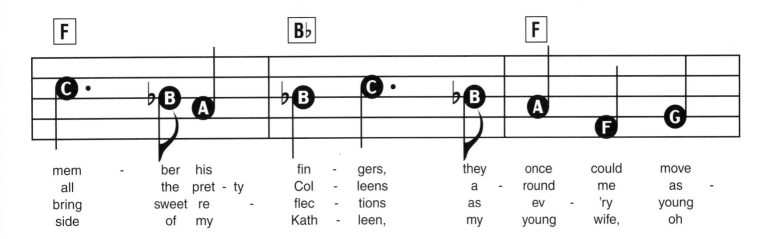

F · · · · Bb · · · F

mem - ber his fin - gers, they once could move
all the pret - ty Col - leens a - round me as -
bring sweet re - flec - tions as ev - 'ry young
side of my Kath - leen, my young wife, oh

C7
C · · · Dm

sharp - er to _____ raise up the
sem - bled loved ___ their bold Phe - lim
joy _____ should, for ____ the mer - ry - heart - ed
place ____ me, then ___ for - get Phe - lim

C7
C F 1-3

mem - 'ry of his dear na - tive land.
Bra - dy, the _____ bard of Ar - magh.
boys _____ make the best of old men.
Bra - dy the _____ bard of Ar -

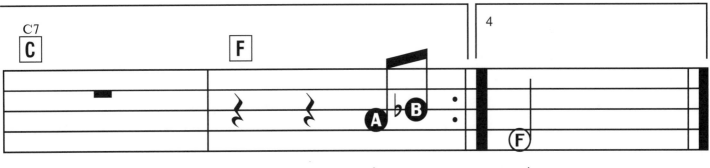

C7
C F 4

At a magh.
Oh, how
And when

Believe Me, If All Those Endearing Young Charms

Registration 3
Rhythm: Waltz

Words and Music by
Thomas Moore

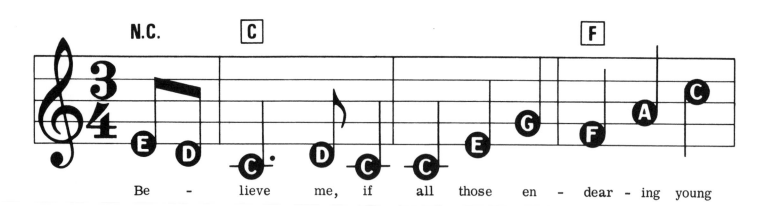

Be - lieve me, if all those en - dear - ing young

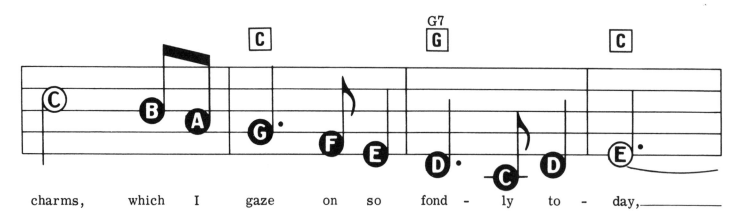

charms, which I gaze on so fond - ly to - day,_____

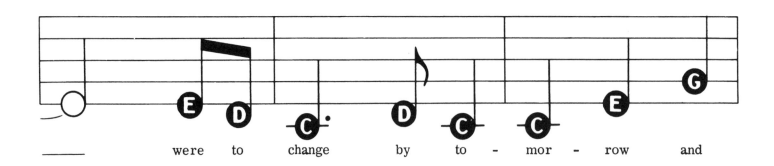

_____ were to change by to - mor - row and

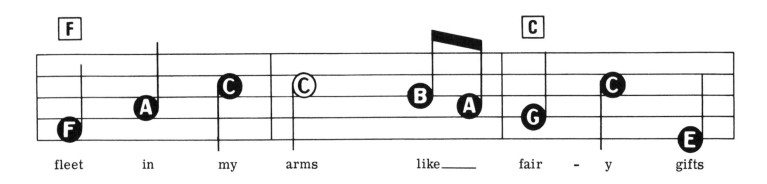

fleet in my arms like_____ fair - y gifts

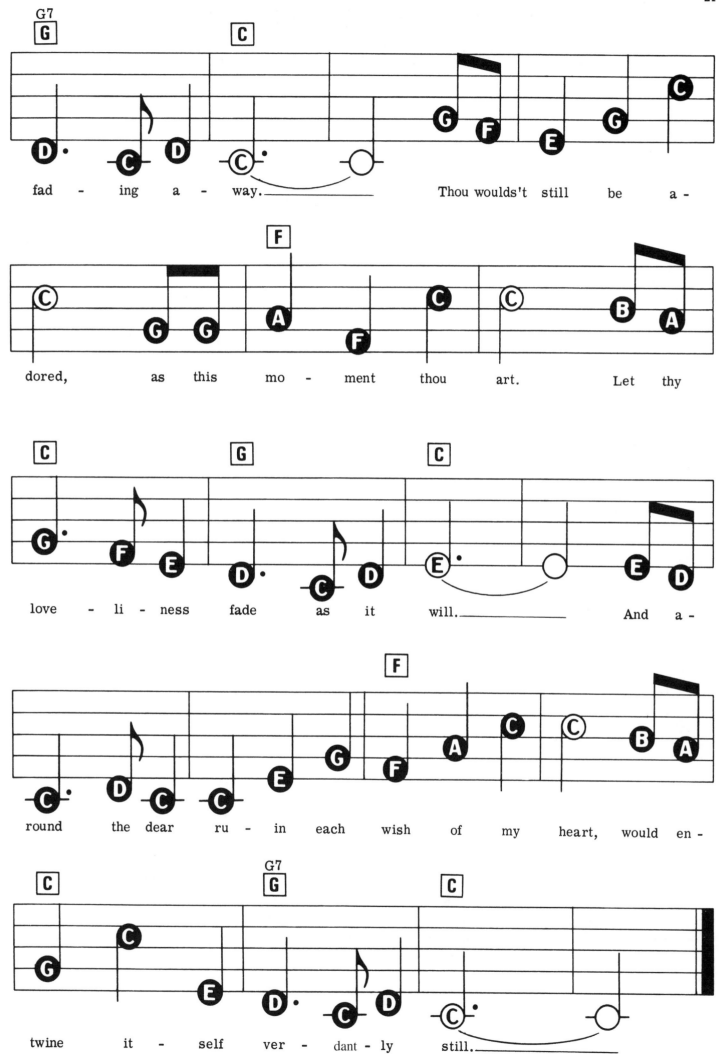

Black Velvet Band

Registration 8
Rhythm: Waltz

Traditional Irish Folk Song

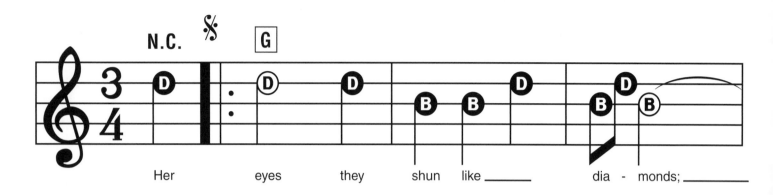

Her eyes they shun like ____ dia - monds; ____

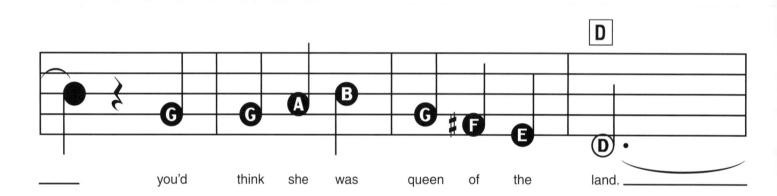

____ you'd think she was queen of the land. ____

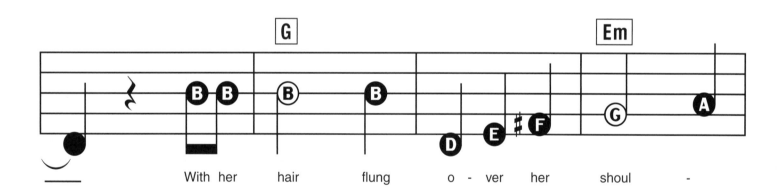

____ With her hair flung o - ver her shoul -

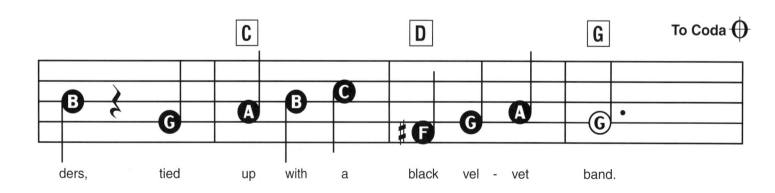

ders, tied up with a black vel - vet band.

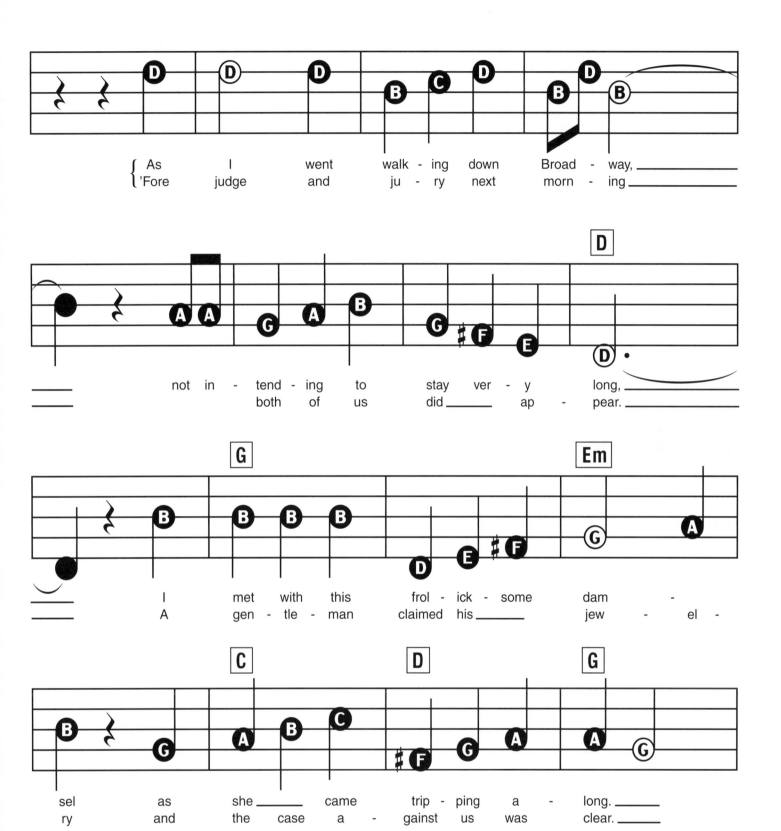

As | I | went | walk - ing down | Broad - way, _____
'Fore | judge | and | ju - ry next | morn - ing _____

_____ | not in - tend - ing | to | stay ver - y | long, _____
_____ | both | of | us | did _____ ap - pear. _____

_____ | I | met with this | frol - ick - some | dam -
_____ | A | gen - tle - man | claimed his _____ | jew - el -

sel | as | she _____ came | trip - ping a - | long. _____
ry | and | the | case a - | gainst us was | clear. _____

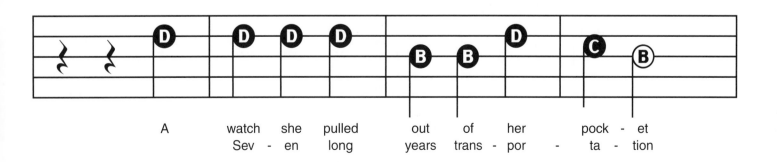

A | watch she pulled | out of her | pock - et
Sev - en long | years trans - por - | ta - tion

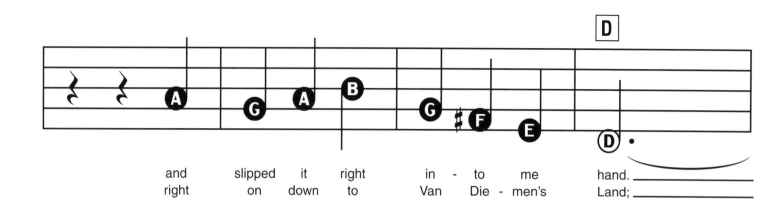

and slipped it right in - to me hand. _____
right on down to Van Die - men's Land; _____

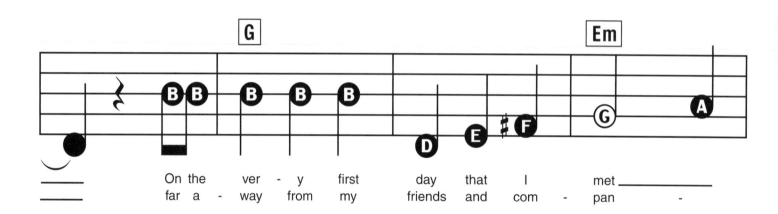

_____ On the ver - y first day that I met _____
_____ far a - way from my friends and com - pan -

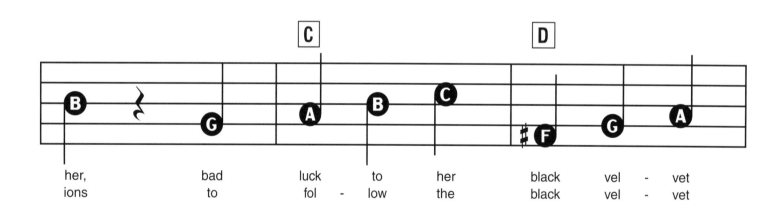

her, bad luck to her the black vel - vet
ions to fol - low the black vel - vet

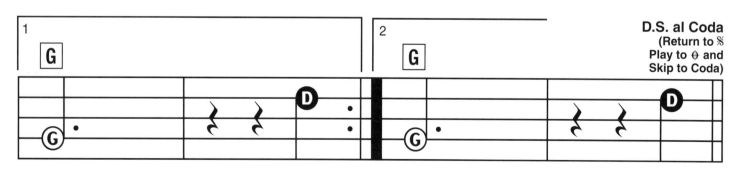

D.S. al Coda
(Return to %
Play to ⊕ and
Skip to Coda)

band. Her band. Her

CODA

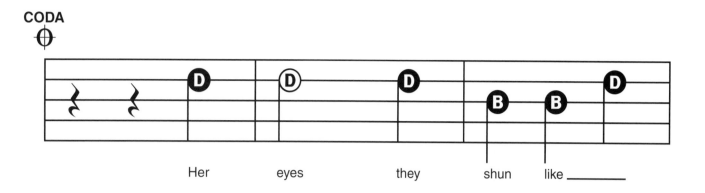

Her eyes they shun like _____

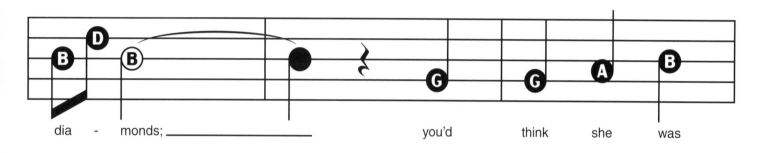

dia - monds; _____ you'd think she was

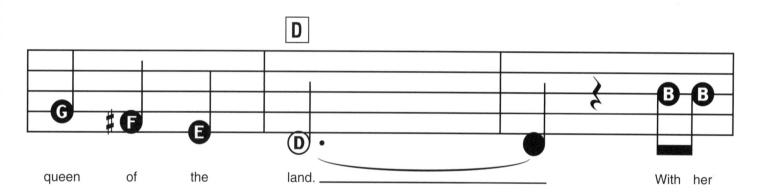

queen of the land. _____ With her

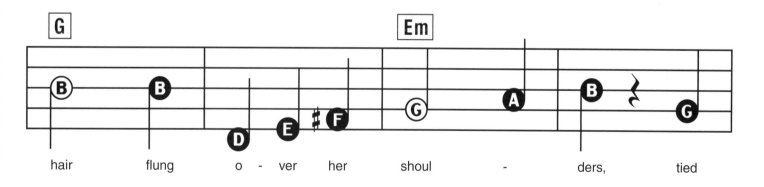

hair flung o - ver her shoul - ders, tied

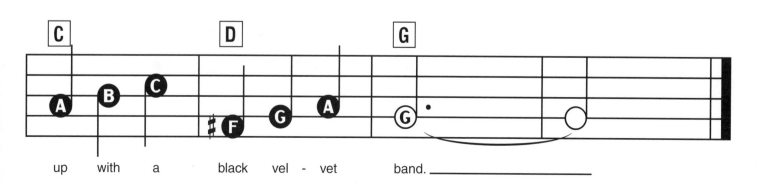

up with a black vel - vet band. _____

The Bold Tenant Farmer

Registration 7
Rhythm: 6/8 March or Jig/Gigue

Traditional Irish Folk Song

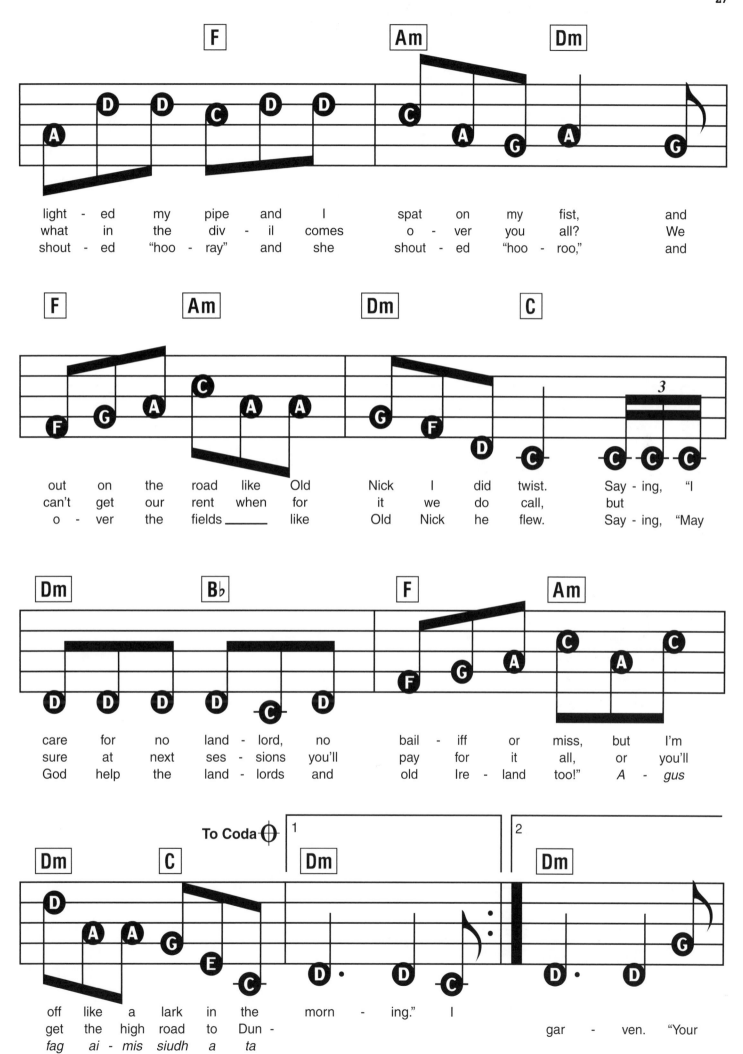

28

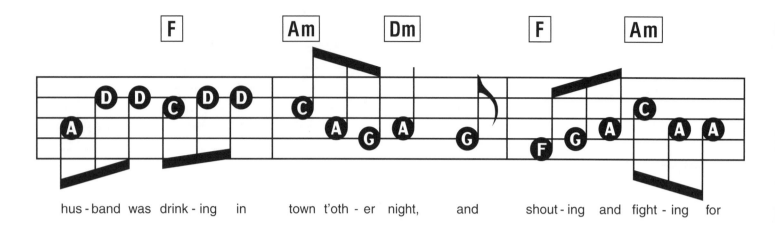

hus-band was drink-ing in town t'oth-er night, and shout-ing and fight-ing for

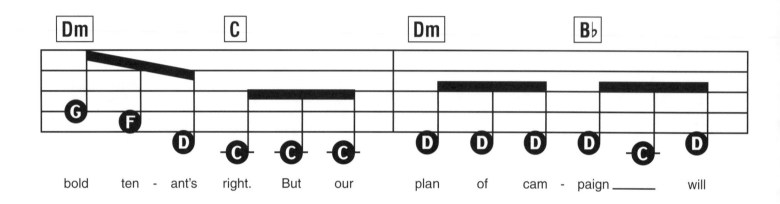

bold ten - ant's right. But our plan of cam - paign _____ will

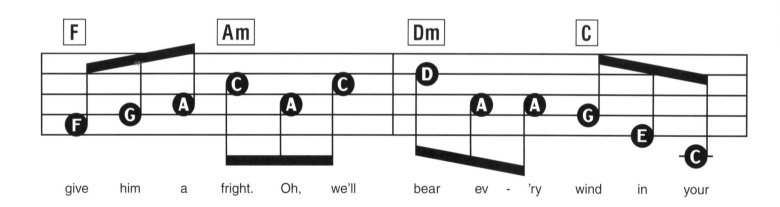

give him a fright. Oh, we'll bear ev - 'ry wind in your

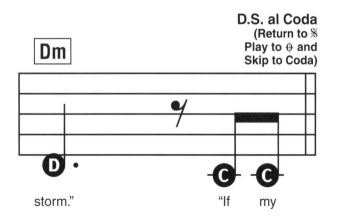

storm." "If my

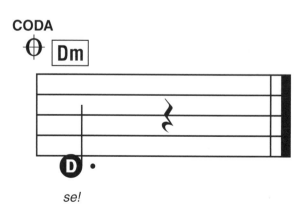

se!

Botany Bay

Registration 1
Rhythm: Waltz

Folk Song

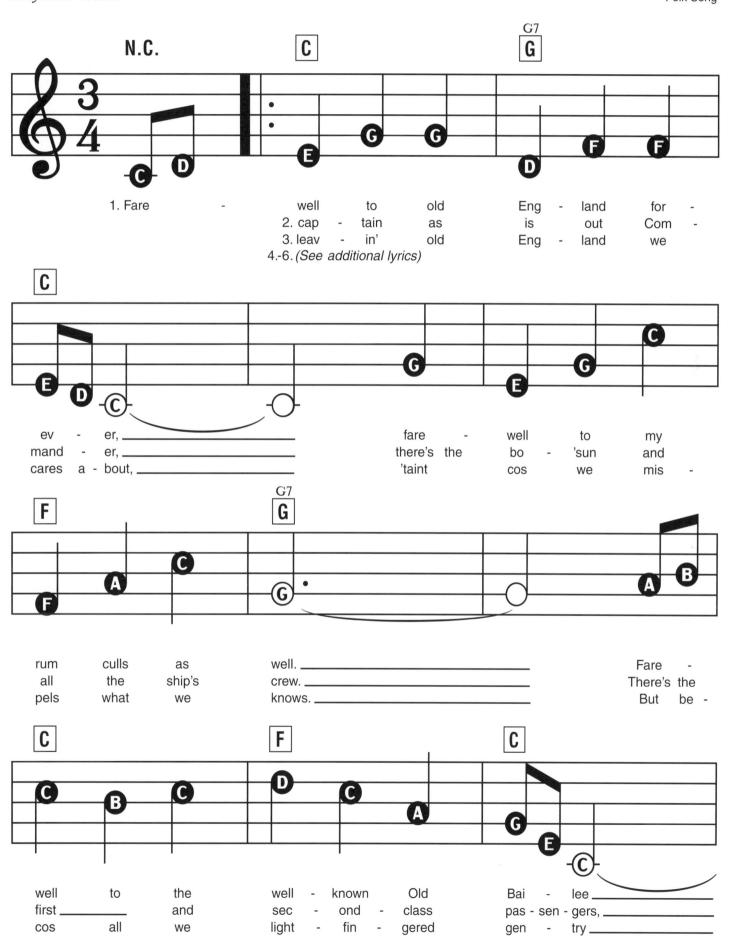

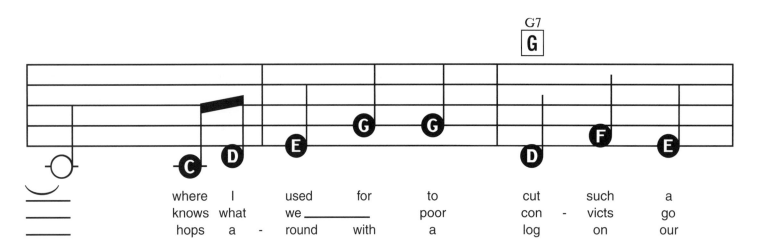

where I used for to cut such a
knows what we _____ poor con - victs go
hops a - round with a log on our

Refrain

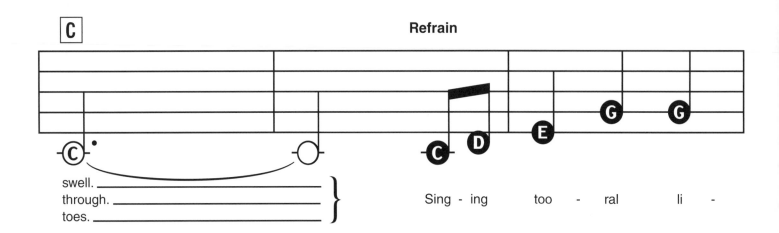

swell. _____
through. _____
toes. _____

Sing - ing too - ral li -

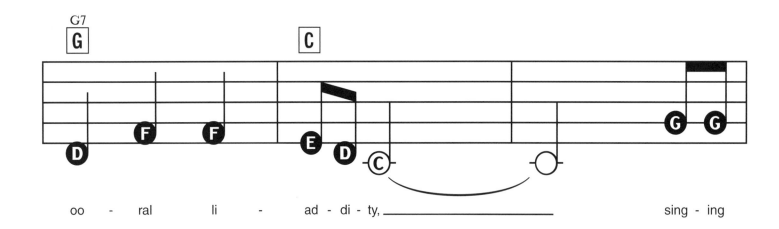

oo - ral li - ad - di - ty, _____ sing - ing

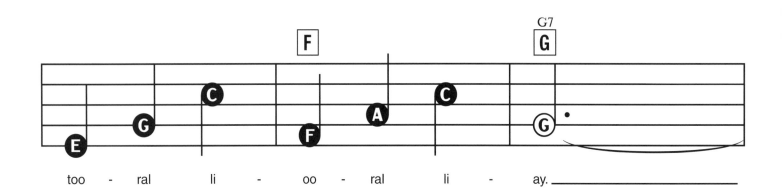

too - ral li - oo - ral li - ay. _____

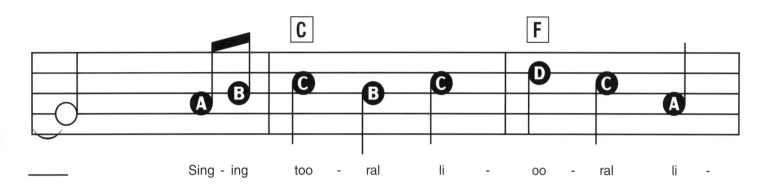

Sing - ing too - ral li - oo - ral li -

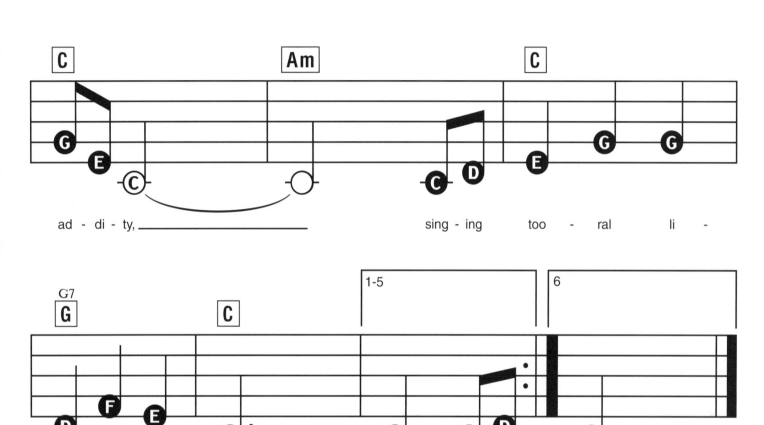

ad - di - ty, _____ sing - ing too - ral li -

oo - ral li - ay. _____

{ There's the
'Taint ____
For ____

Additional Lyrics

4. For seven long years I'll be staying here,
For seven long years and a day.
For meeting a cove in an area
And taking his ticker away.
Refrain

5. Oh, had I the wings of a turtledove!
I'd soar on my pinions so high.
Slap bang to the arms of my Polly love,
And in her sweet presence I'd die.
Refrain

6. Now, all my young Dookies and Duchesses,
Take warning from what I've to say.
Mind all is your own as you touchesses,
Or you'll find us in Botany Bay.
Refrain

The Bonny Boy

Registration 2
Rhythm: Fox Trot

Traditional Irish Folk Song

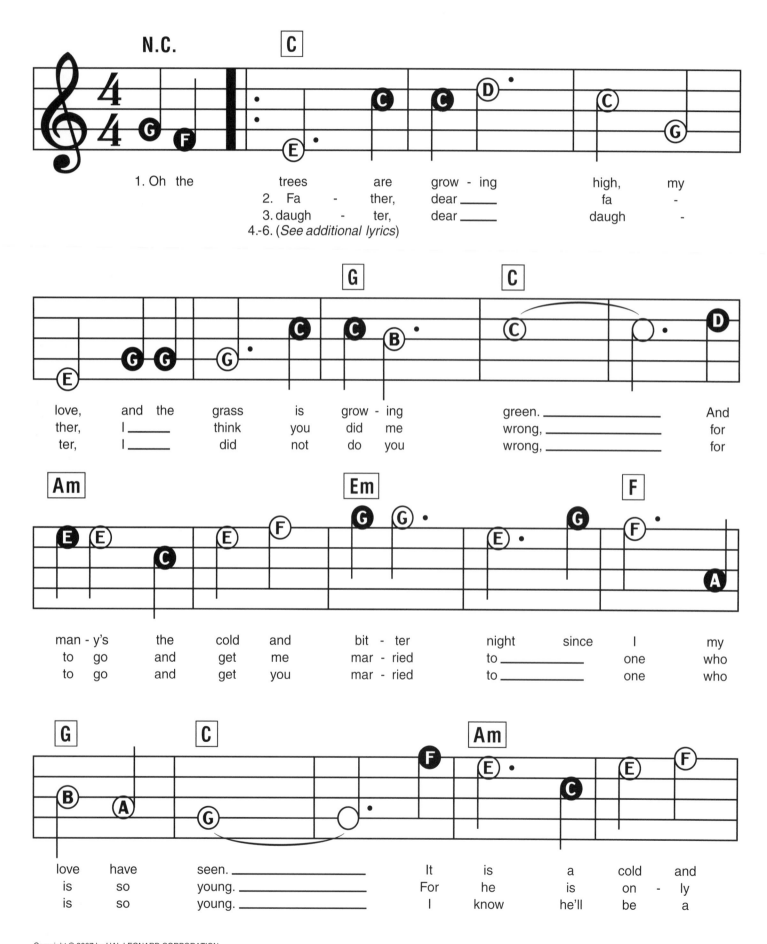

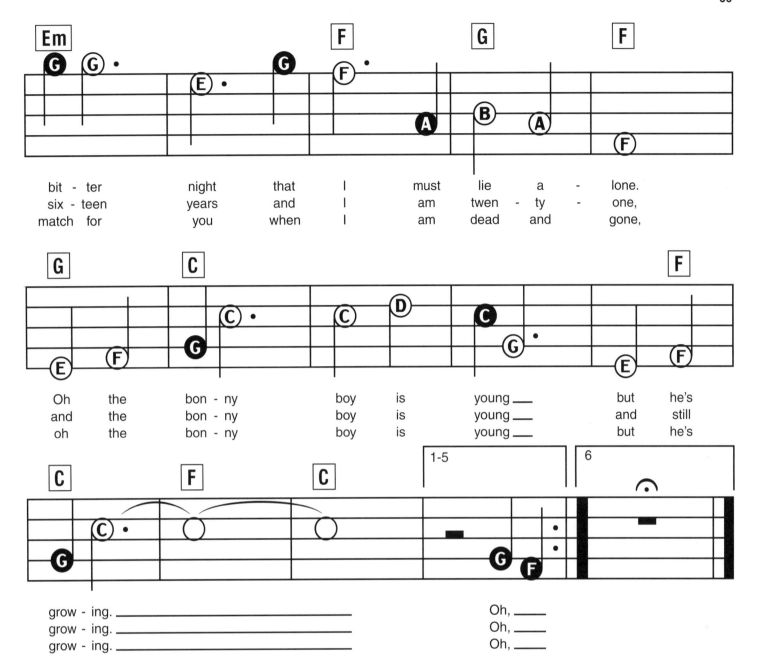

bit - ter　　night　　that　I　　must　lie　a - lone.
six - teen　　years　　and　I　　am　twen - ty - one,
match for　　you　　when　I　　am　dead　and　gone,

Oh　the　bon - ny　　boy　is　young ___　but　he's
and　the　bon - ny　　boy　is　young ___　and　still
oh　the　bon - ny　　boy　is　young ___　but　he's

grow - ing. _____ Oh, ___
grow - ing. _____ Oh, ___
grow - ing. _____ Oh, ___

Additional Lyrics

4. Oh, Father, dear father, I'll tell you what I'll do.
I'll send my love to college for another year or two,
And all around his college cap I'll tie a ribbon blue
Just to show the other girls that he's married.

5. At evening when strolling down by the college wall
You'd see the young collegiates a-playing at the ball.
You'd see him in amongst them there, the fairest of them all.
He's my bonny boy, he's young but he's growing.

6. At the early age of sixteen years he was a married man,
And at the age of seventeen the father of a son.
But at the age of eighteen o'er his grave the grass grew strong.
Cruel death put an end to his growing.

Boston Burglar

Registration 8
Rhythm: Fox Trot

Traditional Irish Folk Song

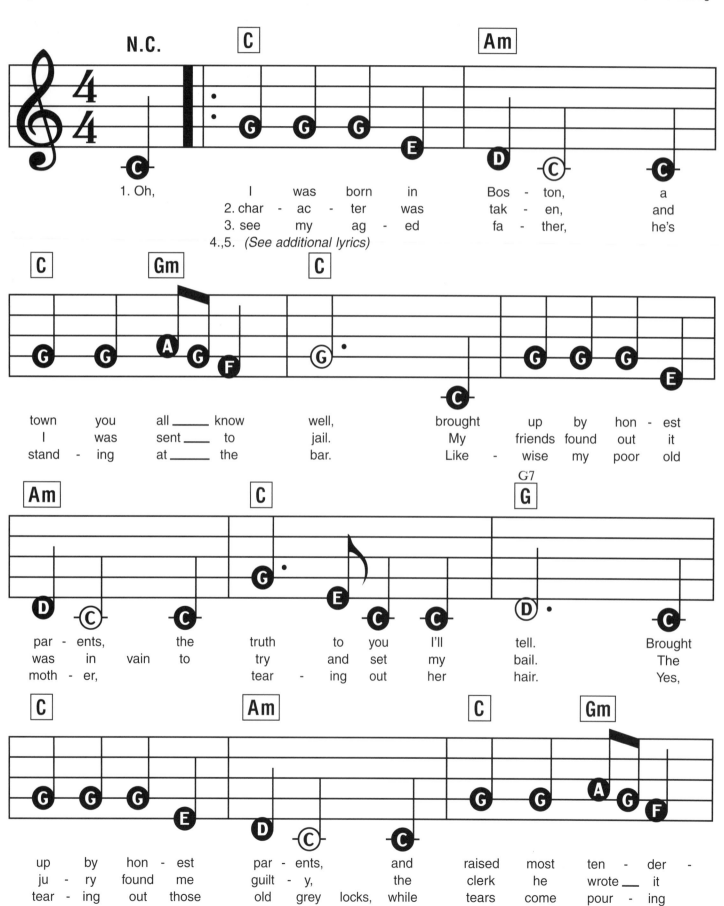

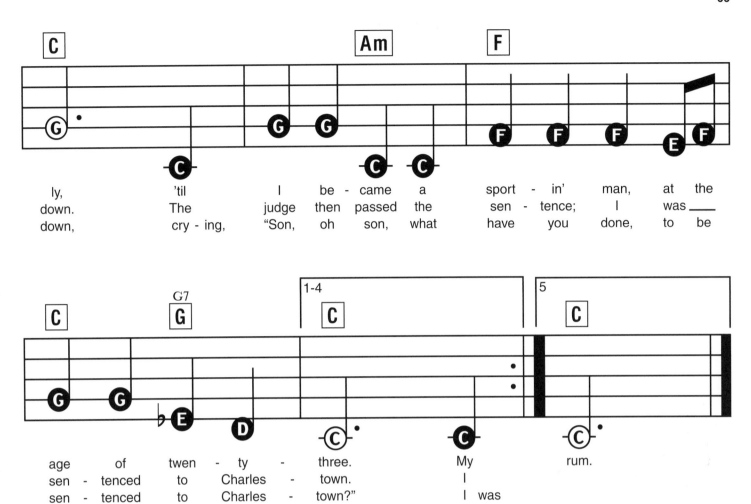

ly,   'til   I   be - came   a   sport - in'   man,   at   the
down.   The   judge then   passed   the   sen - tence;   I   was ____
down,   cry - ing,   "Son, oh   son,   what   have   you   done,   to   be

age   of   twen - ty -   three.   My   rum.
sen - tenced to   Charles - town.   I
sen - tenced to   Charles - town?"   I   was

Additional Lyrics

4. I was put on board an eastern train, one cold December day.
   And ev'ry station that we passed I'd hear the people say,
   "There goes the Boston burglar. In strong chains he is bound.
   For some crime or another, he is going Charlestown."

5. Now there's a girl in Boston, a girl that I love well.
   And when I gain my freedom, along with her I'll dwell.
   Yes, when I gain my freedom, bad company I'll shun.
   Likewise night walking, rambling, and also drinking rum.

Boulavogue

Registration 1
Rhythm: Waltz

Words and Music by
P.J. McCall

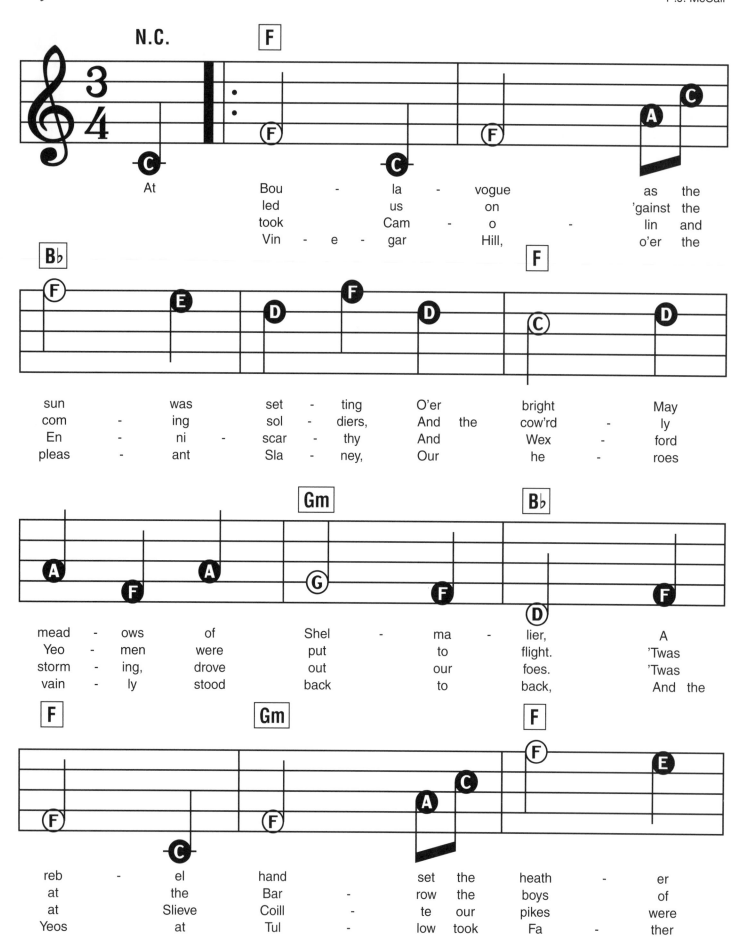

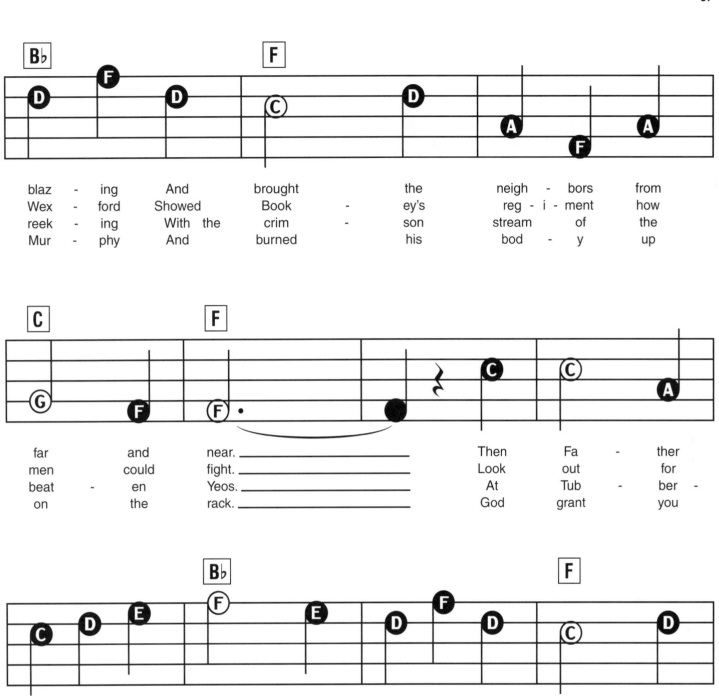

blaz	-	ing	And		brought		the		neigh	-	bors	from
Wex	-	ford	Showed		Book	-	ey's		reg - i - ment			how
reek	-	ing	With the		crim	-	son		stream		of	the
Mur	-	phy	And		burned		his		bod	-	y	up

far	and	near. _____		Then	Fa	-	ther
men	could	fight. _____		Look	out		for
beat	- en	Yeos. _____		At	Tub	-	ber -
on	the	rack. _____		God	grant		you

Mur	-	phy	from	old	Kil	-	cor - mack	Spurred	up		the
hire	-	lings,	King	George	of		Eng - land,	Search	ev	-	'ry
neer	-	ing	and	Bal	-	ly -	el - lis	Full	man	-	y a
glo	-	ry,	brave	Fa	-	ther	Mur - phy,	And	o	-	pen

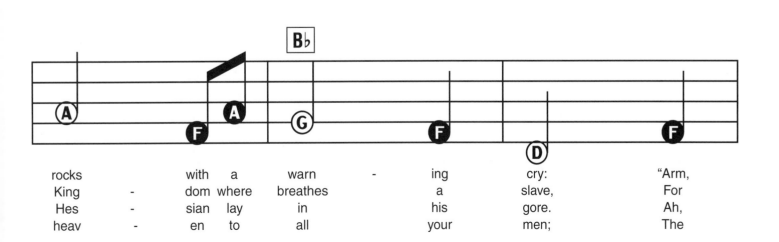

rocks	with	a	warn	-	ing	cry:	"Arm,
King	- dom	where	breathes		a	slave,	For
Hes	- sian	lay	in		his	gore.	Ah,
heav	- en	to	all		your	men;	The

38

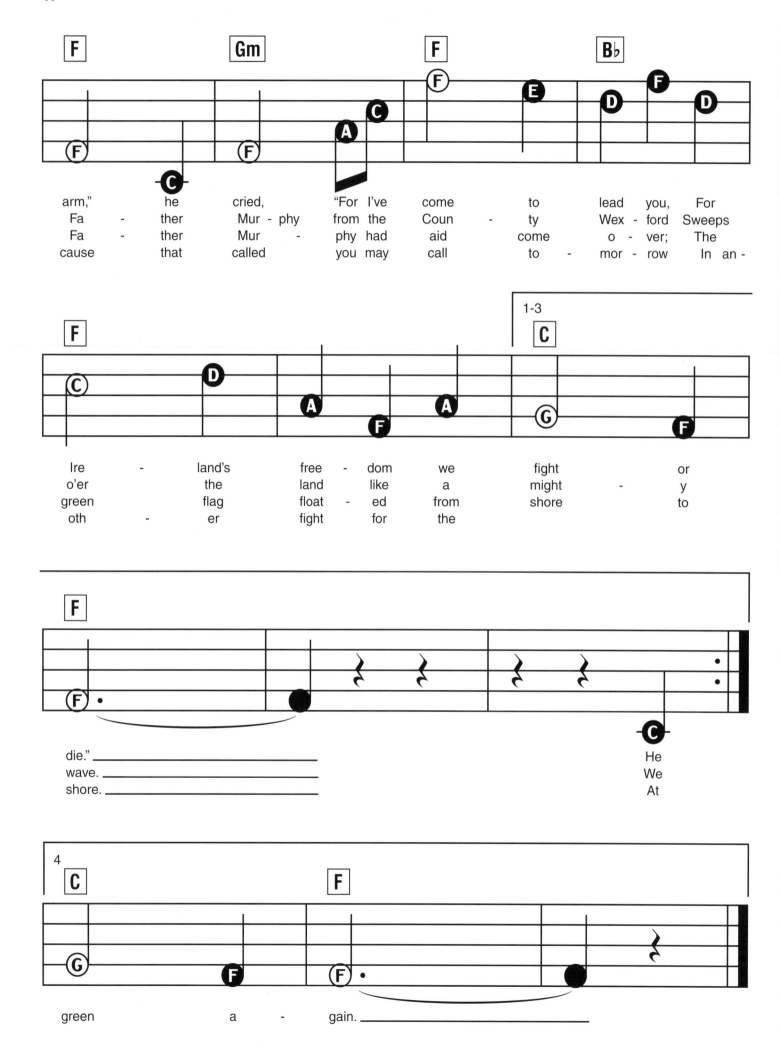

The Boys of Fairhill

Registration 7
Rhythm: Fox Trot

Traditional Irish Folk Song

Come and have a hol - i - day with our hurl - ing club so gay. Your
We'll go down by Sun - day's well, what might hap - pen, who can tell: heads,
Jim - my Bar - ry hooks the ball, we'll hook Jim - my, ball and all.
Kath - y Bar - ry sells cru beens, fair - ly burst - ing at the seams,

souls we will charm and your hearts we will thrill. The
they might ___ roll or some blood it might spill. We'll
"Here's up them all!" says the boys of Fair - hill. The
sure for to cure and more boys sure for to kill. The

girls sure they will charm ___ you. The boys sure they won't harm ___ you.
come back by Black - pool ___ way when we've o - ver - come the fray.
Rock - ies thought they were the stars till they met the Saint Fin - barr's.
stench on Pat - rick's Bridge is wick - ed how does Fa - ther Mat - thew stick it.

"Here's up them all," says the boys of Fair - hill. boys of Fair - hill.

The Boys from the County Armagh

Registration 8
Rhythm: Waltz

Traditional Irish Folk Song

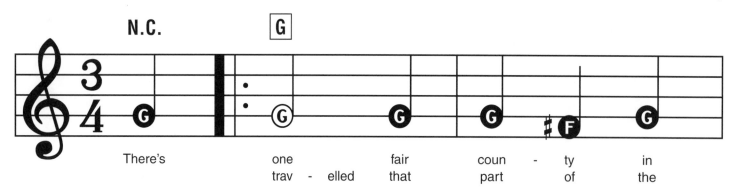

There's one fair coun - ty in
trav - elled that part of the

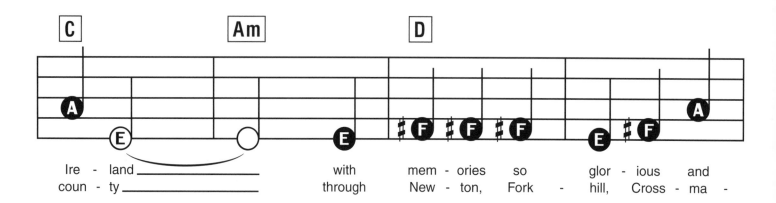

Ire - land with mem - ories so glor - ious and
coun - ty through New - ton, Fork - hill, Cross - ma -

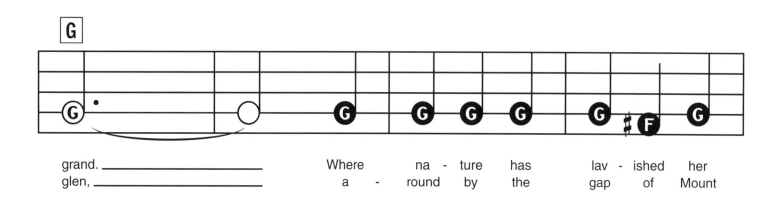

grand. Where na - ture has lav - ished her
glen, a - round by the gap of Mount

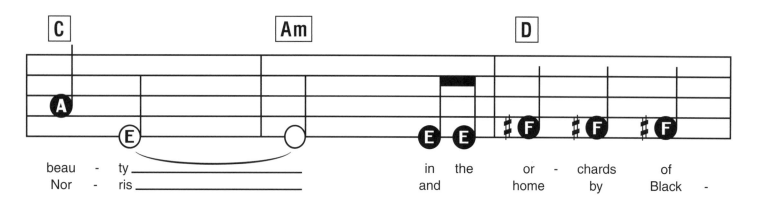

beau - ty in the or - chards of
Nor - ris and home by Black -

41

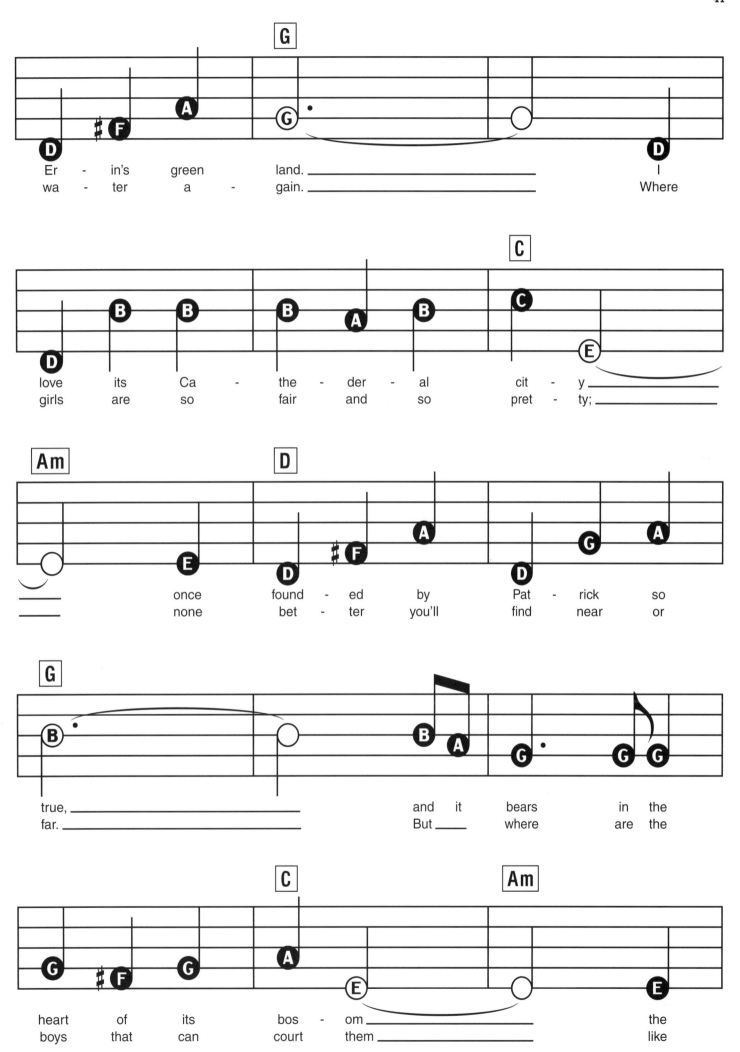

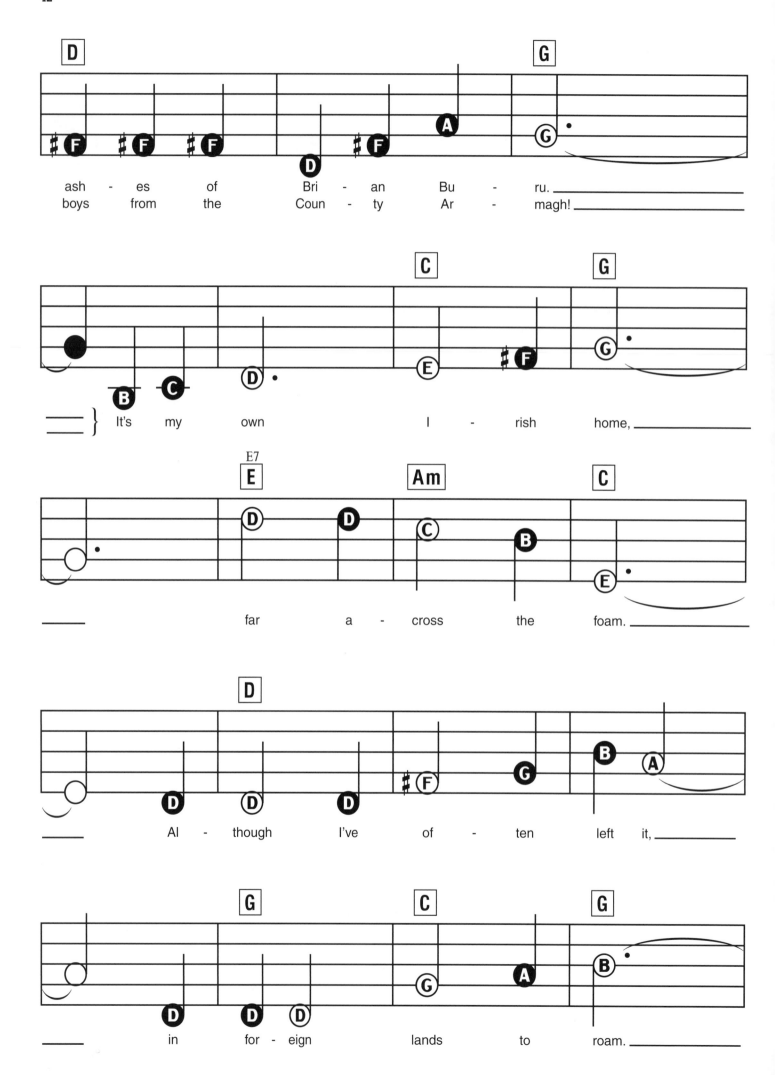

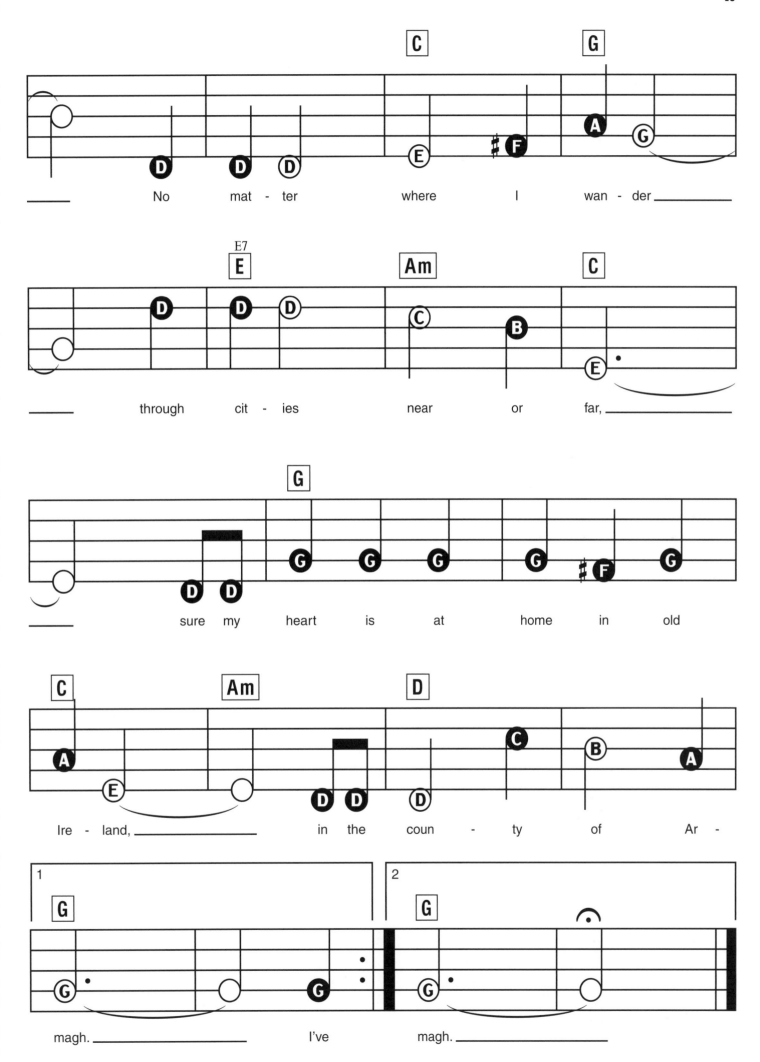

Brennan on the Moor

Registration 4
Rhythm: March or Polka

Traditional

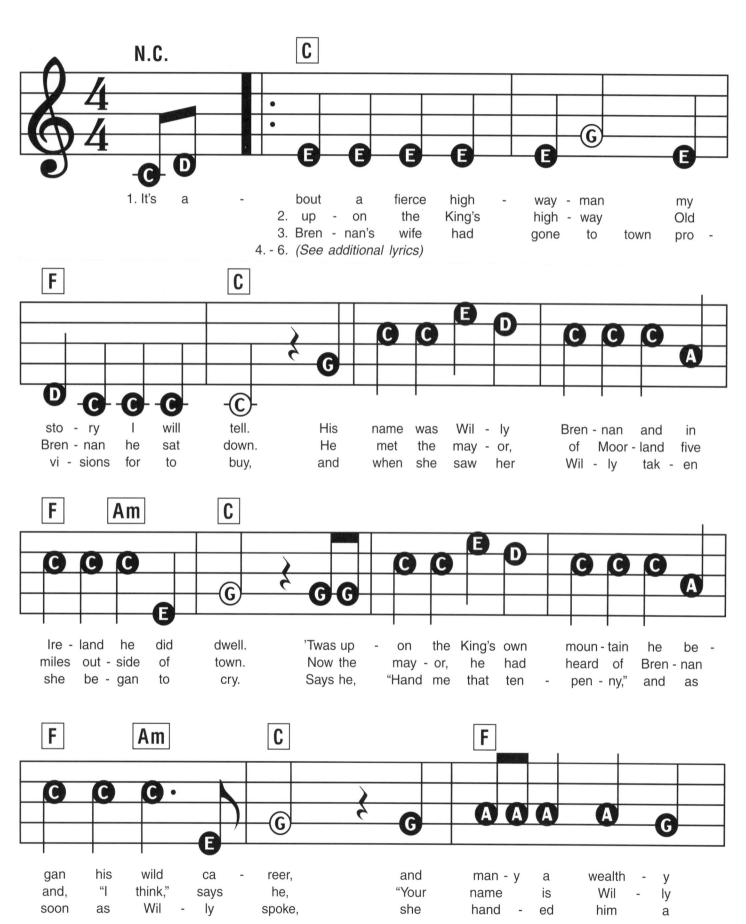

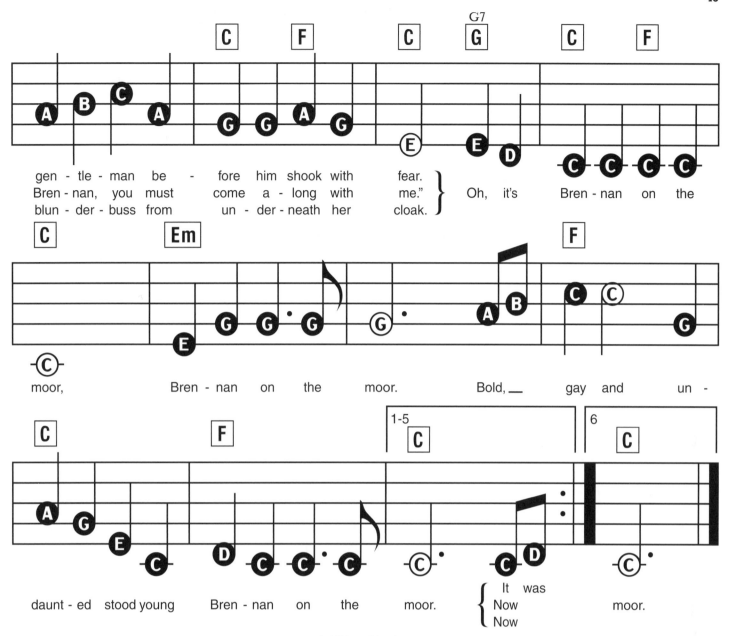

Additional Lyrics

4. Now Brennan got his blunderbuss, my story I'll unfold.
   He caused the mayor to tremble and deliver up his gold.
   Five thousand pounds were offered for his apprehension there,
   But Brennan and the peddler to the mountain did repair.
   Oh, it's Brennan on the moor, Brennan on the moor.
   Bold, gay and undaunted stood young Brennan on the moor.

5. Now Brennan is an outlaw all on some mountain high.
   With infantry and cavalry to take him they did try.
   But he laughed at them and he scorned at them until, it was said,
   By a false-hearted woman he was cruelly betrayed.
   Oh, it's Brennan on the moor, Brennan on the moor.
   Bold, gay and undaunted stood young Brennan on the moor.

6. They hung him at the crossroads; in the chains he swung and died.
   But still they say that in the night some do see him ride.
   They see him with his blunderbuss in the midnight chill;
   Along, along the king's highway rides Willy Brennan still.
   Oh, it's Brennan on the moor, Brennan on the moor.
   Bold, gay and undaunted stood young Brennan on the moor.

A Bunch of Thyme

Registration 2
Rhythm: Fox Trot

Traditional Irish Folk Song

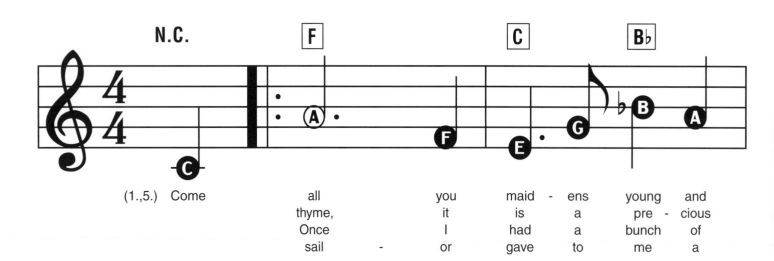

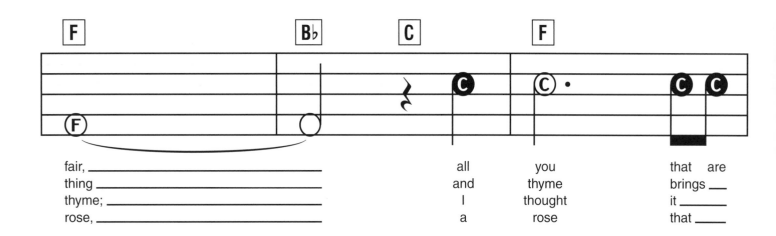

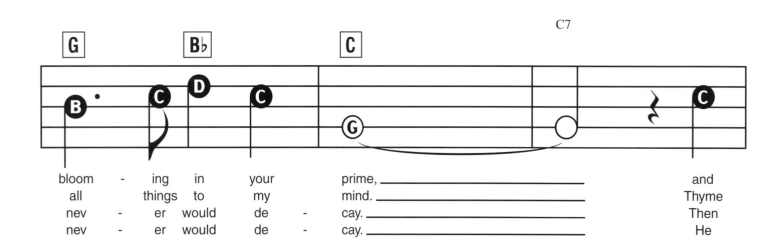

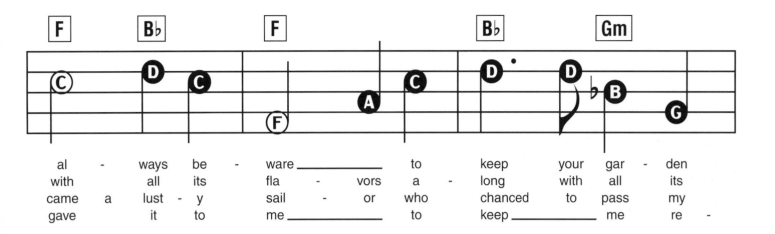

al -	ways	be -	ware _____	to	keep	your	gar -	den
with	all	its	fla -	vors	a -	long	with	all	its
came	a	lust -	y	sail -	or	who	chanced	to	pass	my
gave	it	to	me _____	to	keep _____	me	re -

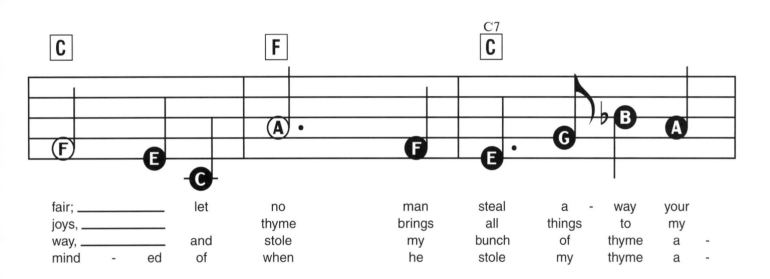

fair; _____	let	no	man	steal	a -	way	your
joys, _____	thyme	brings	all	things	to	my
way, _____	and	stole	my	bunch	of	thyme	a -
mind -	ed	of	when	he	stole	my	thyme	a -

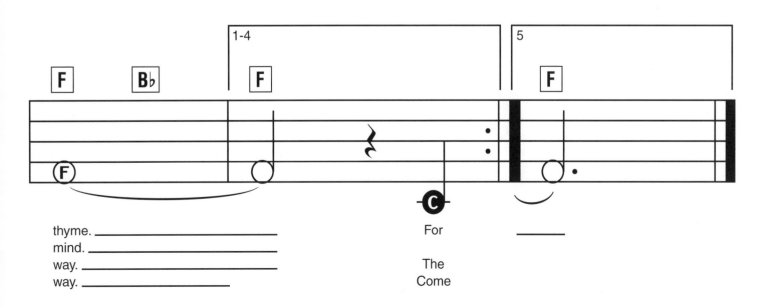

thyme. _____	For _____
mind. _____	
way. _____	The
way. _____	Come

Butcher Boy

Registration 7
Rhythm: Fox Trot

Traditional Irish Folk Song

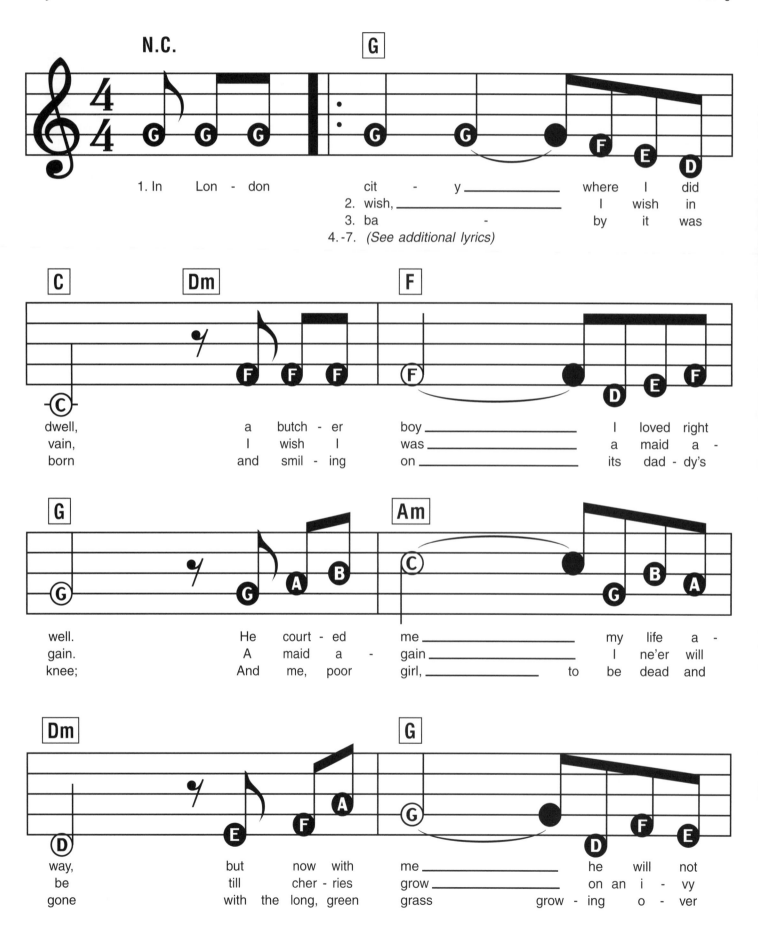

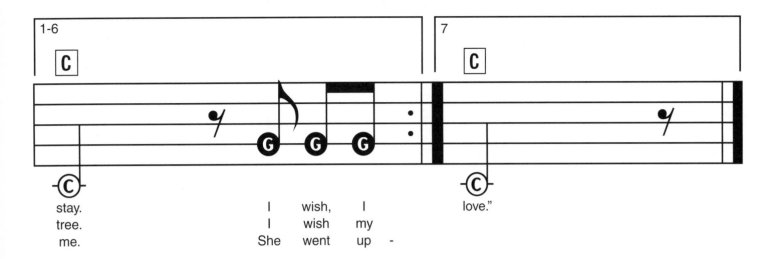

stay.
tree.
me.

I   wish,   I
I   wish my
She went   up -

love."

Additional Lyrics

4. She went upstairs to go to bed,
   And calling to her mother said,
   "Give me a chair till I sit down
   And a pen and ink till I write down."

5. At ev'ry word she dropped a tear,
   At ev'ry line cried, "Willie, dear,
   Oh, what a foolish girl was I
   To be led astray by a butcher boy."

6. He went upstairs and the door he broke;
   He found her hanging from a rope
   He took his knife and he cut her down,
   And in her pocket these words he found:

7. "Oh, make my grave large, wide and deep;
   But a marble stone at my head and feet.
   And in the middle a turtledove,
   That the world may know that I died for love."

Carrickfergus

Registration 7
Rhythm: Fox Trot

Traditional Irish Folk Song

51

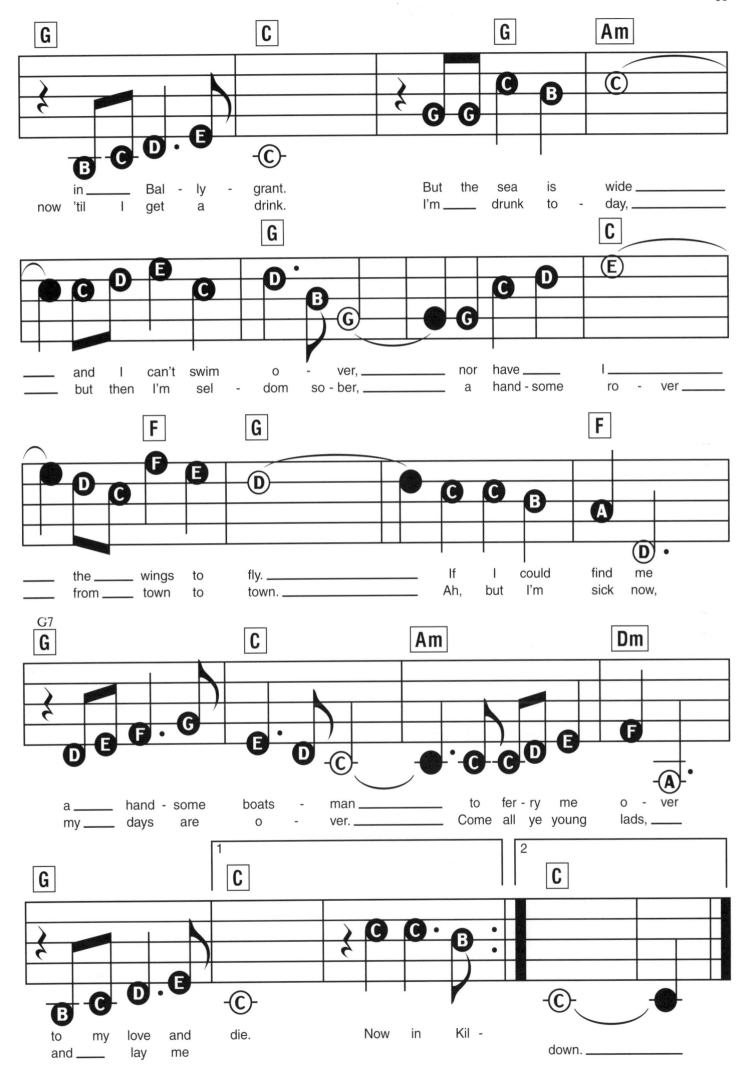

Castle of Dromore

Registration 8
Rhythm: 6/8 March or Jig/Gigue

Traditional Irish Folk Song

53

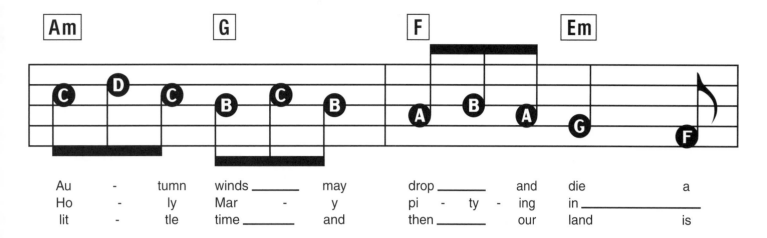

Au - tumn winds _____ may drop _____ and die a
Ho - ly Mar - y pi - ty - ing in _____
lit - tle time _____ and then _____ our land is

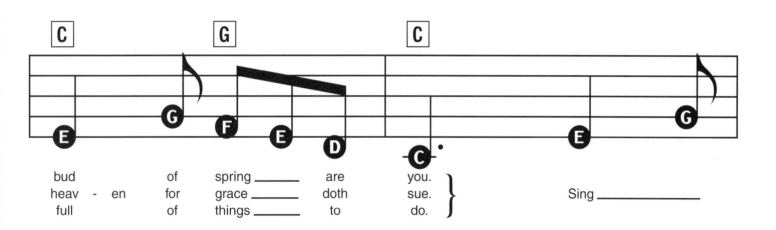

bud of spring _____ are you. }
heav - en for grace _____ doth sue.
full of things _____ to do. }

Sing _____

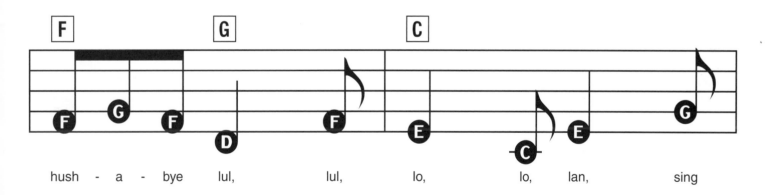

hush - a - bye lul, lul, lo, lo, lan, sing

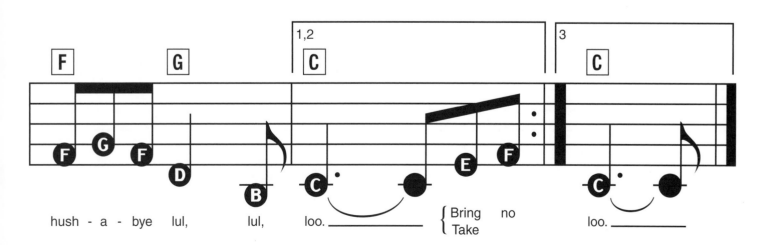

1,2

3

hush - a - bye lul, lul, loo. _____ { Bring no loo. _____
Take

Cliffs of Doneen

Registration 4
Rhythm: Waltz

Traditional Irish Folk Song

55

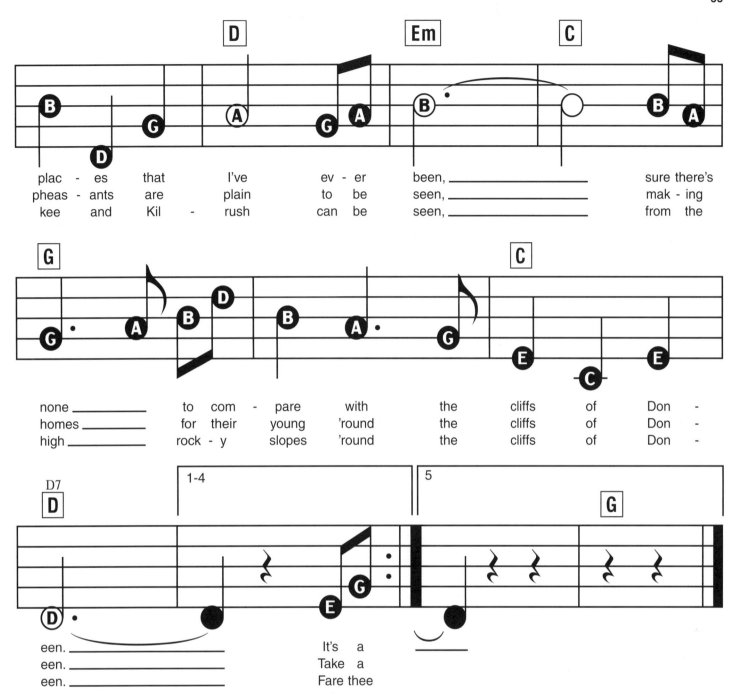

Additional Lyrics

4. Fare thee well to Doneen, fare thee well for a while
   And to all the kind people I'm leaving behind.
   To the streams and the meadows where late I have been,
   And the high rocky slopes 'round the cliffs of Doneen.

5. Fare thee well to Doneen, fare thee well for a while.
   And although we are parted by the raging sea wild,
   Once again I will walk with my Irish colleen
   'Round the high rocky slopes of the cliffs of Doneen.

Cockles and Mussels
(Molly Malone)

Registration 5
Rhythm: Waltz

Traditional Irish Folksong

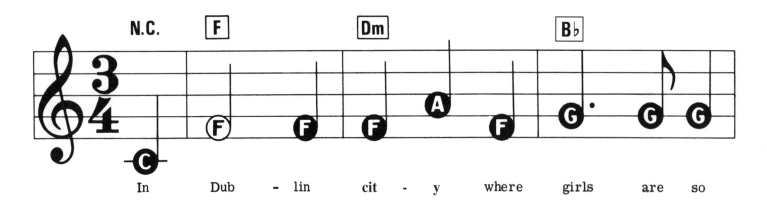

In Dub - lin cit - y where girls are so

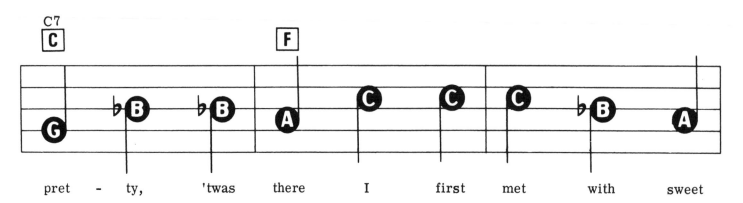

pret - ty, 'twas there I first met with sweet

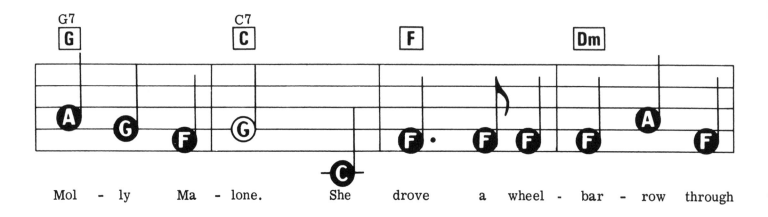

Mol - ly Ma - lone. She drove a wheel - bar - row through

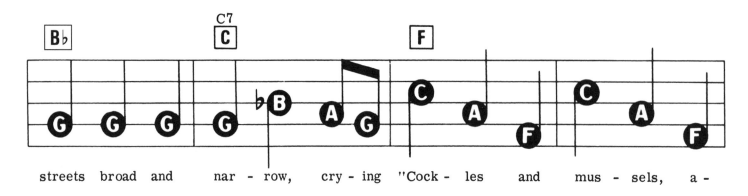

streets broad and nar - row, cry - ing "Cock - les and mus - sels, a -

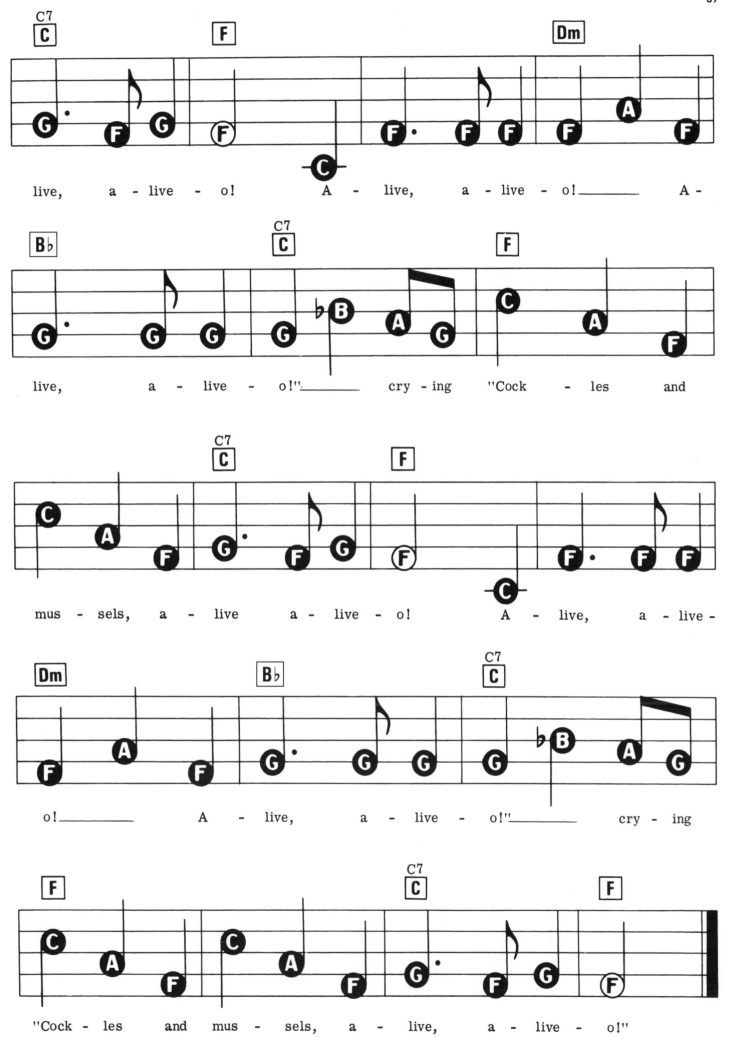

live, a - live - o! A - live, a - live - o!_____ A -

live, a - live - o!"_____ cry - ing "Cock - les and

mus - sels, a - live a - live - o! A - live, a - live -

o!_____ A - live, a - live - o!"_____ cry - ing

"Cock - les and mus - sels, a - live, a - live - o!"

Come Back to Erin

Registration 4
Rhythm: Fox Trot

Irish Folk Song

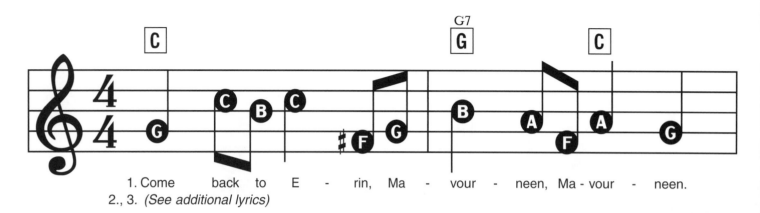

1. Come back to E - rin, Ma - vour - neen, Ma - vour - neen.
2., 3. *(See additional lyrics)*

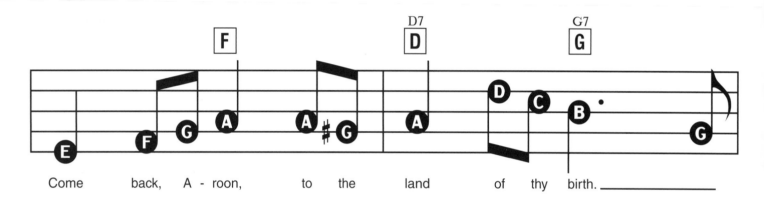

Come back, A - roon, to the land of thy birth. _____

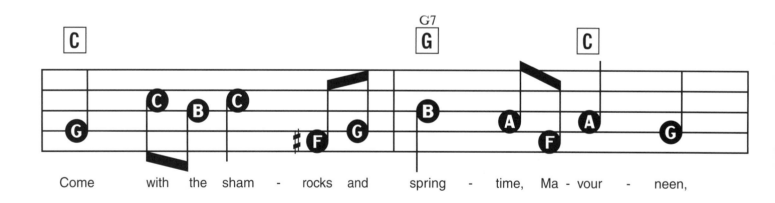

Come with the sham - rocks and spring - time, Ma - vour - neen,

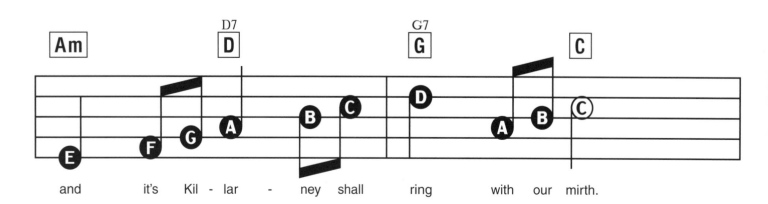

and it's Kil - lar - ney shall ring with our mirth.

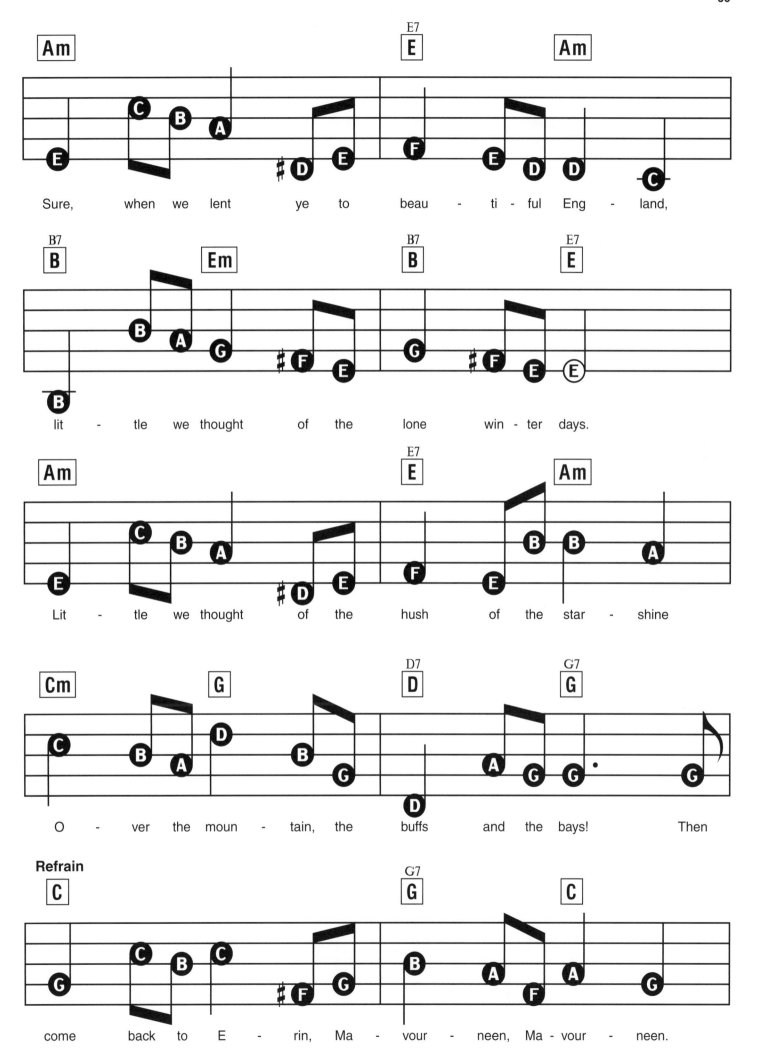

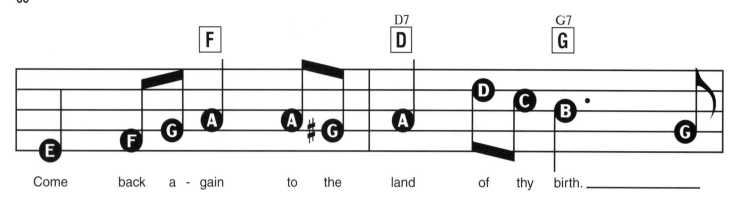

Come back a - gain to the land of thy birth. _____

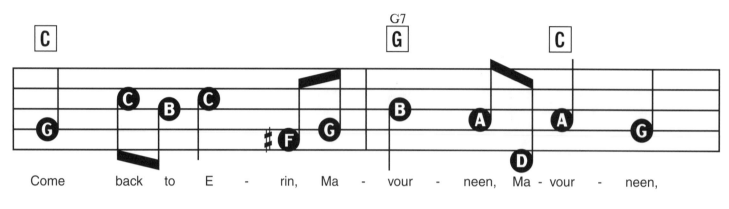

Come back to E - rin, Ma - vour - neen, Ma - vour - neen,

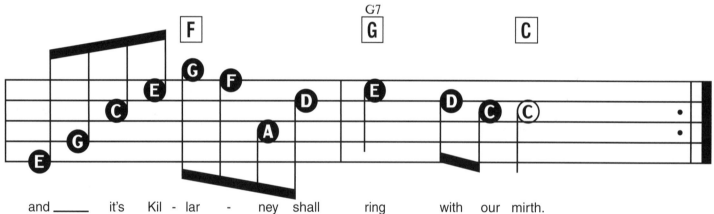

and ____ it's Kil - lar - ney shall ring with our mirth.

Additional Lyrics

2. Over the green sea, Mavourneen, Mavourneen,
   Long shone the white sail that bore thee away
   Riding the white waves that fair summer mornin',
   Just like a Mayflow'r afloat on the bay.
   O! but my heart sank when clouds came between us,
   Like a grey curtain the rain falling down,
   Hid from my sad eyes the path o'er the ocean,
   Far, far away where my colleen had flown.
   Refrain

3. O! may the Angels awakin', and sleepin'
   Watch o'er my bird in the land far away
   And it's my pray'rs will consign to their keepin'
   Care o' my jewel by night and by day.
   When by the fireside I watch the bright embers,
   Then all my heart flies to England and thee,
   Cravin' to know if my darlin' remembers,
   Or if her thoughts may be crossin' to me.
   Refrain

Danny Boy

Registration 10
Rhythm: 8 Beat or Pops

Words by Frederick Edward Weatherly
Traditional Irish Folk Melody

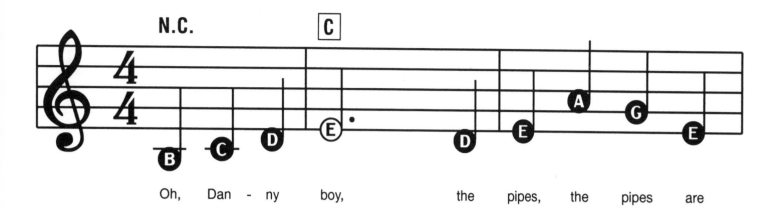

Oh, Dan - ny boy, the pipes, the pipes are

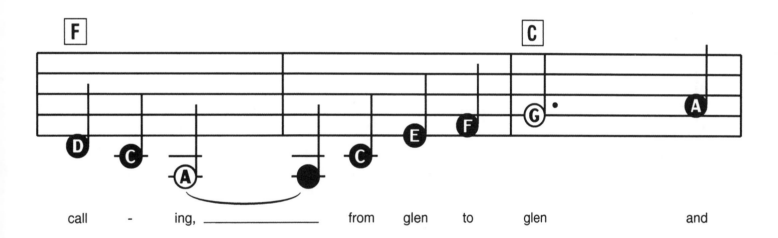

call - ing, _____ from glen to glen and

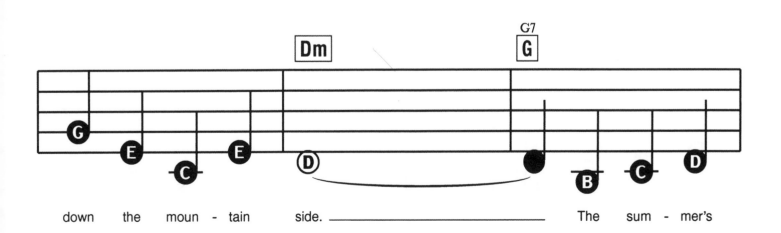

down the moun - tain side. _____ The sum - mer's

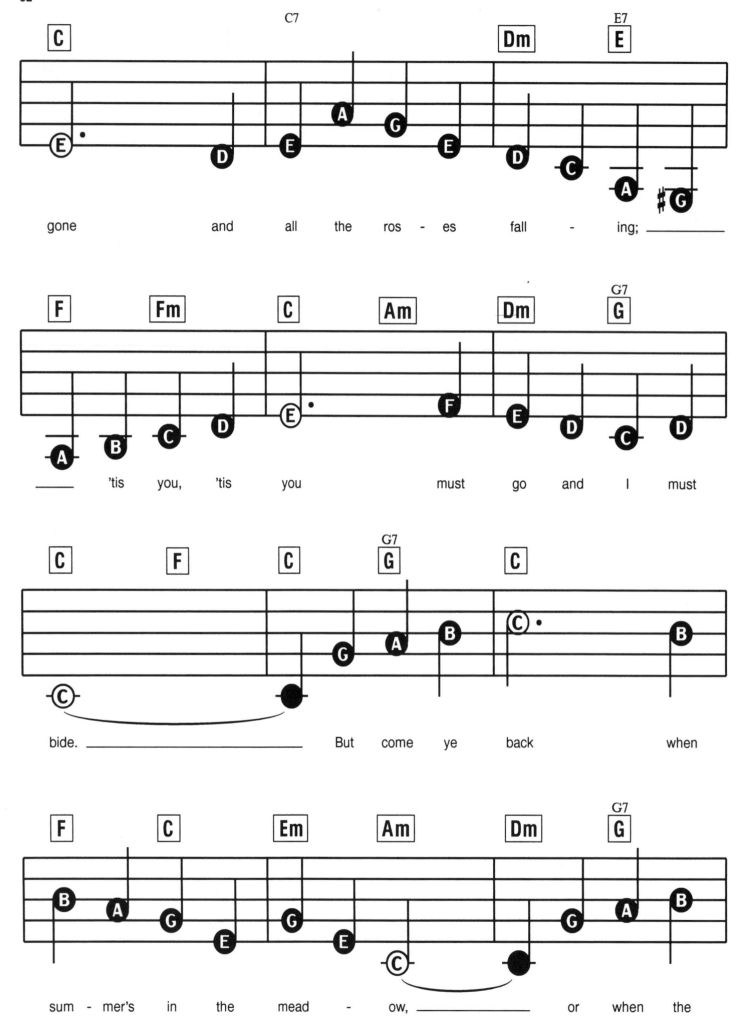

63

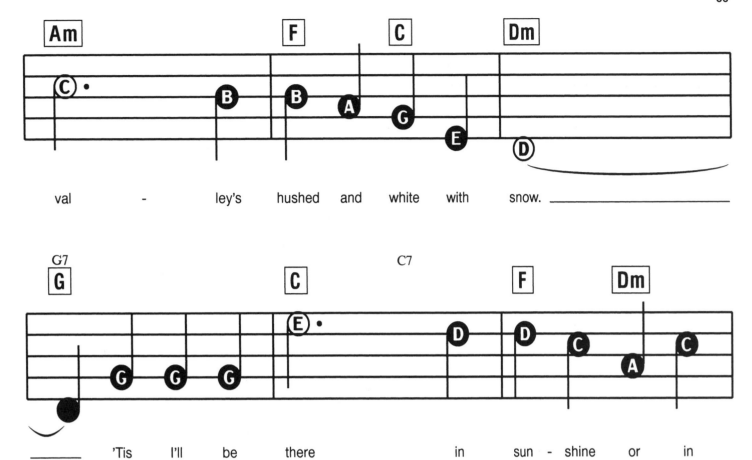

val - ley's hushed and white with snow. _____

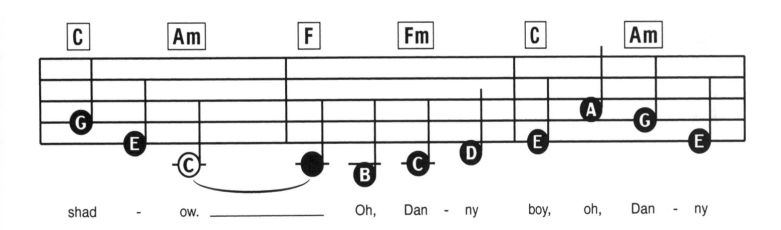

_____ 'Tis I'll be there in sun - shine or in

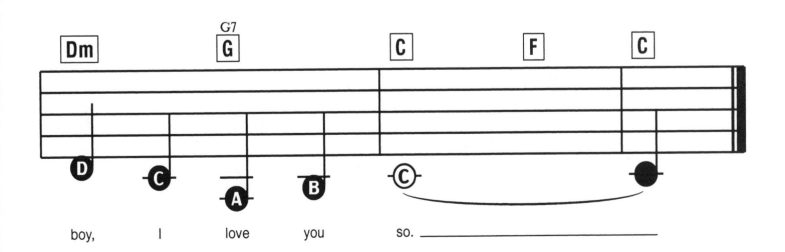

shad - ow. _____ Oh, Dan - ny boy, oh, Dan - ny

boy, I love you so. _____

Come to the Bower

Registration 2
Rhythm: Fox Trot

Traditional Irish Folk Song

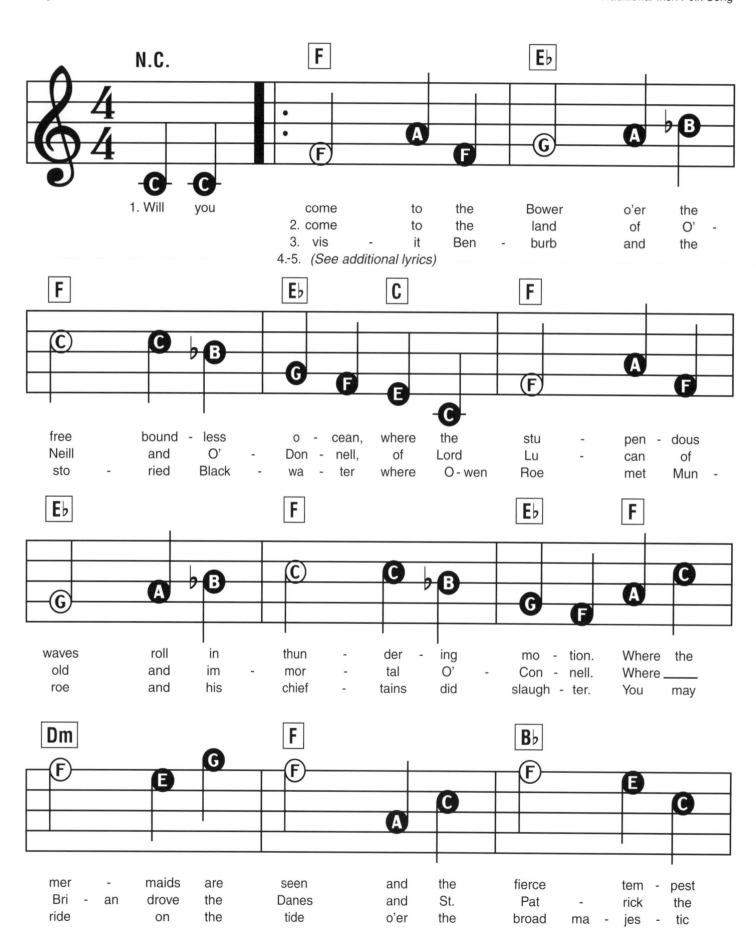

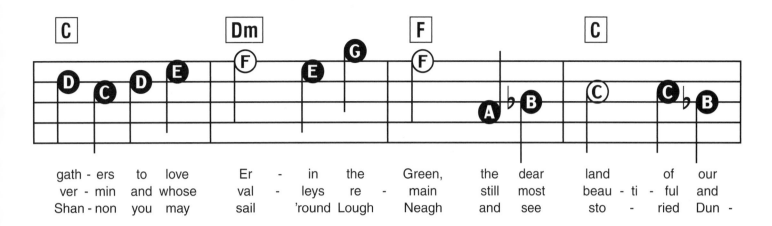

gath - ers to love Er - in the Green, the dear land of our
ver - min and whose val - leys re - main still most beau - ti - ful and
Shan - non you may sail 'round Lough Neagh and see sto - ried Dun -

Refrain

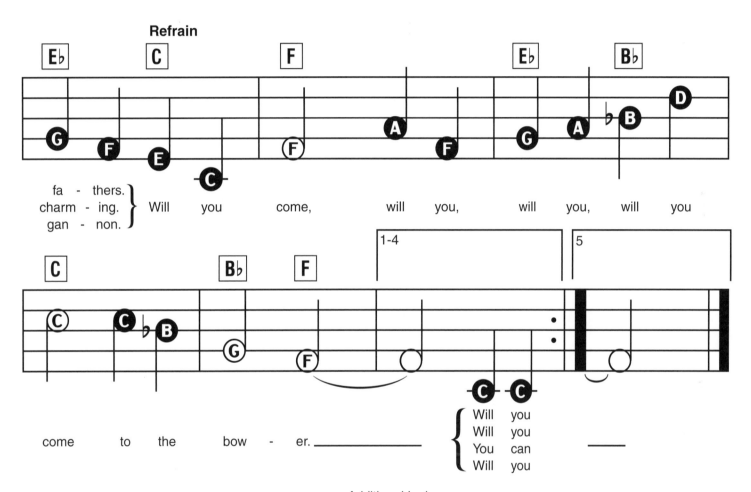

fa - thers.
charm - ing. } Will you come, will you, will you, will you
gan - non.

come to the bow - er. _____

{ Will you
  Will you
  You can
  Will you _____

Additional Lyrics

4. You can visit New Ross gallant Wexford and Gorey,
   Where the green was last seen by proud Saxon and Tory,
   Where the soil is sanctified by the blood of each true man,
   Where they died, satisfied, their enemies they would not run from.
   Refrain

5. Will you come and awake our lost land from its slumbers?
   And her fetters we will break, links that long are encumbered.
   And the air will resound with "Hosannas" to greet you
   On the shore will be found gallant Irishmen to meet you.
   Refrain

The Croppy Boy

Registration 2
Rhythm: Waltz

18th Century Irish Folk Song

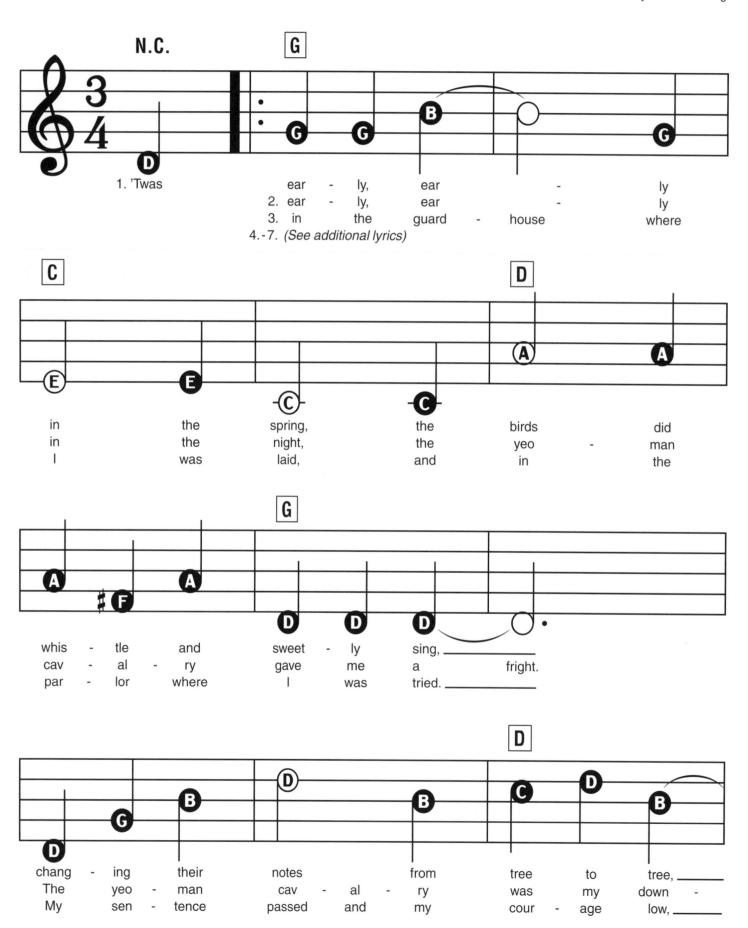

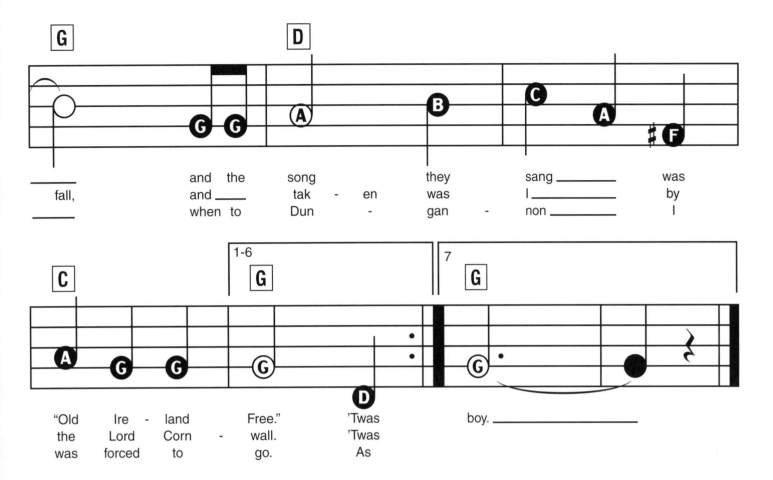

Additional Lyrics

4. As I was passing my father's door, my brother William stood at the door.
   My aged father stood there also, my tender mother her hair she tore.

5. As I was going up Wexford Hill, who could blame me to cry my fill?
   I looked behind and I looked before, my aged mother I shall see no more.

6. As I was mounted on the scaffold high, my aged father was standing by.
   My aged father did me deny, and the name he gave me was the croppy boy.

7. 'Twas in the Dungannon this young man died, and in Dungannon his body lies,
   And you good people that do pass by, oh, shed a tear for the croppy boy.

The Curragh of Kildare

Registration 8
Rhythm: Fox Trot

Traditional Irish Folk Song

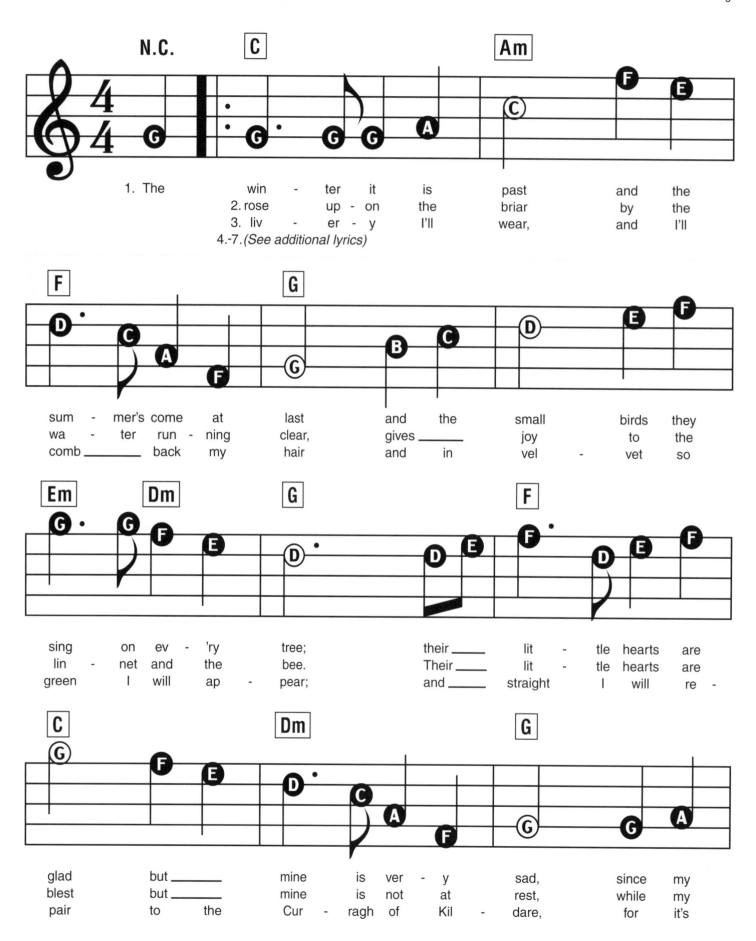

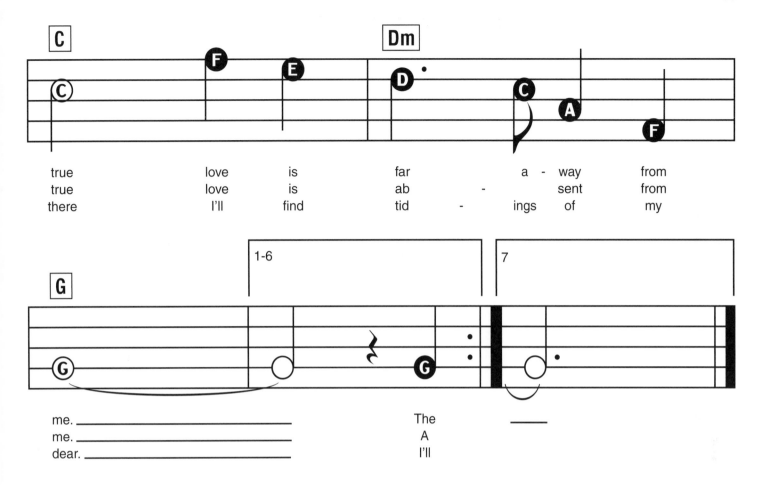

true   love   is   far   a - way   from
true   love   is   ab - sent   from
there   I'll   find   tid - ings   of   my

1-6

7

me. _____ The
me. _____ A
dear. _____ I'll   ____

Additional Lyrics

4. I'll wear a cap of black, with a frill around my neck,
   Gold rings on my fingers I wear;
   It's this undertake, for my true lover's sake,
   He resides at the Curragh of Kildare.

5. I would not think it strange, thus the world for to range,
   If I only got tiding of my dear;
   But here is Cupid's chain, if I'm bound to remain,
   I would spend my whole life in despair.

6. My love is like the sun, that in the firmament does run;
   And always proves constant and true;
   But his is like the moon, that wanders up and down,
   And ev'ry month is new.

7. All you that are in love, and cannot it remove.
   I pit the pains you endure;
   For experience let me know, that your hearts are full of woe,
   And a woe that no mortal can cure.

Dicey Reilly

Registration 7
Rhythm: Fox Trot

Traditional Irish Folk Song

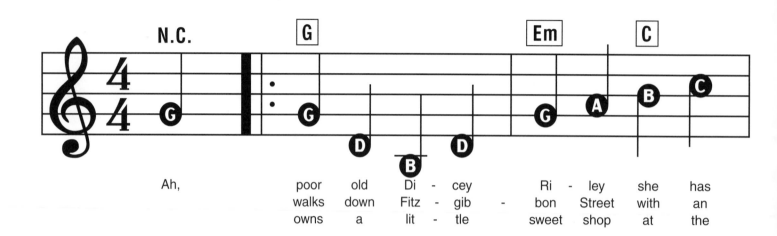

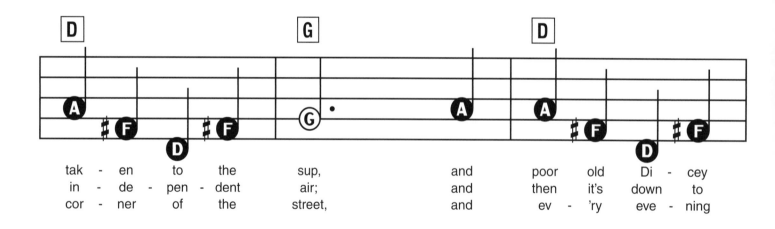

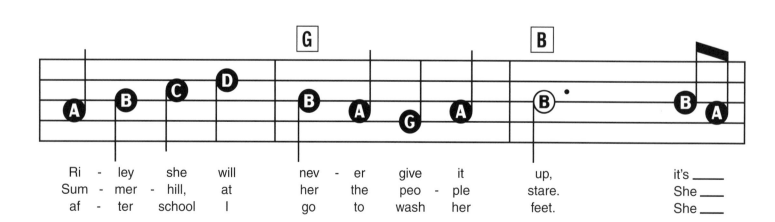

71

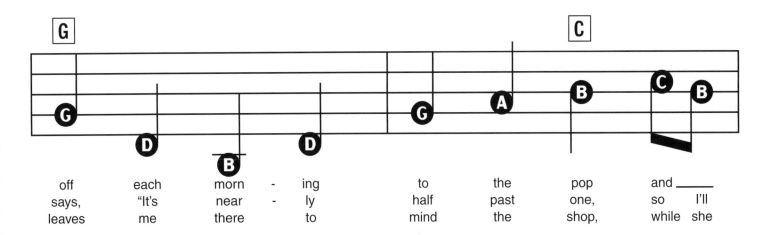

off each morn - ing to the pop and ____
says, "It's near - ly half past one, so I'll
leaves me there to mind the shop, while she

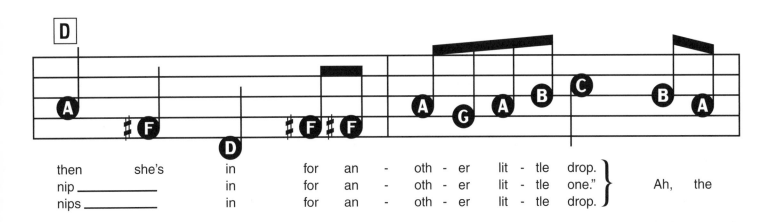

then she's in for an - oth - er lit - tle drop.
nip ____ in for an - oth - er lit - tle one." Ah, the
nips ____ in for an - oth - er lit - tle drop.

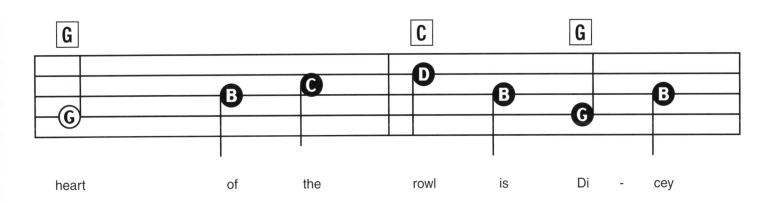

heart of the rowl is Di - cey

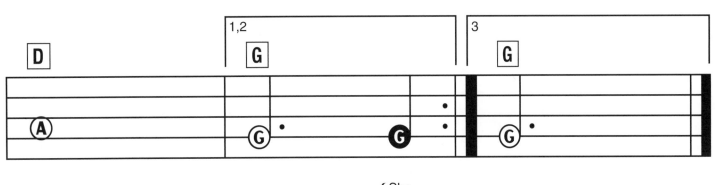

Ri - ley. She / She ley.

Do You Want Your Old Lobby

Registration 1
Rhythm: Waltz

Traditional Irish Folk Song

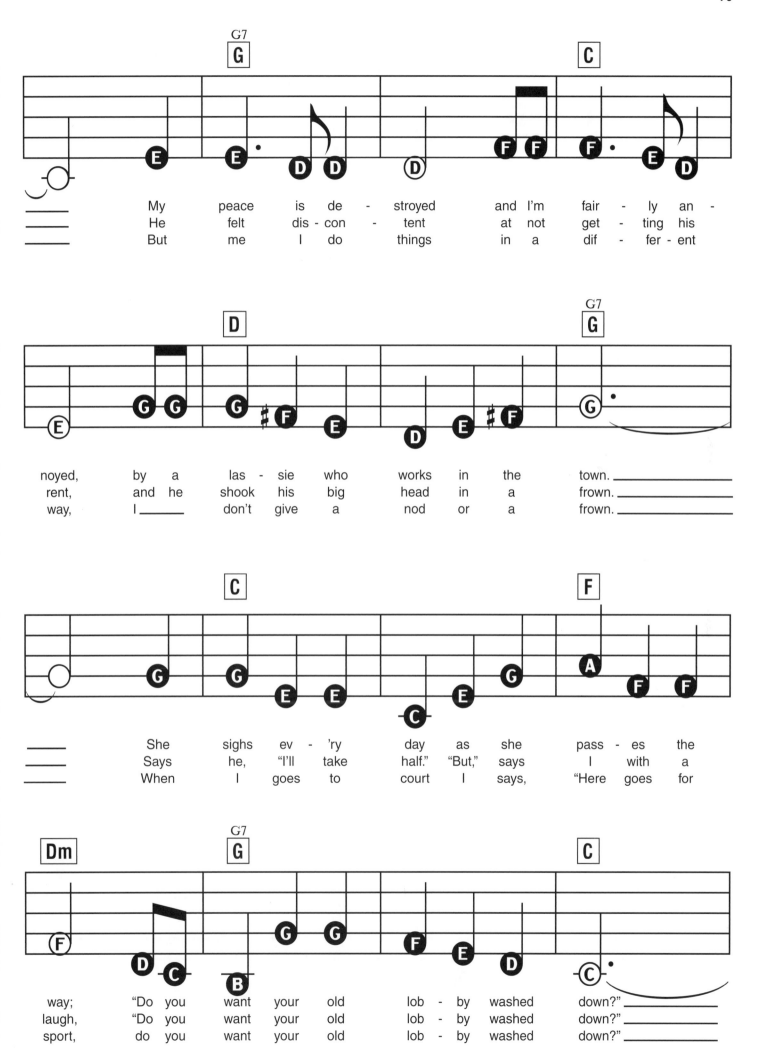

74

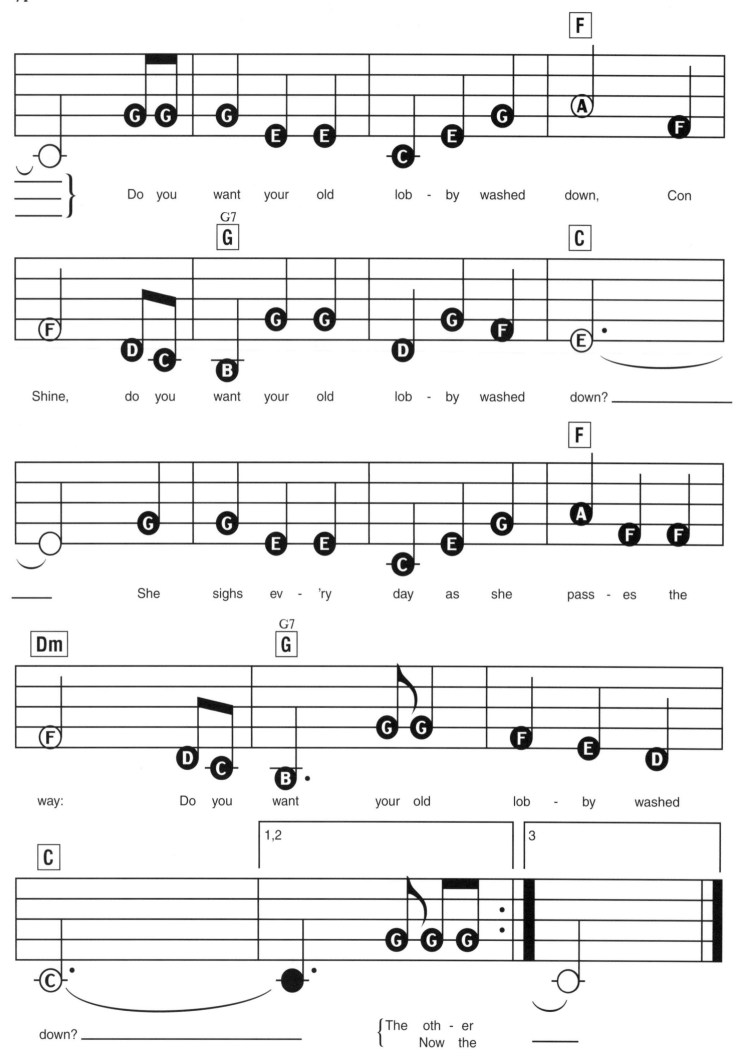

Fiddler's Green

Registration 2
Rhythm: Waltz

Traditional Irish Folk Song

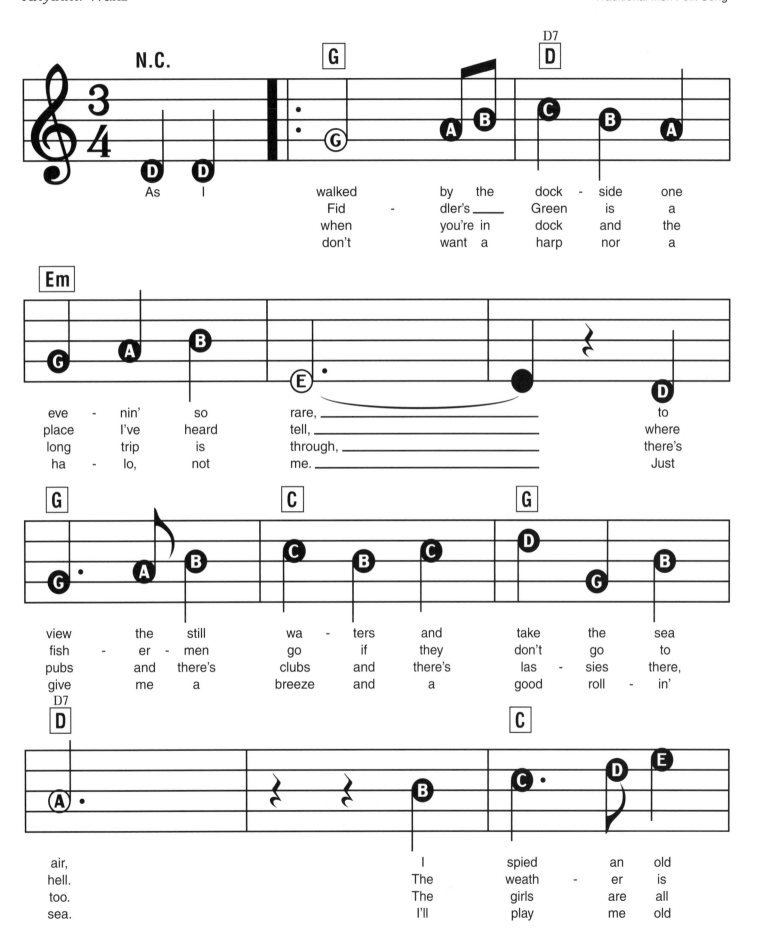

76

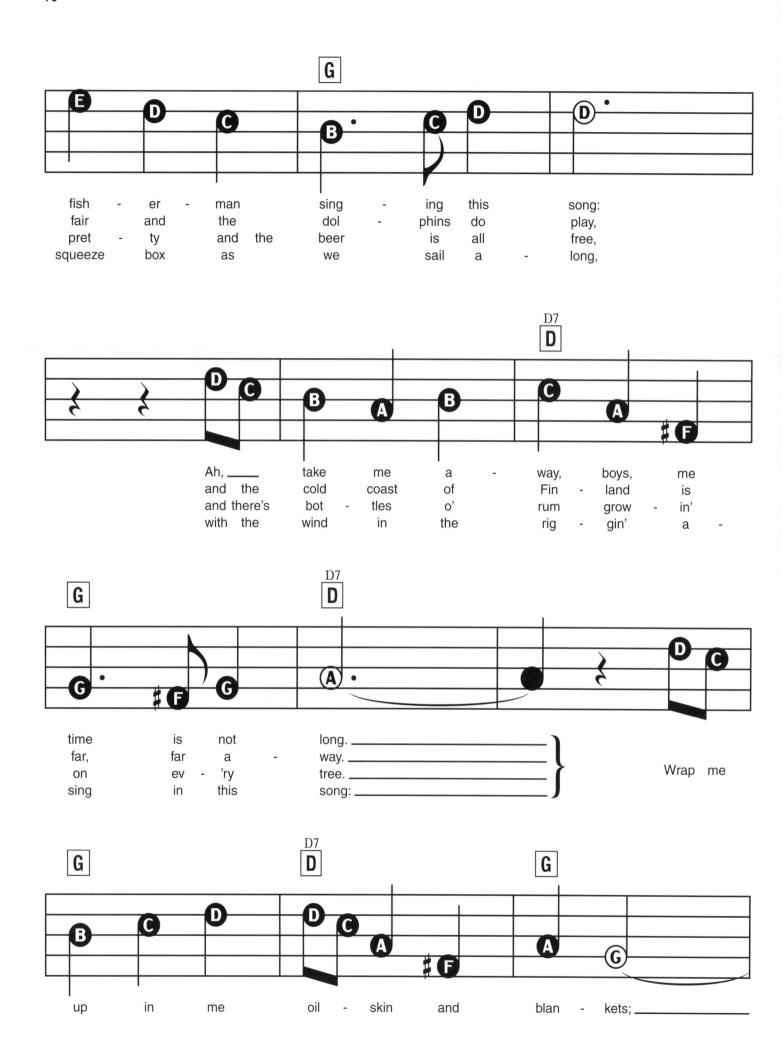

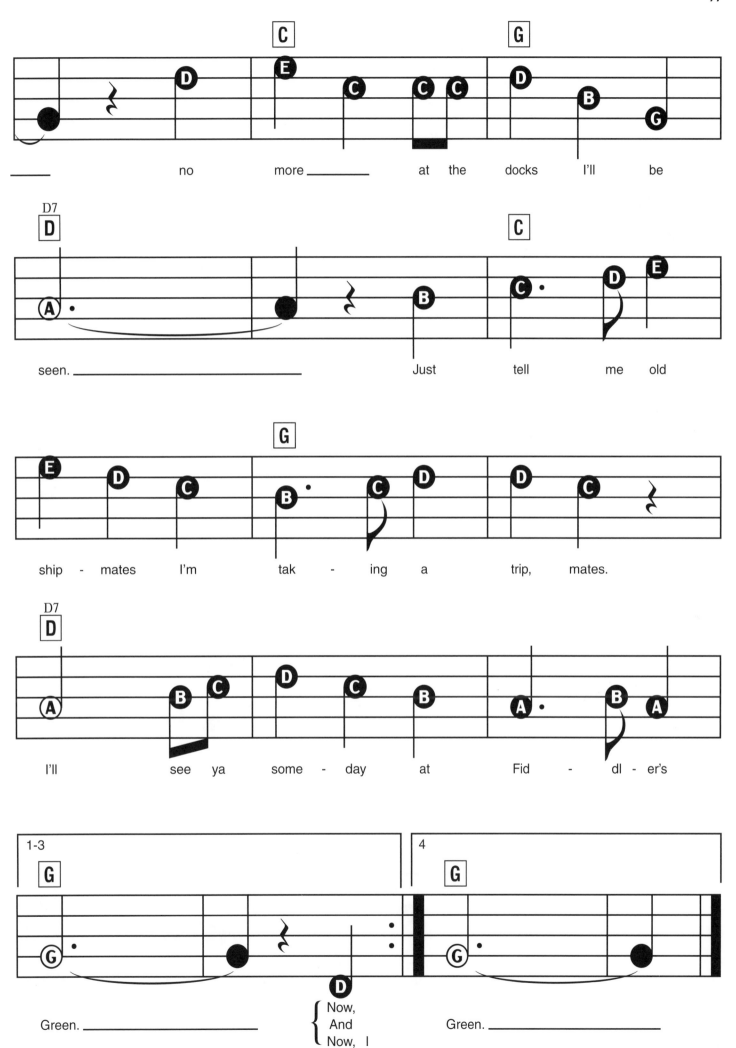

Down by the Salley Gardens

Registration 4
Rhythm: Ballad

Traditional Irish Folk Song

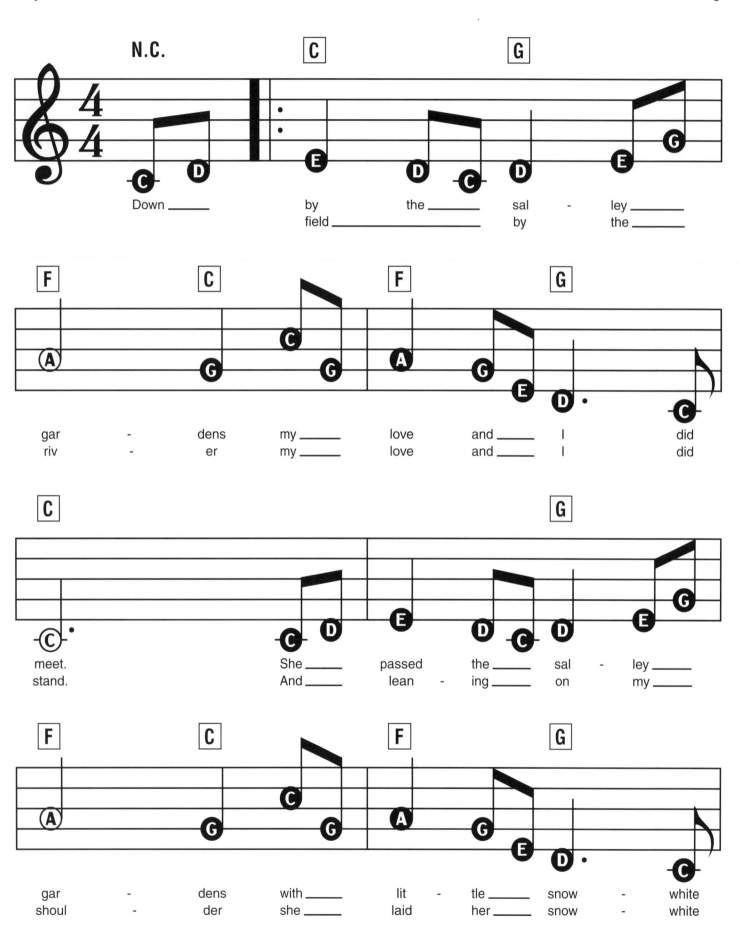

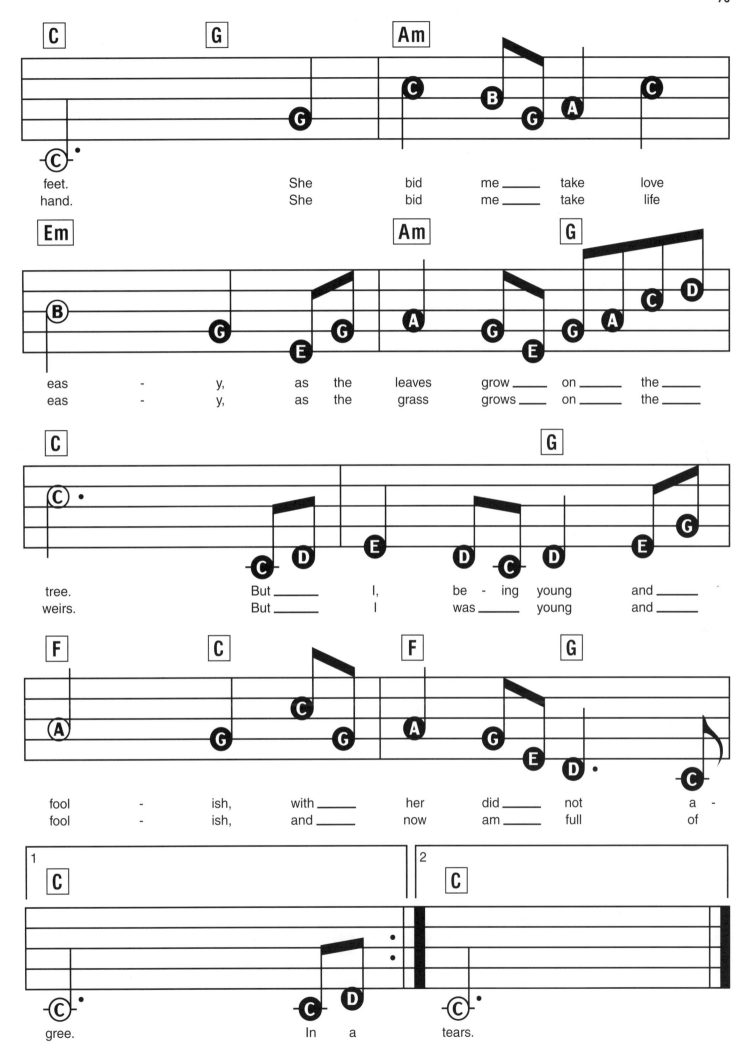

Easy and Slow

Registration 7
Rhythm: Waltz

Traditional Irish Folk Song

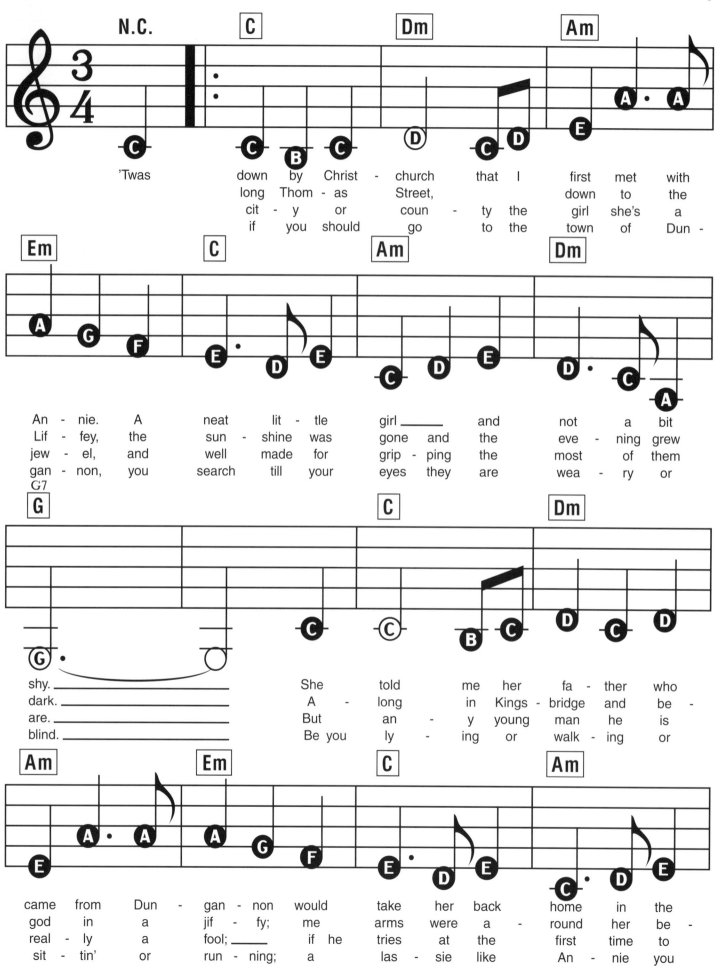

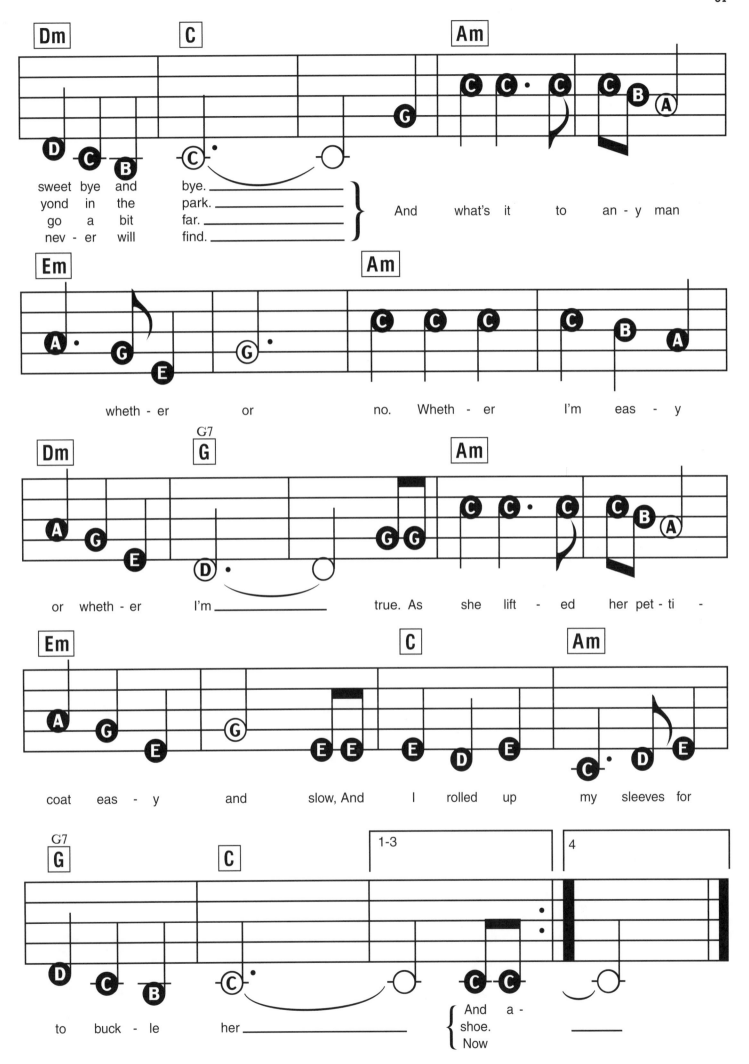

The Enniskillen Dragoon

Registration 8
Rhythm: Fox Trot

Traditional Irish Folk Song

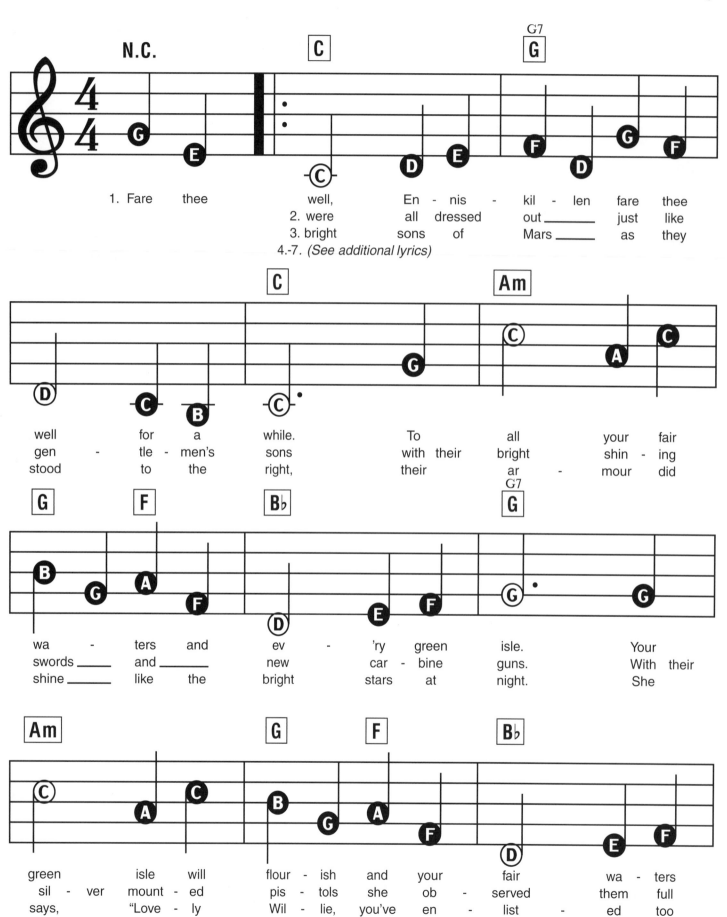

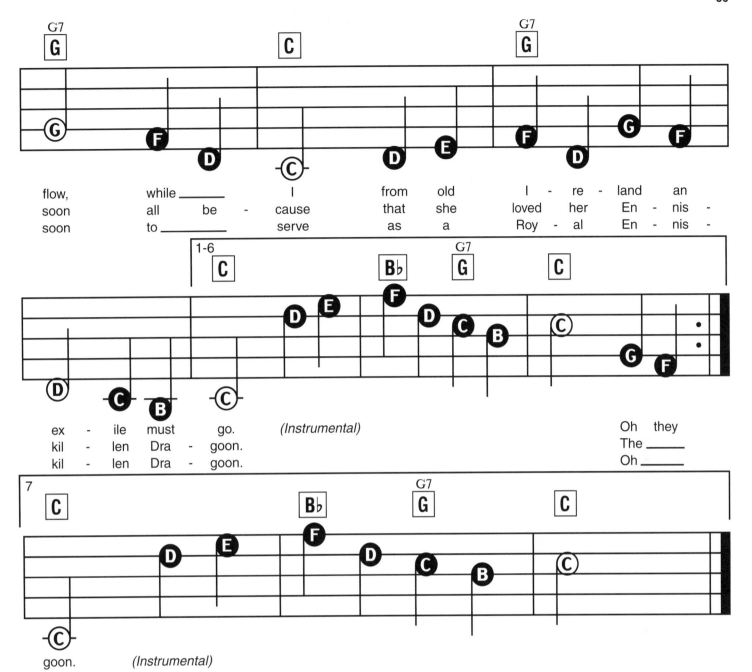

flow,   while ____   I   from   old   I   -   re   -   land   an
soon   all   be   -   cause   that   she   loved   her   En   -   nis -
soon   to ____   serve   as   a   Roy   -   al   En   -   nis -

ex   -   ile   must   go.   *(Instrumental)*   Oh   they
kil   -   len   Dra   -   goon.   The ____
kil   -   len   Dra   -   goon.   Oh ____

goon.   *(Instrumental)*

Additional Lyrics

4. "Oh beautiful Flora, your pardon I crave,
   From now and forever I will act as your slave.
   Your parents insult you both morning and noon
   For fear you should wed your Enniskillen Dragoon."

5. "Oh now dearest Willie, you should mind what you say
   Until I'm of age my parents I must obey.
   But when you're leaving Ireland they will surely change their tune
   Saying, the Lord be he with you Enniskillen Dragoon."

6. Farewell Enniskillen, fare thee well for a while
   And all around the borders of Erin's green isle
   And when the wars are over I'll return in full bloom
   And they'll all welcome home their Enniskillen Dragoon.

7. Now the war is over, they've returned home at last.
   The regiment's in Dublin and Willie got a pass.
   Last Sunday they were married and bold Willie was the groom
   And now she enjoys her Enniskillen Dragoon.

Finnegan's Wake

Registration 3
Rhythm: Fox Trot

Traditional Irish Folk Song

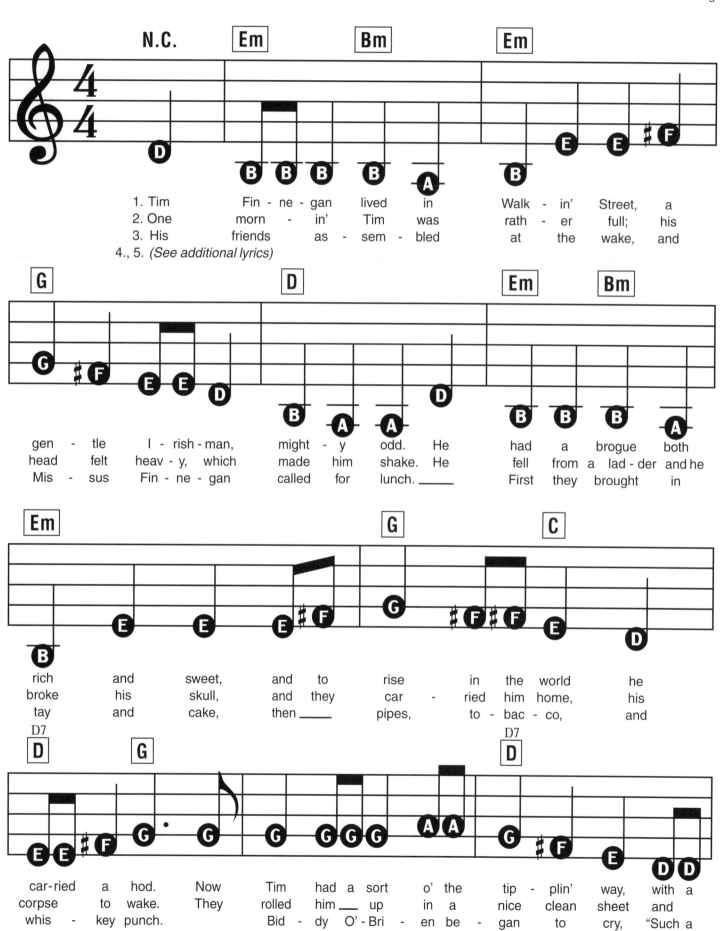

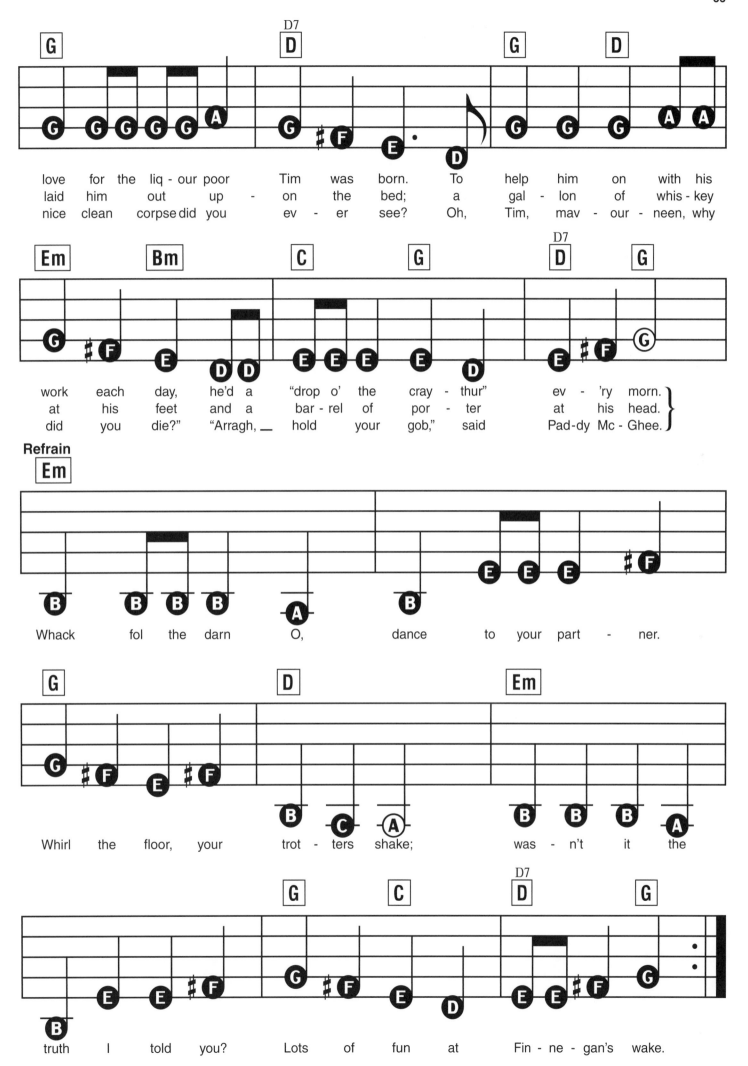

Additional Lyrics

4. Then Maggie O'Connor took up the job,
   "Oh Biddy," says she, "you're wrong, I'm sure."
   Biddy, she gave her a belt in the gob
   And left her sprawlin' on the floor.
   And then the war did soon engage,
   'Twas woman to woman and man to man.
   Shillelaigh law was all the rage,
   And a row and ruction soon began.
   Refrain

5. Then Mickey Maloney ducked his head
   When a noggin of whiskey flew at him.
   It missed, and falling on the bed,
   The liquor scattered over Tim!
   The corpse revives; see how he rises!
   Timothy, rising from the bed,
   Said, "Whirl your whiskey around like blazes,
   Thanum an Dhul! Do you think I'm dead?"
   Refrain

Follow Me up to Carlow

Registration 8
Rhythm: 6/8 March or Jig/Gigue

Traditional Irish Folk Song

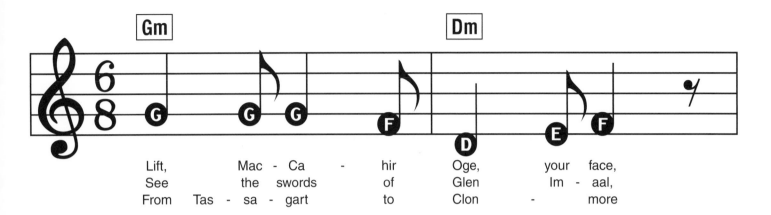

Lift, Mac Ca - hir Oge, your face,
See the swords of Glen Im - aal,
From Tas - sa - gart to Clon - more

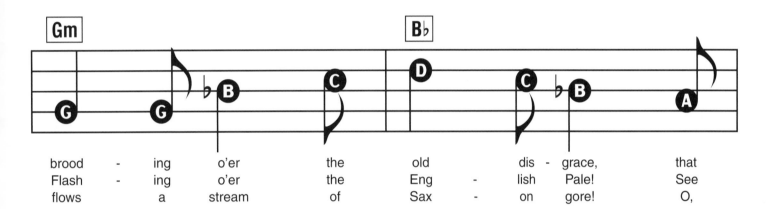

brood - ing o'er the old dis - grace, that
Flash - ing o'er the Eng - lish Pale! See
flows a stream of Sax - on gore! O,

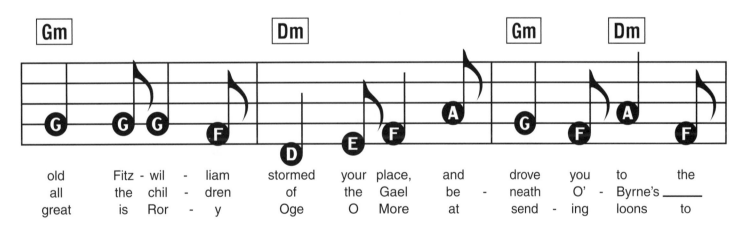

old Fitz - wil - liam stormed your place, and drove you to the
all the chil - dren of the Gael be - neath O' - Byrne's ____
great is Ror - y Oge O More at send - ing loons to

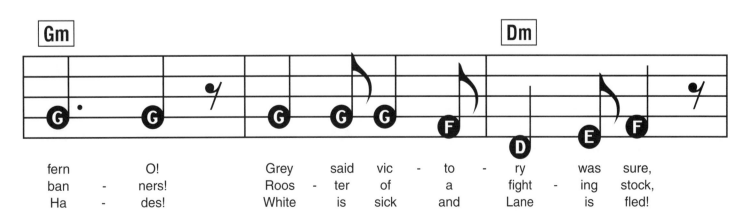

fern O! Grey said vic - to - ry was sure,
ban - ners! Roos - ter of a fight - ing stock,
Ha - des! White is sick and Lane is fled!

88

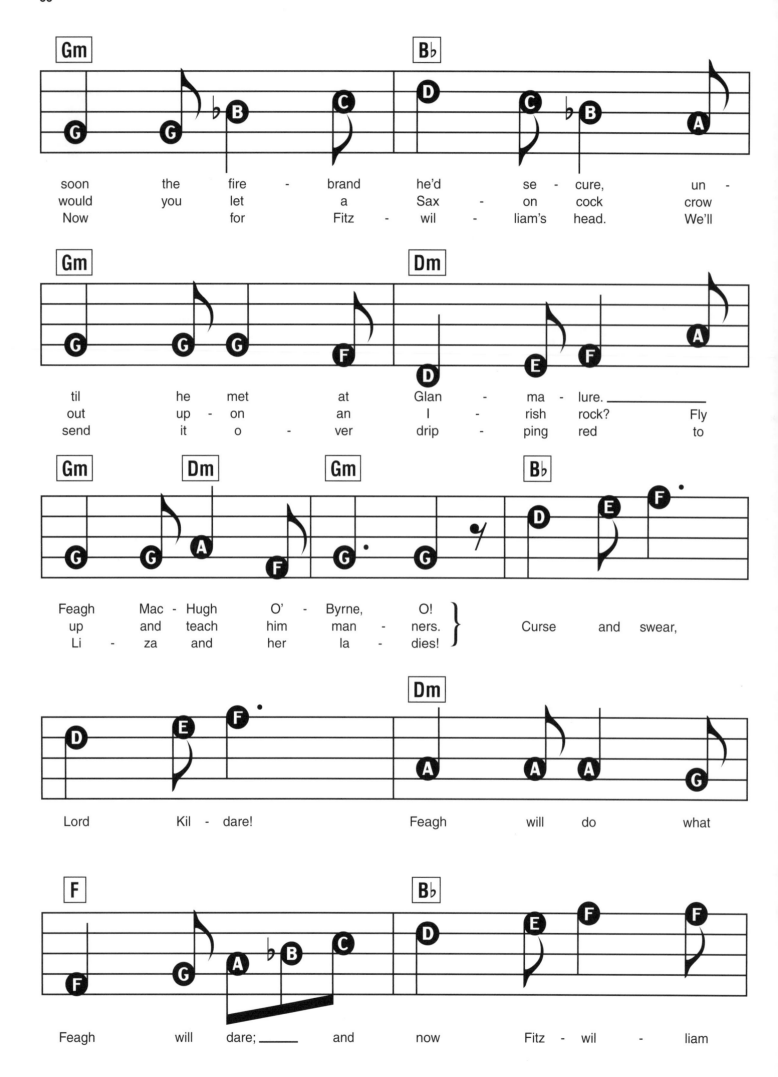

89

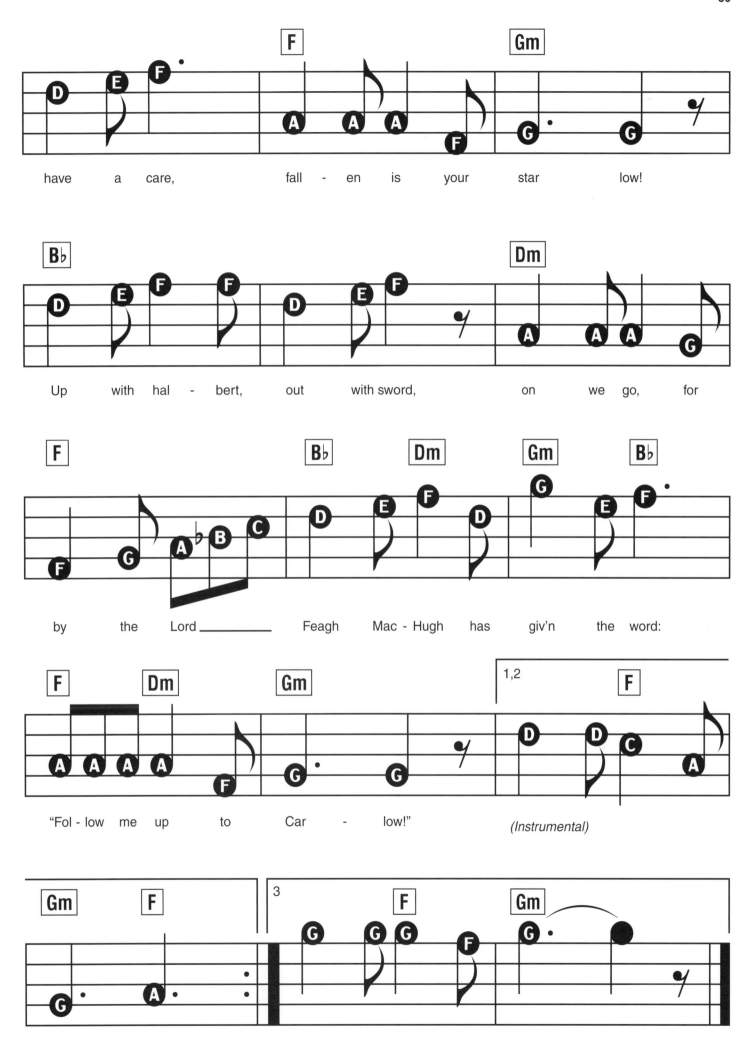

The Foggy Dew

Registration 8
Rhythm: Waltz

Traditional Irish Folk Song

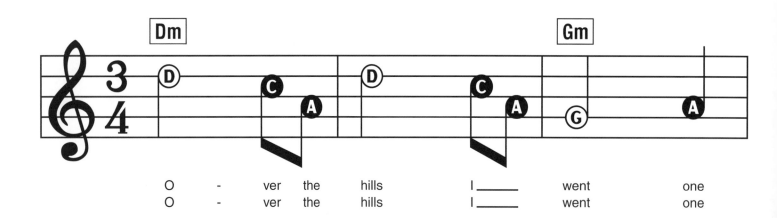

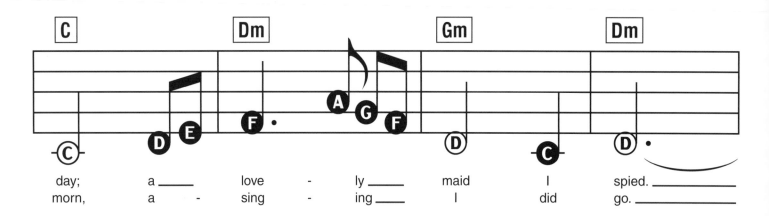

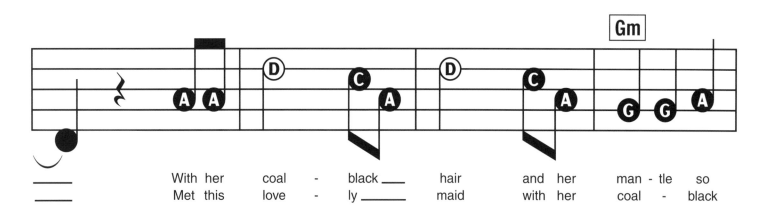

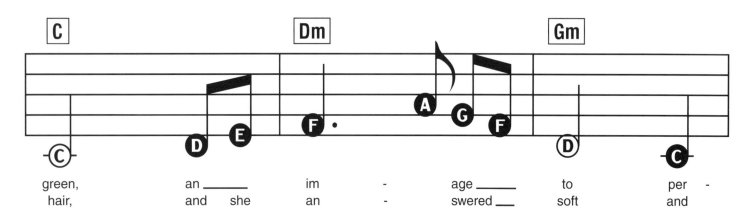

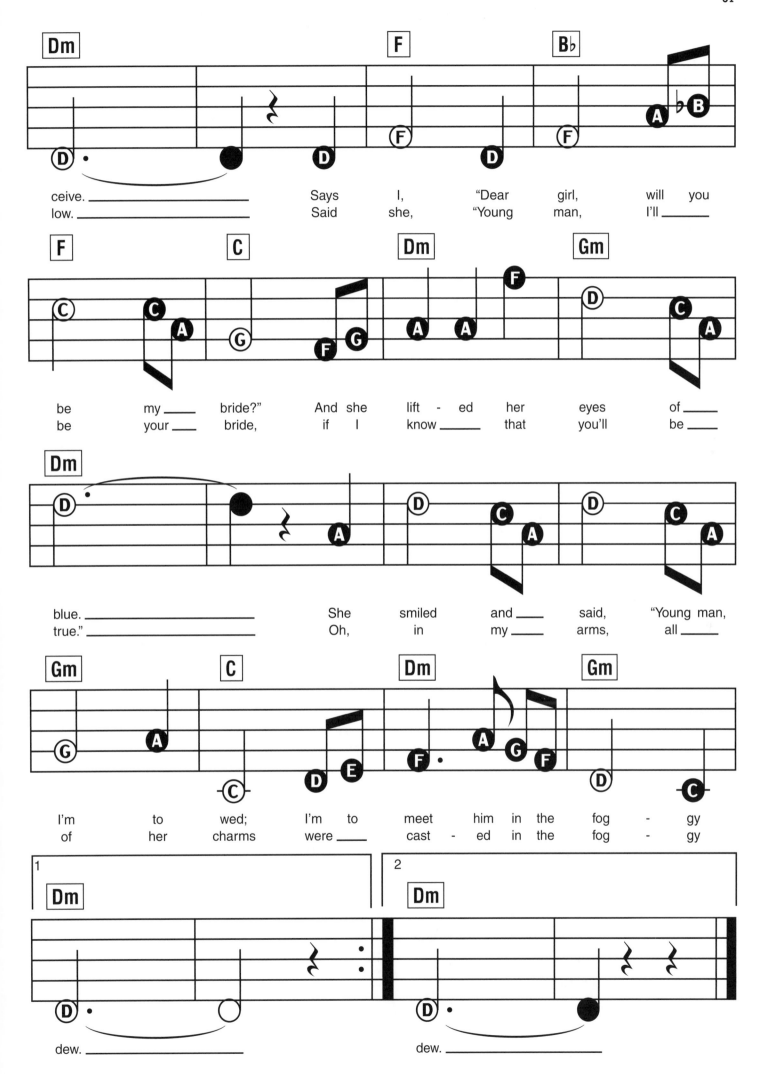

The Galway Races

Registration 4
Rhythm: Fox Trot

Traditional Irish Folk Song

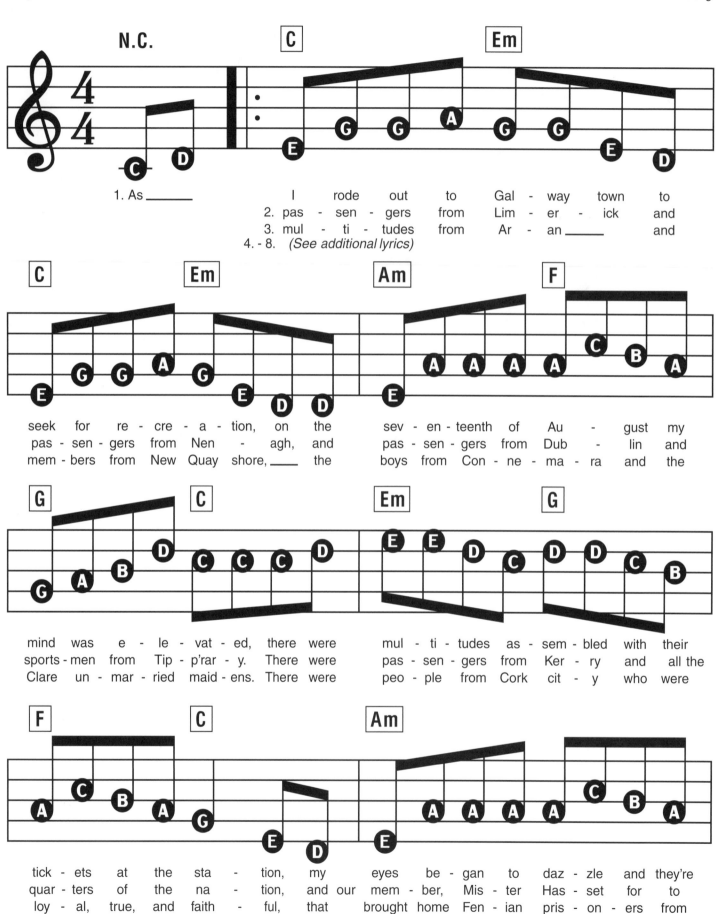

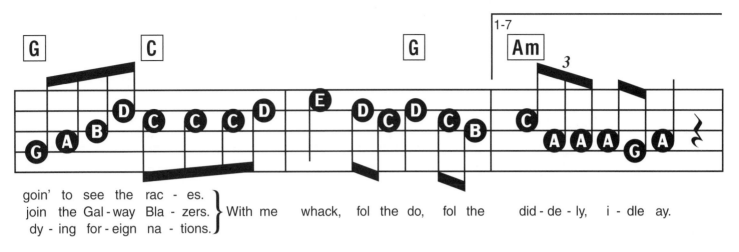

goin' to see the rac - es.
join the Gal - way Bla - zers.
dy - ing for - eign na - tions.
With me whack, fol the do, fol the did - de - ly, i - dle ay.

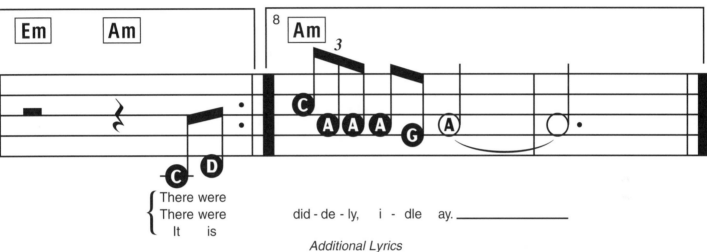

There were
There were
It is

did - de - ly, i - dle ay. _____

Additional Lyrics

4. It is there you'll see confectioners with sugar sticks and dainties,
The lozenges and oranges and lemonade and raisins,
And gingerbread and spices to accommodate the ladies,
And a big crubeen for threepence to be picking while you're able,
With me whack, fol the do, fol the diddely, idle ay.

5. It is there you'll see the gamblers, the thimbles and the garters,
And the sporting Wheel-of-Fortune with the four and twenty quarters.
There were others without scruple pelting wattles at poor Maggy,
And her father well contented to be looking at his daughter.
With me whack, fol the do, fol the diddely, idle ay.

6. It is there you'll see the pipers and the fiddlers competing,
And the nimble-footed dancers, and they trippin' on the daisies,
And others cryin' cigars and bill for all the races,
With the colors of the jockeys and the prize and horse's ages.
With me whack, fol the do, fol the diddely, idle ay.

7. It's there you'd see the jockeys and they mounted on most stately,
The pink and blue, the red and green, the emblem of our nation,
When the bell was rung for starting all the horses seemed impatient,
I thought they never stood on ground, their speed was so amazing.
With me whack, fol the do, fol the diddely, idle ay.

8. There was half a million people there of all denominations,
The Catholic, the Protestant, the Jew and Presbyterian.
There was yet no animosity, no matter what persuasion,
But fortune and hospitality inducing fresh acquaintance.
With me whack, fol the do, fol the diddely, idle ay.

The Galway Shawl

Registration 4
Rhythm: Waltz

Traditional Irish Folk Song

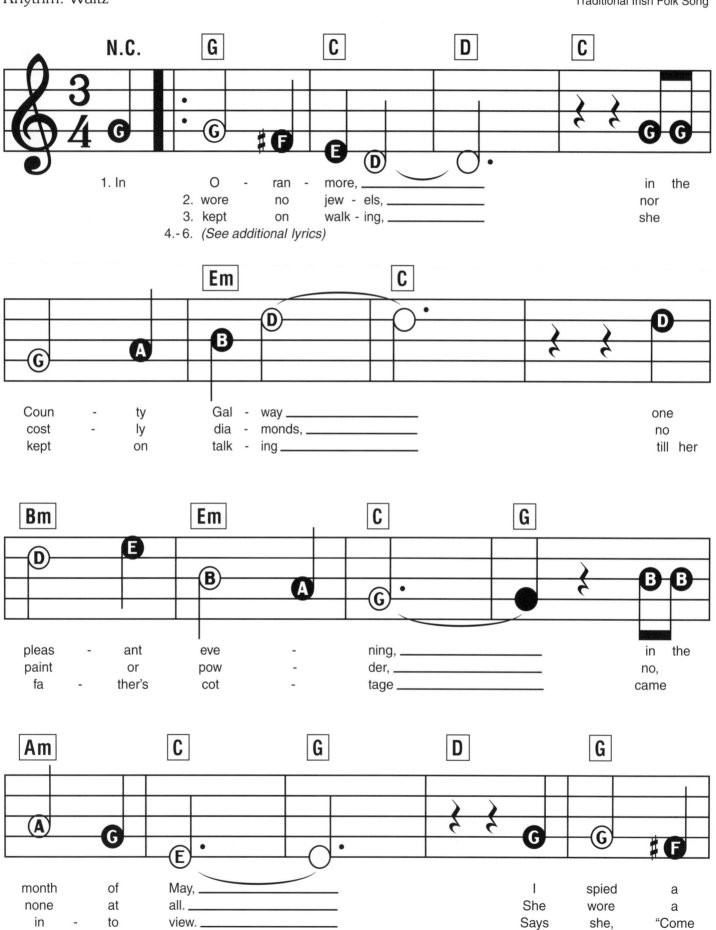

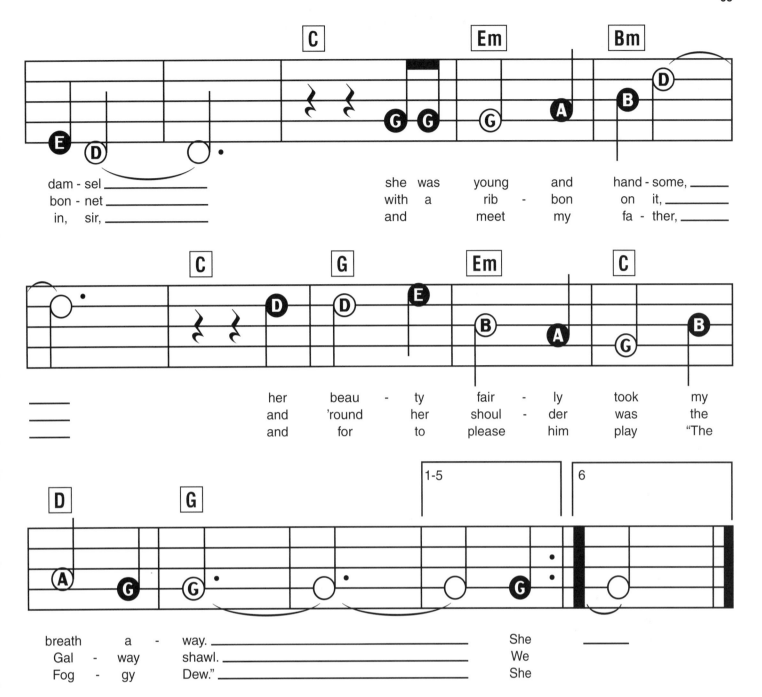

dam - sel _____ she was young and hand - some, _____
bon - net _____ with a rib - bon on it, _____
in, sir, _____ and meet my fa - ther, _____

_____ her beau - ty fair - ly took my
_____ and 'round her shoul - der was the
_____ and for to please him play "The

breath a - way. _____ She _____
Gal - way shawl. _____ We
Fog - gy Dew." _____ She

Additional Lyrics

4. She sat me down beside the fire,
   I could see her father, he was six feet tall.
   And soon her mother had the kettle singing,
   All I could think of was the Galway shawl.

5. I played "The Blackbird" and "The Stack of Barley,"
   "Rodney's Glory," and "The Foggy Dew."
   She sang each note like an Irish linnet
   Whilst the tears stood in her eyes of blue.

6. "Twas early, early, all in the morning,
   When I hit the road for old Donegal.
   She said, "Goodbye, Sir," she cried and kissed me,
   And my heart remained with the Galway shawl.

Green Grow the Rashes, O

Registration 1
Rhythm: March

Traditional Irish Folk Song

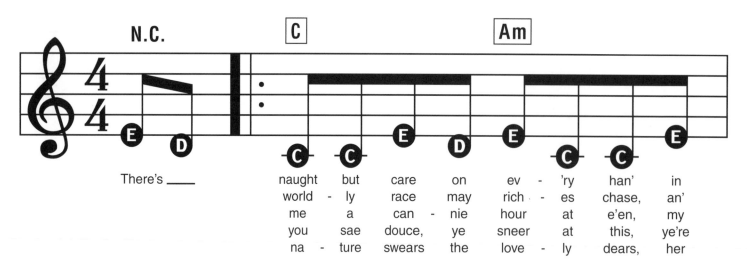

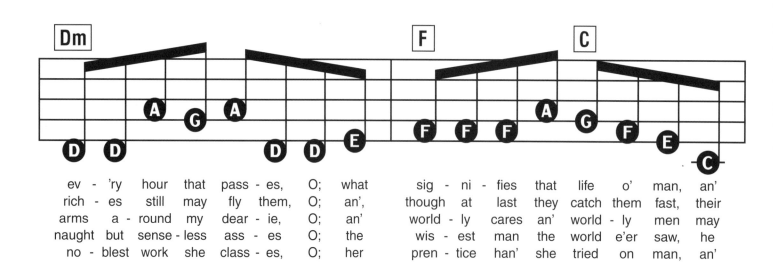

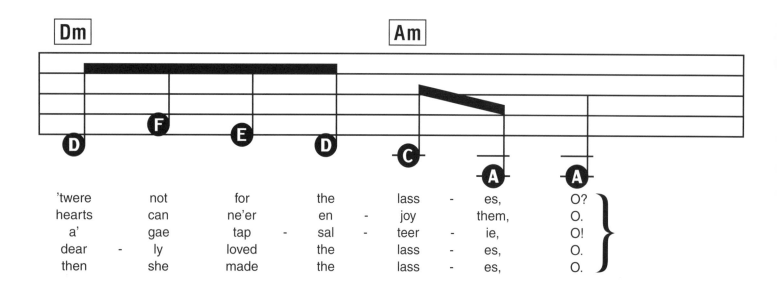

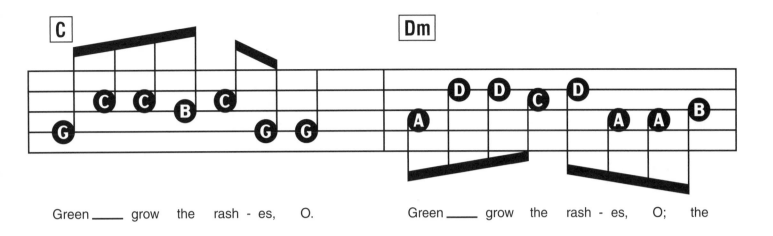

Green _____ grow the rash - es, O.   Green _____ grow the rash - es, O; the

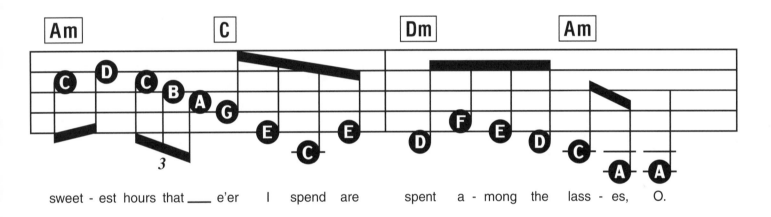

sweet - est hours that ___ e'er   I   spend are   spent a - mong the lass - es, O.

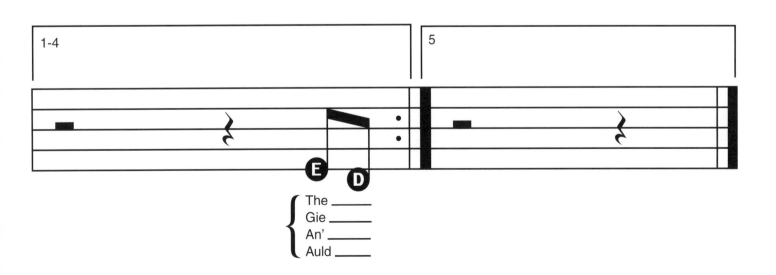

The _____
Gie _____
An' _____
Auld _____

Henry My Son

Registration 7
Rhythm: March

Traditional Irish Folk Song

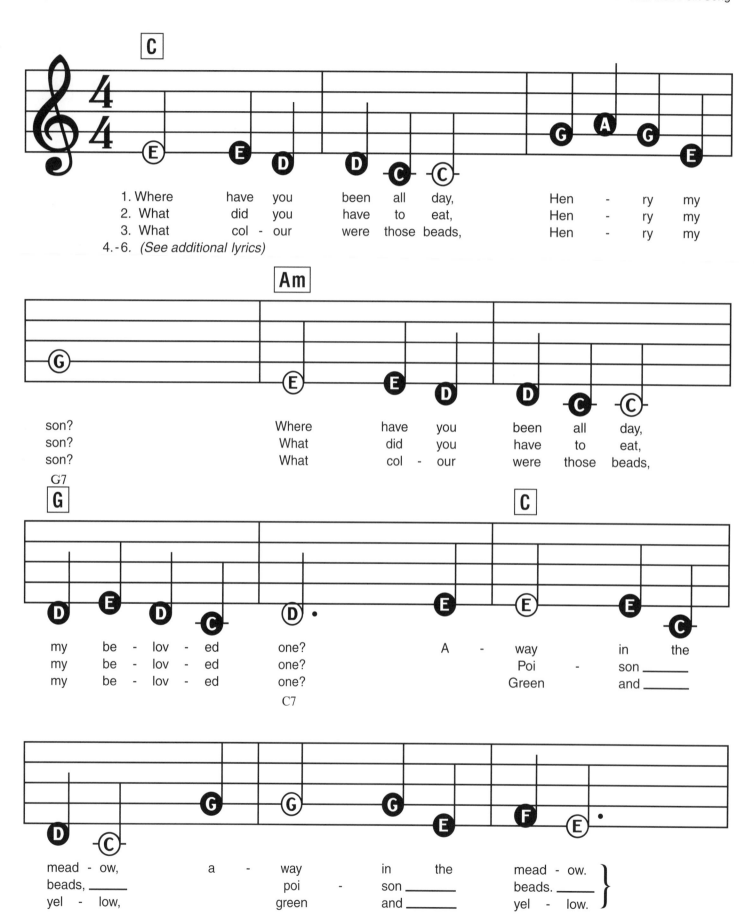

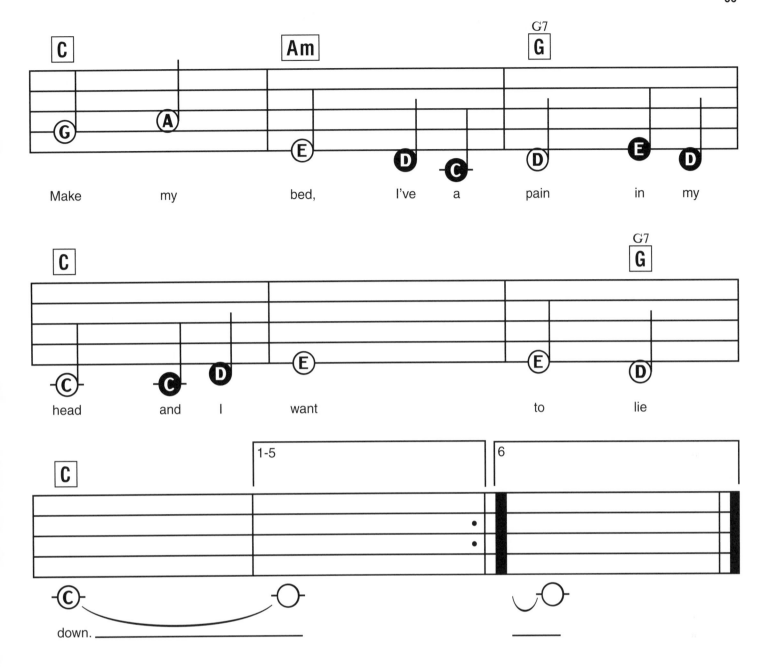

Make my bed, I've a pain in my

head and I want to lie

down.

1-5   6

Additional Lyrics

4. What will you leave your mother, Henry my son?
   What will you leave your mother, my beloved one?
   A woolen blanket, a woolen blanket.
   Make my bed, I've a pain in my head and I want to lie down.

5. What will you leave your children, Henry my son?
   What will you leave your children, my beloved one?
   The keys of heaven, the keys of heaven.
   Make my bed, I've a pain in my head and I want to lie down.

6. And what will you leave your sweetheart, Henry my son?
   What will you leave your sweetheart, my beloved one?
   A rope to hang her, a rope to hang her.
   Make my bed, I've a pain in my head and I want to lie down.

High Germany

Registration 8
Rhythm: Fox Trot

Traditional Irish Folk Song

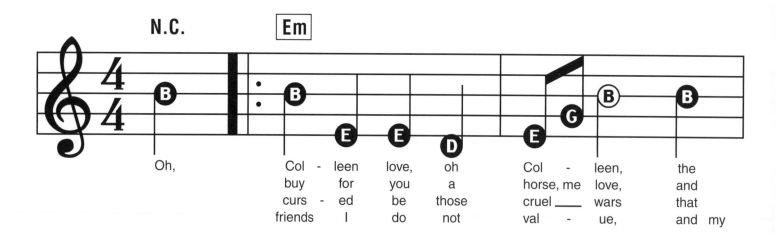

Oh,
Col - leen love, oh Col - leen, the
buy for you a horse, me love, and
curs - ed be those cruel ___ wars that
friends I do not val - ue, and my

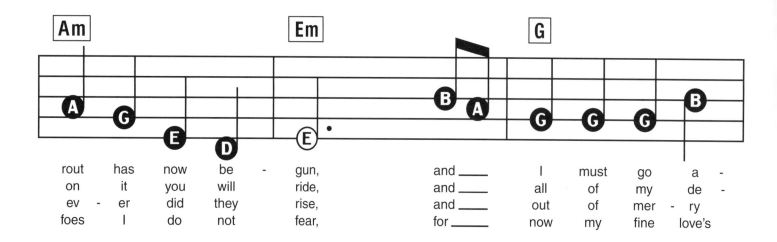

rout has now be - gun, and ___ I must go a
on it you will ride, and ___ all of my de -
ev - er did they rise, and ___ out of mer - ry
foes I do not fear, for ___ now my fine love's

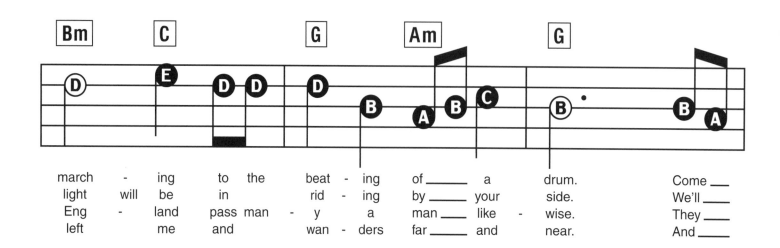

march - ing to the beat - ing of ___ a drum. Come ___
light will be in rid - ing by ___ your side. We'll ___
Eng - land pass man - y a man ___ like - wise. They ___
left me and wan - ders far ___ and near. And ___

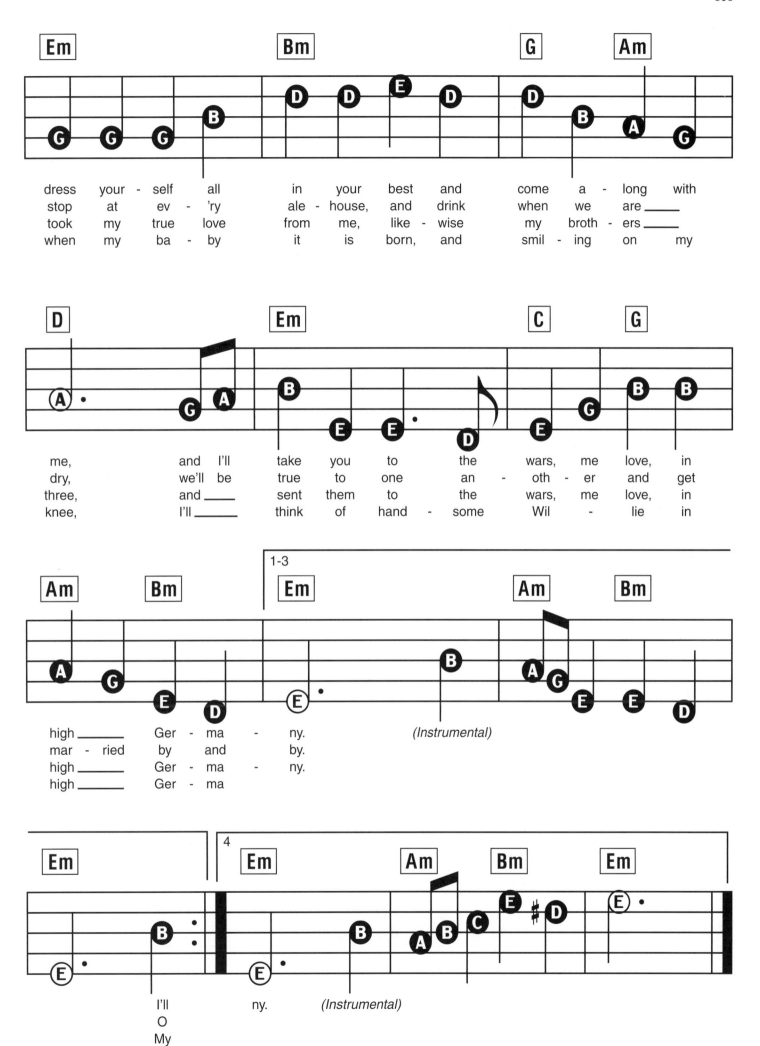

Highland Paddy

Registration 7
Rhythm: March

Traditional Irish Folk Song

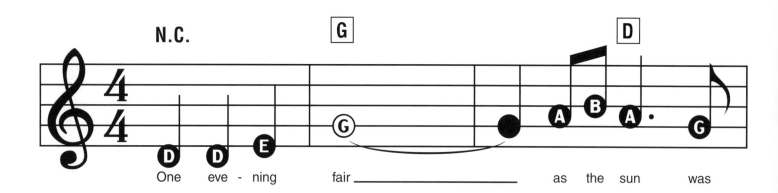

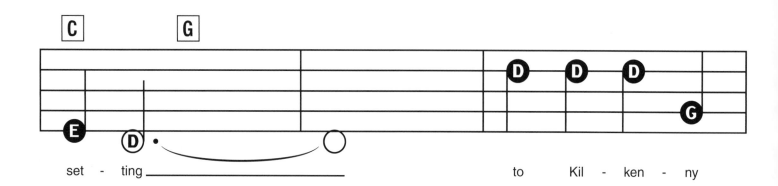

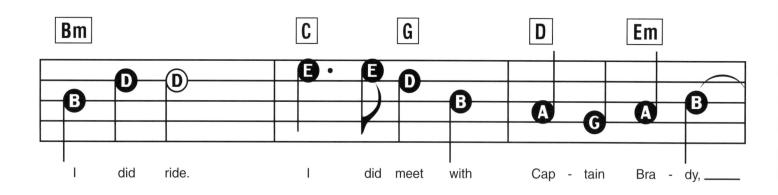

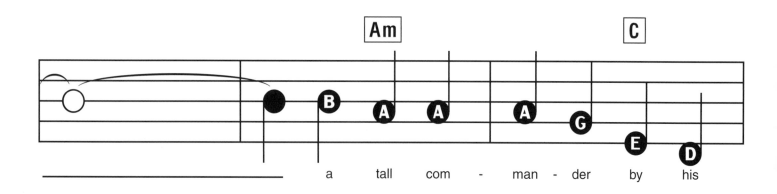

103

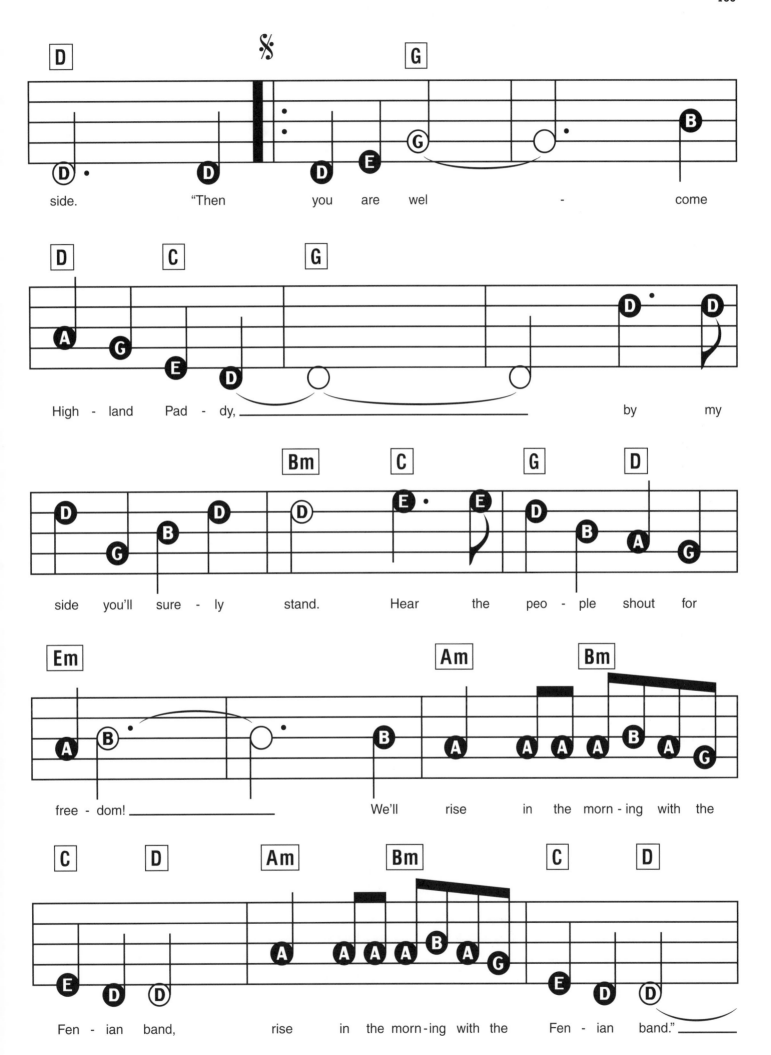

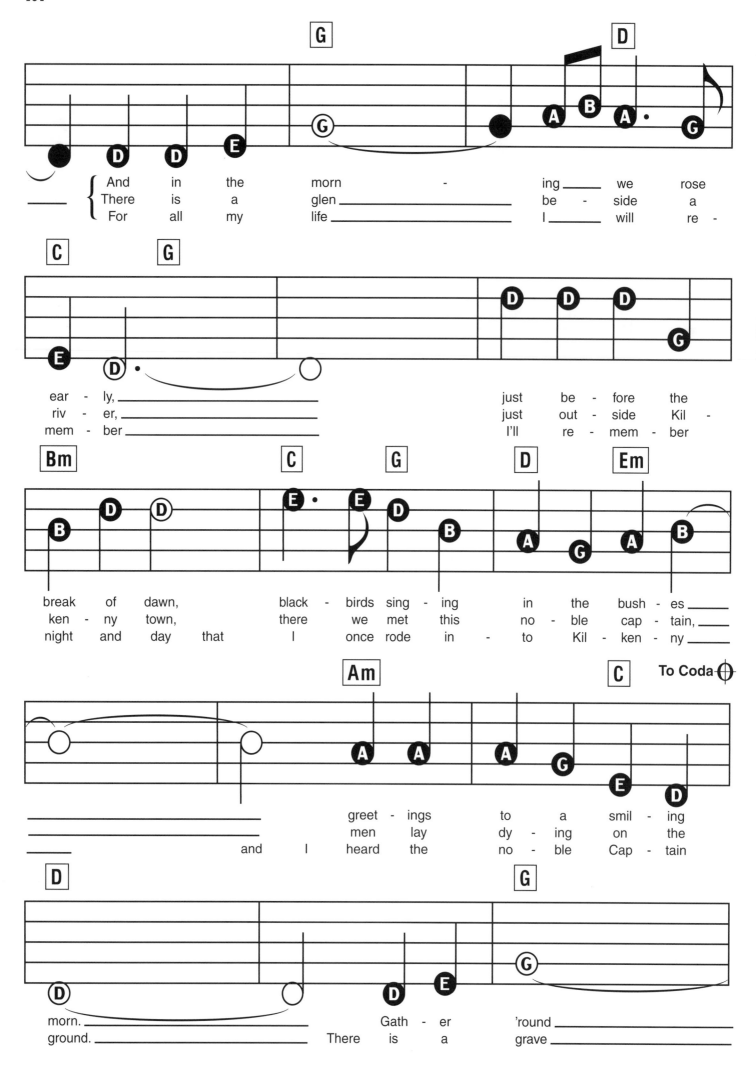

104

105

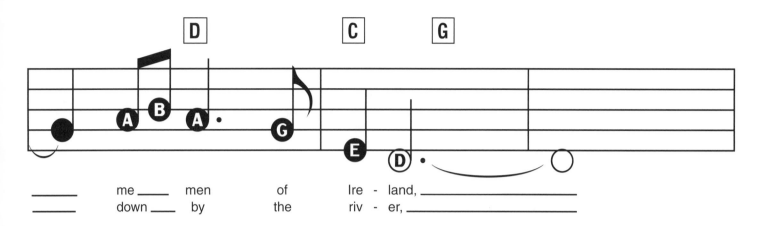

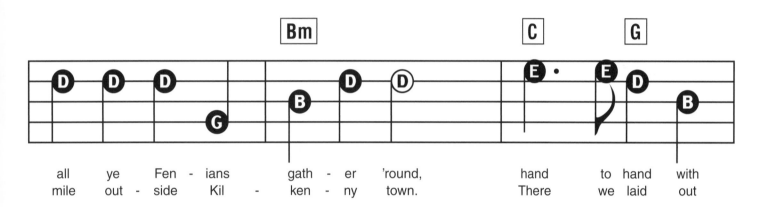

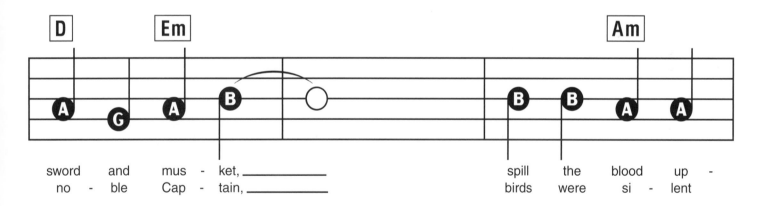

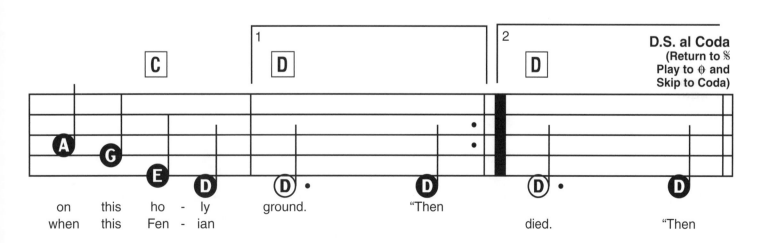

106

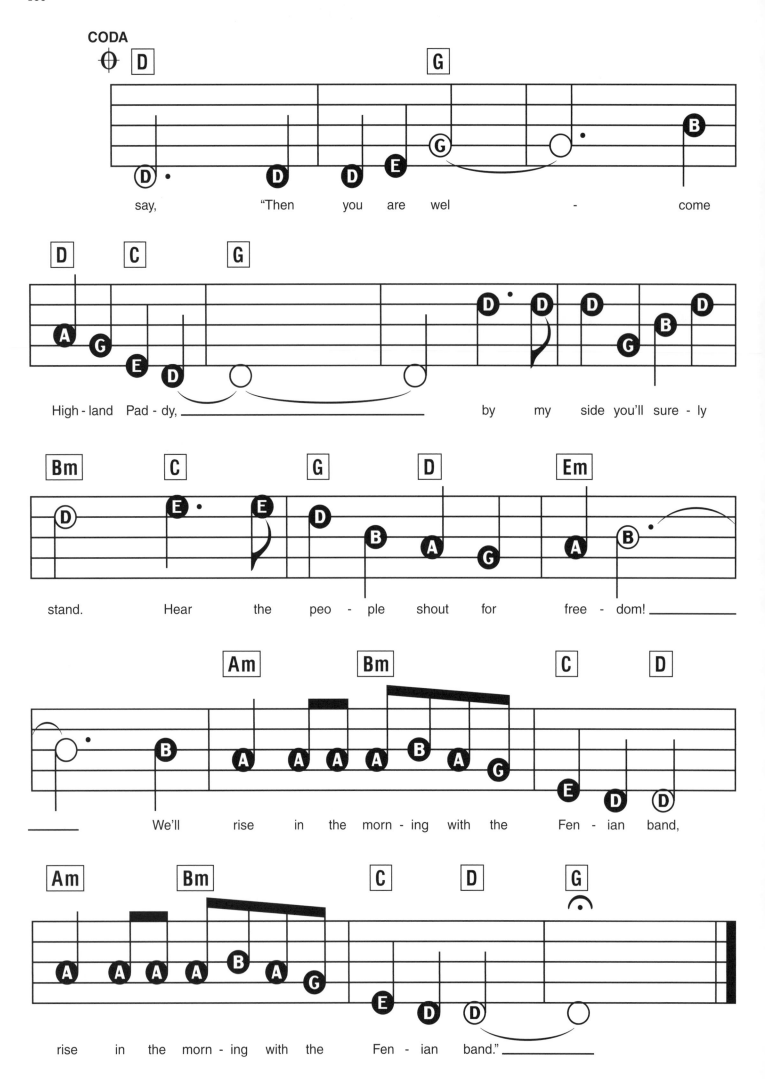

The Holy Ground

Registration 1
Rhythm: Fox Trot

Traditional Irish Folk Song

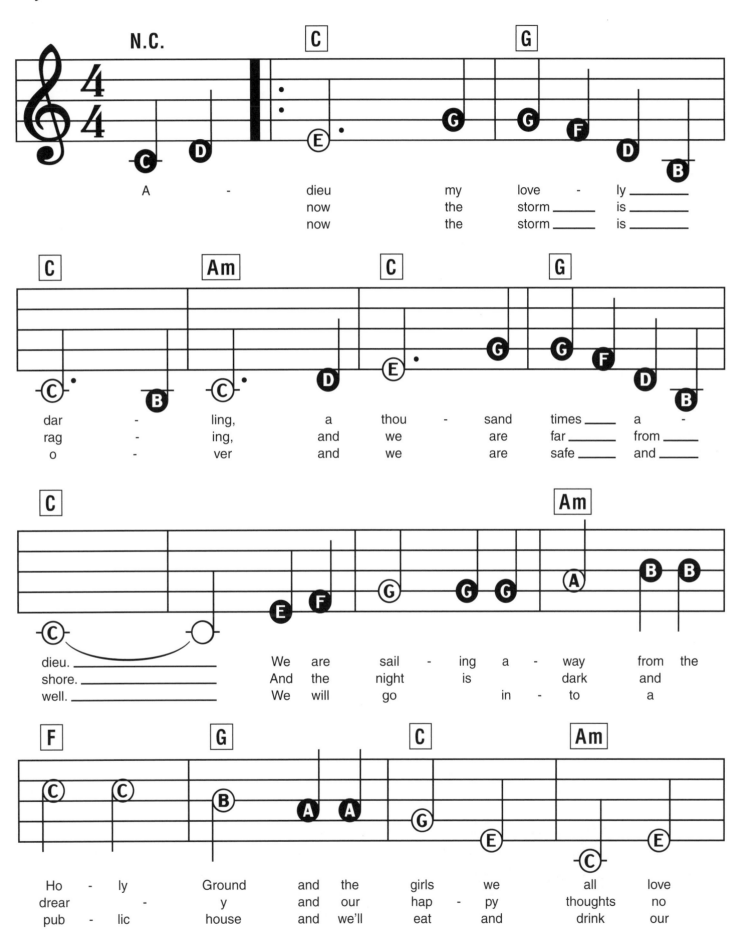

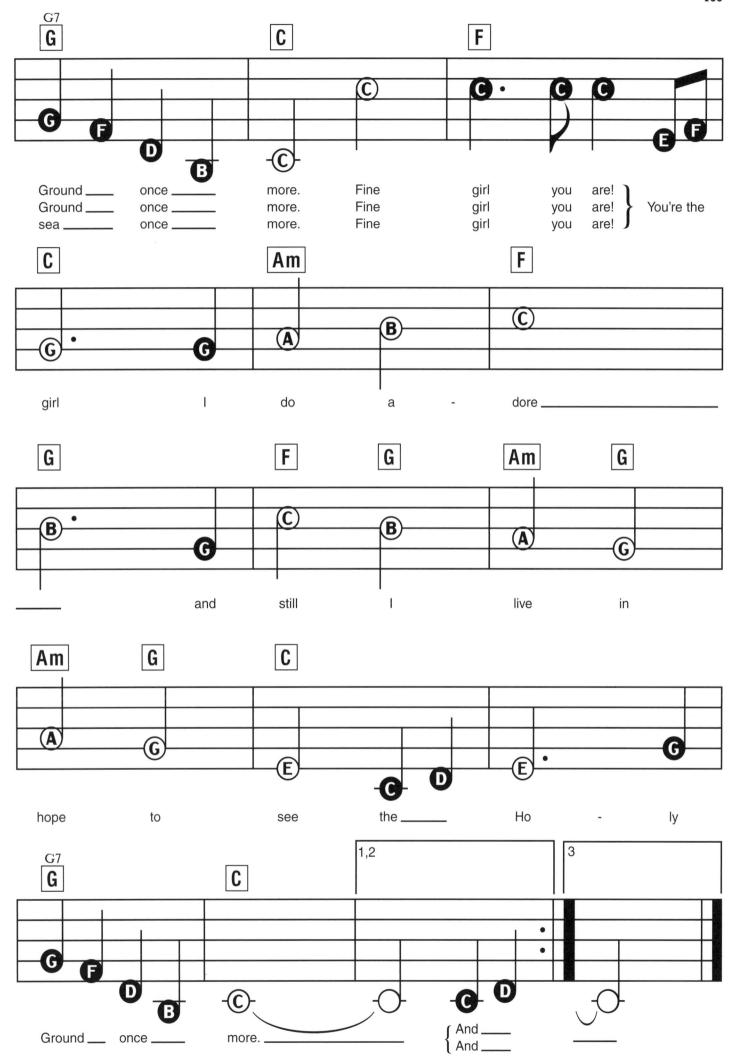

The Hills of Kerry

Registration 10
Rhythm: Waltz

Traditional Irish Folk Song

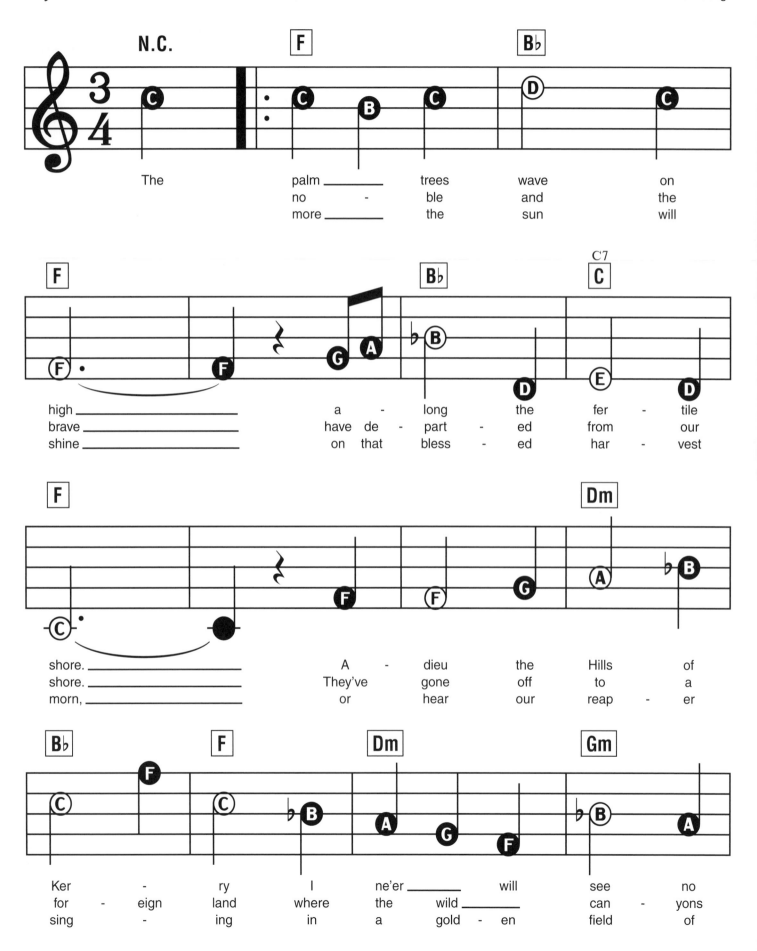

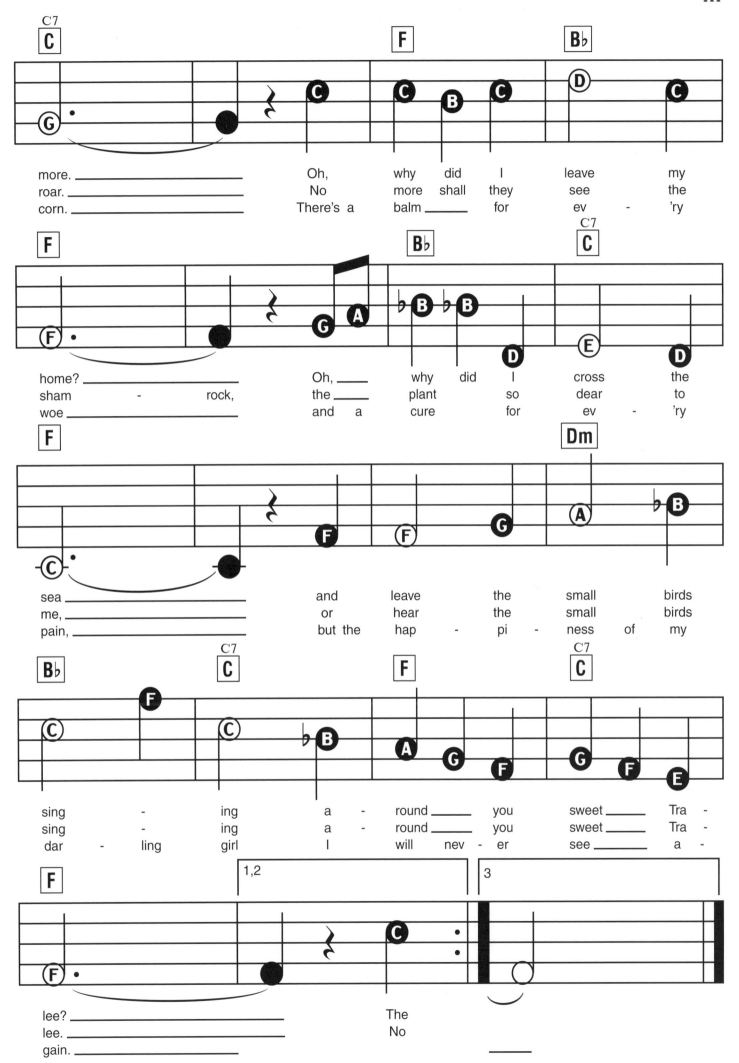

The Humour Is on Me Now

Registration 1
Rhythm: 6/8 March or Jig/Gigue

Traditional Irish Folk Song

1. As _____ I went out one morn - ing, it
2. qui - et you fool - ish daugh - ter, and
3. who are you to turn me, that
4. deed I'll tell my moth - er the
5.-8. *(See additional lyrics)*

be - ing the month of May, a farm - er and his
hold your sim - ple tongue. You're bet - ter free and
mar - ried young your - self, and took my dar - ling
aw - ful things you say, in - deed I'll tell my

daugh-ter _____ I spied up - on my way. And the
sin - gle, _____ and hap - py while you're young. But the
moth - er _____ from off the sin - gle shelf? Ah sure,
moth - er _____ this ver - y bless - ed day. Och, now

girl sat down quite calm - ly to the milk - ing of her
daugh - ter shook her shoul - ders and _____ milked her pa - tient
daugh - ter dear, so ais - y, and _____ milk your pa - tient
daugh - ter, have a heart, dear, you'll _____ start a fear - ful

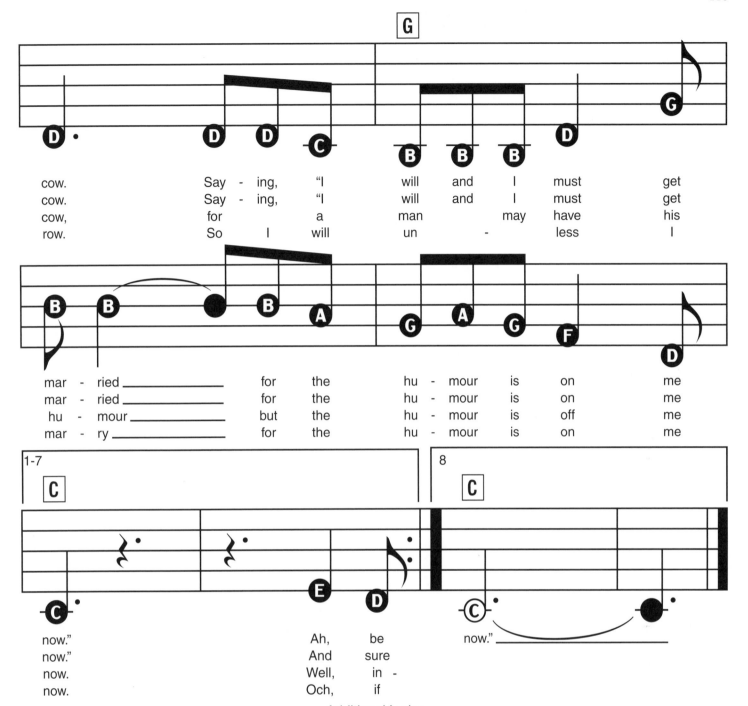

cow.   Say - ing, "I   will and I must get
cow.   Say - ing, "I   will and I must get
cow,   for   a   man may have his
row.   So I will   un - less I

mar - ried _____ for the hu - mour is on me
mar - ried _____ for the hu - mour is on me
hu - mour _____ but the hu - mour is off me
mar - ry _____ for the hu - mour is on me

1-7   C

8   C

now."
now."
now.
now.

Ah, be
And sure
Well, in -
Och, if

now." _____

Additional Lyrics

5. Och, if you must be married will you tell me who's the man?
And quickly she did answer, "There's William, James and John,
A carpenter, a tailor, and a man to milk the cow,
For I will and I must get married and the humour is on me now."

6. A carpenter's a sharp man, and a tailor's hard to face,
With his legs across the table and his threads about the place.
And sure John's a fearful tyrant and never lacks a row,
But I will and I must be married for the humour is on me now.

7. Well, if you must be married, will you tell me what you'll do?
"Sure I will," the daughter answered, "just the same as you.
I'll be mistress of my dairy and my butter and my cow."
And your husband too, I'll venture, for the humour is on you now.

8. So at last the daughter married and married well-to-do,
And loved her darling husband for a month, a year or two.
But John was all a tyrant and she quickly rued her vow,
Saying, "I'm sorry that I married for the humour is off me now."

I Know My Love

Registration 2
Rhythm: Waltz

Traditional Irish Folk Song

I Never Will Marry

Registration 7
Rhythm: Waltz

Traditional Folk Song

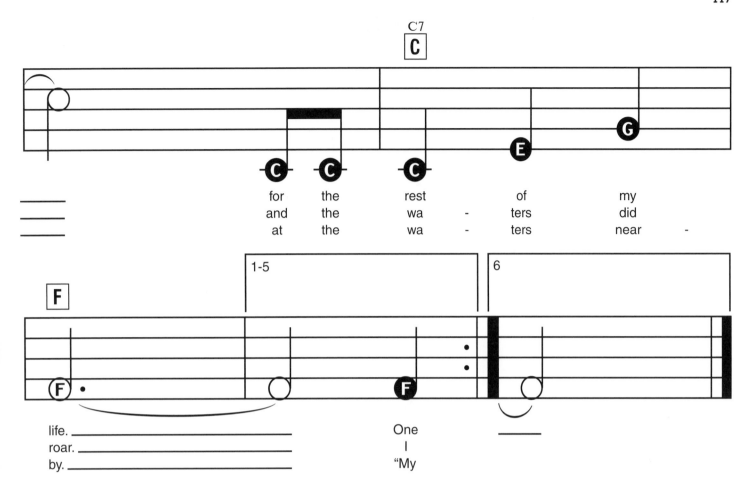

for the rest of my
and the wa - ters did
at the wa - ters near -

life. _____ One
roar. _____ I
by. _____ "My

Additional Lyrics

4. "My love's gone and left me, he's the one I adore.
   I never will see him, no never, no more."

5. "The shells in the ocean will be my deathbed,
   And the fish in the water swim over my head."

6. She plunged her fair body in the water so deep.
   And she closed her pretty blue eyes in the water to sleep.

I Once Loved a Lass

Registration 1
Rhythm: Waltz

Traditional Irish Folk Song

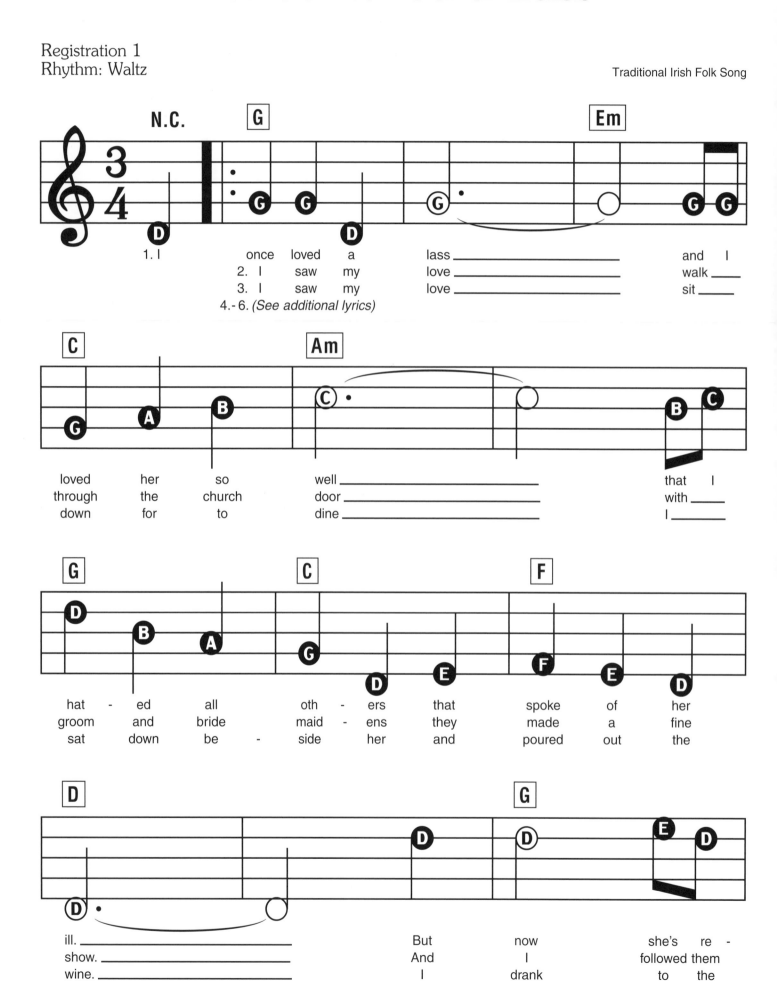

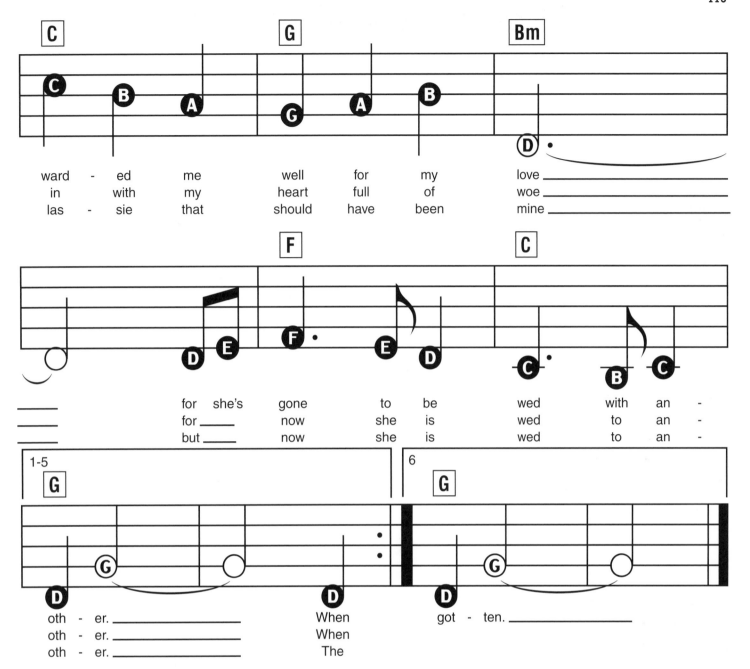

Additional Lyrics

4. The men in yon forest, they ask it of me
   How many strawberries grow in the salt sea?
   And I ask of them back with a tear in my eye
   How many ships sail in the forest?

5. So dig me a grave and dig it so deep
   And cover me over with flowers so sweet
   And I will turn in for to take a long sleep
   And maybe in time I'll forget her.

6. They dug him a grave and they dug it so deep
   They covered him over with flowers so sweet
   And he has turned in for to take a long sleep
   And maybe by now he's forgotten.

I'll Take You Home Again, Kathleen

Registration 1
Rhythm: Fox Trot

Words and Music by
Thomas Westendorf

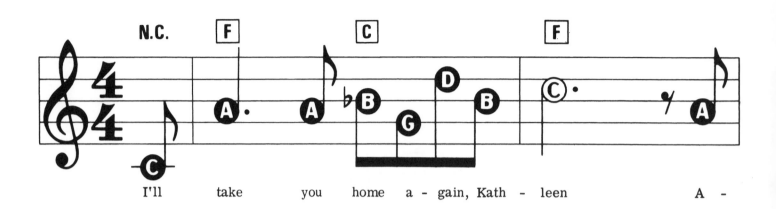

I'll take you home a - gain, Kath - leen A -

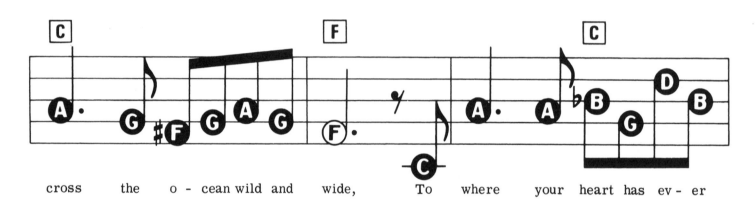

cross the o - cean wild and wide, To where your heart has ev - er

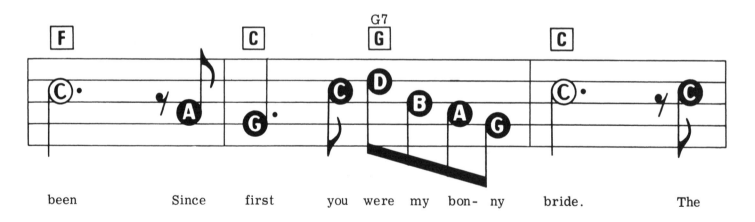

been Since first you were my bon - ny bride. The

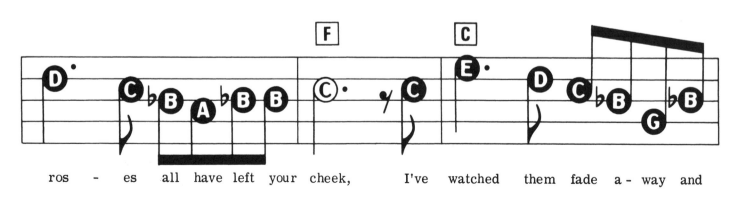

ros - es all have left your cheek, I've watched them fade a - way and

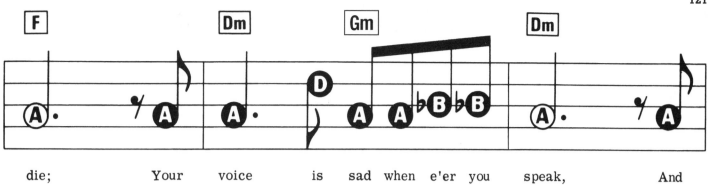

die; Your voice is sad when e'er you speak, And

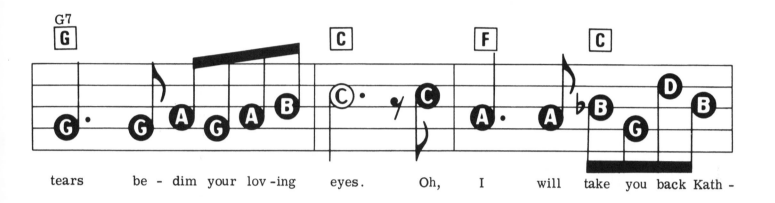

tears be - dim your lov -ing eyes. Oh, I will take you back Kath -

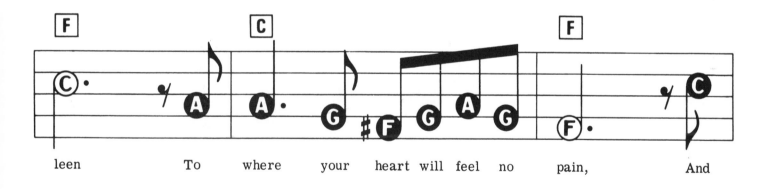

leen To where your heart will feel no pain, And

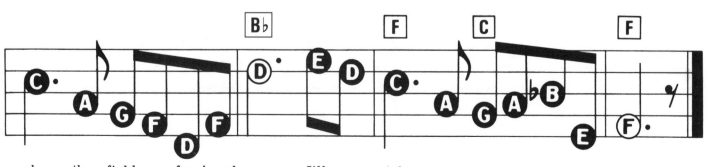

when the fields are fresh and green, I'll___ take you to your home a - gain.

I'll Tell Me Ma

Registration 2
Rhythm: Fox Trot

Traditional Irish Folk Song

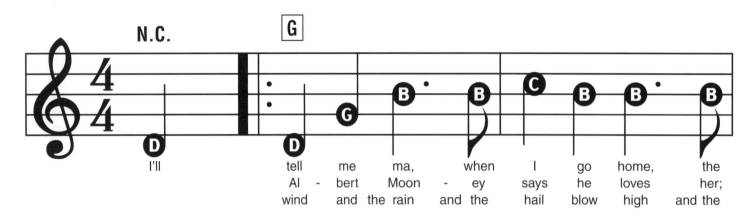

I'll tell me ma, when I go home, the
Al - bert Moon - ey says he loves her;
wind and the rain and the hail blow high and the

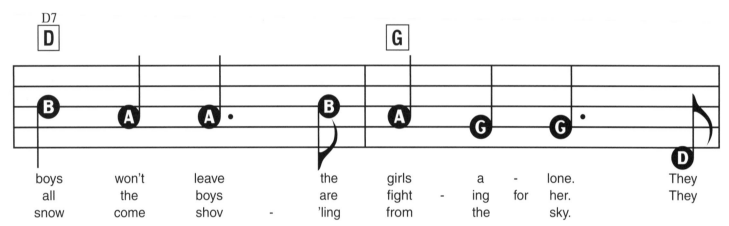

boys won't leave the girls a - lone. They
all the boys are fight - ing for her. They
snow come shov - 'ling from the sky.

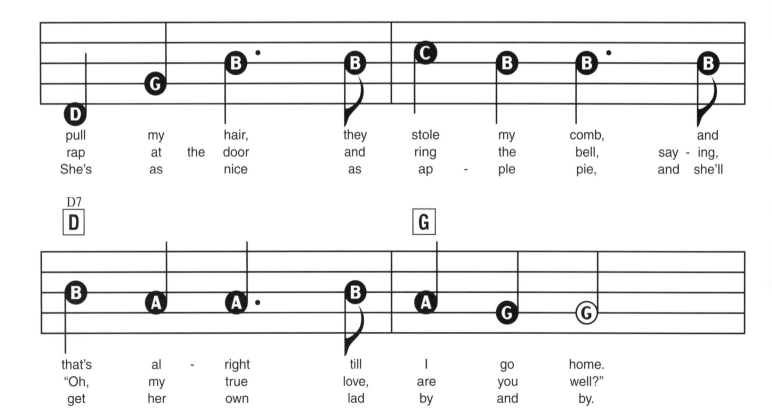

pull my hair, they stole my comb, and
rap at the door and ring the bell, say - ing,
She's as nice as ap - ple pie, and she'll

that's al - right till I go home.
"Oh, my true love, are you well?"
get her own lad by and by.

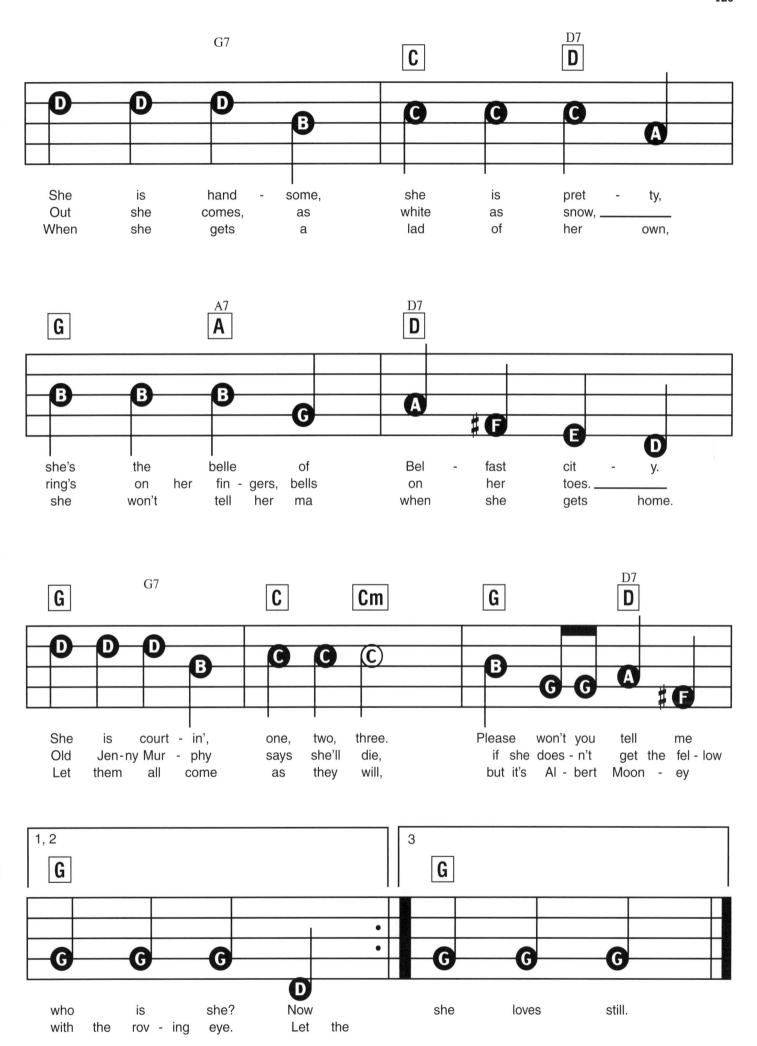

I'm a Rover and Seldom Sober

Registration 8
Rhythm: Waltz

Traditional Irish Folk Song

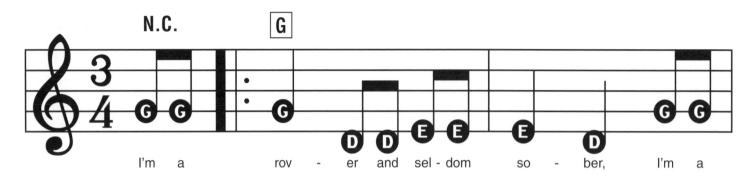

I'm a rov - er and sel - dom so - ber, I'm a

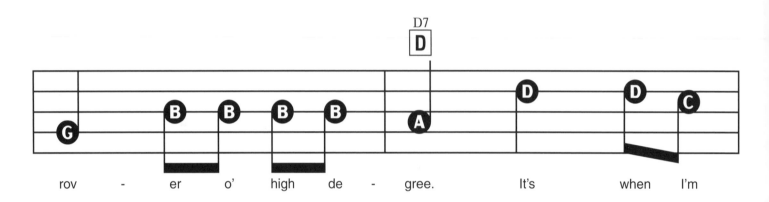

rov - er o' high de - gree. It's when I'm

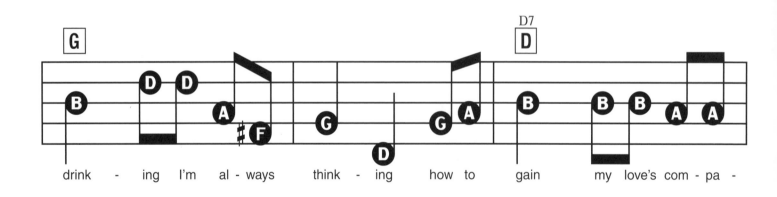

drink - ing I'm al - ways think - ing how to gain my love's com - pa -

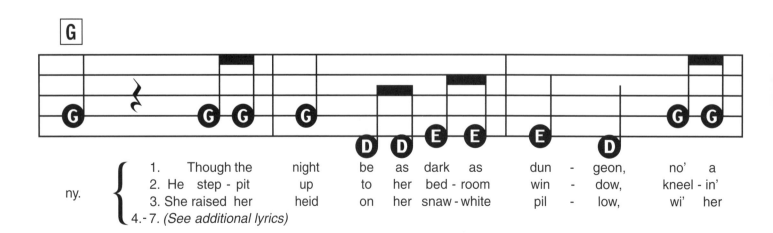

ny.

1. Though the night be as dark as dun - geon, no' a
2. He step - pit up to her bed - room win - dow, kneel - in'
3. She raised her heid on her snaw - white pil - low, wi' her
4.-7. *(See additional lyrics)*

125

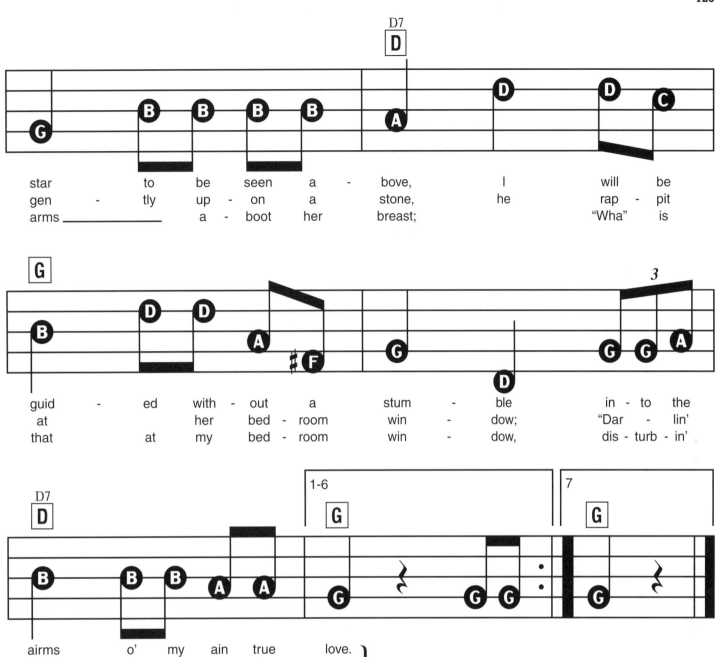

star   to   be seen a - bove,   I   will be
gen - tly up - on a   stone,   he   rap - pit
arms _____ a - boot her breast;   "Wha" is

guid - ed   with - out a stum - ble   in - to the
at   her bed - room win - dow;   "Dar - lin'
that at my bed - room win - dow,   dis - turb - in'

airms o' my ain true love.   I'm a   love."
dear, do you lie a - lone?"
me   at my lang night's rest?"

Additional Lyrics

4. "It's only me, your ain true lover;
   Open the door and let me in,
   For I hae come on a lang journey
   And I'm near drenched to the skin."

5. She opened the door wi' the greatest pleasure,
   She opened the door and she let him in;
   They baith shook hands and embraced each other,
   Until the mornin' they lay as one.

6. The cocks were crawin', the birds were whistlin',
   The burns they ran free abune the brae;
   "Remember, lass, I'm a ploughman laddie
   And the fairmer I must obey."

7. "Noo, my lass, I must gang and leave thee,
   And though the hills they are high above,
   I will climb them wi' greater pleasure
   Since I been in the airms o' my love."

The Irish Rover

Registration 2
Rhythm: Fox Trot

Traditional Irish Folk Song

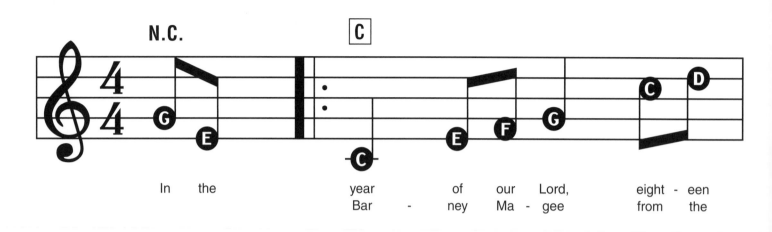

In the year of our Lord, eight - een
Bar - ney Ma - gee from the

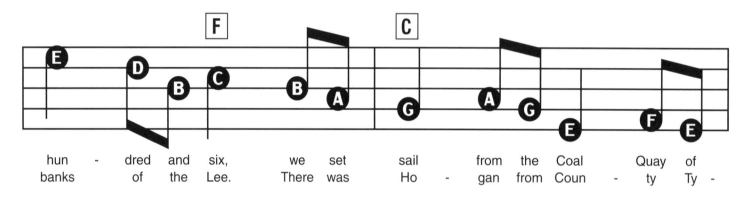

hun - dred and six, we set sail from the Coal Quay of
banks of the Lee. There was Ho - gan from Coun - ty Ty -

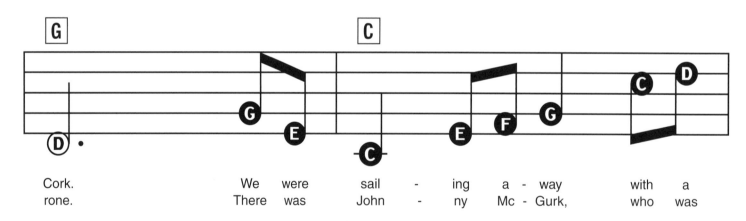

Cork. We were sail - ing a - way with a
rone. There was John - ny Mc - Gurk, who was

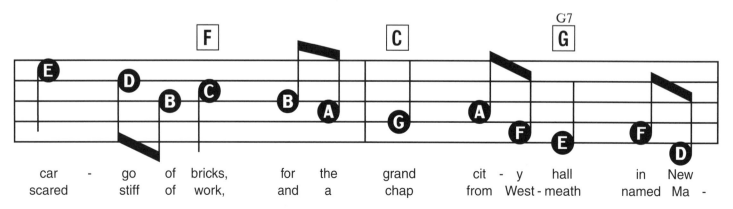

car - go of bricks, for the grand cit - y hall in New
scared stiff of work, and a grand chap from West - meath named Ma -

127

Isn't It Grand, Boys?

Registration 3
Rhythm: Waltz

Traditional Irish Folk Song

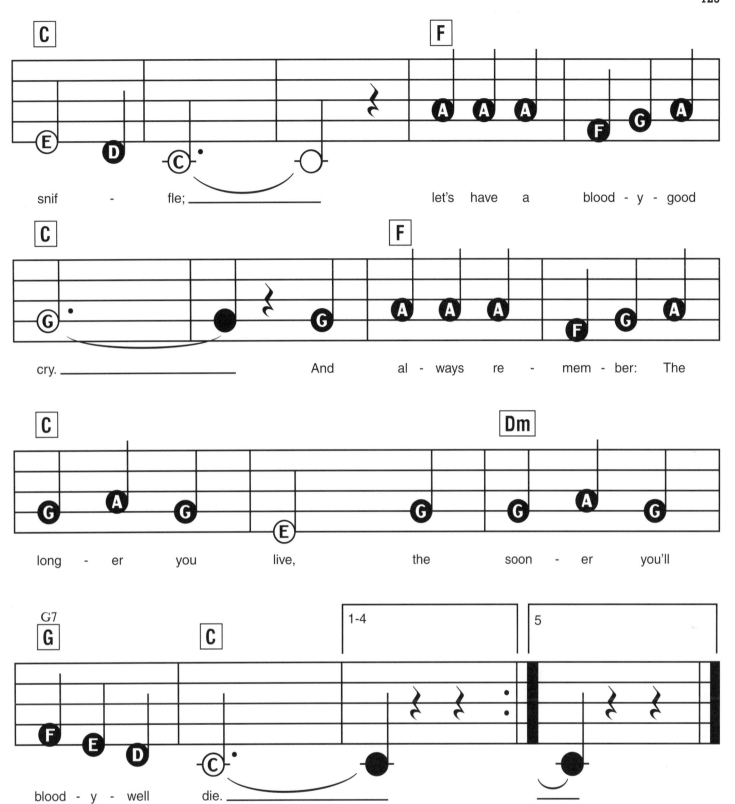

C   **F**

snif - fle; _____ let's have a blood - y - good

C   **F**

cry. _____ And al - ways re - mem - ber: The

C   **Dm**

long - er you live, the soon - er you'll

G7
G   **C**   1-4   5

blood - y - well die. _____

Additional Lyrics

4. Look at the preacher,
   Bloody-nice fellow.
   Isn't it grand, boys,
   To be bloody-well dead?

5. Look at the widow,
   Bloody-great female.
   Isn't it grand, boys,
   To be bloody-well dead?

James Connolly

Registration 2
Rhythm: Waltz

Traditional Irish Folk Song

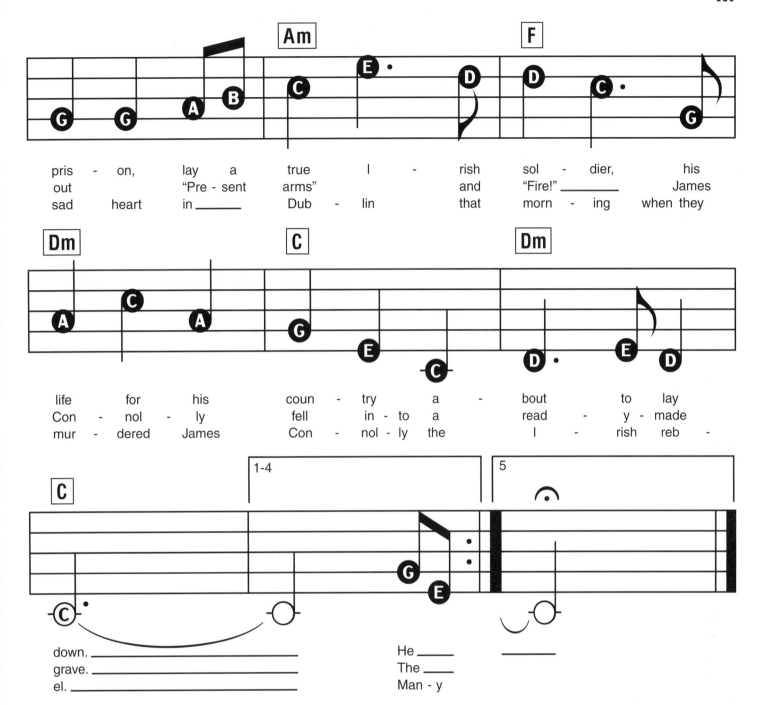

pris - on, lay a true I - rish sol - dier, his
out "Pre - sent arms" and "Fire!" _____ James
sad heart in _____ Dub - lin that morn - ing when they

life for his coun - try a - bout to lay
Con - nol - ly fell in - to a read - y - made
mur - dered James Con - nol - ly the I - rish reb -

down. _____ He _____ _____
grave. _____ The _____
el. _____ Man - y

Additional Lyrics

4. Many years have rolled by since the Irish Rebellion
   When the guns of Britannia they loudly did speak.
   And the bold IRA they stood shoulder to shoulder
   And the blood from their bodies flowed down Sackville Street.

5. The Four Courts of Dublin the English bombarded
   The spirit of freedom they tried hard to quell.
   But above all the din came the cry "No Surrender!"
   'Twas with voice of James Connolly, the Irish rebel.

Johnny, I Hardly Knew Ye

Registration 8
Rhythm: 6/8 March or Jig/Gigue

Traditional Irish Folk Song

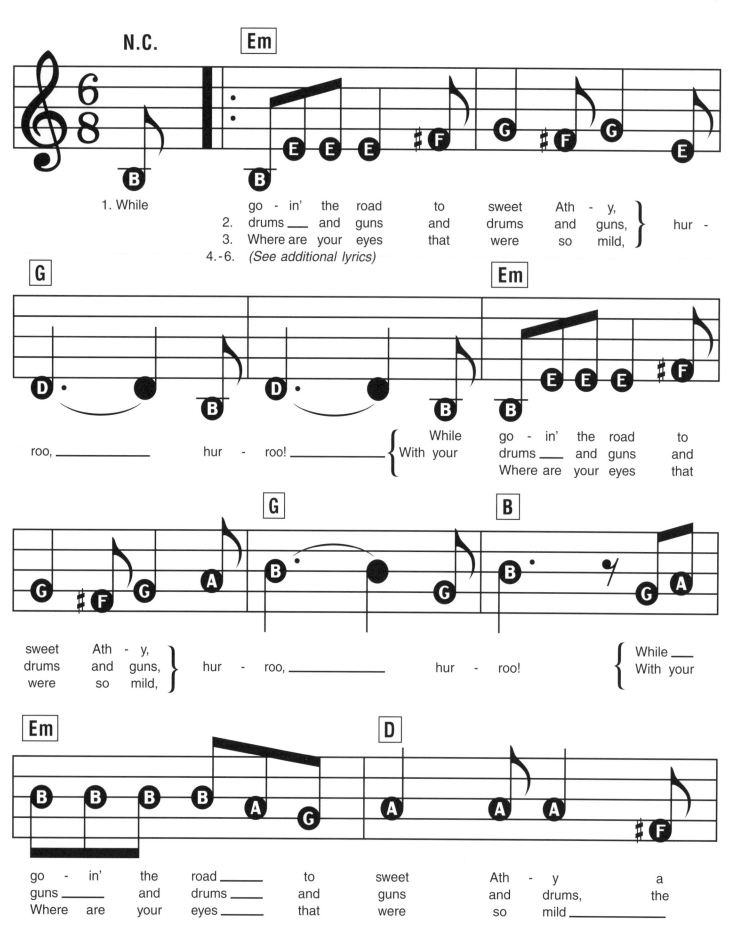

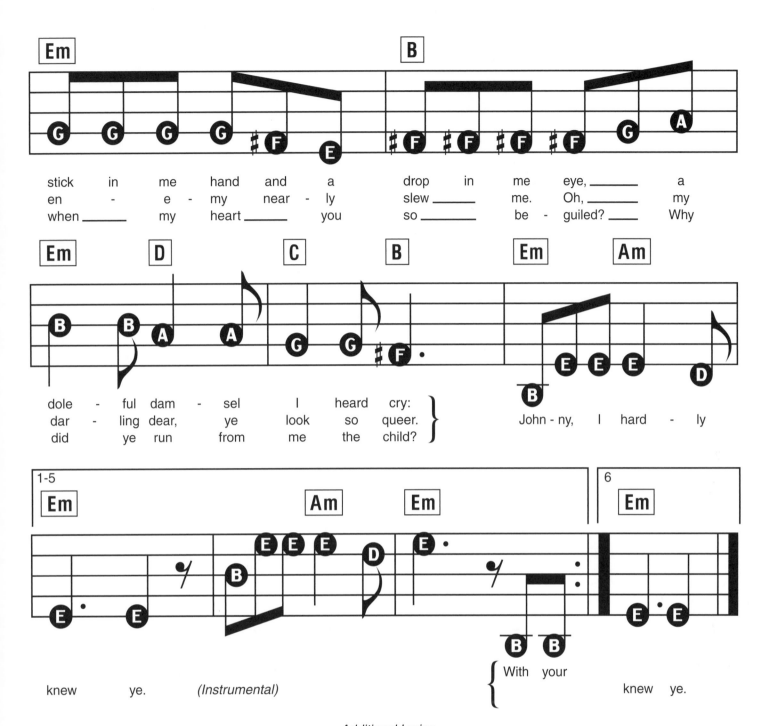

Additional Lyrics

4. Where are your legs that used to run, hurroo, hurroo!
   Where are your legs that used to run, hurroo, hurroo!
   Where are your legs that used to run
   When you went for to carry a gun?
   Indeed your dancing days are done,
   Johnny, I hardly knew ye.

5. I'm happy for to see you home, hurroo, hurroo!
   I'm happy for to see you home, hurroo, hurroo!
   I'm happy for to see you home
   All from the island of Sulloon,
   So low in flesh, so high in bone.
   Johnny, I hardly knew ye.

6. Ye haven't an arm, ye haven't a leg, hurroo, hurroo!
   Ye haven't an arm, ye haven't a leg, hurroo, hurroo!
   Ye haven't an arm, ye haven't a leg,
   Ye're an armless, boneless, chickenless egg,
   Ye'll have to put with a bowl out to beg.
   Johnny, I hardly knew ye.

Johnson's Motor Car

Registration 4
Rhythm: Fox Trot

Traditional Irish Folk Song

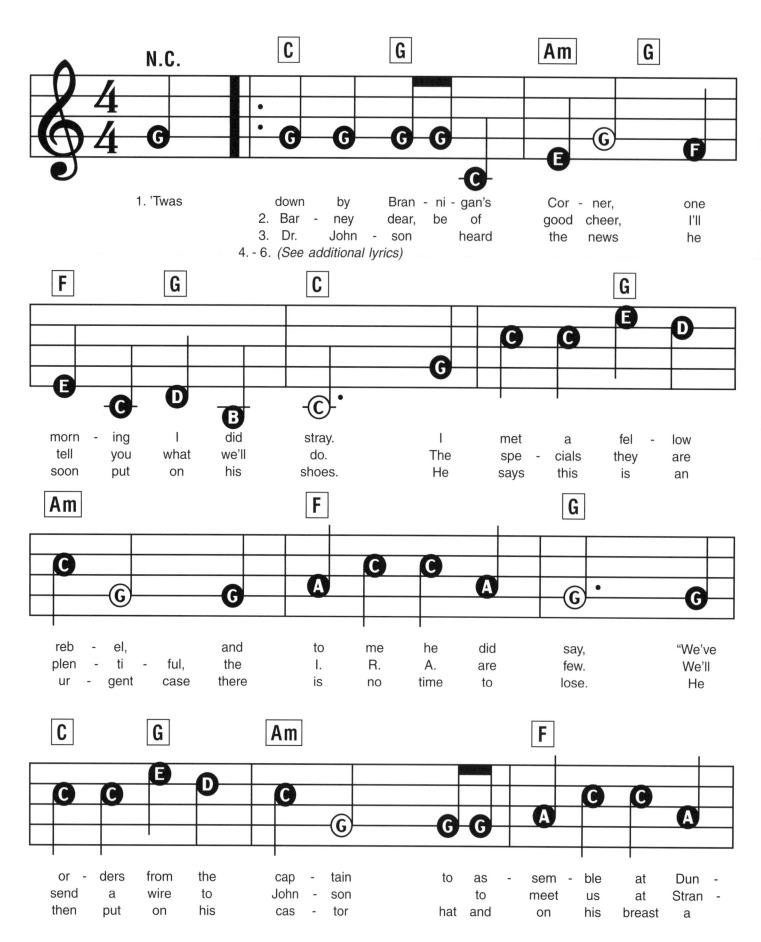

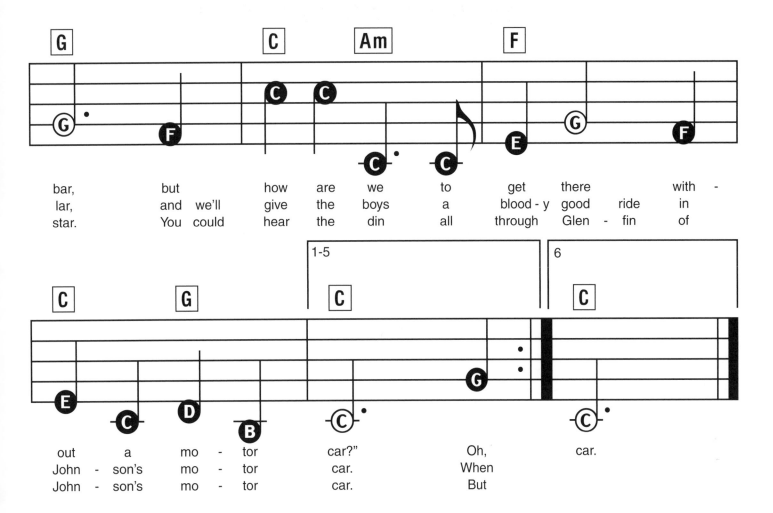

bar,	but	how	are	we	to	get	there	with -
lar,	and we'll	give	the	boys	a	blood - y	good	ride in
star.	You could	hear	the	din	all	through	Glen - fin	of

out	a	mo - tor	car?"	Oh,	car.
John - son's	mo - tor	car.	When	
John - son's	mo - tor	car.	But	

Additional Lyrics

4. But when he got to the railway bridge, some rebels he saw there.
   Old Johnson knew the game was up, for at him they did stare.
   he said, "I have a permit, to travel near and far."
   "To hell with your English permit, we want your motor car."

5. "What will my loyal brethren think, when they hear the news,
   My car it has been commandeered, by the rebels at dunluce."
   "We'll give you a receipt for it, all signed by Captain Barr.
   And when Ireland gets her freedom, boy, you'll get your motor car."

6. Well, we put that car in motion and filled it to the brim,
   With guns and bayonets shining which made old Johnson grim,
   And Barney hoisted a Sinn Fein flag, and it fluttered like a star,
   And we gave three cheers for the I.R.A. and Johnson's motor car.

I Know Where I'm Goin'

Registration 2
Rhythm: Ballad or Fox Trot

Scottish Folk Song

The Jolly Beggarman

Registration 1
Rhythm: Fox Trot

Traditional Irish Folk Song

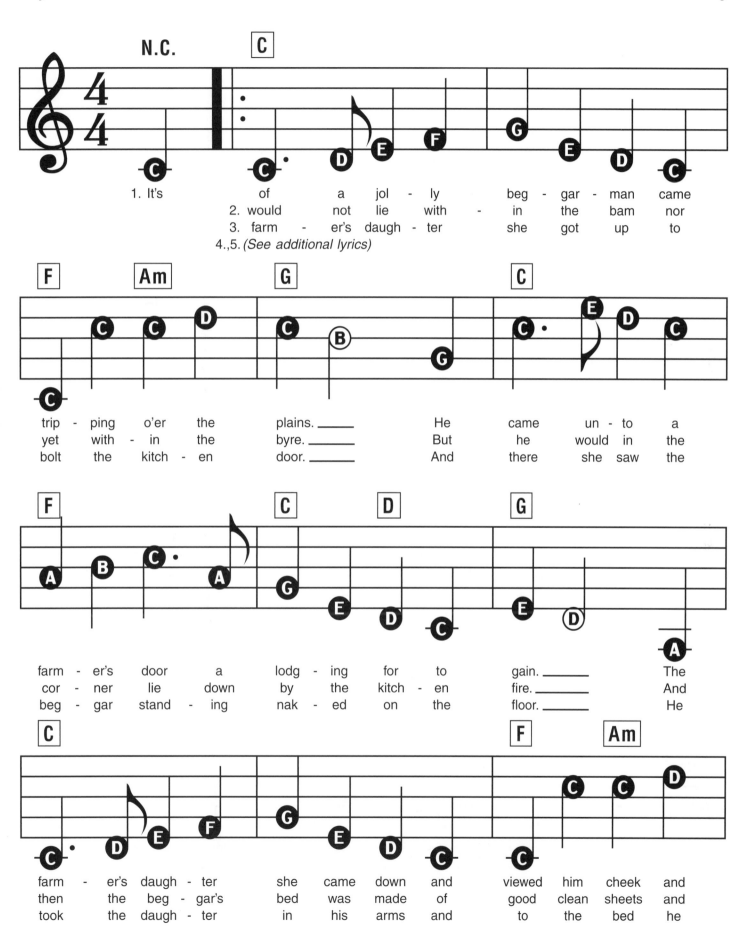

138

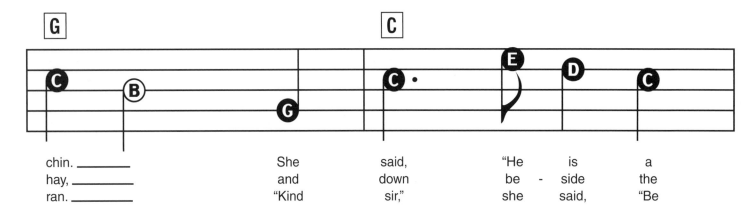

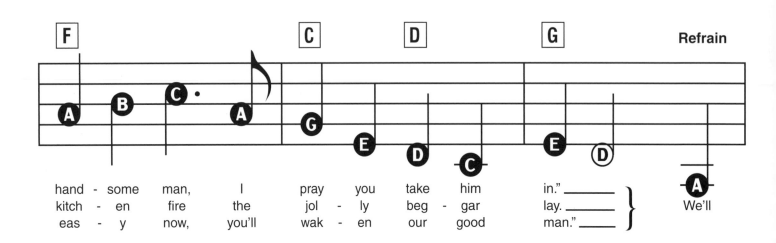

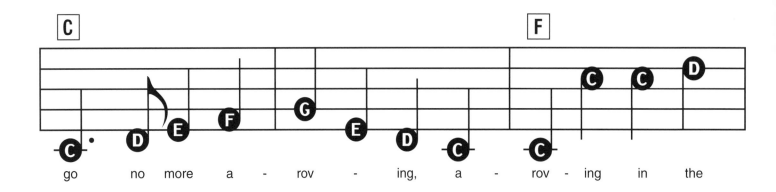

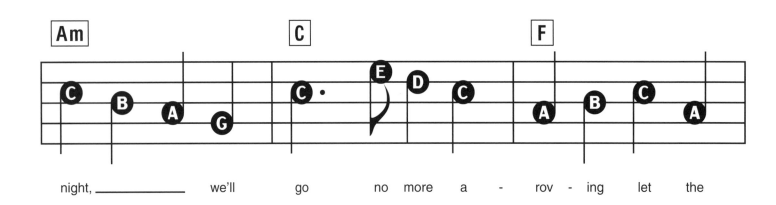

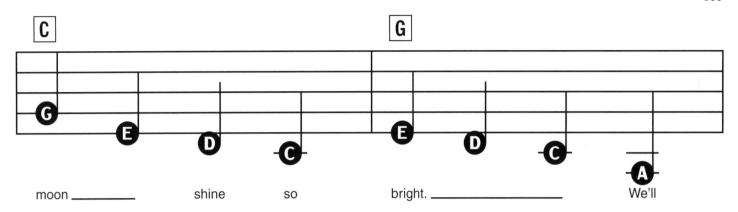

moon _____ shine so bright. _____ We'll

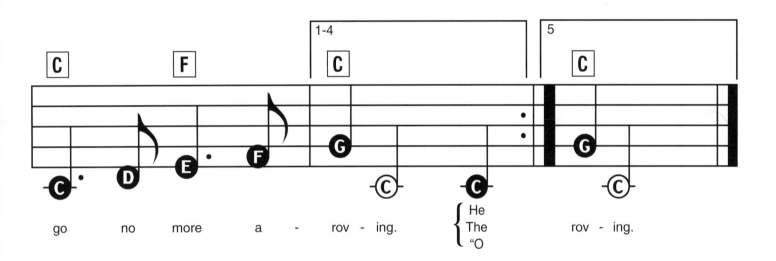

go no more a - rov - ing.

{ He
{ The
{ "O

rov - ing.

Additional Lyrics

4. "O no, you are no beggar man, you are some gentleman
For you have stole my maidenhead and I am quite undone."
"I am no lord, I am no squire, of beggars I be one
And beggars they be robbers all and you are quite undone."
Refrain

5. The farmer's wife came down the stairs, awakened from her sleep.
She saw the beggar and the girl and she began to weep.
She took the bed in both her hands and threw it at the wall
Saying, "Go you with the beggarman, your maidenhead and all!"
Refrain

Jug of Punch

Registration 1
Rhythm: Waltz

Ulster Folk Song

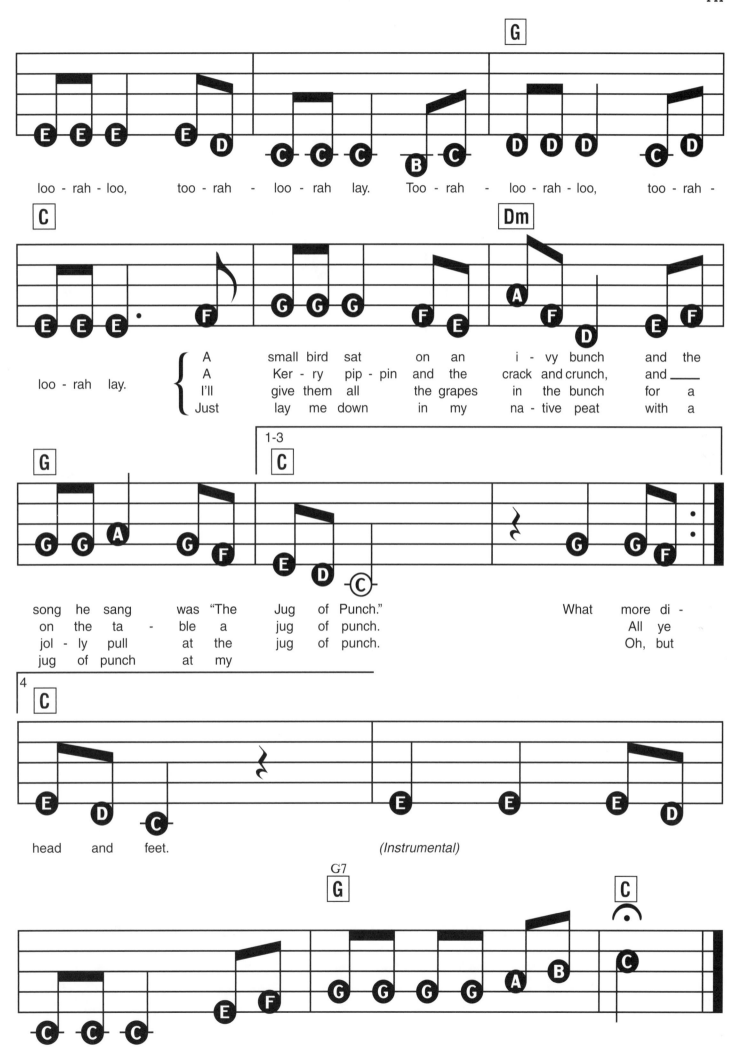

The Juice of the Barley

Registration 4
Rhythm: Waltz

Traditional Irish Folk Song

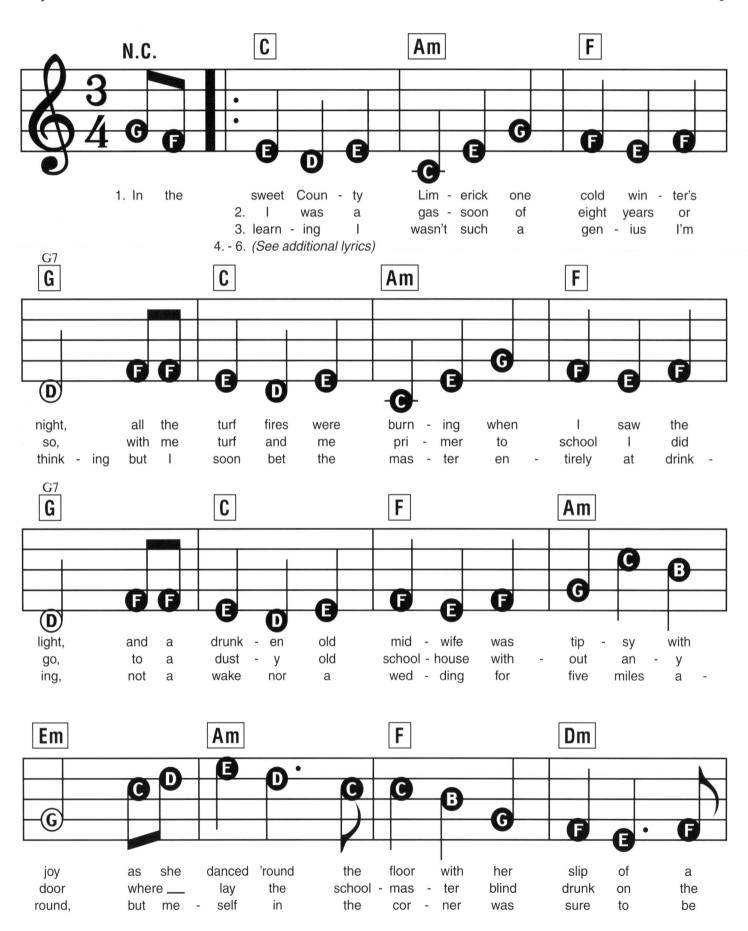

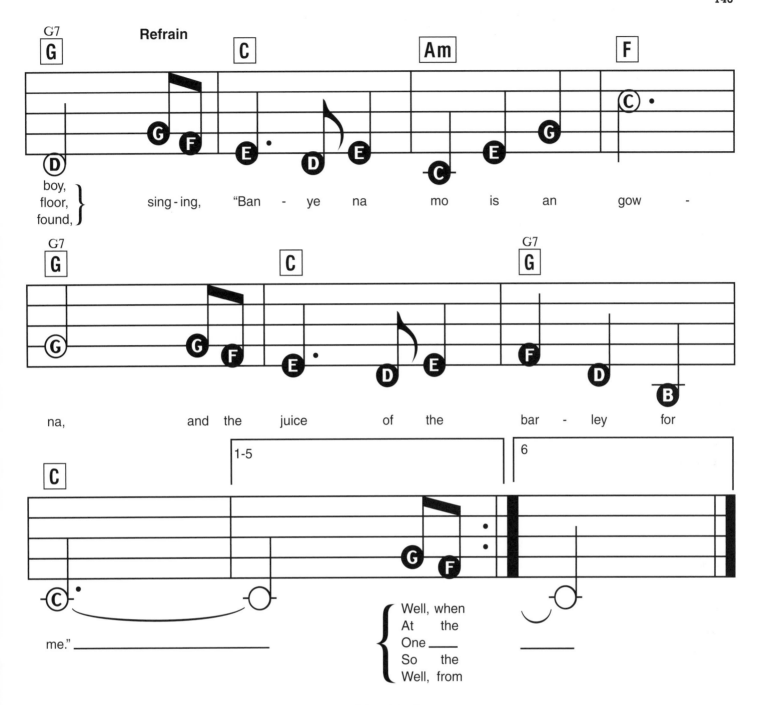

Additional Lyrics

4. One Sunday the priest read me out from the altar
   Saying, "You'll end up your days with your neck in a halter.
   And you'll dance a fine jig betwixt heaven and hell."
   And the words they did frighten, the truth for to tell.
   Refrain

5. So the very next morning as the dawn it did break,
   I went down to the vestry the pledge for to take.
   And there in that room sat the priests in a bunch
   'Round a big roaring fire drinking tumblers of punch.
   Refrain

6. Well, from that day to this I have wandered alone
   I'm a Jack of all Trades and a master of none.
   With the sky for me roof and the earth for me floor
   And I'll dance out me days drinking whiskey galore.
   Refrain

Kelly of Killane

Registration 8
Rhythm: Fox Trot

Traditional Irish Folk Song

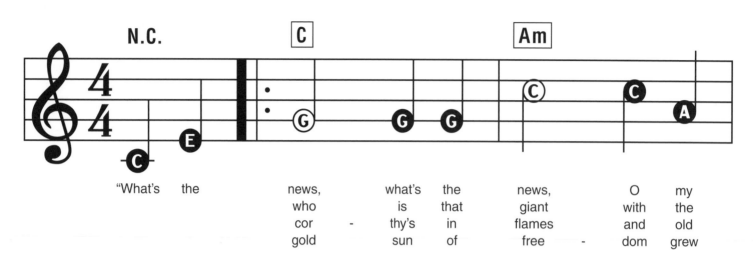

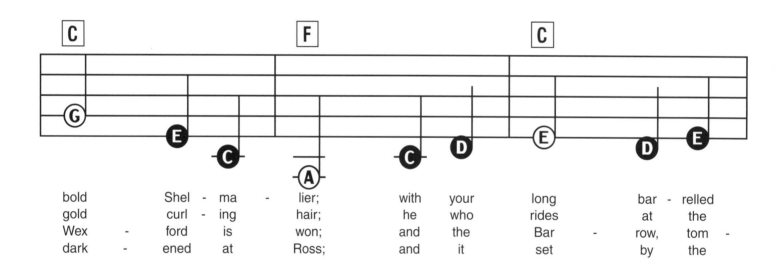

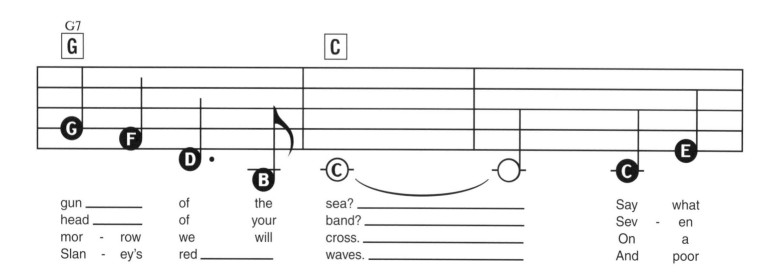

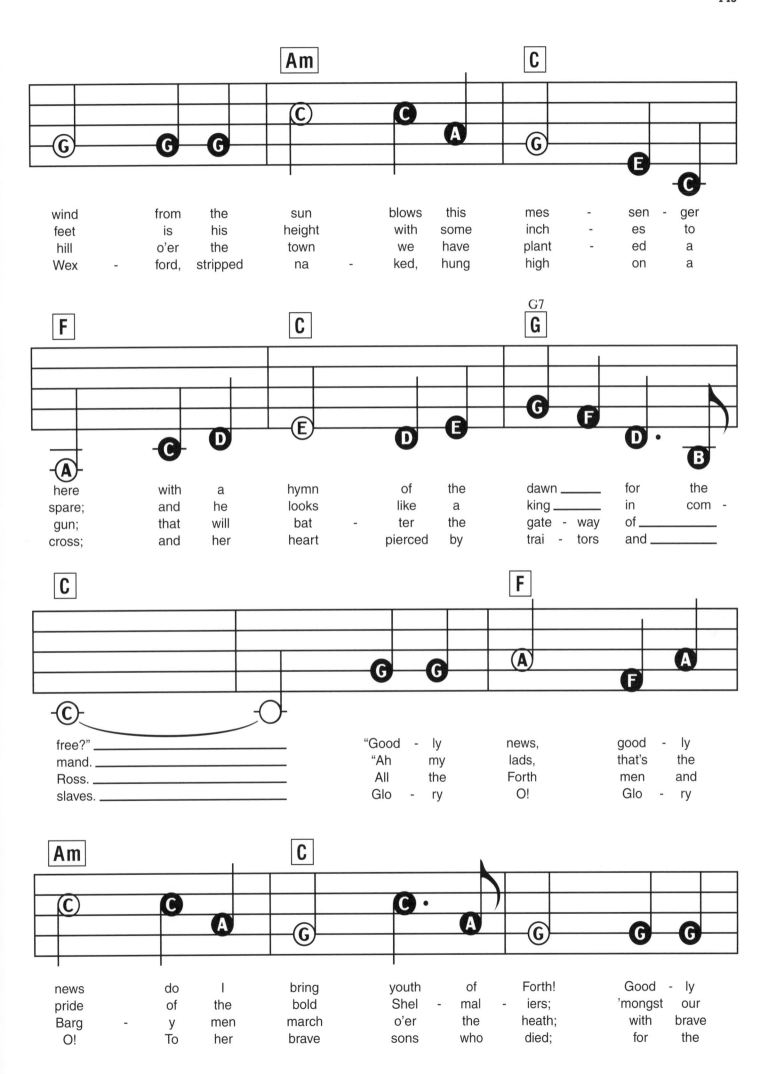

145

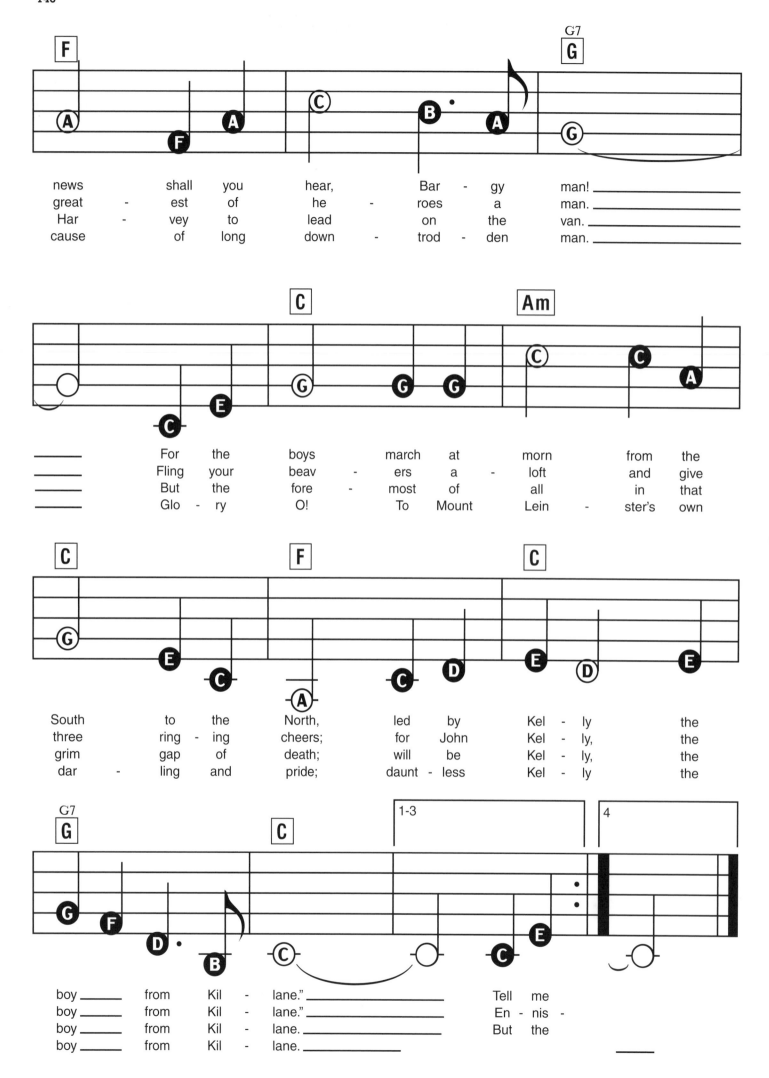

The Little Beggarman

Registration 4
Rhythm: 6/8 March or Jig/Gigue

Traditional Irish Folk Song

148

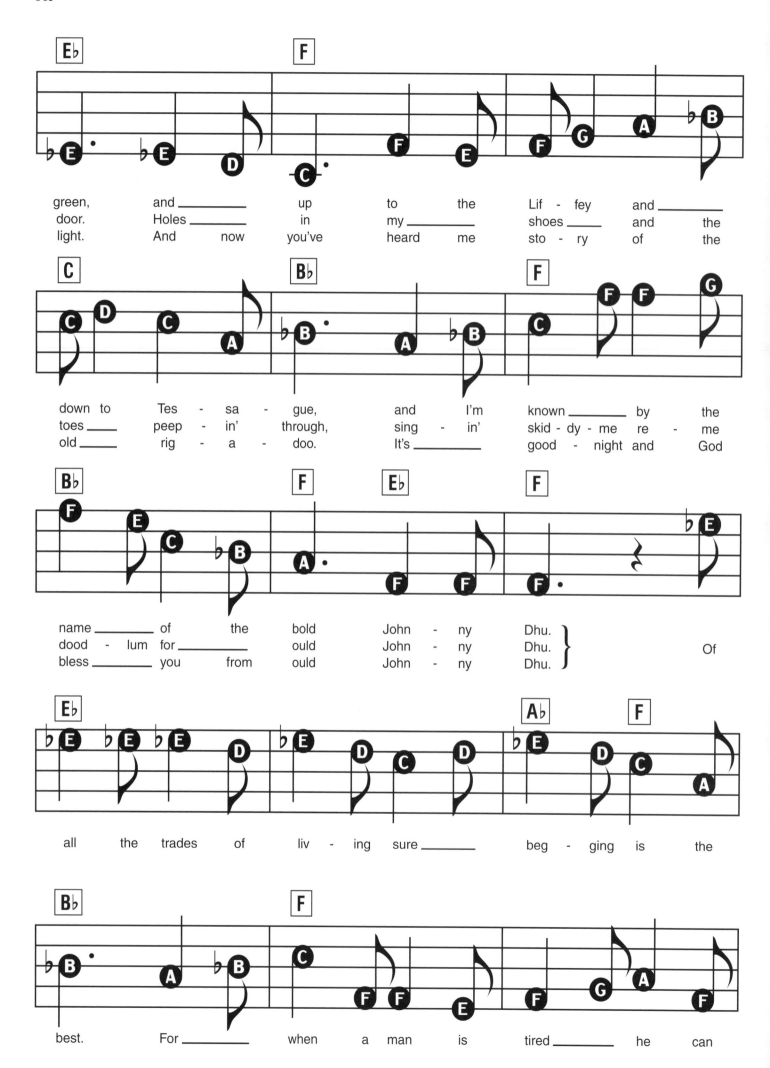

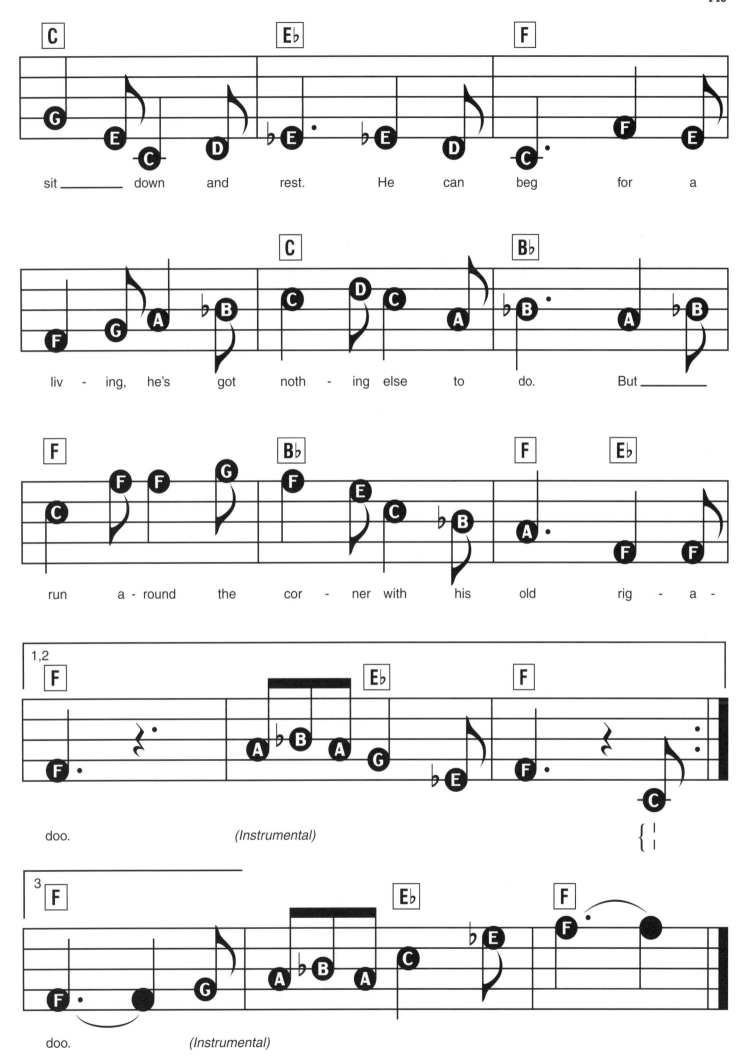

The Kerry Recruit

Registration 7
Rhythm: Waltz

Traditional Irish Folk Song

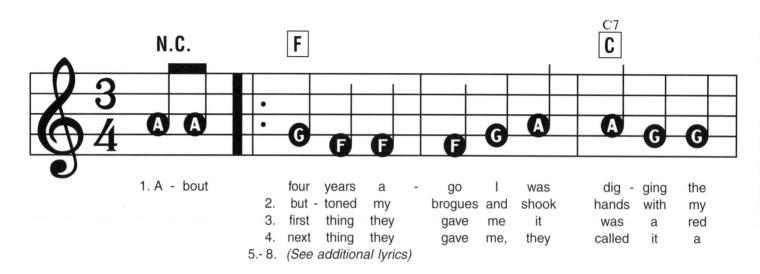

1. A - bout four years a - go I was dig - ging the
2. but - toned my brogues and shook hands with my
3. first thing they gave me it was a red
4. next thing they gave me, they called it a
5.- 8. *(See additional lyrics)*

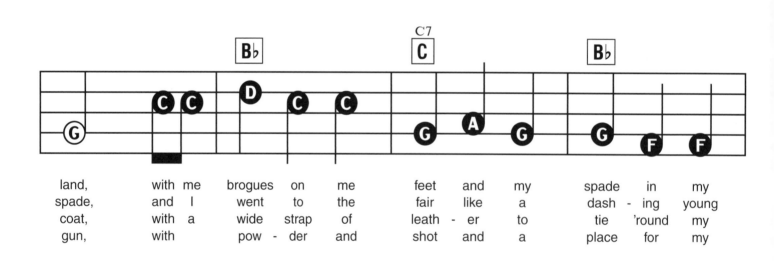

land, with me brogues on me feet and my spade in my
spade, and I went to the fair like a dash - ing young
coat, with a wide strap of leath - er to tie 'round my
gun, with pow - der and shot and a place for my

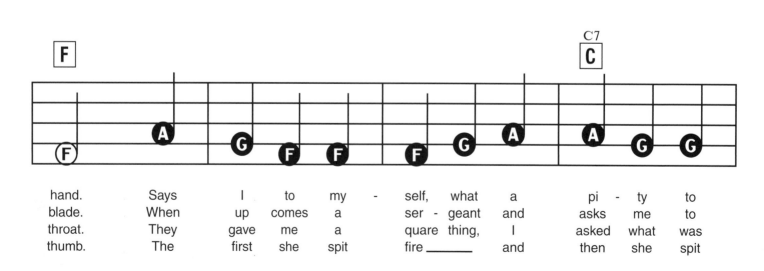

hand. Says I to my - self, what a pi - ty to
blade. When up comes a ser - geant and asks me to
throat. They gave me a quare thing, I asked what was
thumb. The first she spit fire _____ and then she spit

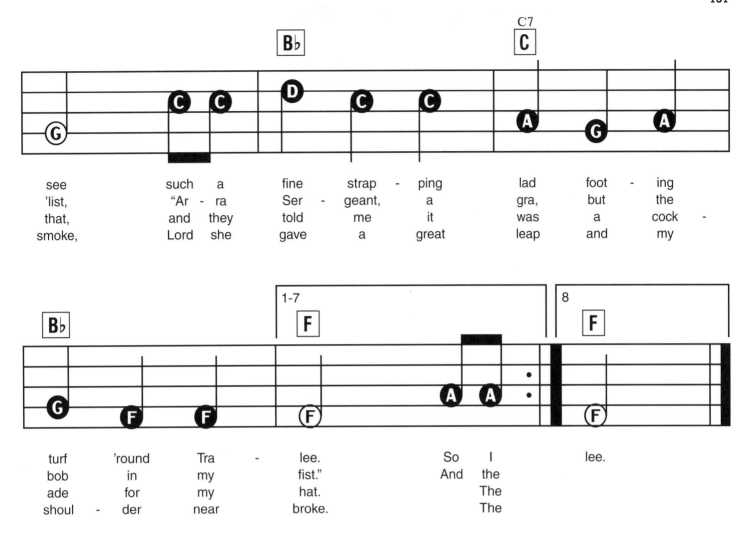

see	such	a	fine	strap	-	ping	lad	foot	-	ing
'list,	"Ar	- ra	Ser	- geant,		a	gra,	but		the
that,	and	they	told	me		it	was	a		cock -
smoke,	Lord	she	gave	a		great	leap	and		my

turf	'round	Tra	-	lee.		So	I	lee.
bob	in	my		fist."		And	the	
ade	for	my		hat.		The		
shoul	- der	near		broke.		The		

Additional Lyrics

5. The next place they sent me was down to the sea,
   On board of a warship bound for the Crimea.
   Three sticks in the middle all rowled 'round with sheets.
   Faith, she walked through the water without any feet.

6. We fought at the Alma, likewise Inkermann,
   But the Russians they whaled us at the Redan.
   In scaling the walls there myself lost my eye,
   And a big Russian bullet ran off with my thigh.

7. It was there I lay bleeding, stretched on the cold ground,
   Heads, legs, and arms were scattered all around.
   Says I, if my man or my cleavens were nigh,
   They'd bury me decent and raise a loud cry.

8. They brought me the doctor, who soon staunched my blood,
   And he gave me an elegant leg made of wood.
   They gave me a medal and tenpence a day,
   Contented with Sheila, I'll live on half pay.

Lanigan's Ball

Registration 4
Rhythm: 6/8 March or Jig/Gigue

Traditional Irish Folk Song

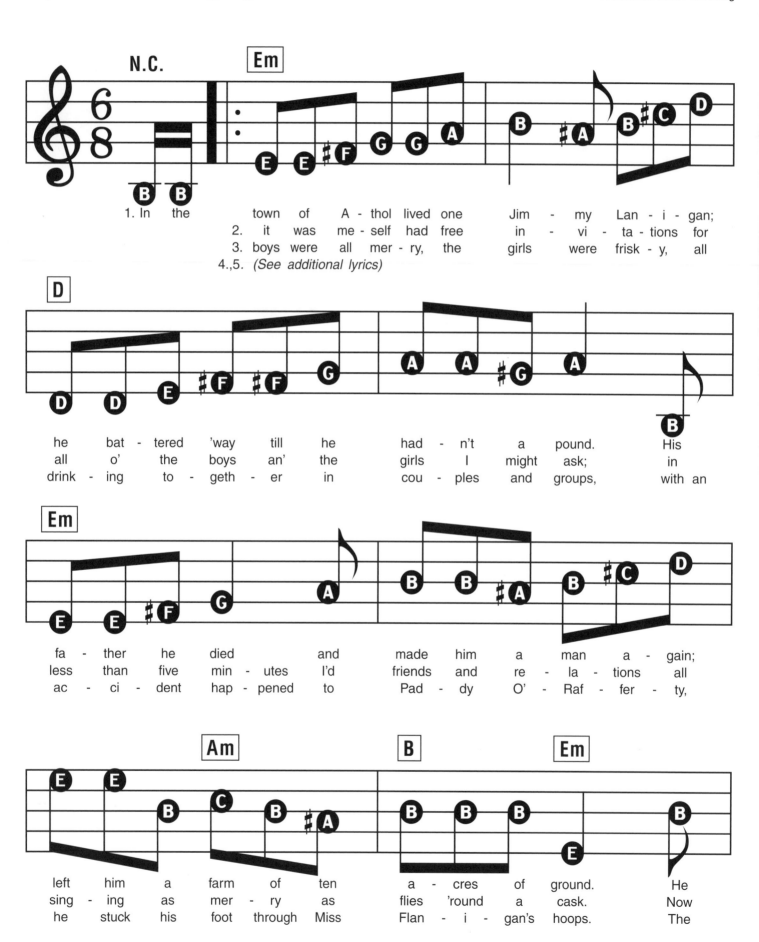

1. In the town of A - thol lived one Jim - my Lan - i - gan;
2. it was me - self had free in - vi - ta - tions for
3. boys were all mer - ry, the girls were frisk - y, all
4.,5. *(See additional lyrics)*

he bat - tered 'way till he had - n't a pound. His
all o' the boys an' the girls I might ask; in
drink - ing to - geth - er in cou - ples and groups, with an

fa - ther he died and made him a man a - gain;
less than five min - utes I'd friends and re - la - tions all
ac - ci - dent hap - pened to Pad - dy O' - Raf - fer - ty,

left him a farm of ten a - cres of ground. He
sing - ing as mer - ry as flies 'round a cask. Now
he stuck his foot through Miss Flan - i - gan's hoops. The

153

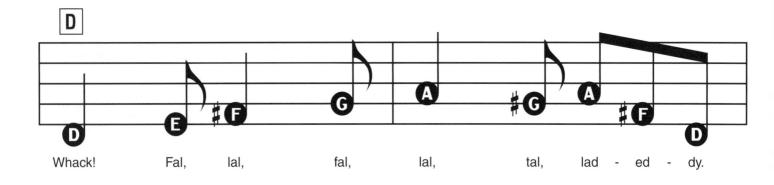

Whack! Fal, lal, fal, lal, tal, lad - ed - dy.

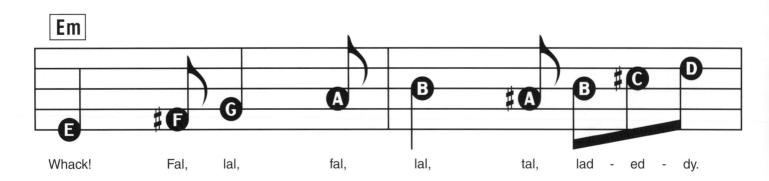

Whack! Fal, lal, fal, lal, tal, lad - ed - dy.

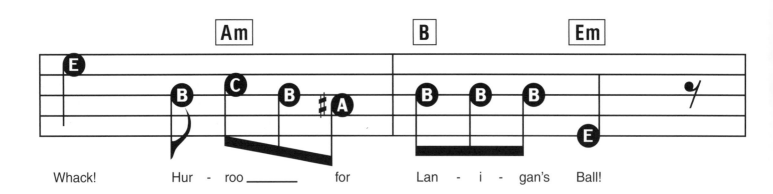

Whack! Hur - roo _____ for Lan - i - gan's Ball!

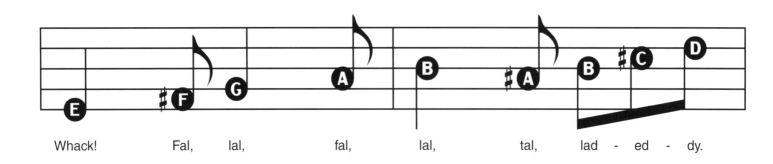

Whack! Fal, lal, fal, lal, tal, lad - ed - dy.

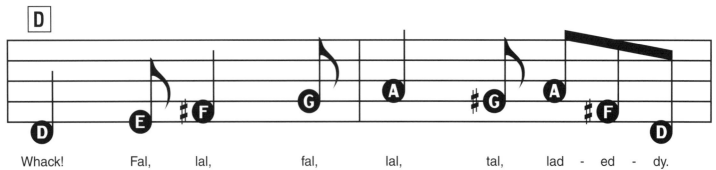

Whack! Fal, lal, fal, lal, tal, lad - ed - dy.

155

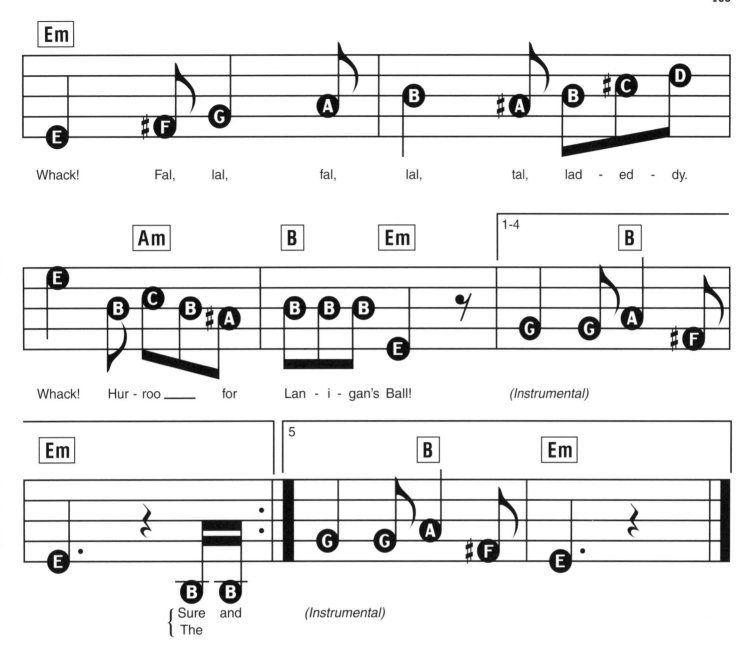

Additional Lyrics

4. Oh, arrah, boys, but thin was the 'ruption; meself got a wollop from Phelim McCoo.
   Soon I replied to his nate introduction and we kicked up the divil's own phililaloo.
   Casey, the piper, he was nearly strangled; he squeezed up his bags, chaunters and all.
   The girls in their ribbons all got entangled, and that put a stop to Lanigan's Ball.
   Refrain

5. In the midst of the row, Miss Kavanagh fainted; her face all the while was as red as the rose.
   The ladies declared her cheeks they were painted, but she'd taken a drop too much, I suppose.
   Paddy McCarty, so hearty and able, when he saw his dear colleen stretched out in the hall,
   He pulled the best leg from out under the table and broke all the chiney at Lanigan's Ball.
   Refrain

The Lark in the Clear Air

Registration 5
Rhythm: None

Words and Music by
Sir Samuel Ferguson

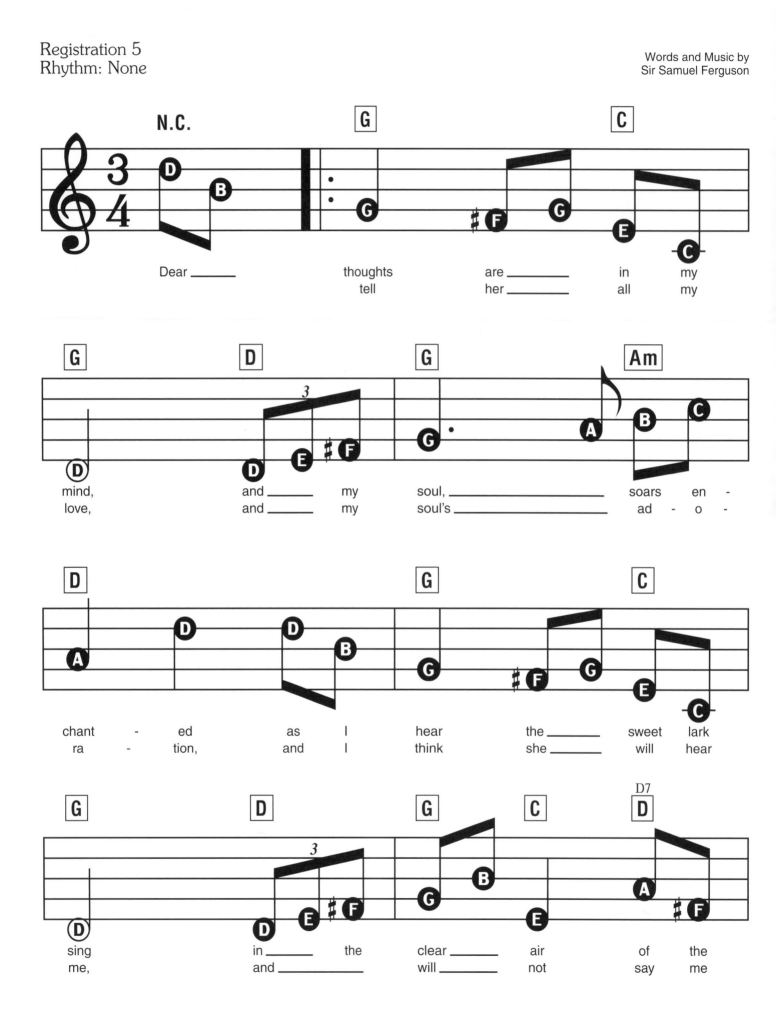

157

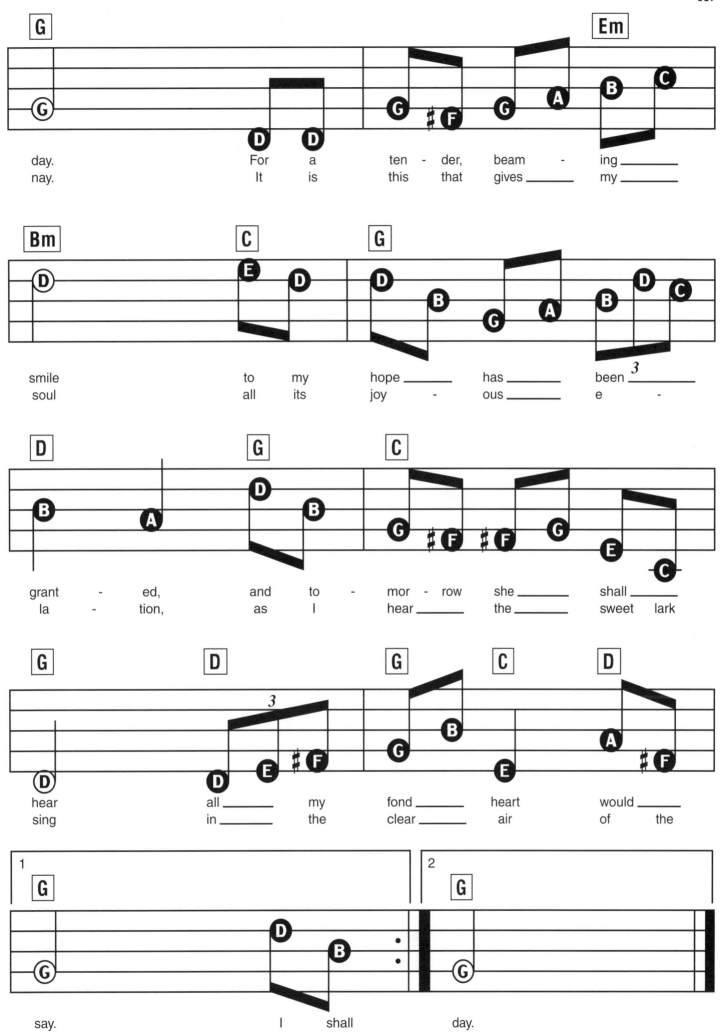

Lark in the Morning

Registration 8
Rhythm: 6/8 March or Jig/Gigue

Traditional Irish Folk Song

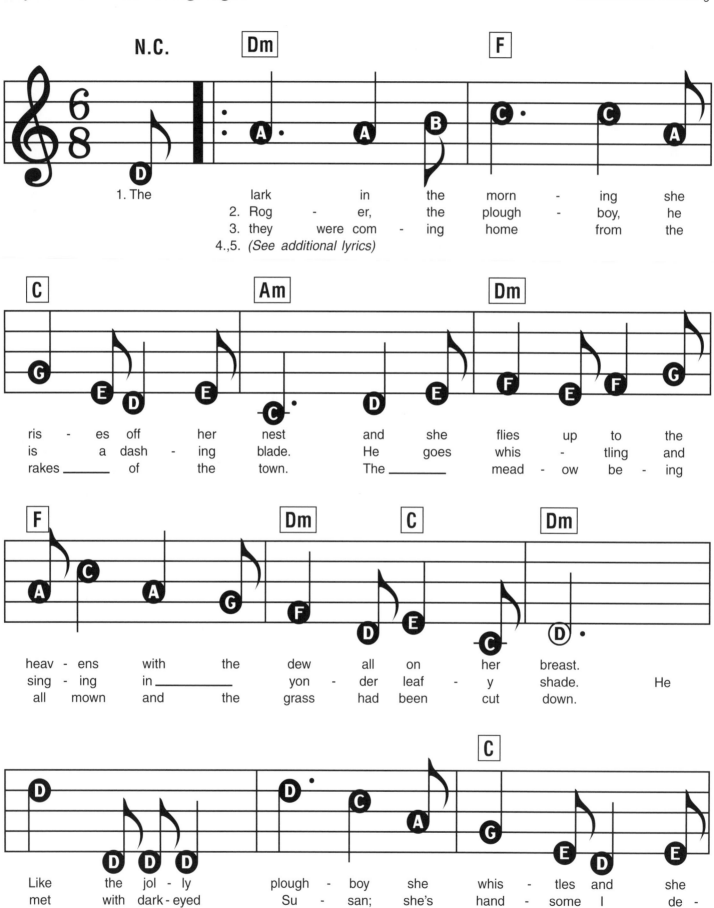

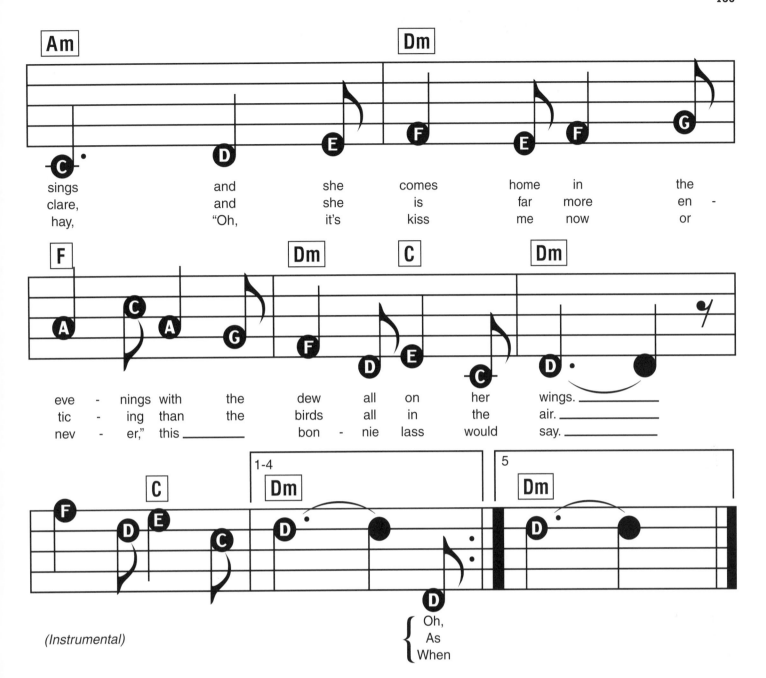

(Instrumental)

{ Oh,
As
When

Additional Lyrics

4. When twenty long weeks were over and had passed,
   Her mammy asked the reason why she thickened 'round the waist.
   "It was the pretty ploughboy," this lassie then did say,
   "For he asked me for to tumble all in the new-mown hay."

5. Here's a health to you ploughboys wherever you may be
   That like to have a bonnie lass a-sitting on each knee.
   With a pint of good strong porter he'll whistle and he'll sing,
   And the ploughboy is as happy as a prince or as a king.

Leaving of Liverpool

Registration 1
Rhythm: Ballad or Fox Trot

Irish Sea Chanty

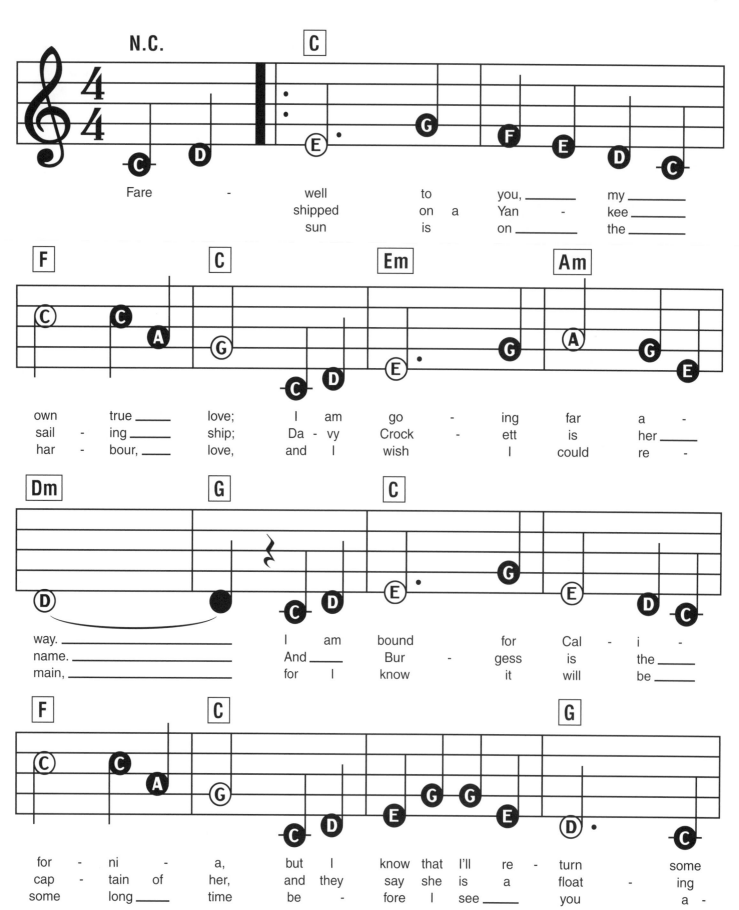

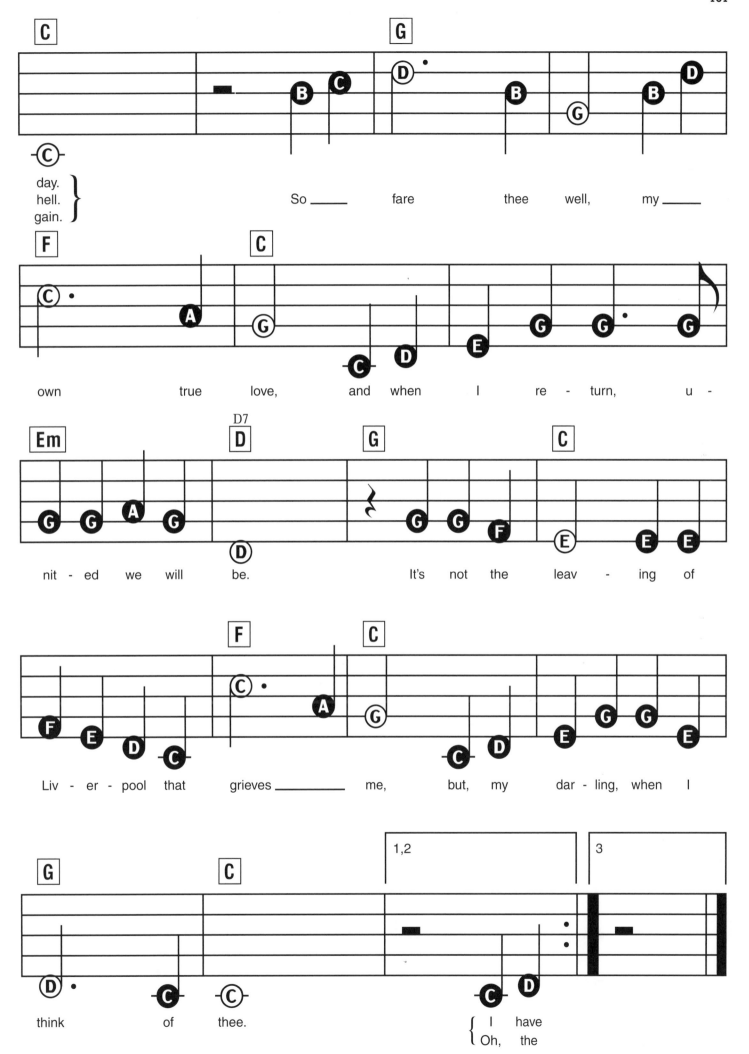

day.
hell.
gain.

So _____ fare thee well, my _____

own true love, and when I re - turn, u -

nit - ed we will be. It's not the leav - ing of

Liv - er - pool that grieves _____ me, but, my dar - ling, when I

think of thee.

1,2

3

I have
Oh, the

Love Is Teasing

Registration 8
Rhythm: Waltz

Traditional Irish Folk Song

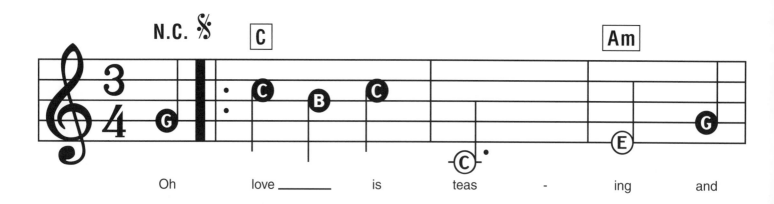

Oh love _____ is teas - ing and

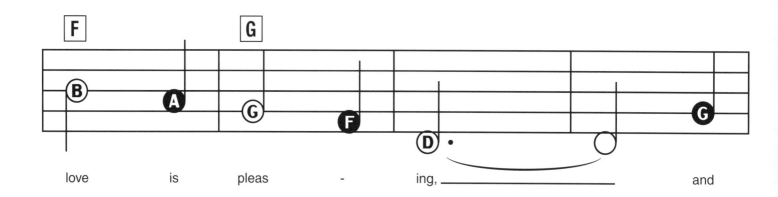

love is pleas - ing, _____ and

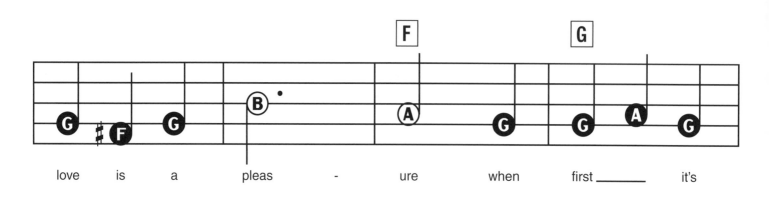

love is a pleas - ure when first _____ it's

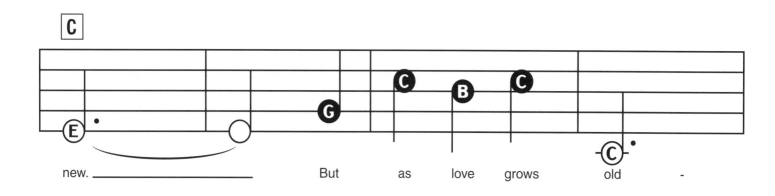

new. _____ But as love grows old -

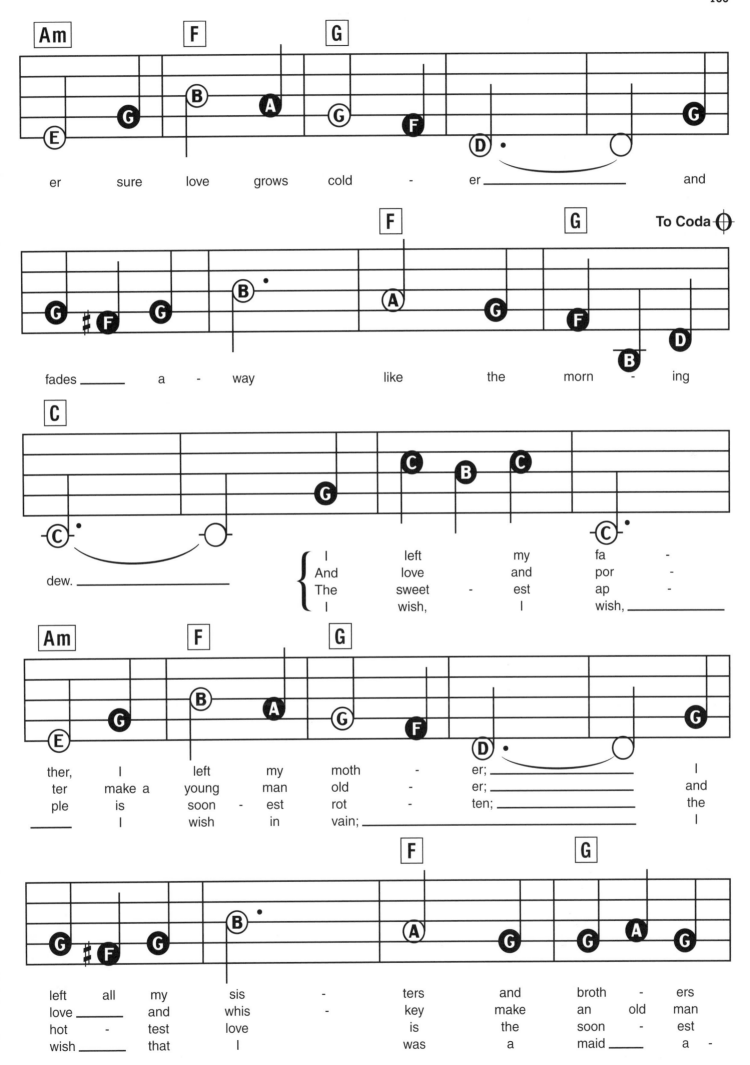

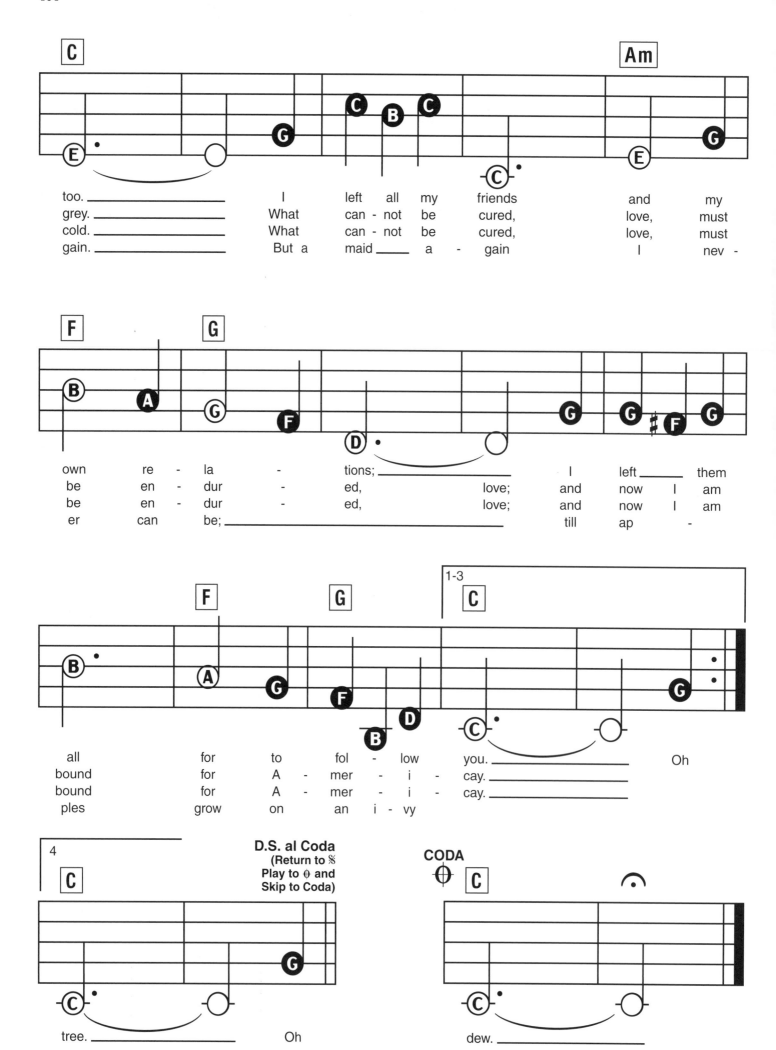

MacNamara's Band

Registration 5
Rhythm: 6/8 March

Words by John J. Stamford
Music by Shamus O'Connor

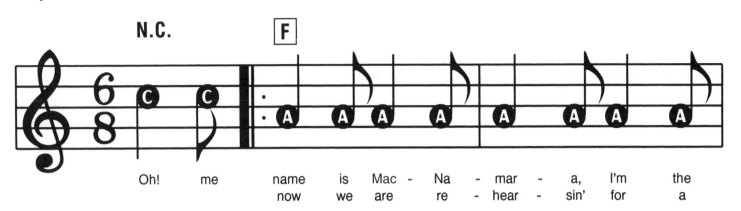

Oh! me name is Mac - Na - mar - a, I'm the
now we are re - hear - sin' for a

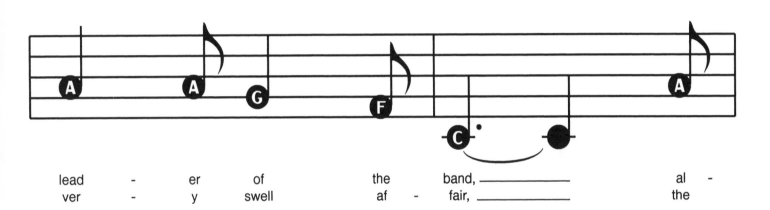

lead - er of the band, _____ al -
ver - y swell af - fair, _____ the

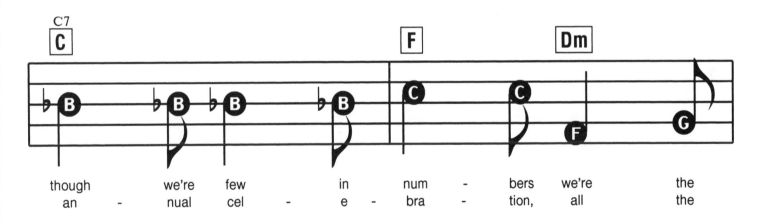

though we're few in num - bers we're the
an - nual cel - e - bra - tion, all the

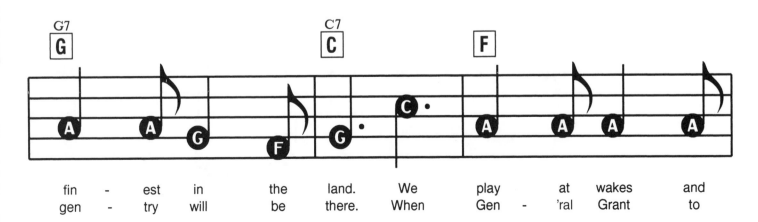

fin - est in the land. We play at wakes and
gen - try will be there. When Gen - 'ral Grant to

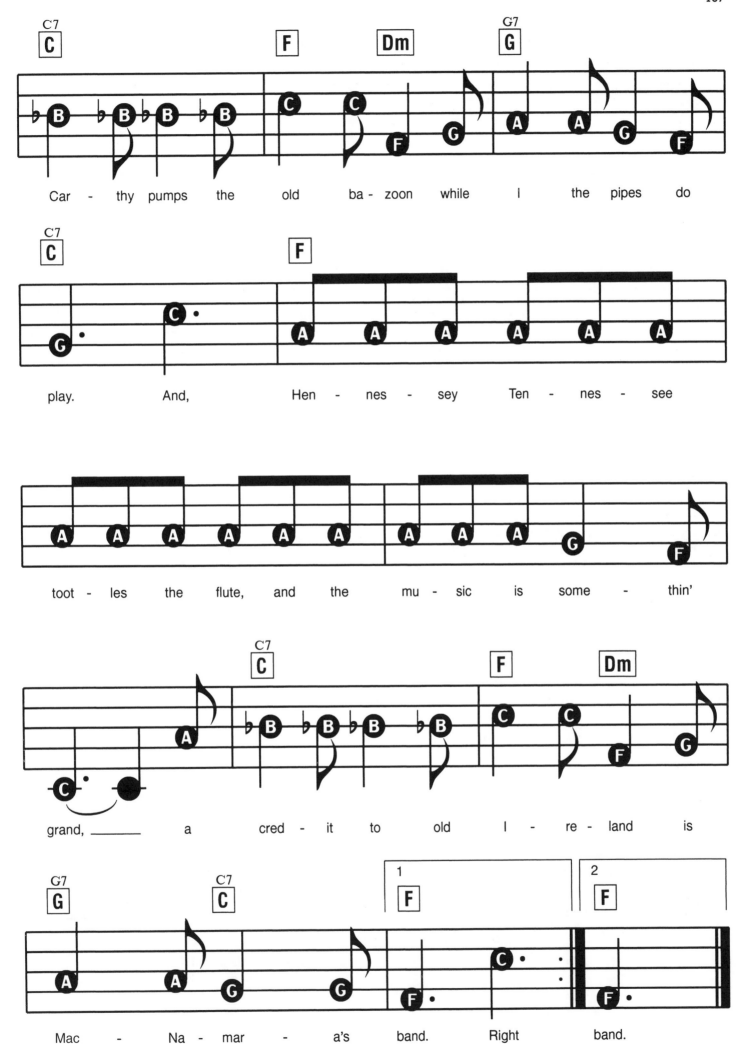

Lowlands Low

Registration 4
Rhythm: Fox Trot

Traditional Irish Folk Song

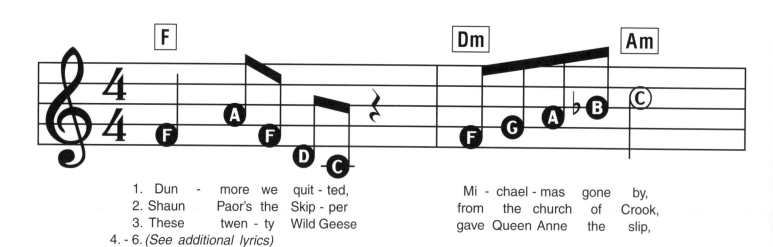

1. Dun - more we quit - ted,   Mi - chael - mas gone   by,
2. Shaun   Paor's the   Skip - per   from the church of   Crook,
3. These   twen - ty   Wild Geese   gave Queen Anne   the   slip,
4. - 6. *(See additional lyrics)*

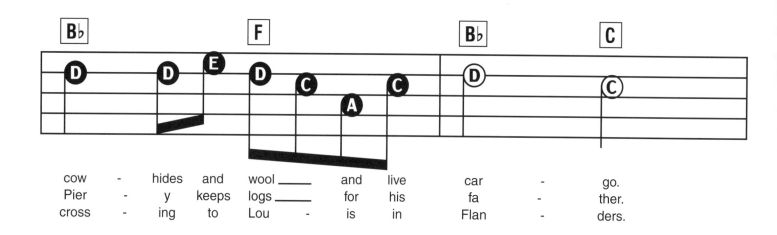

cow - hides and   wool ____ and   live   car - go.
Pier - y   keeps   logs ____ for his   fa - ther.
cross - ing   to Lou - is   in   Flan - ders.

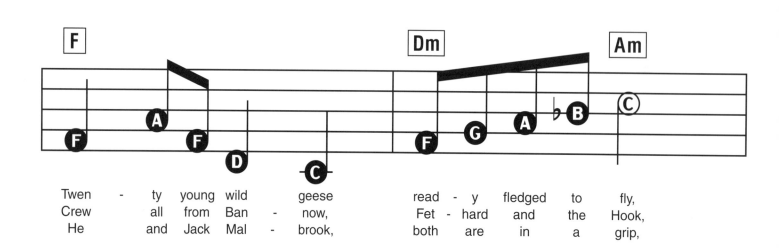

Twen - ty young wild   geese   read - y fledged to   fly,
Crew   all from Ban - now,   Fet - hard and   the   Hook,
He   and Jack Mal - brook,   both   are   in   a   grip,

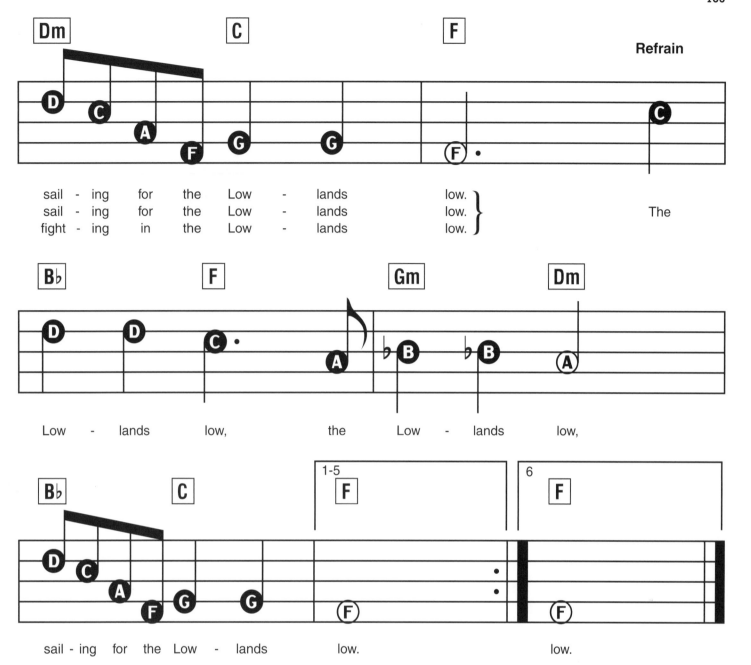

Refrain

sail - ing for the Low - lands low.
sail - ing for the Low - lands low.
fight - ing in the Low - lands low.

The

Low - lands low, the Low - lands low,

sail - ing for the Low - lands low.

low.

Additional Lyrics

4. Close lay a rover, off the Isle of Wight,
   Either a Salce or Saxon.
   Out through a sea mist we bade them good night,
   Sailing for the Lowlands low.
   Refrain

5. Ready with priming we'd our galliot gun,
   Muskets and pikes in good order.
   We should be riddled, captives would be none.
   Death! Or else the Lowlands low.
   Refrain

6. Pray, holy Brendan, Turk or Algerine,
   Dutchman nor Saxon may sink us.
   We'll bring back Geneva Rack and Rhenish wine,
   Safely from the Lowlands low.
   Refrain

The Meeting of the Waters

Registration 8
Rhythm: Waltz

Traditional Irish Folk Song

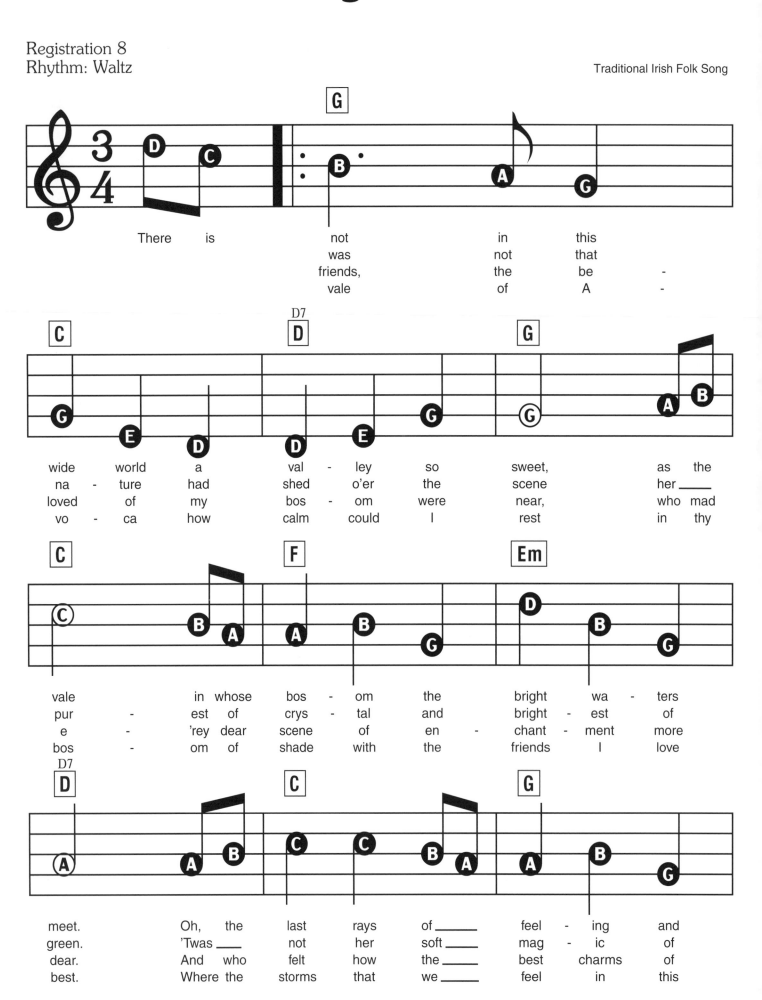

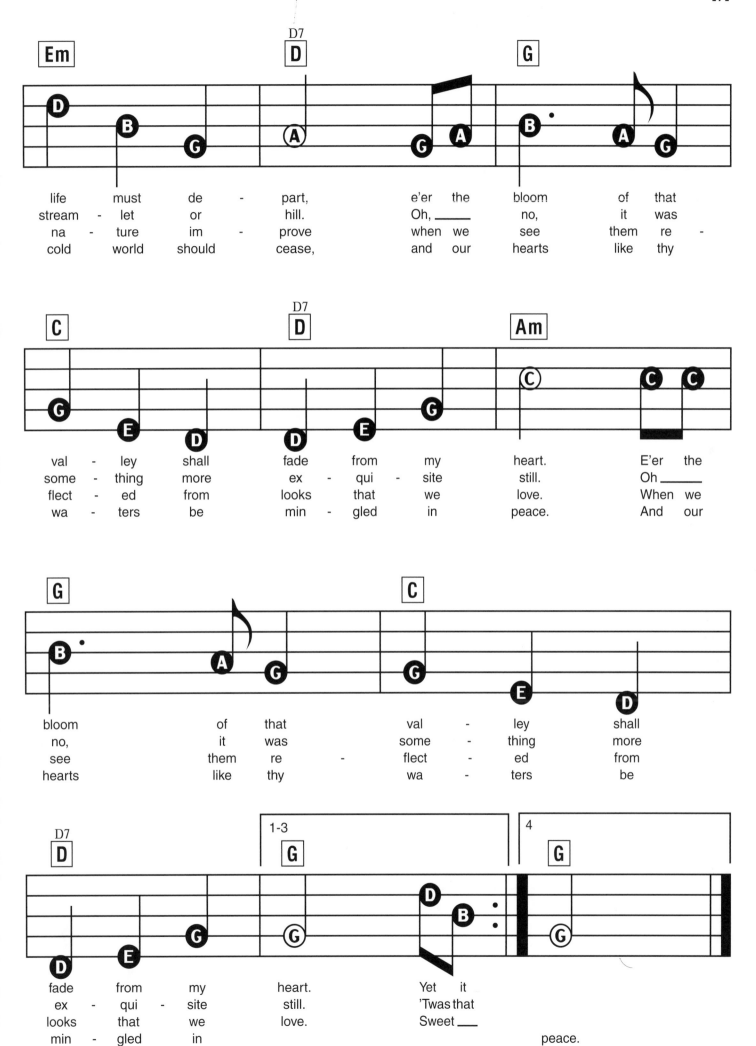

The Mermaid

Registration 4
Rhythm: Fox Trot

18th Century Sea Chantey

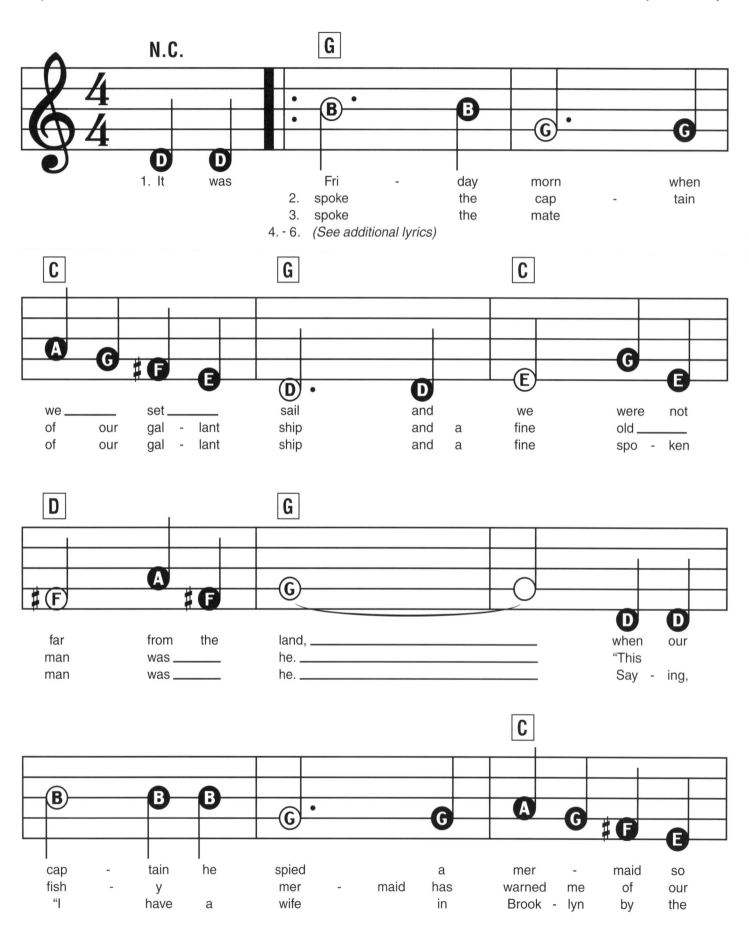

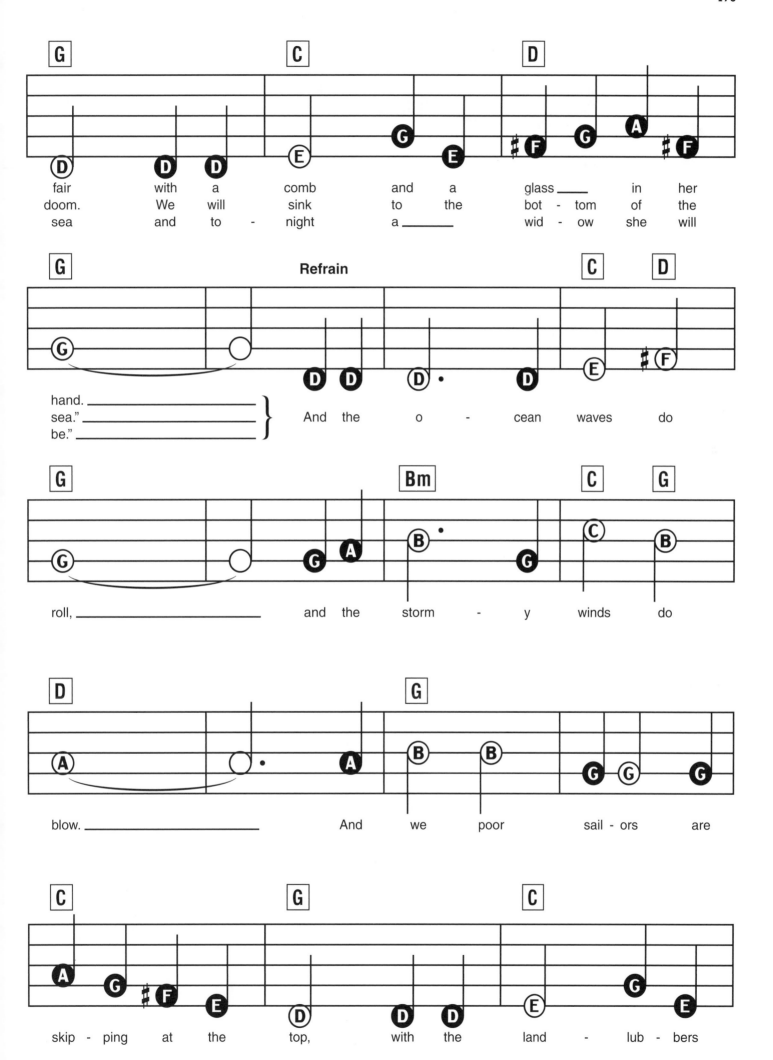

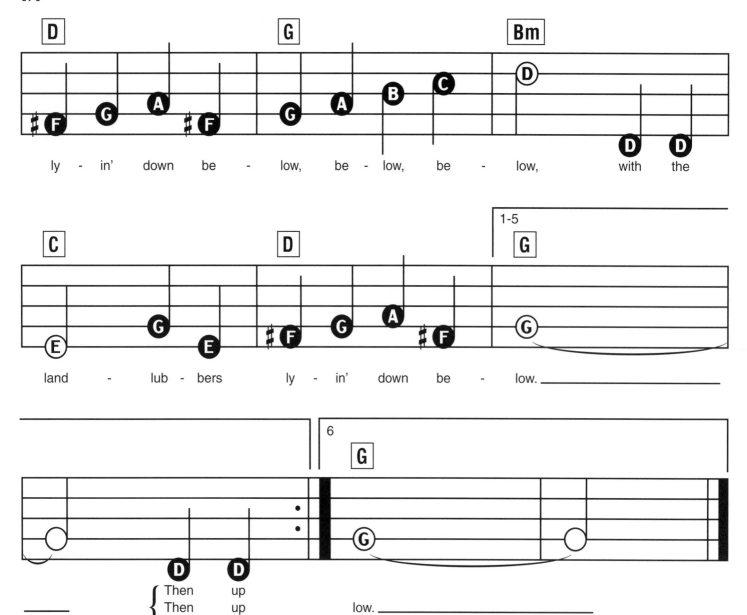

Additional Lyrics

4. Then up spoke the cabin boy of our gallant ship and a brave young lad was he.
   "I have a sweetheart in Salem by the sea and tonight she'll be weeping for me."
   Refrain

5. Then up spoke the cook of our gallant ship and a crazy old butcher was he.
   "I care so much more for my skillets and my pans than I do for the bottom of the sea."
   Refrain

6. Then three times around spun our gallant ship and three times around spun she.
   Three times around spun our gallant ship and she sank to the bottom of the sea.
   Refrain

The Merry Ploughboy

Registration 1
Rhythm: 6/8 March or Jig/Gigue

Traditional Irish Folk Song

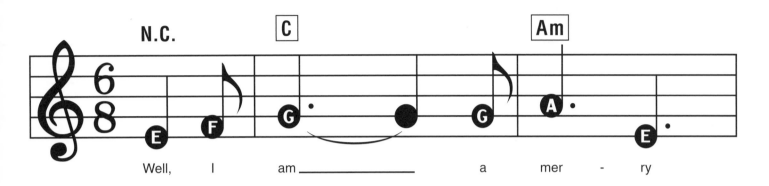

Well, I am _____ a mer - ry

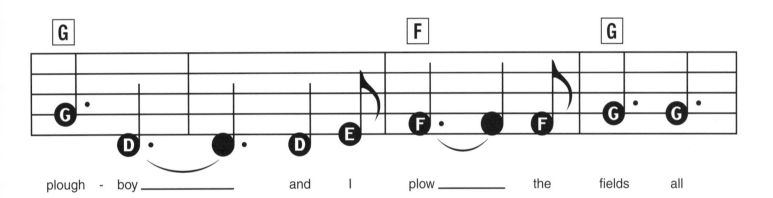

plough - boy _____ and I plow _____ the fields all

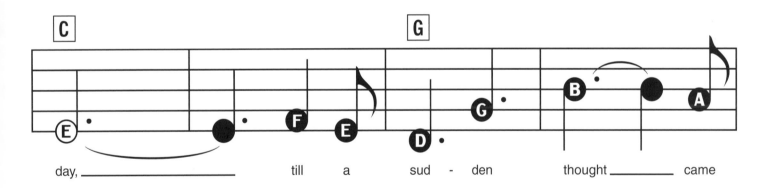

day, _____ till a sud - den thought _____ came

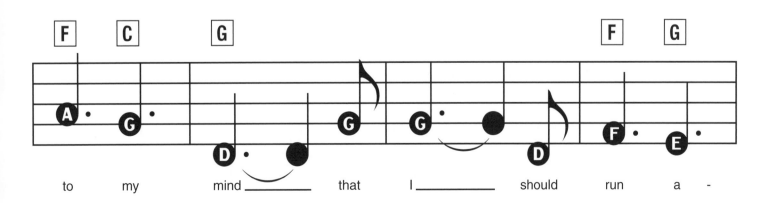

to my mind _____ that I _____ should run a -

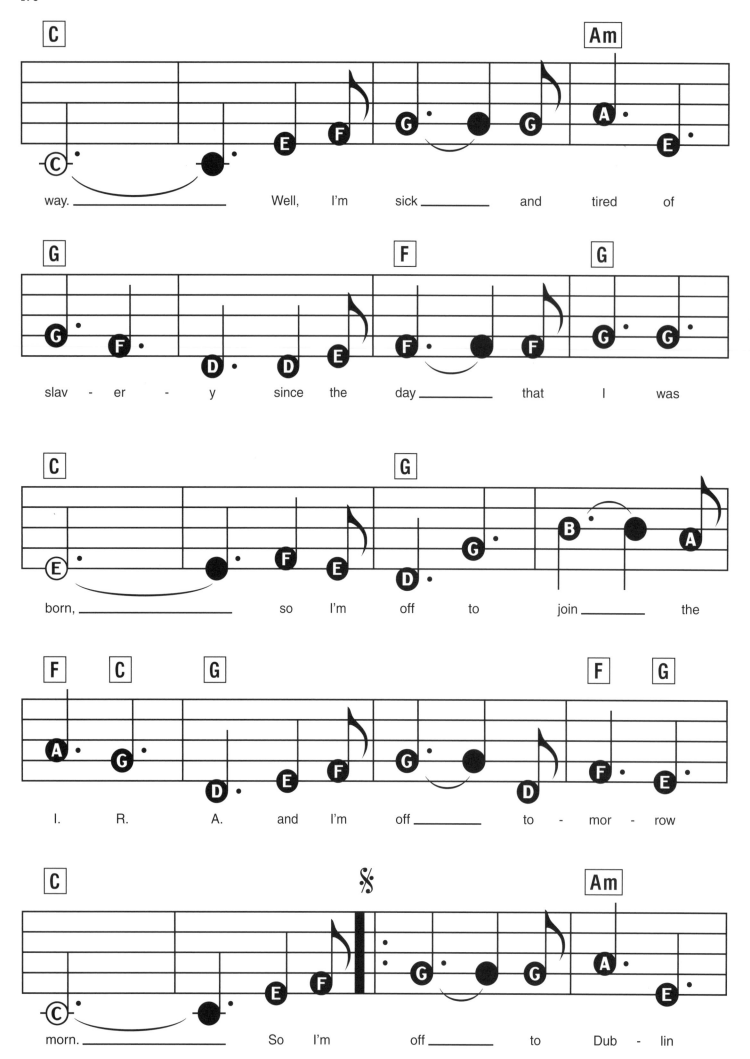

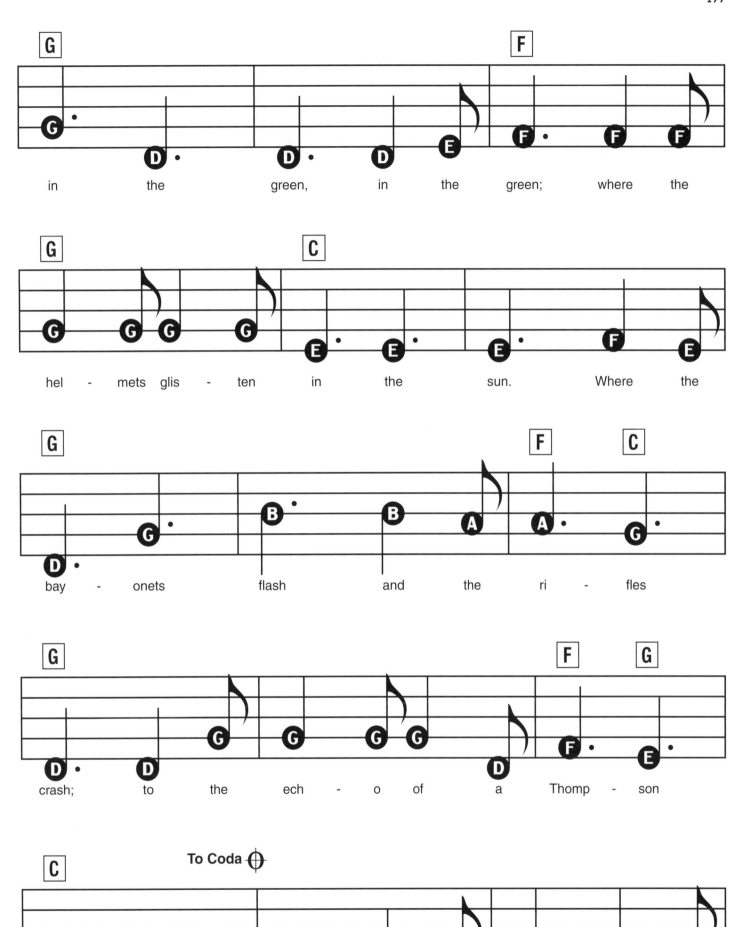

178

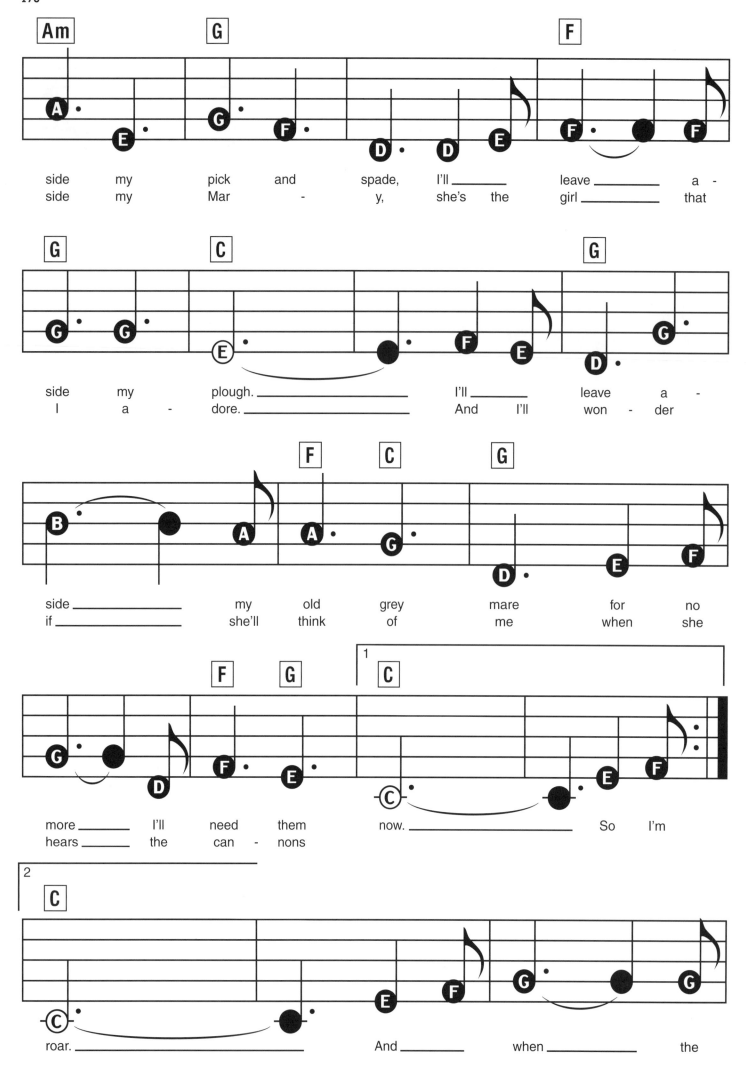

Minstrel Boy

Registration 8
Rhythm: Fox Trot

Traditional

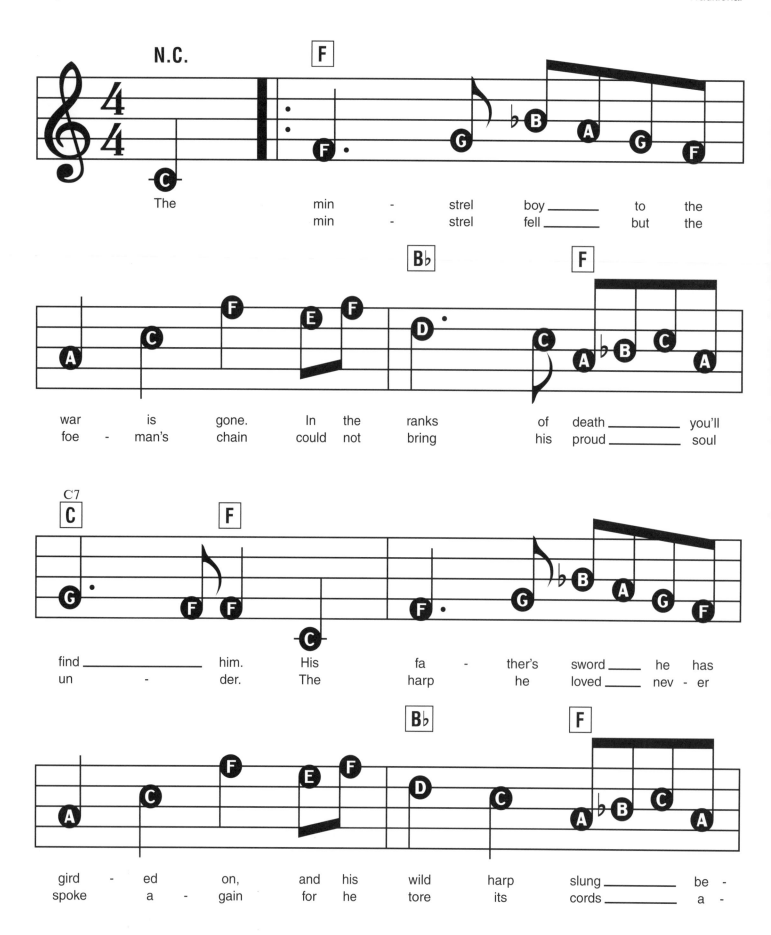

181

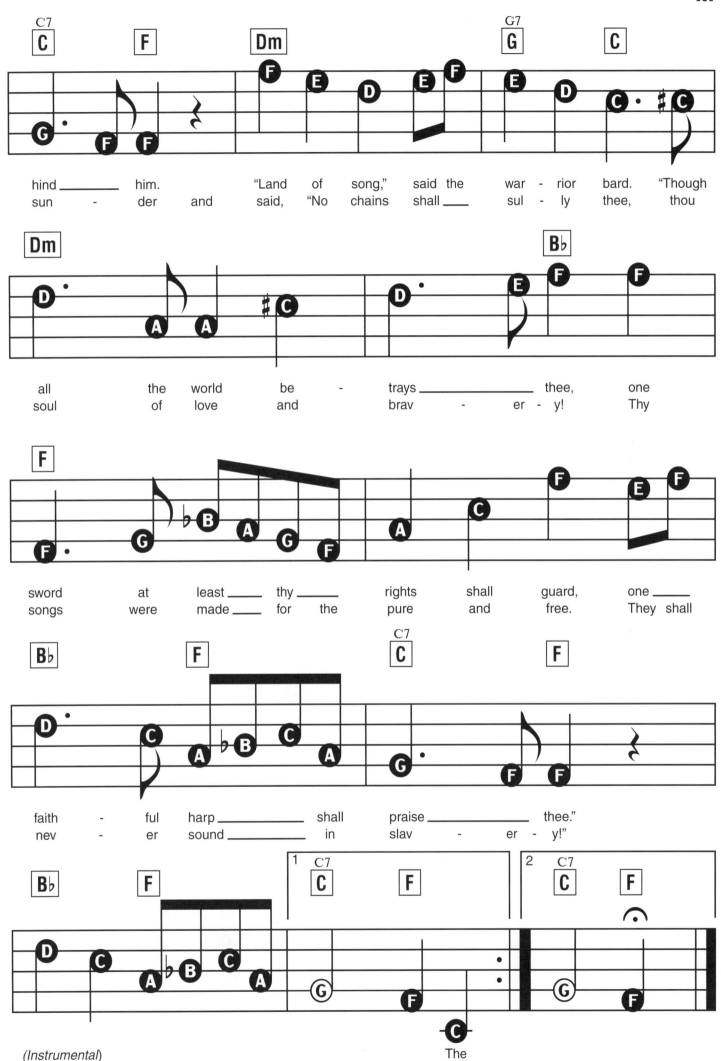

(Instrumental)

The Mountains of Mourne

Registration 2
Rhythm: Waltz

Words by Percy French
Traditional Irish Melody

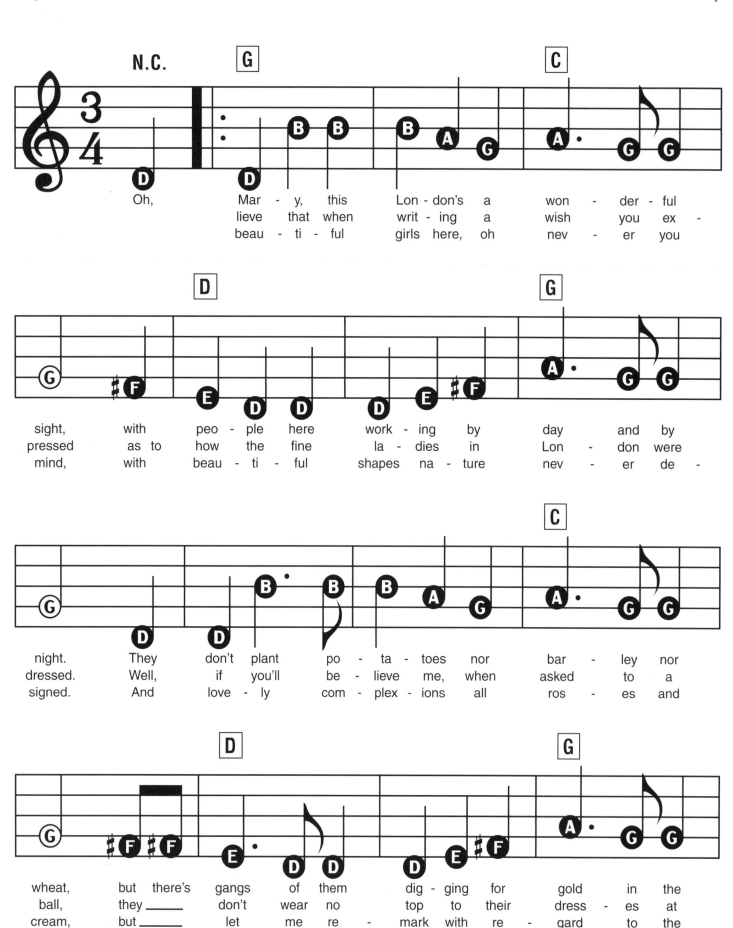

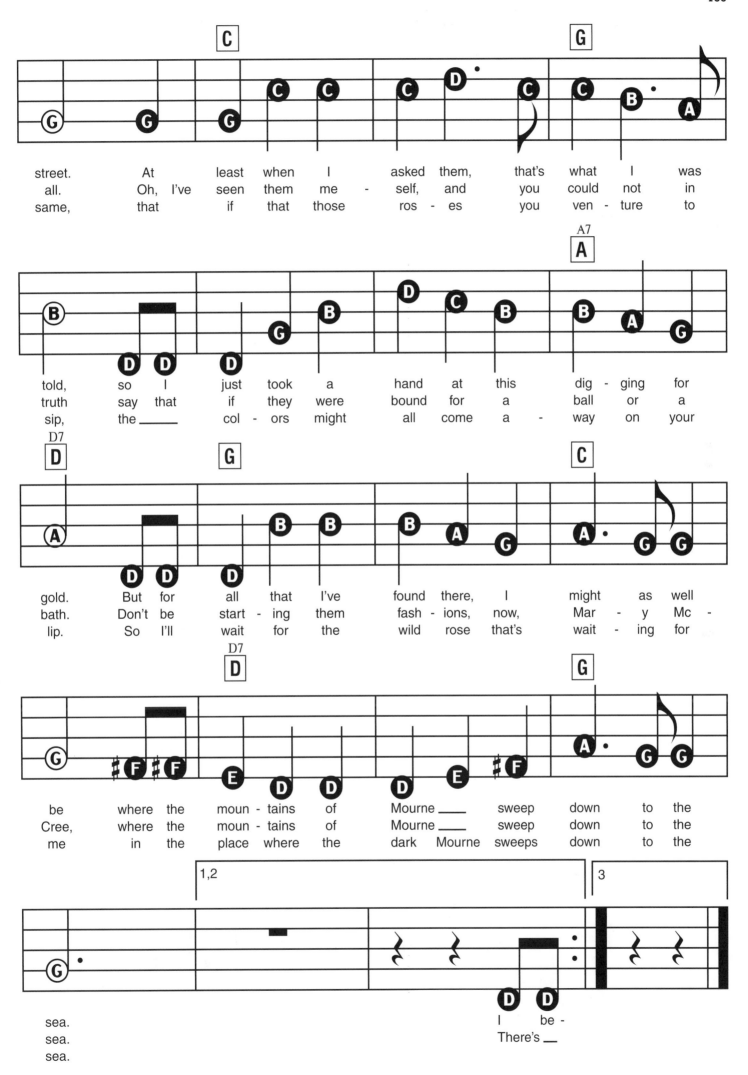

Mrs. McGrath

Registration 2
Rhythm: March or Fox Trot

Traditional Irish Folk Song

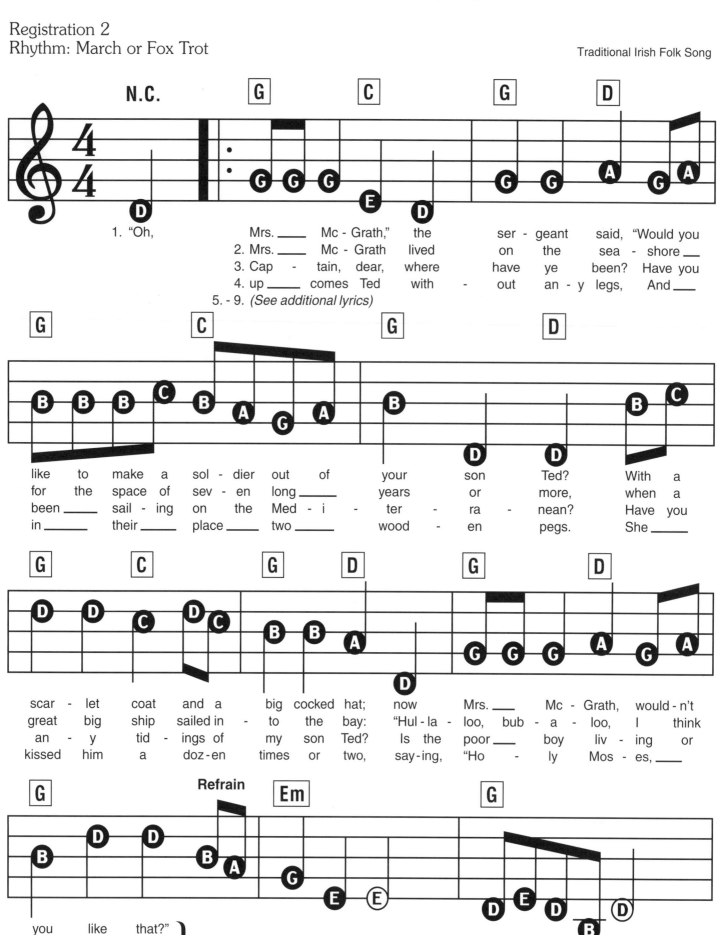

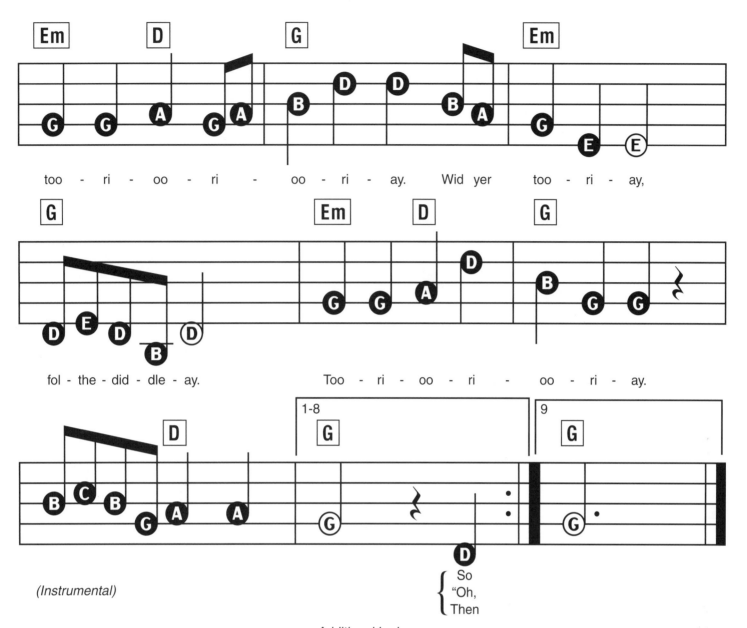

too - ri - oo - ri - oo - ri - ay. Wid yer too - ri - ay,

fol - the - did - dle - ay. Too - ri - oo - ri - oo - ri - ay.

(Instrumental)

So
"Oh,
Then

Additional Lyrics

5. "Oh, then were ye drunk or were ye blind
That ye left yer two fine legs behind?
Or was it walking upon the sea
Wore yer two fine legs from the knees away?"
Refrain

6. "Oh, I wasn't drunk and I wasn't blind,
But I left me two fine legs behind;
For a cannon ball on the fifth of May
Took me two fine legs from the knees away."
Refrain

7. "Oh, then, Teddy me boy," the widow cried,
"Yer two fine legs were yer mama's pride.
Them stumps of a tree wouldn't do at all,
Why didn't ye run from the big cannon ball?"
Refrain

8. "All foreign wars I do proclaim
Between Don John and the King of Spain.
But by heavens I'll make them rue the time
That they swept the legs from a child of mine."
Refrain

9. "Oh then, if I had ye back again,
I'd never let ye go to fight the King of Spain.
For I'd rather my Ted as he used to be
Than the King of France and his whole Navy."
Refrain

Muirsheen Durkin

Registration 7
Rhythm: Fox Trot

Traditional Irish Folk Song

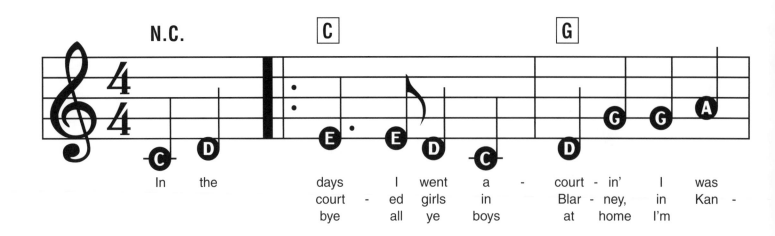

In the days I went a - court - in' I was
court - ed girls in Blar - ney, in Kan -
bye all ye boys at home I'm

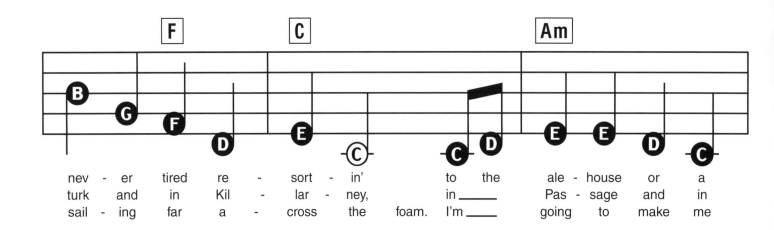

nev - er tired re - sort - in' to the ale - house or a
turk and in Kil - lar - ney, in _____ Pas - sage and in
sail - ing far a - cross the foam. I'm _____ going to make me

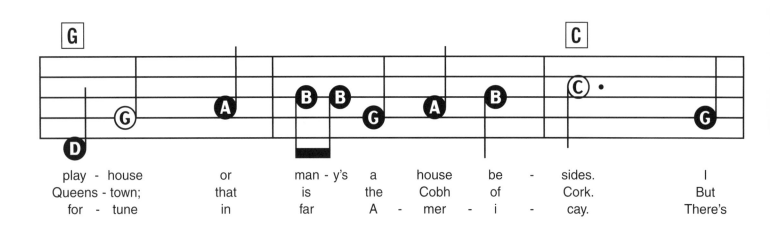

play - house or man - y's a house be - sides. I
Queens - town; that is the Cobh of Cork. But
for - tune in far A - mer - i - cay. There's

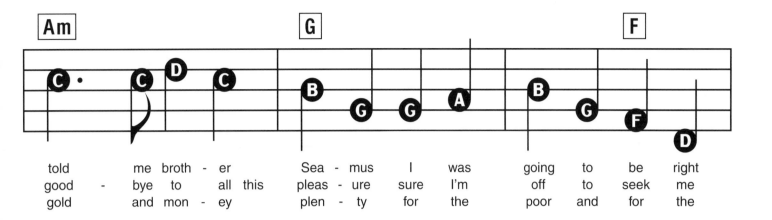

told — me broth - er Sea - mus I was going to be right
good - bye to all this pleas - ure sure I'm off to seek me
gold and mon - ey plen - ty for the poor and for the

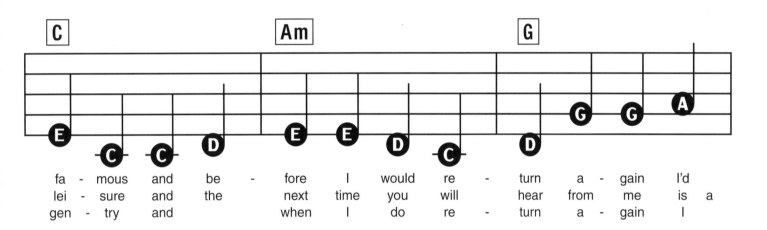

fa - mous and be - fore I would re - turn a - gain I'd
lei - sure and the next time you will hear from me is a
gen - try and when I do re - turn a - gain I

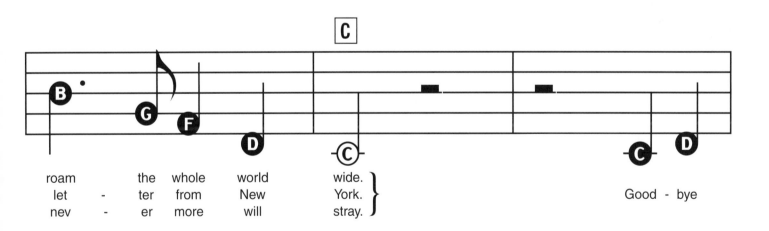

roam the whole world wide. }
let - ter from New York. } Good - bye
nev - er more will stray. }

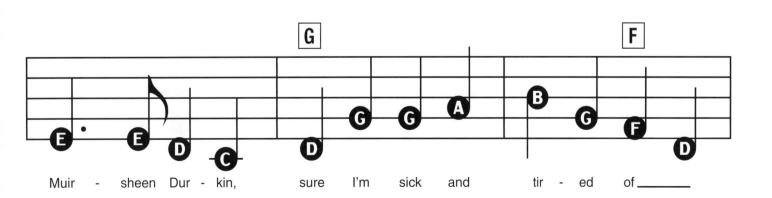

Muir - sheen Dur - kin, sure I'm sick and tir - ed of _____

188

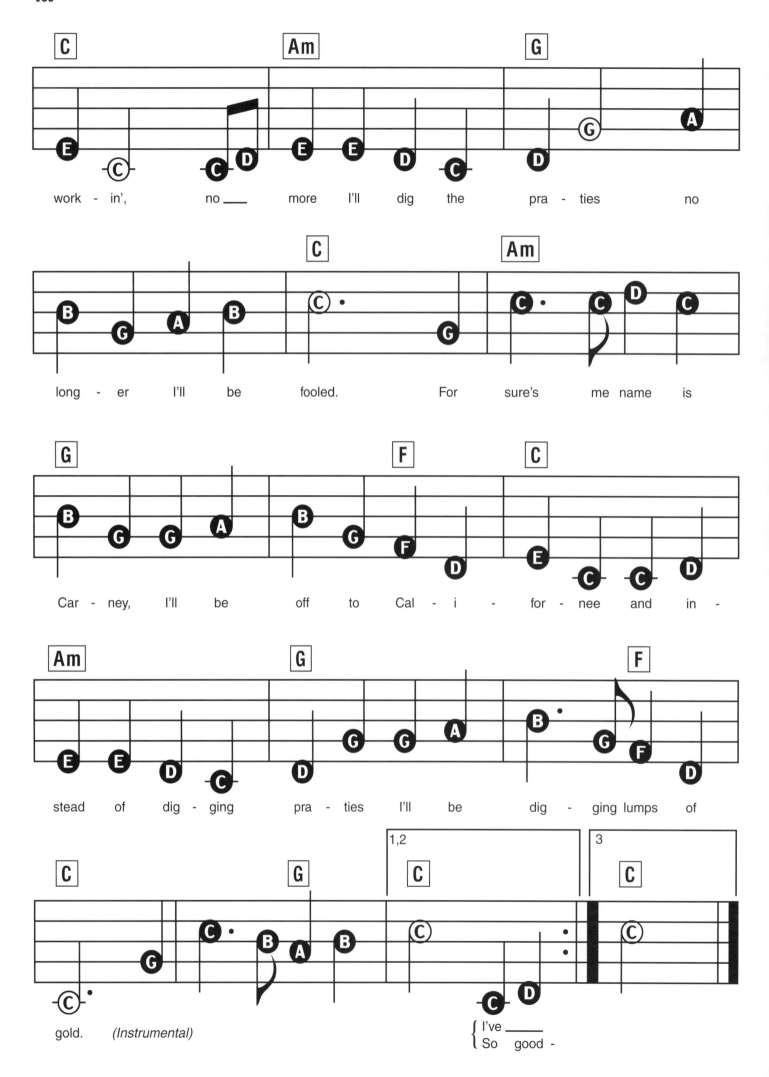

A Nation Once Again

Registration 7
Rhythm: Fox Trot

Words and Music by
Thomas Davis

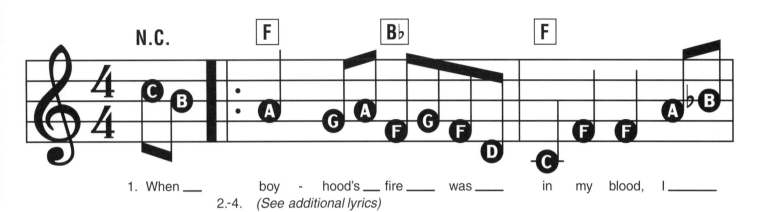

1. When ___ boy - hood's ___ fire ___ was ___ in my blood, I _____
2.-4. *(See additional lyrics)*

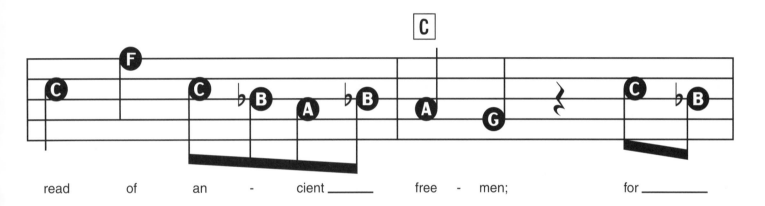

read of an - cient _____ free - men; for _____

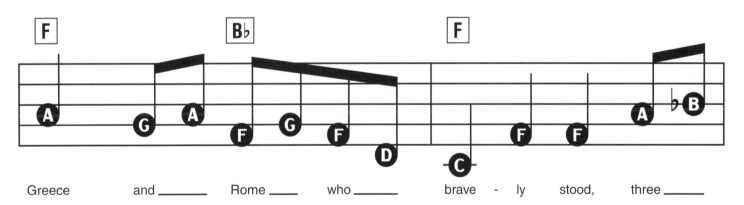

Greece and _____ Rome ___ who _____ brave - ly stood, three _____

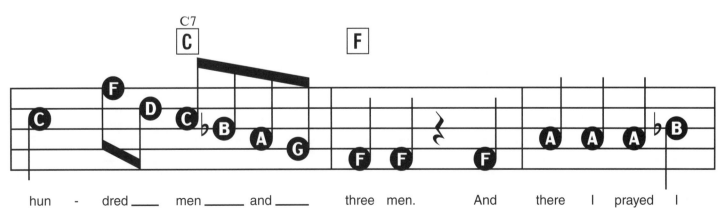

hun - dred ___ men ___ and ___ three men. And there I prayed I

190

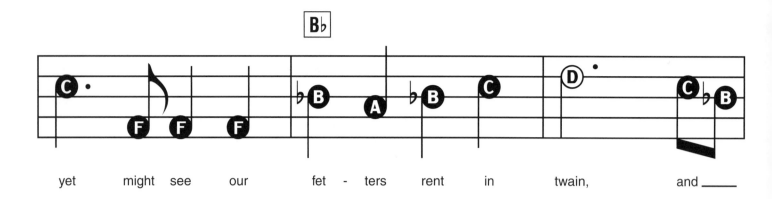

yet might see our fet - ters rent in twain, and ____

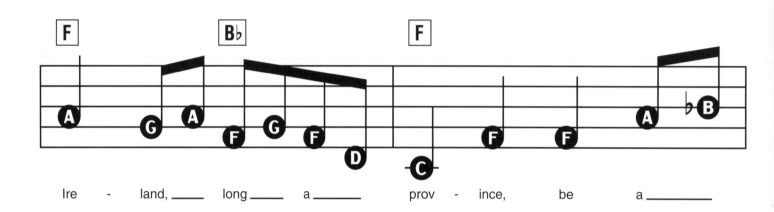

Ire - land, ____ long ____ a ____ prov - ince, be a _____

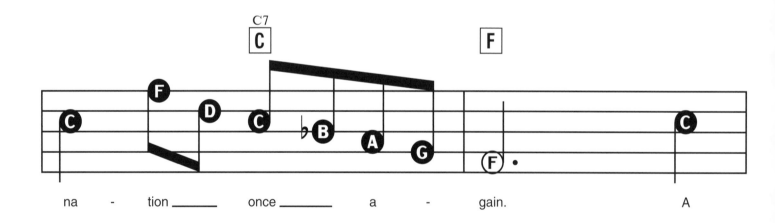

na - tion ____ once ____ a - gain. A

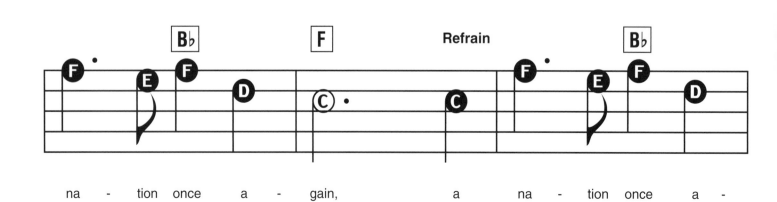

na - tion once a - gain, a na - tion once a -

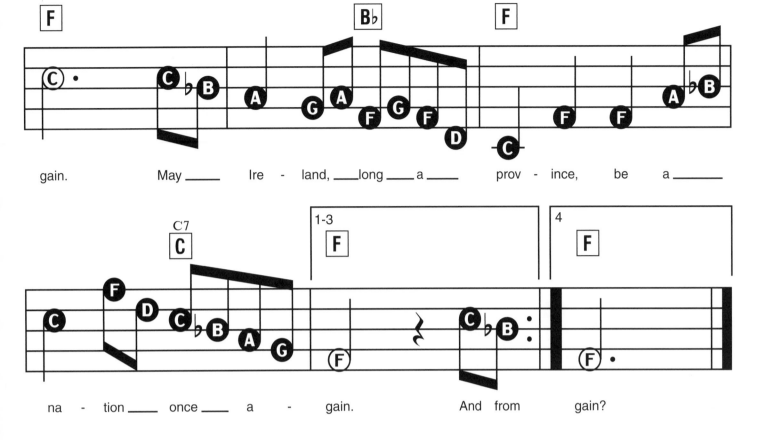

gain.   May ____ Ire - land, ___long ___a ___ prov - ince,   be   a _____

na - tion ___ once ___ a - gain.   And from   gain?

Additional Lyrics

2. And from that time, through wildest woe,
That hope has shown a far light;
Nor could love's brightest summer glow
Outshine that solemn starlight.
It seemed to watch above my head
In forum, field and fane;
Its angel voice sang 'round my bed,
"A nation once again."
Refrain

3. It whispered too, that "Freedom's Ark"
And service high and holy,
Would be profaned by feelings dark
And passions vain or lowly;
For freedom comes from God's right hand,
And needs a Godly train,
And righteous men must make our land
A nation once again.
Refrain

4. So as I grew from boy to man,
I bent me at that bidding;
My spirit of each selfish plan
And cruel passion ridding.
For thus I hoped some day to aid.
Oh! Can such hope be vain
When my dear country shall be made
A nation once again?
Refrain

My Singing Bird

Registration 4
Rhythm: Fox Trot

Traditional

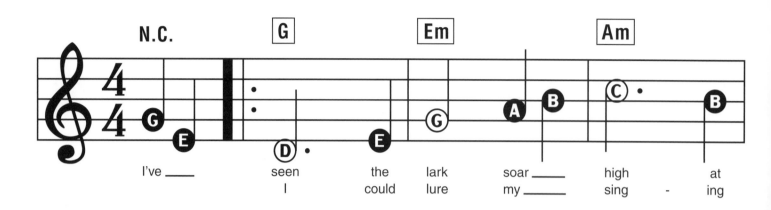

I've ____ seen the lark soar ____ high at
I could lure my ____ sing - ing

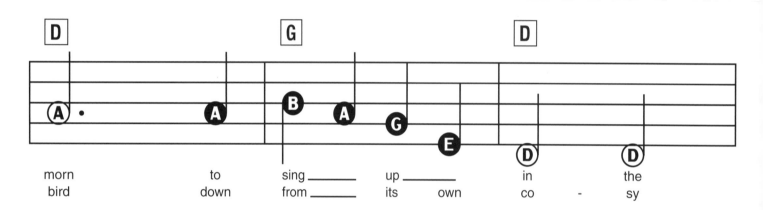

morn to sing ____ up ____ in the
bird down from ____ its own co - sy

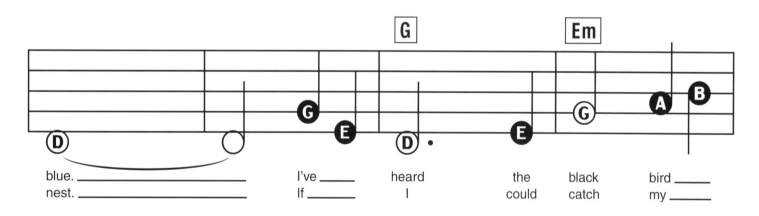

blue. ____ I've ____ heard the black bird ____
nest. ____ If ____ I could catch my ____

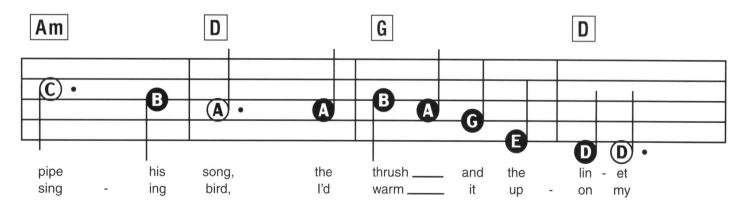

pipe his song, the thrush ____ and the lin - et
sing - ing bird, I'd warm ____ it up - on my

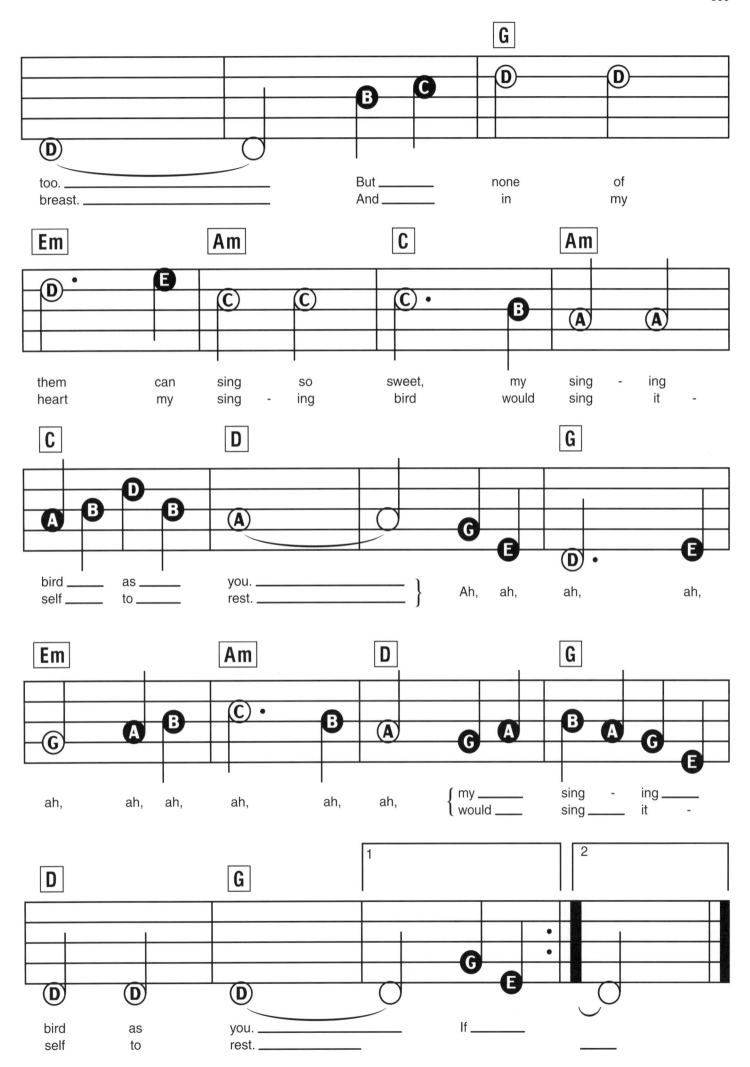

My Wild Irish Rose

Registration 2
Rhythm: Waltz

E+G, Waltz.
109

L Galaxy EP Pian
R1 Violin
R2 Tenor Sax
R3 Organ.

Words and Music by
Chauncey Olcott

Channa A2 St. Km 2

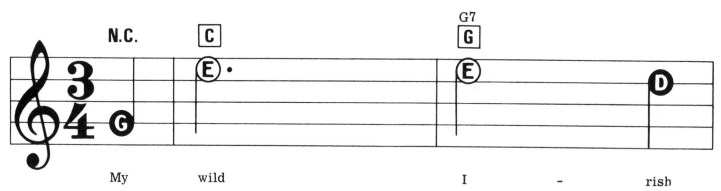

My wild I - rish

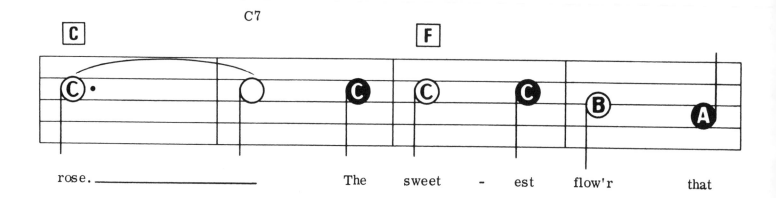

rose. _____ The sweet - est flow'r that

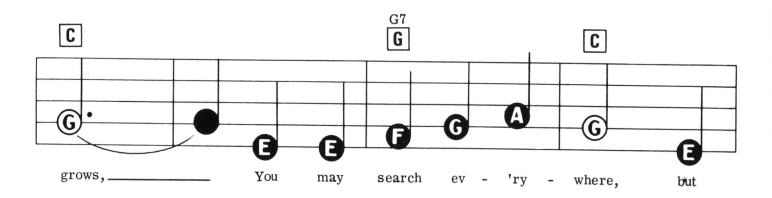

grows, _____ You may search ev - 'ry - where, but

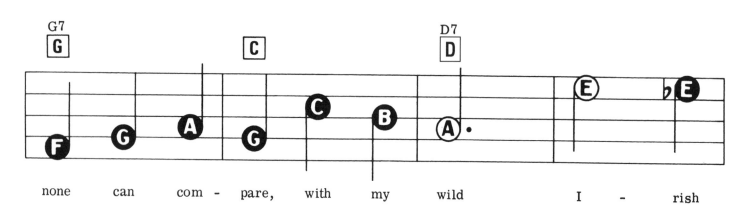

none can com - pare, with my wild I - rish

195

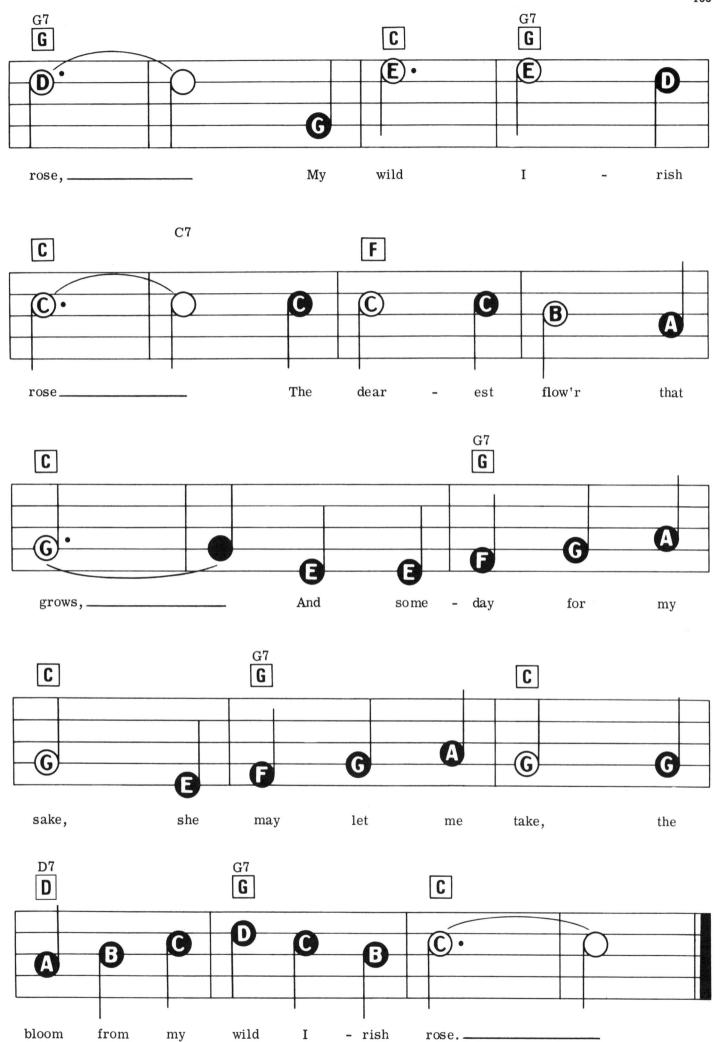

The Nightingale

Registration 2
Rhythm: Waltz

Traditional Irish Folk Song

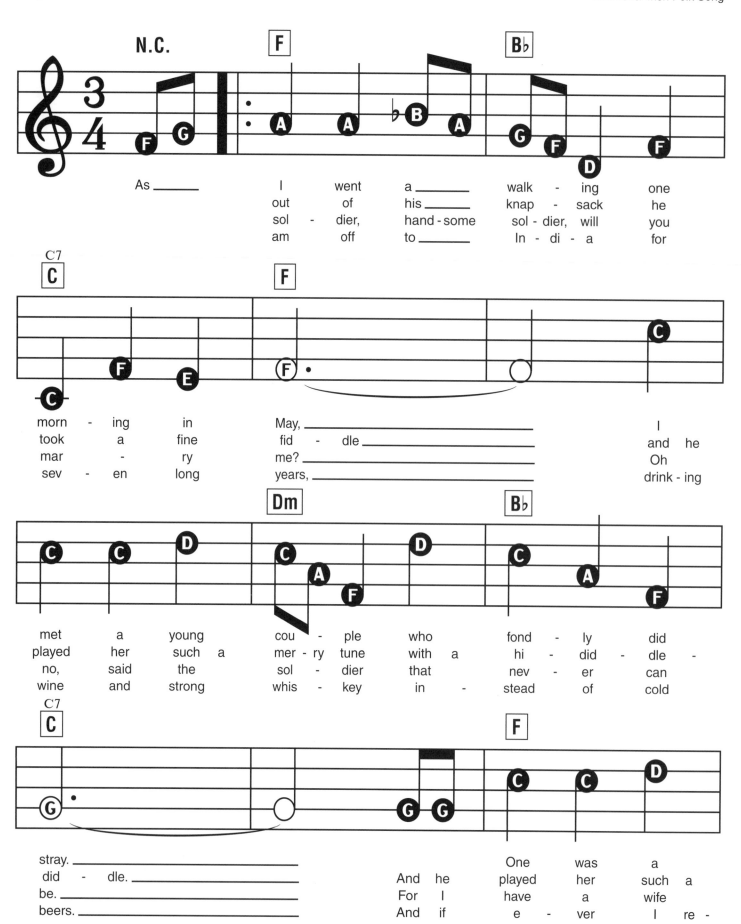

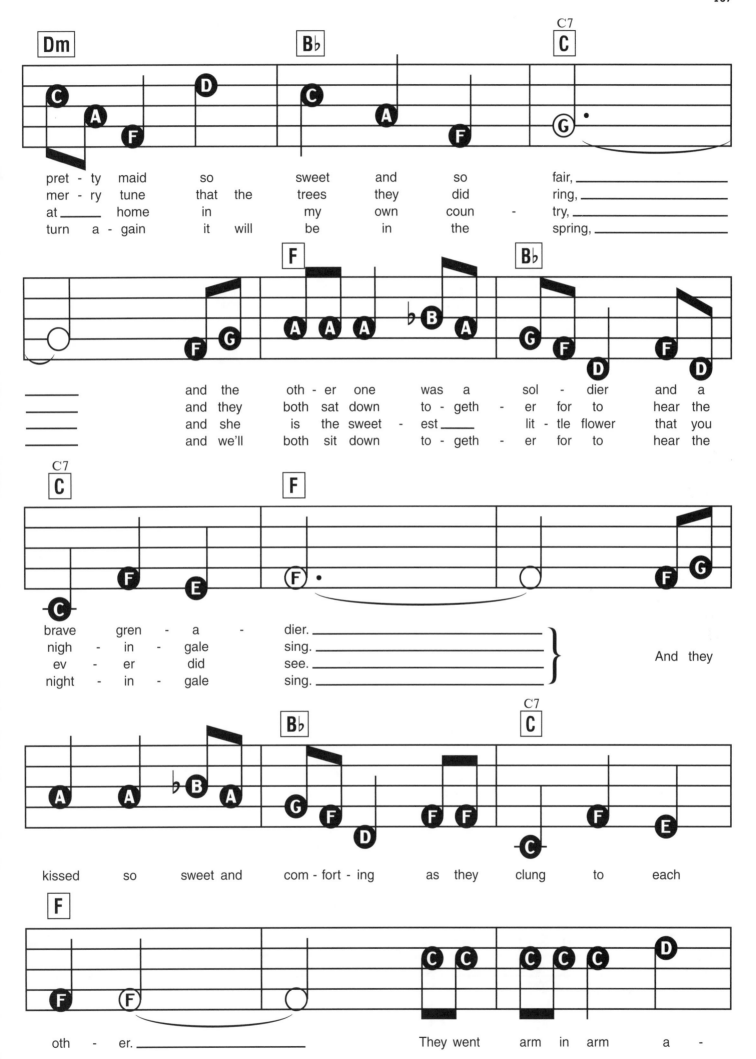

198

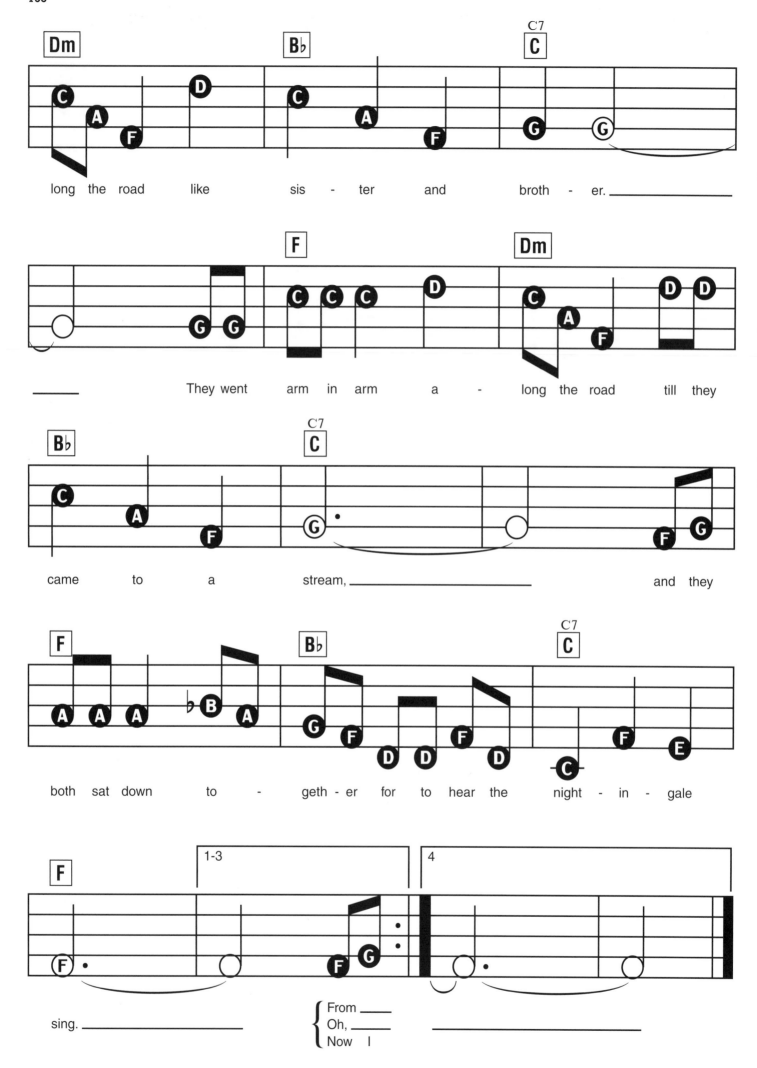

Paddy's Green Shamrock Shore

Registration 2
Rhythm: Waltz

Traditional Irish Folk Song

1. Oh fare thee well sweet
2. ship she lies at
3. Lon - don - der - ry we
4. - 6. (See additional lyrics)

Ire - land my own dear
an - chor now; she's stand - ing
did set sail, it be - ing the

na - tive home. It
by the quay. May
fourth of May. On a

breaks my heart, to see friends
for - tune bright shine down each
stur - dy ship to cov - er the

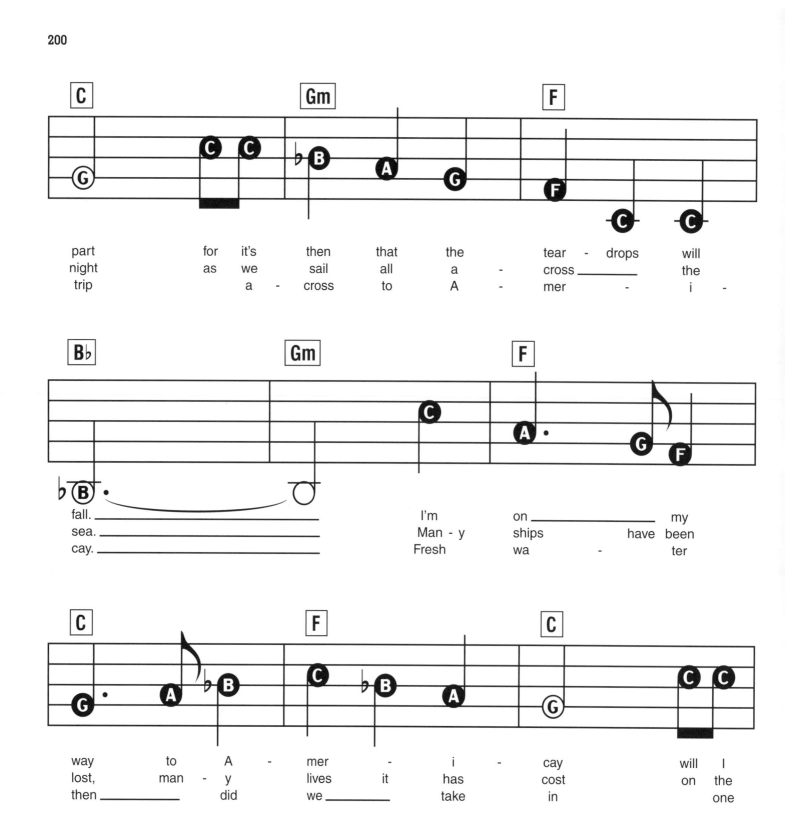

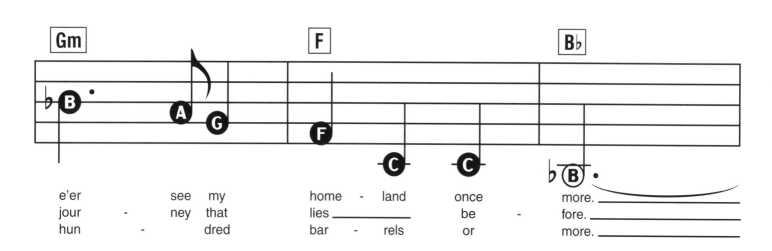

201

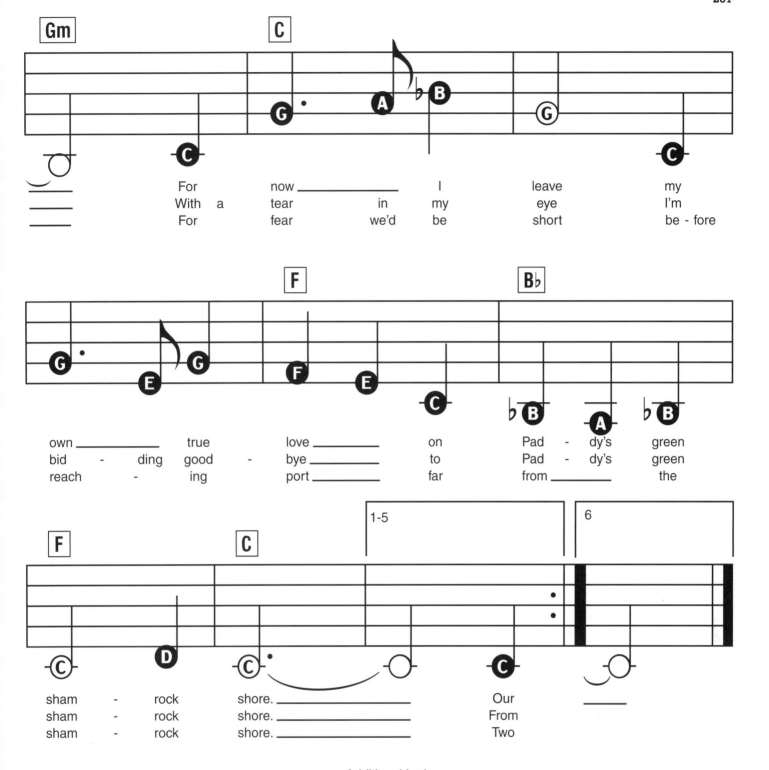

Additional Lyrics

4. Two of our anchors we did weigh before we left the quay
All down the river we were towed till we came to the open sea.
We saw that night the grandest sight we ever saw before,
The sun going down 'tween sea and sky far from Paddy's green shamrock shore.

5. Early next morn, sea-sick and forlorn, not one of us was free
And I myself was confined to bed with no one to pity me.
No father or mother or sister or brother to raise my head when sore,
That made me think of the family I left back on Paddy's green shamrock shore.

6. So are thee well my own true love I think of you night and day.
A place in my mind you surely will find although I'm so far away.
Though I am alone and away from my home I'll think of the good time before,
Until the day I can make my way back to Paddy's green shamrock shore.

O'Donnell Aboo

Registration 8
Rhythm: March or Fox Trot

Words and Music by
M.J. McCann

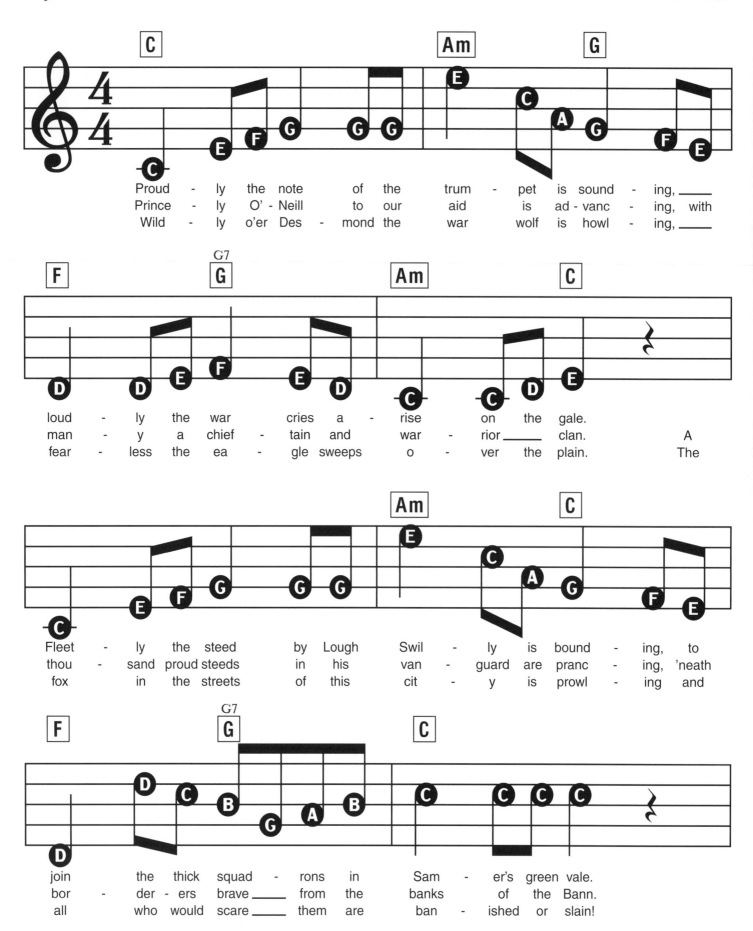

Oft in the Stilly Night

Registration 4
Rhythm: 6/8 March or Jig/Gigue

Irish Folk Song

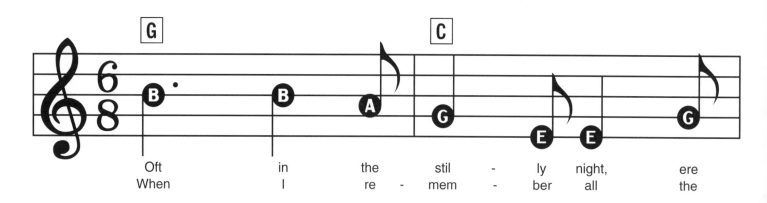

Oft in the stil - ly night, ere
When I re - mem - ber all the

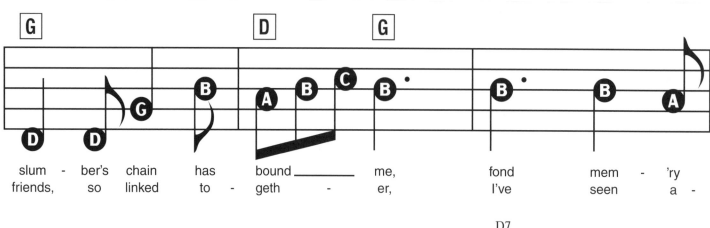

slum - ber's chain has bound _____ me, fond mem - 'ry
friends, so linked to - geth - er, I've seen a -

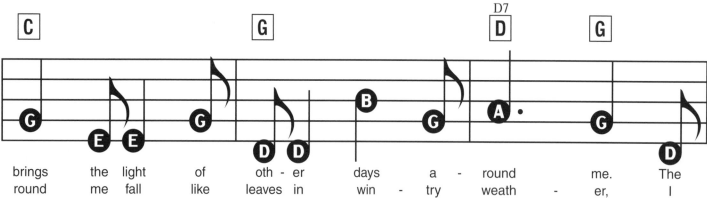

brings the light of oth - er days a - round me. The
round me fall like leaves in win - try weath - er, I

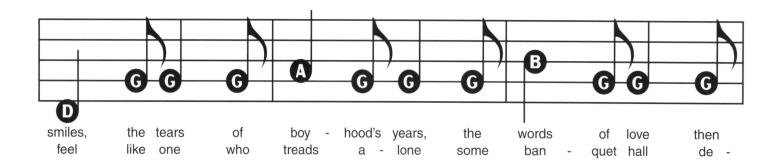

smiles, the tears of boy - hood's years, the words of love then
feel like one who treads a - lone some ban - quet hall de -

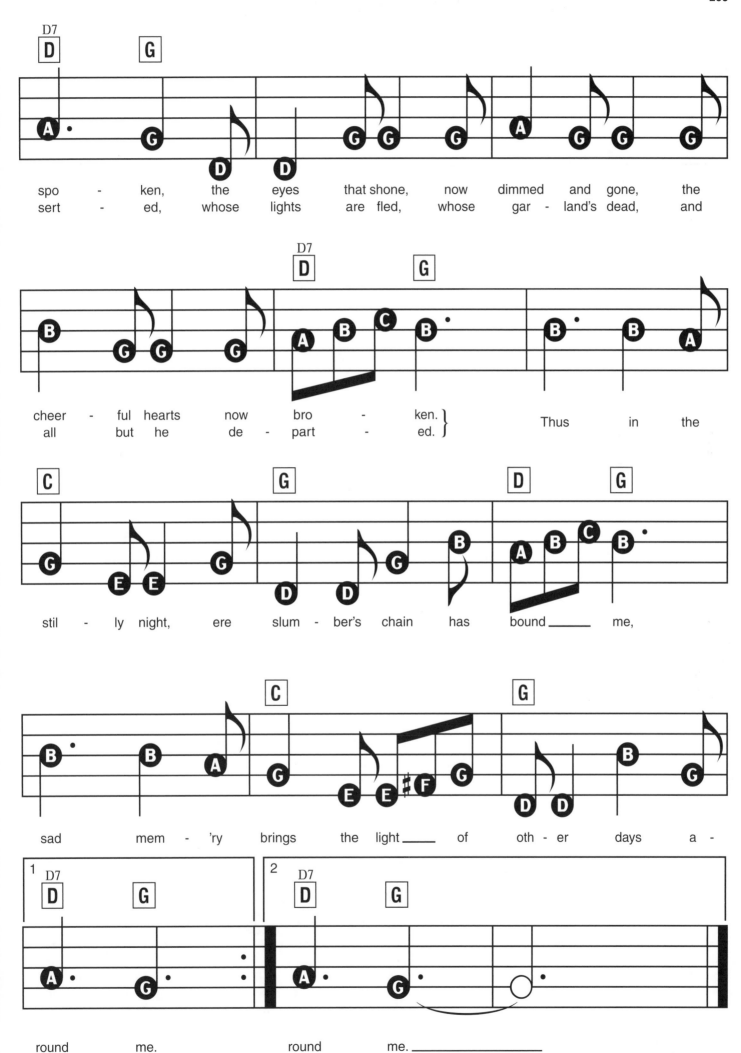

Old Maid in the Garret

Registration 2
Rhythm: Fox Trot

Traditional Irish Folk Song

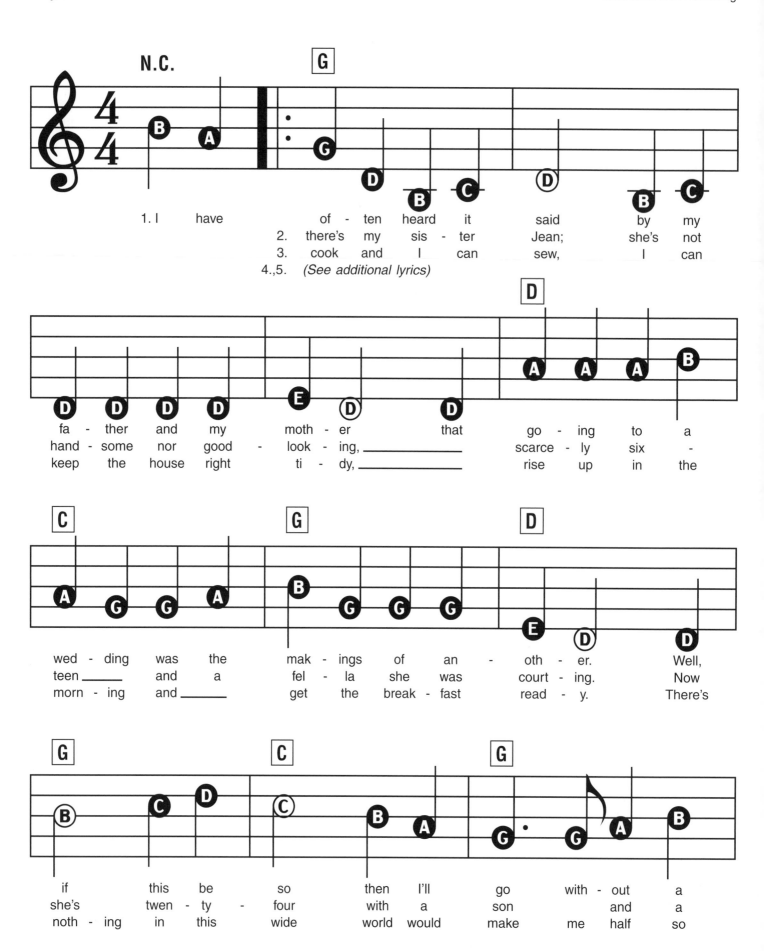

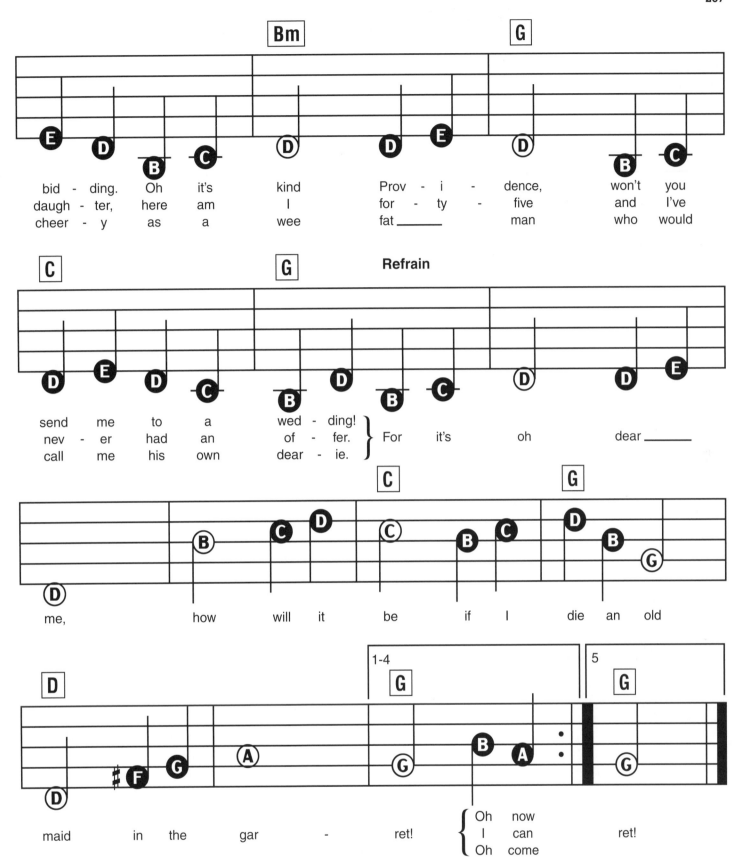

Additional Lyrics

4. Oh come landsman or come townsman, come tinker or come tailor,
   Come fiddler, come dancer, come ploughman or come sailor.
   Come rich man, come poor man, come fool or come witty,
   Come any man at all who would marry me for pity.
   Refrain

5. Oh well I'm away to home for there's nobody heeding,
   There's nobody heeding to poor old Annie's pleading.
   For I'm away home to my own wee-bit garret
   If I can't get a man then I'll surely get a parrot!
   Refrain

The Old Orange Flute

Registration 1
Rhythm: 6/8 March or Jig/Gigue

Traditional Irish Folk Song

1. In the coun - ty Ty - rone near the town of Dun - gan - non, where
2. Bob, the de - ceiv - er, he took us all in, _____ he
3. chap - el on Sun - day to a - tone for past deeds, __ said
4., 5. *(See additional lyrics)*

man - y the ruc - tions me - self had a han' - in, Bob
mar - ried a Pa - pist named Brid - get Mc - Ginn, _____ turned
Pa - ters and A - ves and count - ed his beads, _____ till

Wil - liam - son lived, a weav - er by trade, and
Pap - ish him - self, and for - sook the old cause, that
af - ter some time at the priests own de - sire he

all of us thought him a stout Or - ange blade. On the
gave us our free - dom, re - li - gion, and laws. Now the
went with the old flute to play in the choir. He

Additional Lyrics

4. Bob jumped and he started and got in a flutter
   And threw the old flute in the blessed holy water.
   He thought that this charm would bring some other sound;
   When he tried it again it played "Croppies Lie Down."
   Now for all he could whistle and finger and blow,
   To play Papish music he found it no go.
   "Kick the Pope" and "Boil Water" it freely would sound,
   But one Papish squeak in it couldn't be found.

5. At the council of priests that was held the next day
   They decided to banish the old flute away.
   They couldn't knock heresy out of its head,
   So they bought Bob a new one to play in the stead.
   Now the old flute was doomed and its fate was pathetic,
   'Twas fastened and burned at the stake as heretic.
   As the flames soared around it they heard a strange noise;
   'Twas the old flute still whistling "The Protestant Boys."

The Old Woman from Wexford

Registration 7
Rhythm: 6/8 March or Jig/Gigue

Traditional Irish Folk Song

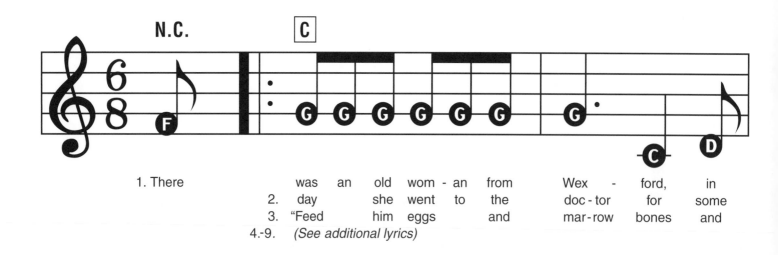

1. There   was an old wom - an from   Wex - ford,   in
2.   day   she went to the   doc - tor   for   some
3.   "Feed   him eggs   and   mar - row bones   and
4.-9. *(See additional lyrics)*

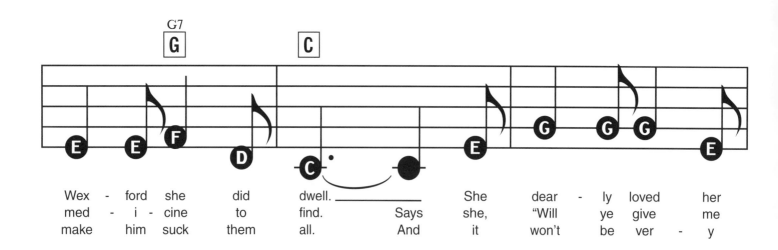

Wex - ford she did   dwell. _____   She dear - ly loved   her
med - i - cine to   find.   Says   she, "Will ye give   me
make him suck them   all.   And   it won't be ver - y

Refrain

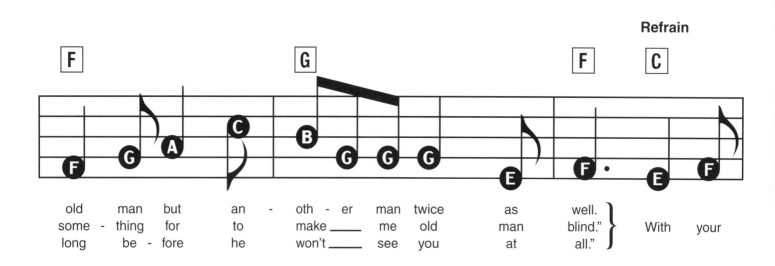

old   man but   an - oth - er man twice as   well. }   With   your
some - thing for   to   make ___ me old man blind." }
long be - fore   he   won't ___ see you at   all." }

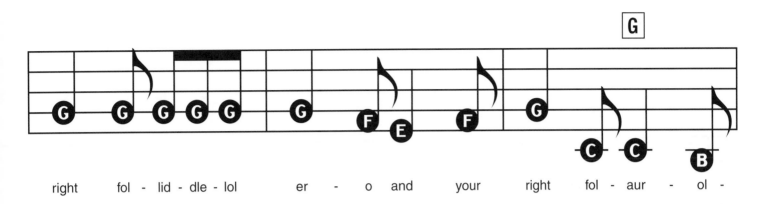

right   fol - lid - dle - lol   er - o and   your   right   fol - aur - ol -

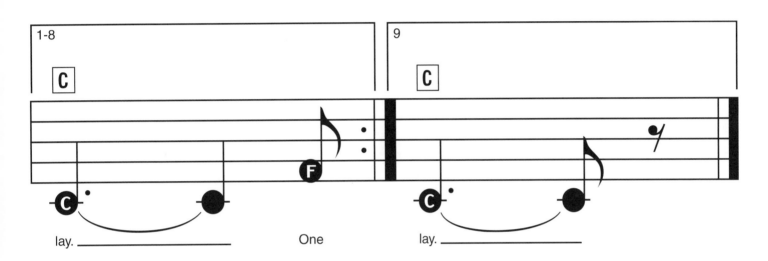

lay. _____   One   lay. _____

Additional Lyrics

4. The doctor wrote a letter and he signed it with his hand
   And he sent it to the old man so that he would understand.
   Refrain

5. She fed him eggs and marrow bones and made him suck them all
   And it wasn't very long before he couldn't see the wall.
   Refrain

6. Said he, "I'd like to drown myself but that would be a sin."
   Said she, "I'll come along with you and help to push you in."
   Refrain

7. The woman she stepped back a bit to rush and push him in,
   But the old man quickly stepped aside and she went tumbling in.
   Refrain

8. How loudly she did holler oh, how loudly she did call,
   "Yerra hold your whist old woman sure I can't see you at all."
   Refrain

9. Now eggs and eggs and marrowbones may make your old man blind,
   But if you want to drown him you must creep up from behind.
   Refrain

Paddy Works on the Railway

Registration 7
Rhythm: March

Traditional

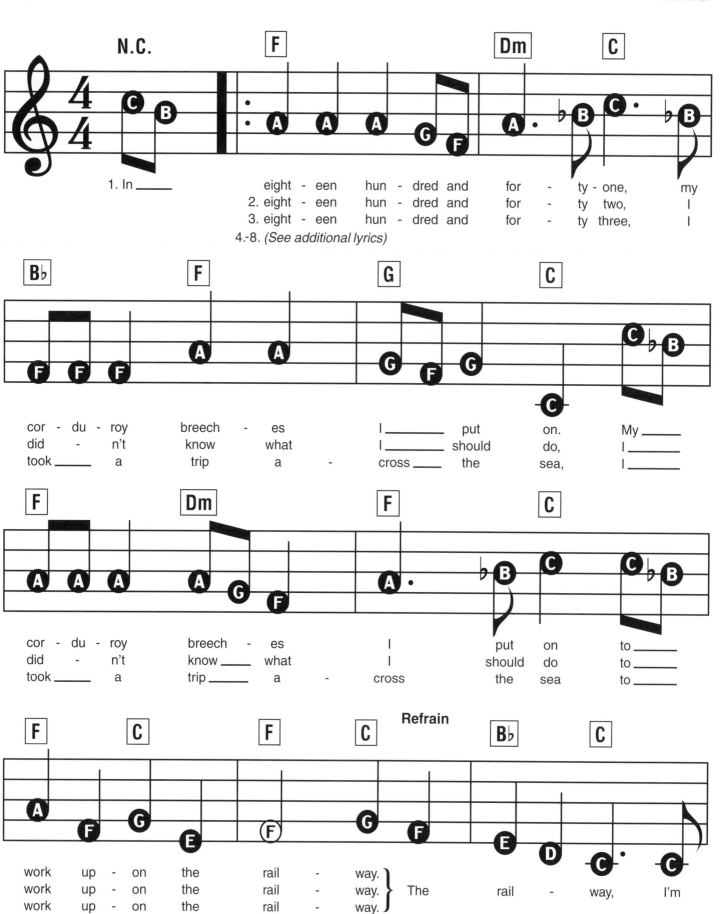

1. In _____ eight - een hun - dred and for - ty-one, my
2. eight - een hun - dred and for - ty two, I
3. eight - een hun - dred and for - ty three, I
4.-8. *(See additional lyrics)*

cor - du - roy breech - es I _____ put on. My _____
did - n't know what I _____ should do, I _____
took _____ a trip a - cross _____ the sea, I _____

cor - du - roy breech - es I put on to _____
did - n't know _____ what I should do to _____
took _____ a trip _____ a - cross the sea to _____

Refrain

work up - on the rail - way.
work up - on the rail - way. } The rail - way, I'm
work up - on the rail - way.

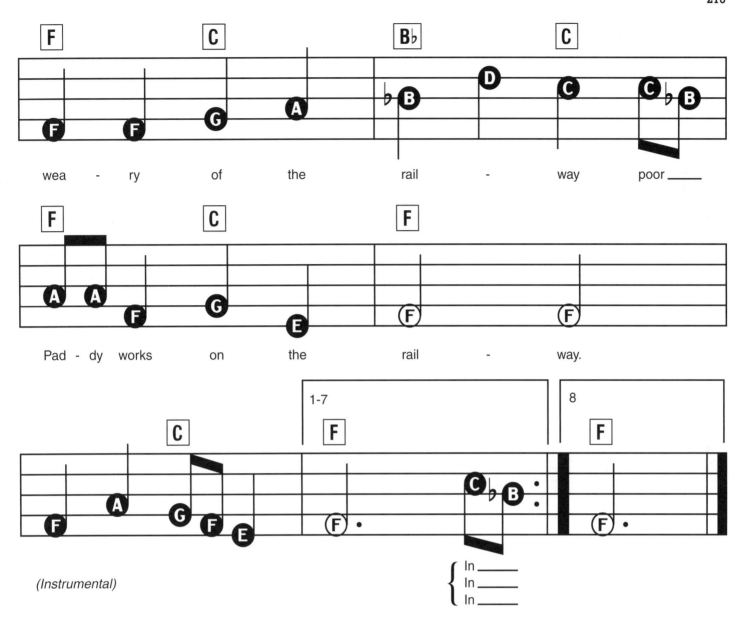

wea - ry of the rail - way poor_____

Pad - dy works on the rail - way.

1-7

8

(Instrumental)

{ In_____
In_____
In_____

Additional Lyrics

4. In eighteen hundred and forty-four, I landed on Columbia's shore,
   I landed on Columbia's shore, to work upon the railway.
   Refrain

5. In eighteen hundred and forty-five, when Daniel O'Connell was alive,
   When Daniel O'Connell was alive, to work upon the railway.
   Refrain

6. In eighteen hundred and forty-six, I changed my trade to carrying bricks,
   I changed my trade to carrying bricks, to work upon the railway.
   Refrain

7. In eighteen hundred and forty-seven, poor Paddy was thinking of going to heaven,
   Poor Paddy was thinking of going to heaven, to work upon the railway.
   Refrain

8. In eighteen hundred and forty-eight, I learnt to take my whiskey straight,
   I learnt to take my whiskey straight, to work upon the railway.
   Refrain

The Parting Glass

Registration 7
Rhythm: Fox Trot

Irish Folk Song

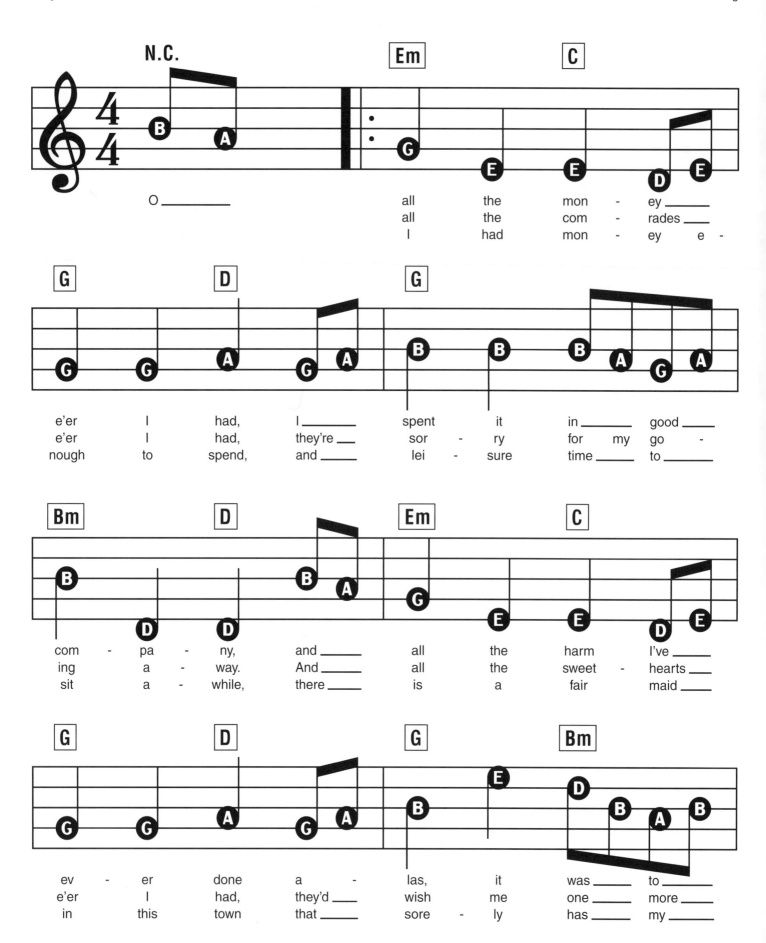

215

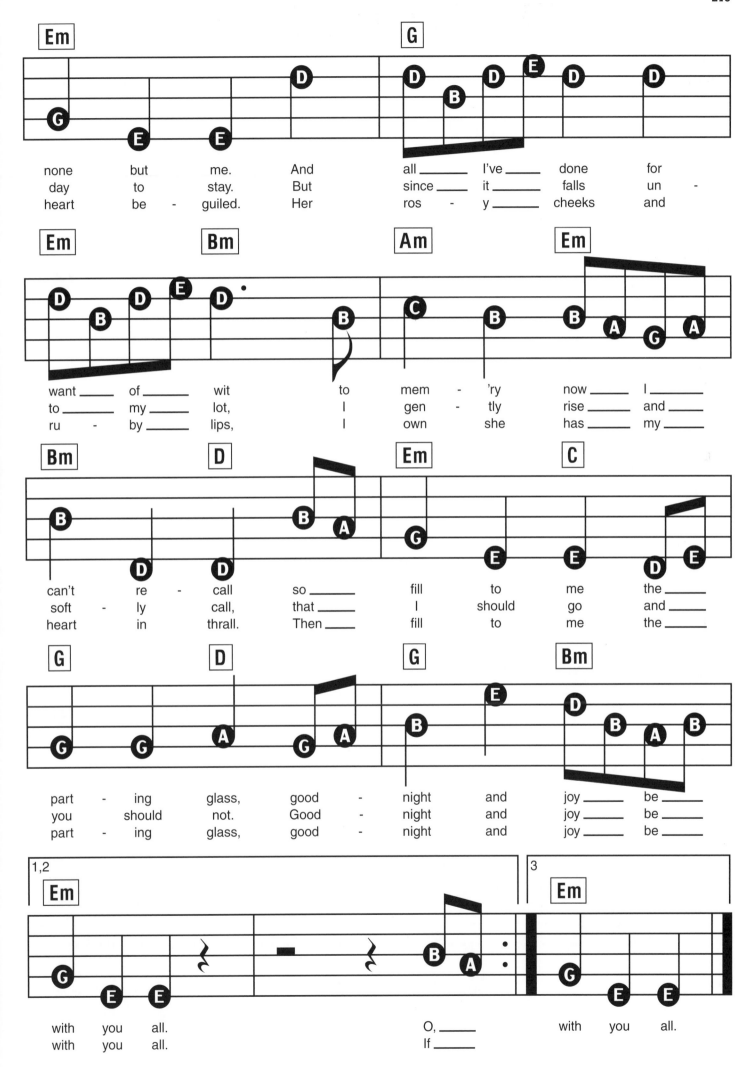

The Patriot Game

Registration 3
Rhythm: Waltz

Traditional Irish Folk Song

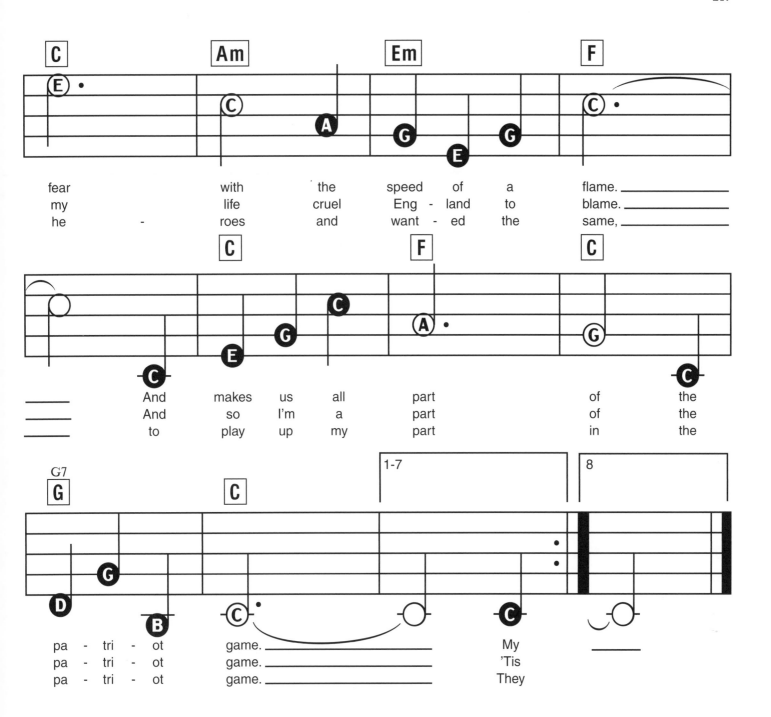

fear with the speed of a flame. _____
my life cruel Eng - land to blame. _____
he - roes and want - ed the same, _____

_____ And makes us all part of the
_____ And so I'm a part of the
_____ to play up my part in the

pa - tri - ot game. _____ My
pa - tri - ot game. _____ 'Tis
pa - tri - ot game. _____ They

Additional Lyrics

4. They told me how Connolly was shot in a chair.
His wounds from the battle all bleeding and bare,
His fine body twisted, all battered and lame.
They soon made him part of the patriot game.

5. I joined a battalion from dear Bally Bay,
And gave up my boyhood so happy and gay.
For now as a soldier I'd drill and I'd train,
To play my full part in the patriot game.

6. This Ireland of mine has for long been half free.
Six countries are under John Bull's tyranny.
And still De Valera is greatly to blame
For shirking his part in the patriot game.

7. I don't mind a bit if I shoot down police,
They're lackeys for war never guardians of peace.
But yet at deserters I'm never let aim,
Those rebels who sold out the patriot game.

8. And now as I lie with my body all holes
I think of those traitors who bargained and sold.
I'm sorry my rifle has not done the same
For the quisling who sold out the patriot game.

The Queen of Connemara

Registration 7
Rhythm: 6/8 March or Jig/Gigue

Traditional Irish Folk Song

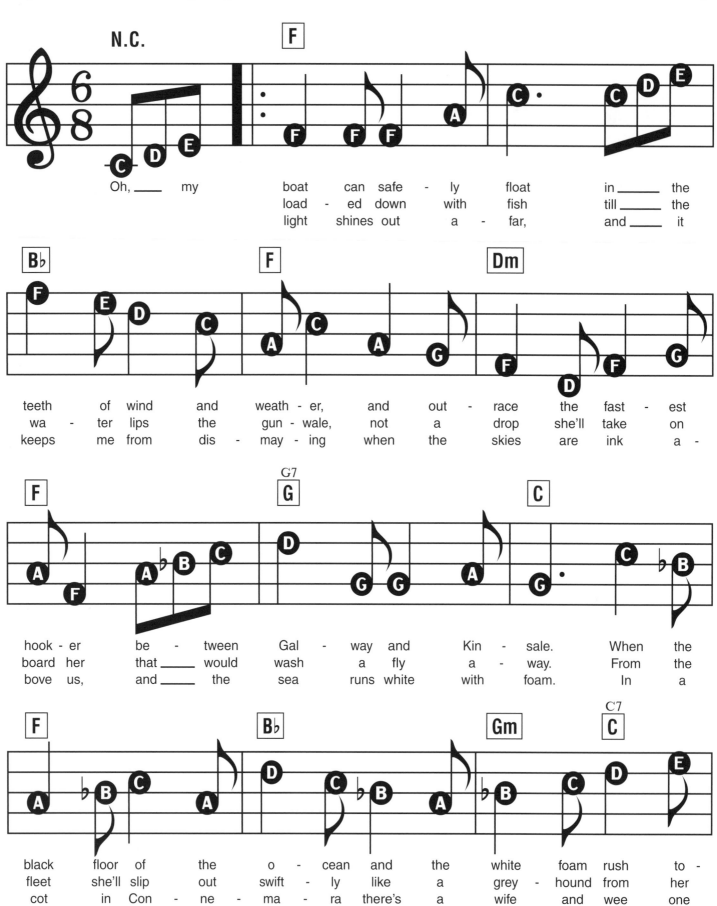

Oh, ___ my boat can safe - ly float in ___ the
load - ed down with fish till ___ the
light shines out a - far, and ___ it

teeth of wind and weath - er, and out - race the fast - est
wa - ter lips the gun - wale, not a drop she'll take on
keeps me from dis - may - ing not when the skies are ink a -

hook - er be - tween Gal - way and Kin - sale. When the
board her that ___ would wash a fly a - way. From the
bove us, and ___ the sea runs white with foam. In a

black floor of the o - cean and the white foam rush to her
fleet she'll slip out swift - ly like a grey - hound from her
cot in Con - ne - ma - ra there's a wife and wee one

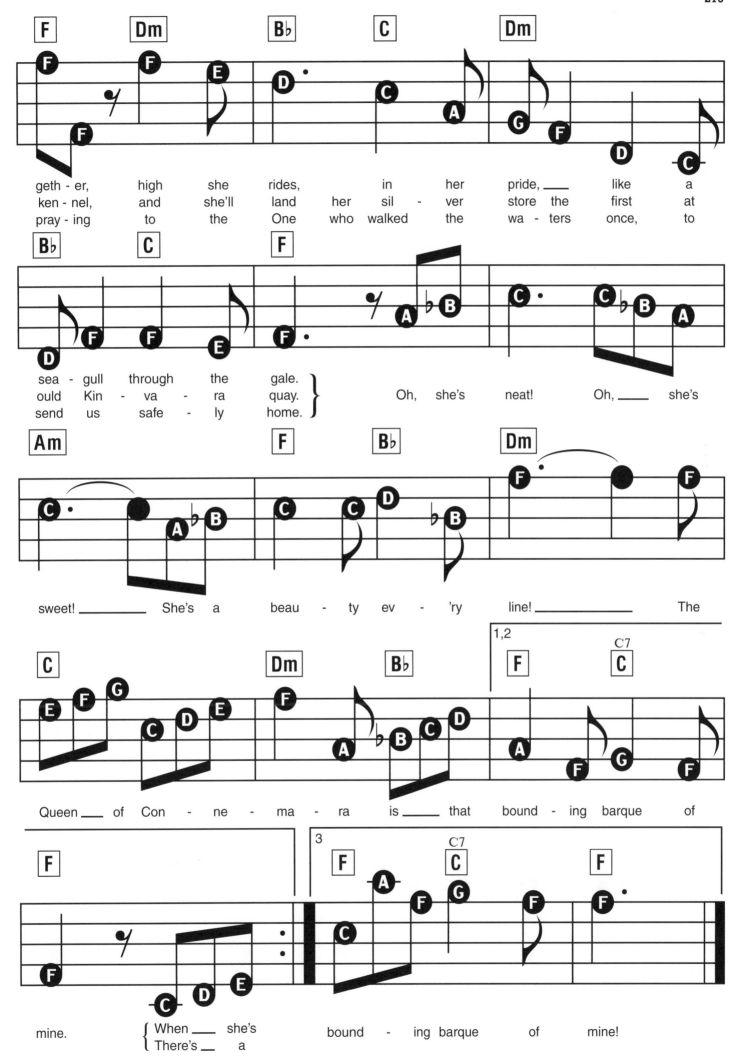

The Raggle-Taggle Gypsy

Registration 4
Rhythm: Fox Trot

Traditional

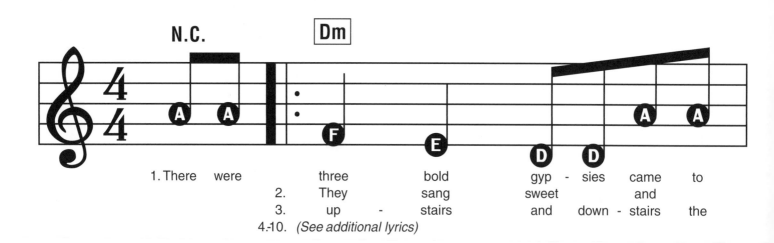

1. There were three bold gyp - sies came to
2. They sang sweet and
3. up - stairs and down - stairs the

4.-10. *(See additional lyrics)*

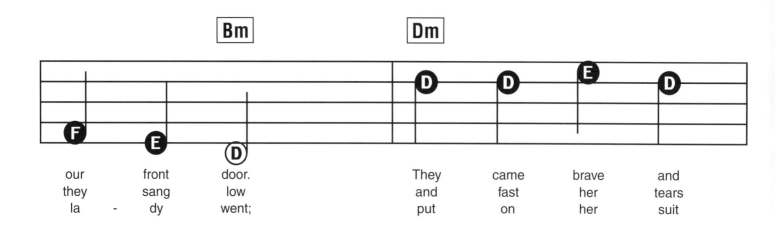

our front door.
they sang low
la - dy went;

They came brave and
and fast her tears
put on her suit

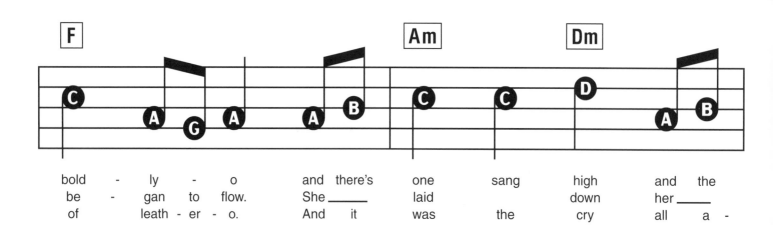

bold - ly - o and there's one sang high and the
be - gan to flow. She _____ laid down her _____
of leath - er - o. And it was the cry all a -

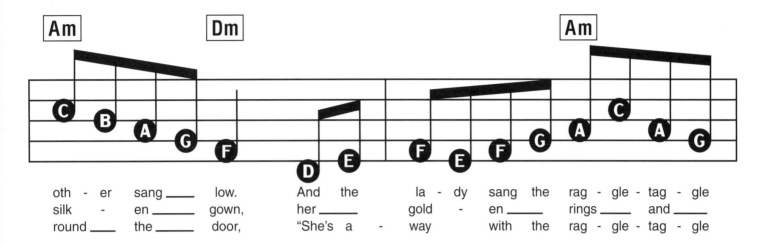

oth - er sang ____ low. And the la - dy sang the rag - gle - tag - gle
silk - en ____ gown, her ____ gold - en ____ rings ____ and ____
round ____ the ____ door, "She's a - way with the rag - gle - tag - gle

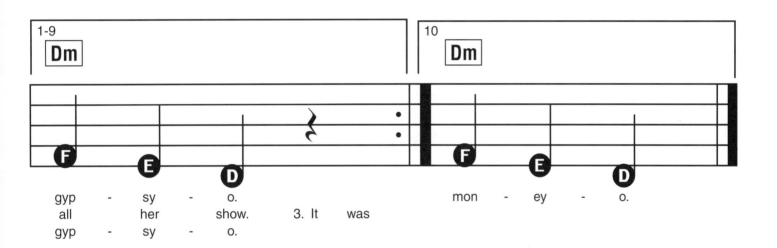

gyp - sy - o.
all her show. 3. It was
gyp - sy - o.

mon - ey - o.

Additional Lyrics

4. It was late that night when the lord came home inquiring for his lady-o.
   The servant's voice rang around the house, "She is gone with the raggle-taggle gypsy-o."

5. "Oh then saddle for me, my milk white steed; the black horse is not speedy-o.
   And I will ride and I'll seek me bride who's away with the raggle-taggle gypsy-o."

6. Oh then he rode high and he rode low; he rode north and south also,
   But when he came to a wide open field it is there that he spotted his lady-o.

7. "Oh then why did you leave your house and your land; why did you leave your money-o?
   And why did you leave your newly wedded lord to be off with the raggle-taggle gypsy-o?"

8. "Yerra what do I care for me house and me land and what do I care for money-o.
   And what do I care for my newly-wedded lord; I'm away with the raggle-taggle gypsy-o?"

9. "And what do I care for my goose-feathered bed with blankets drawn so comely-o.
   Tonight I'll sleep in the wide open field all along with the raggle-taggle gypsy-o."

10. "Oh for you rode east when I rode west; you rode high and I rode low,
    I'd rather have a kiss from the yellow gypsy's lips than all your land and money-o."

Red Is the Rose

Registration 10
Rhythm: Waltz

Irish Folk Song

223

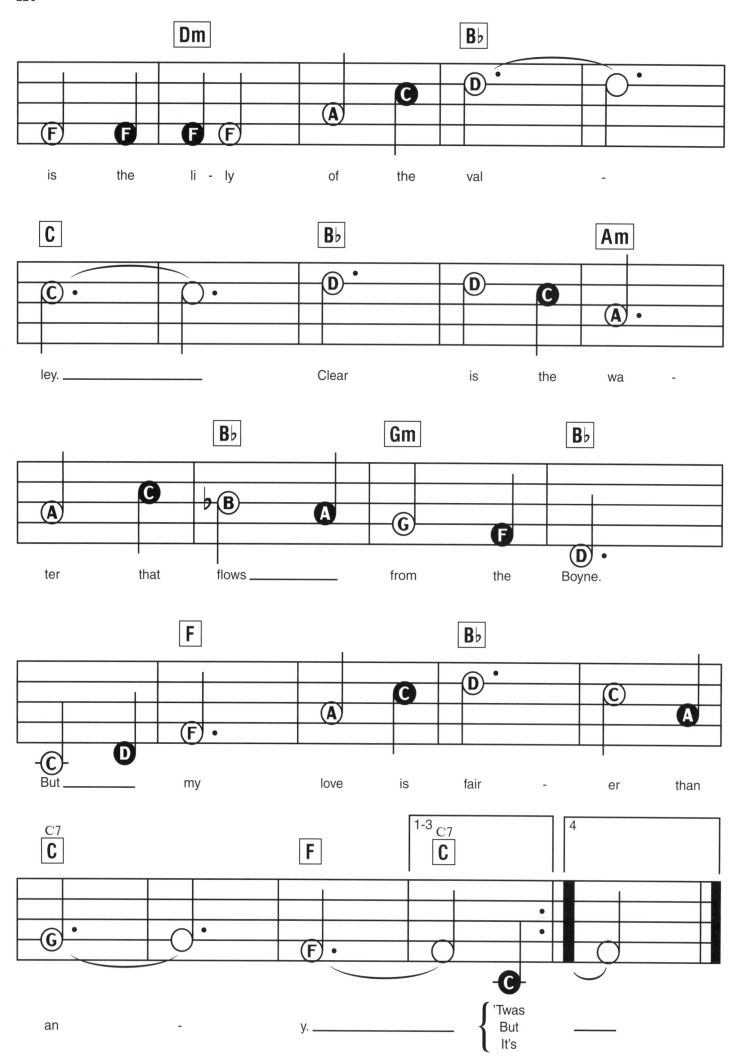

224

The Rocks of Bawn

Registration 2
Rhythm: Waltz

Traditional Irish Folk Song

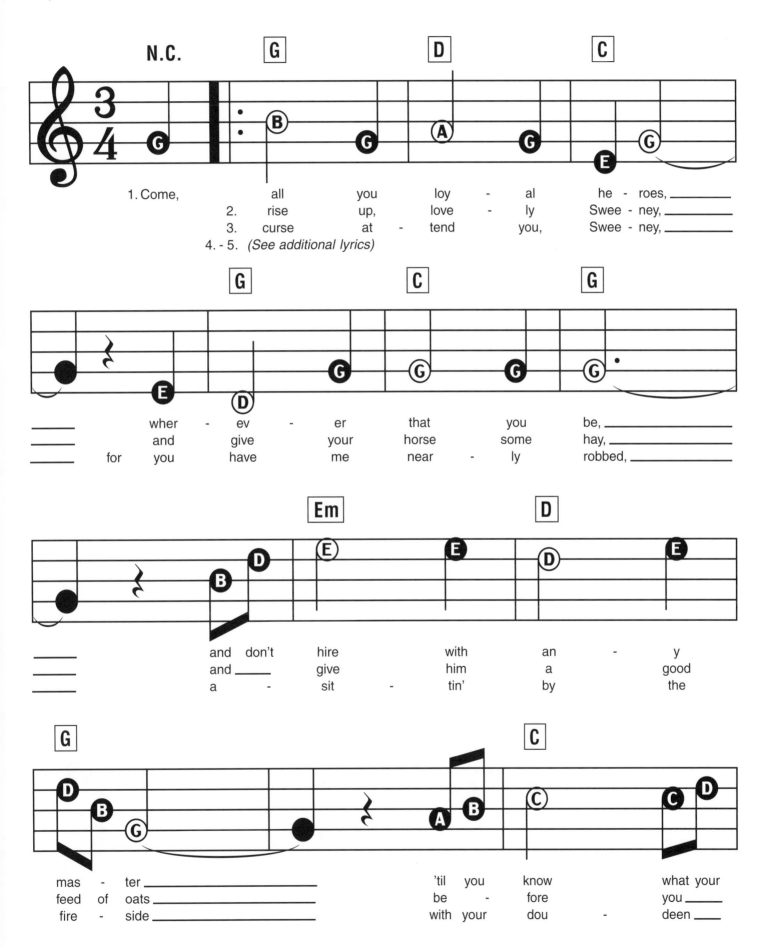

226

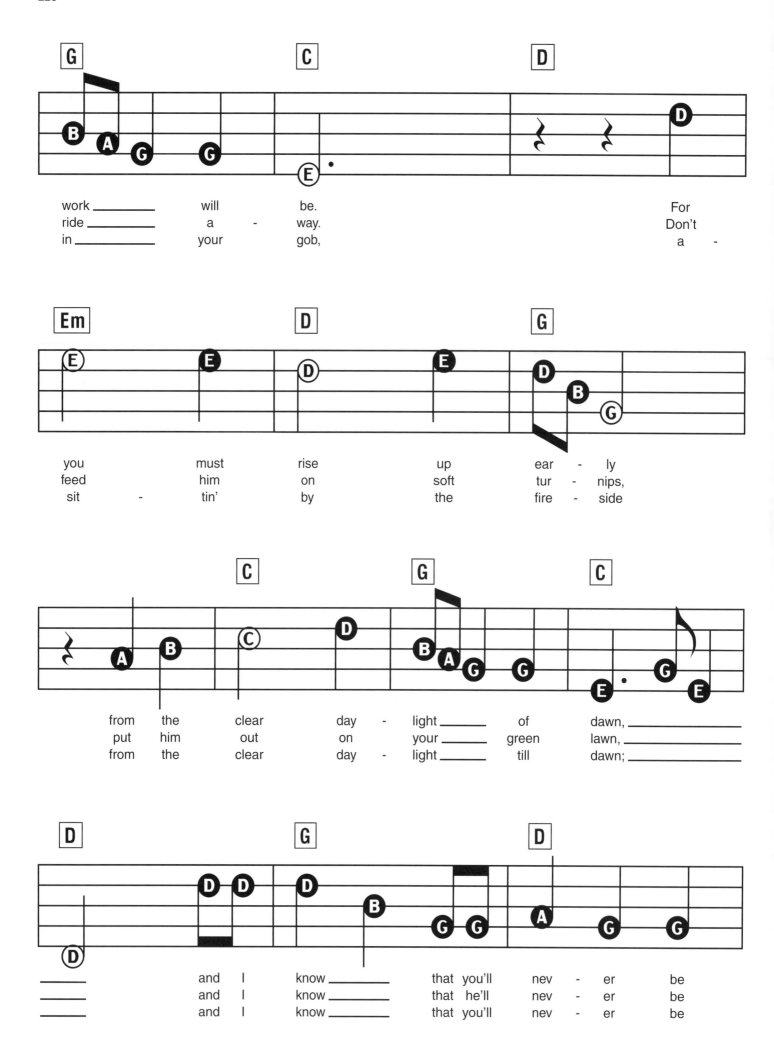

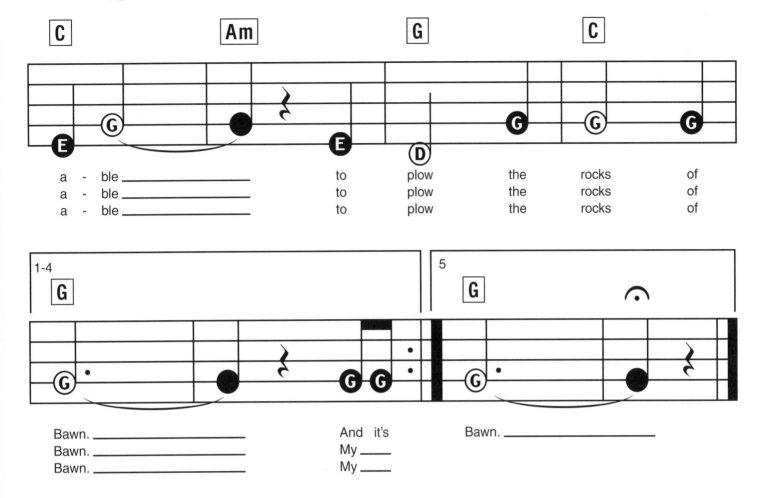

Additional Lyrics

4. My shoes they are well worn out, my stockings they are thin,
And my heart is always trembling for fear that they'll let in.
And my heart is always trembling for the clear daylight of dawn,
Afraid I'll never be able to plow the rocks of Bawn.

5. I wish the Queen of England would write to me in time
And place me in some regiment in all my youth and prime.
I'd fight for Ireland's glory from the clear daylight of dawn,
And I never would return again to plow the rocks of Bawn.

The Rising of the Moon

Registration 8
Rhythm: Fox Trot

Traditional Irish Folk Song

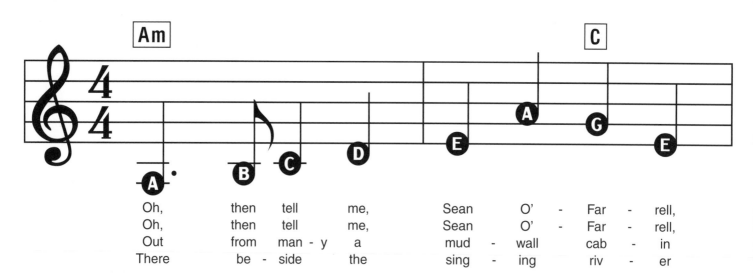

Oh,	then	tell	me,	Sean	O' -	Far -	rell,
Oh,	then	tell	me,	Sean	O' -	Far -	rell,
Out	from	man - y	a	mud -	wall	cab -	in
There	be - side	the		sing -	ing	riv -	er

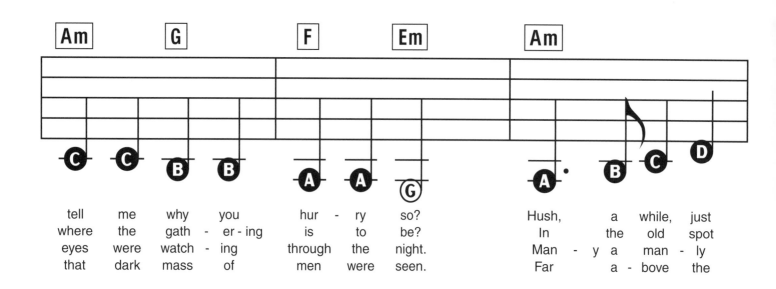

tell	me	why	you	hur -	ry	so?	Hush, a while, just
where	the	gath - er - ing	is	to	be?	In the old spot
eyes	were	watch - ing	through	the	night.	Man - y a man - ly
that	dark	mass	of	men	were	seen.	Far a - bove the

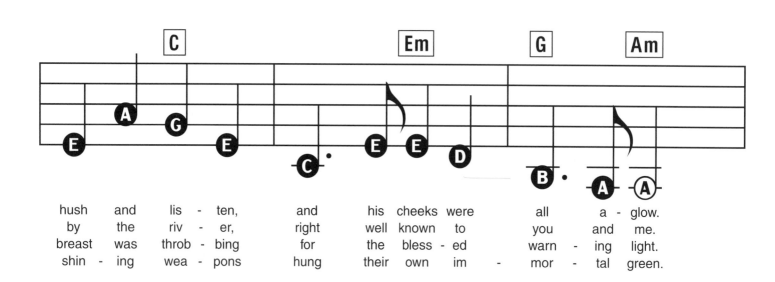

hush	and	lis - ten,	and	his	cheeks were	all a -	glow.
by	the	riv - er,	right	well	known to	you and	me.
breast	was	throb - bing	for	the	bless - ed	warn - ing	light.
shin - ing	wea - pons	hung	their	own	im -	mor - tal	green.

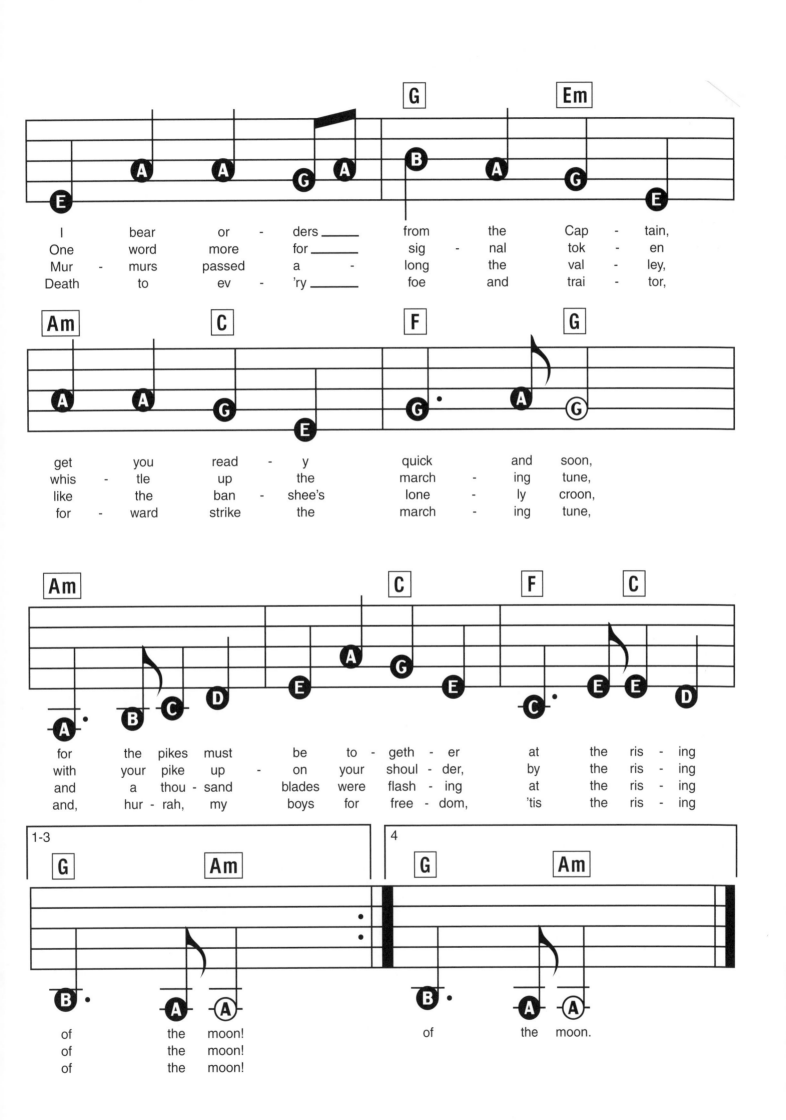

Wild Rover

Traditional Irish Folk Song

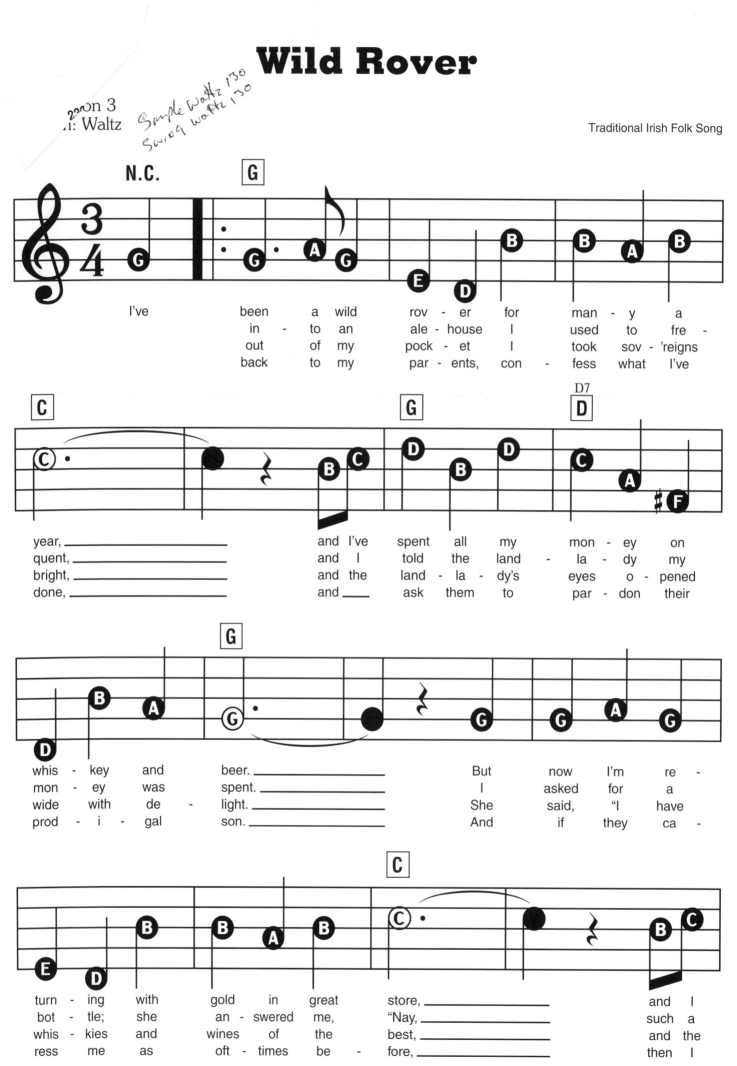

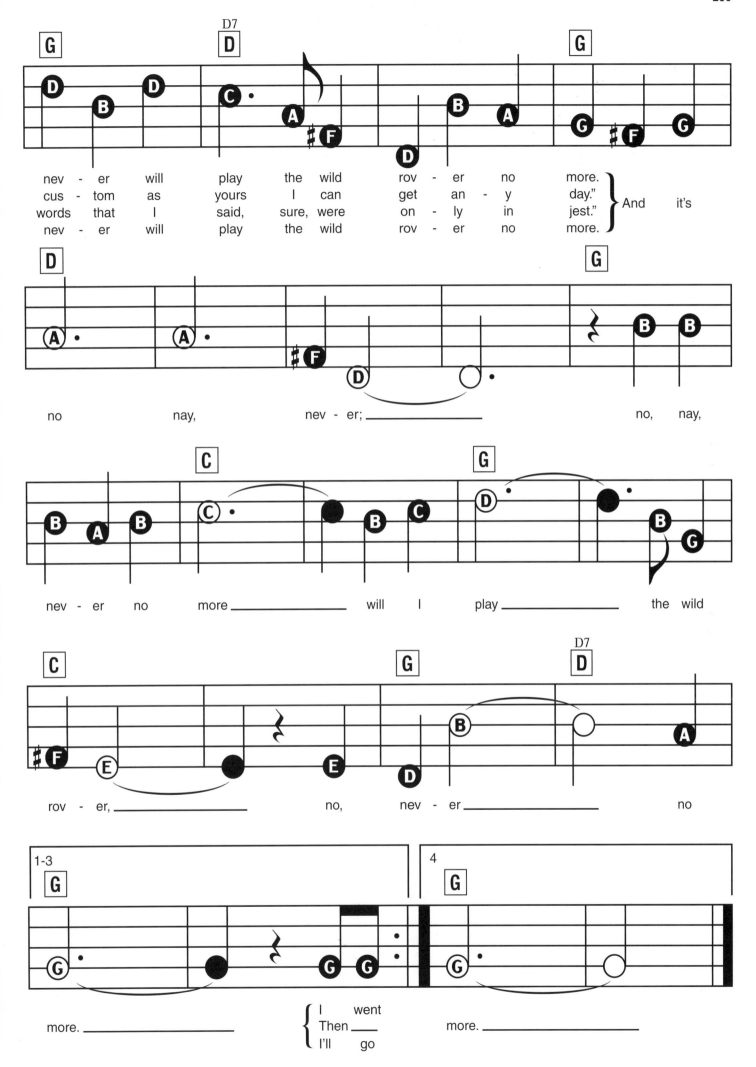

Roddy McCorley

Registration 8
Rhythm: Fox Trot

Traditional Irish Folk Song

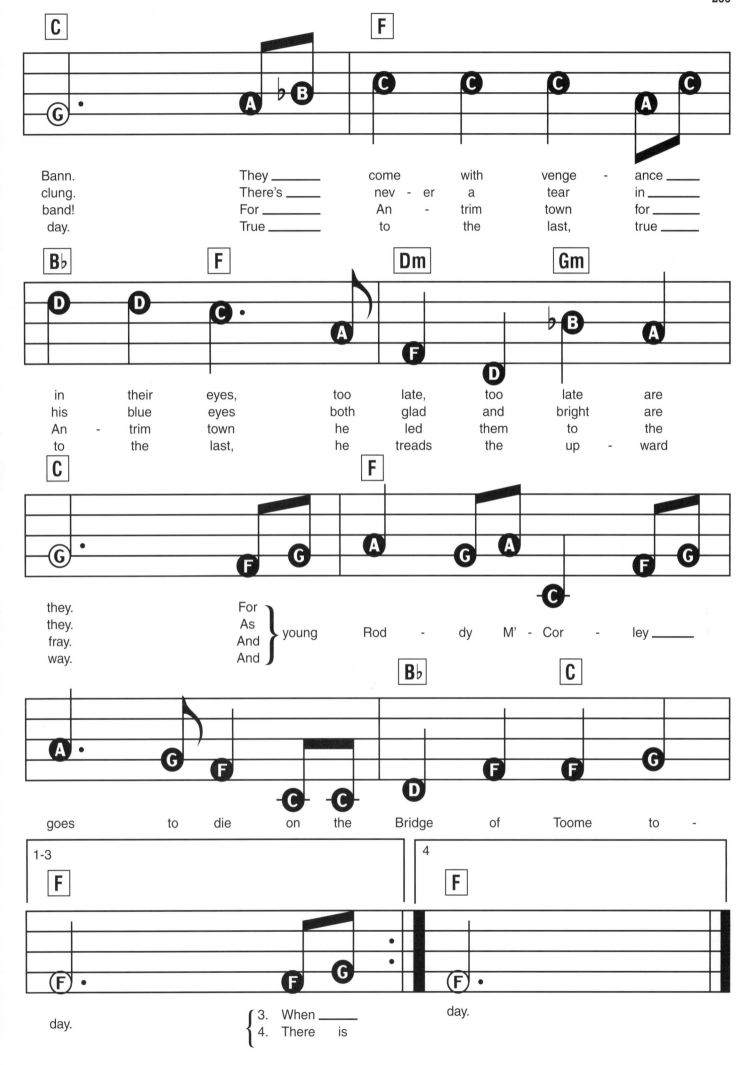

The Rose of Allendale

Registration 7
Rhythm: Ballad or Fox Trot

Traditional Irish Folk Song

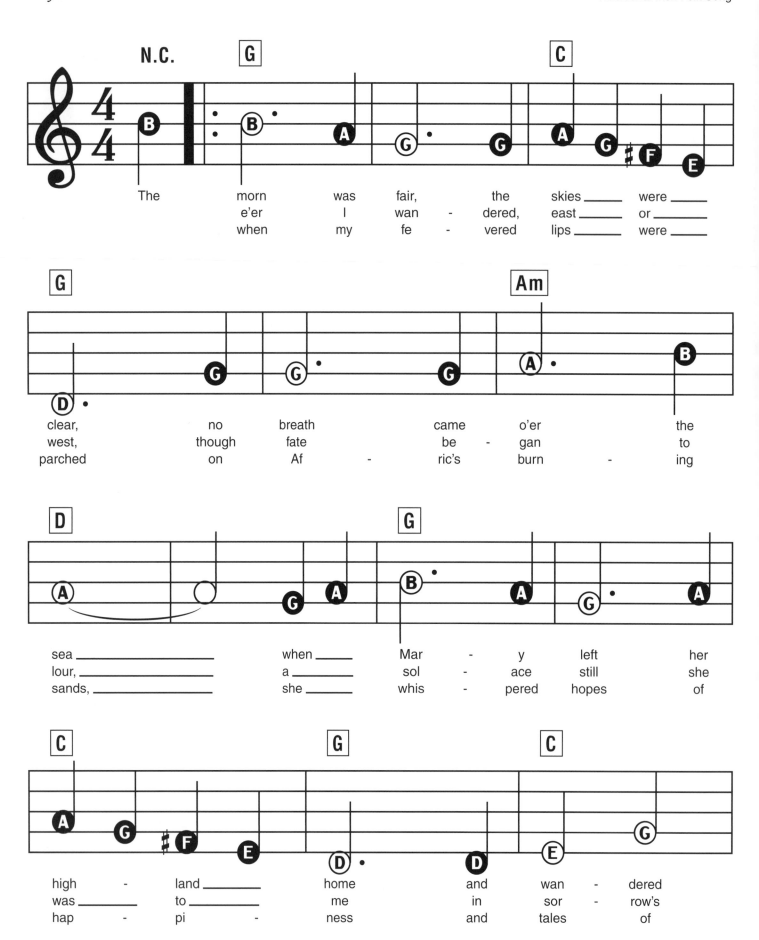

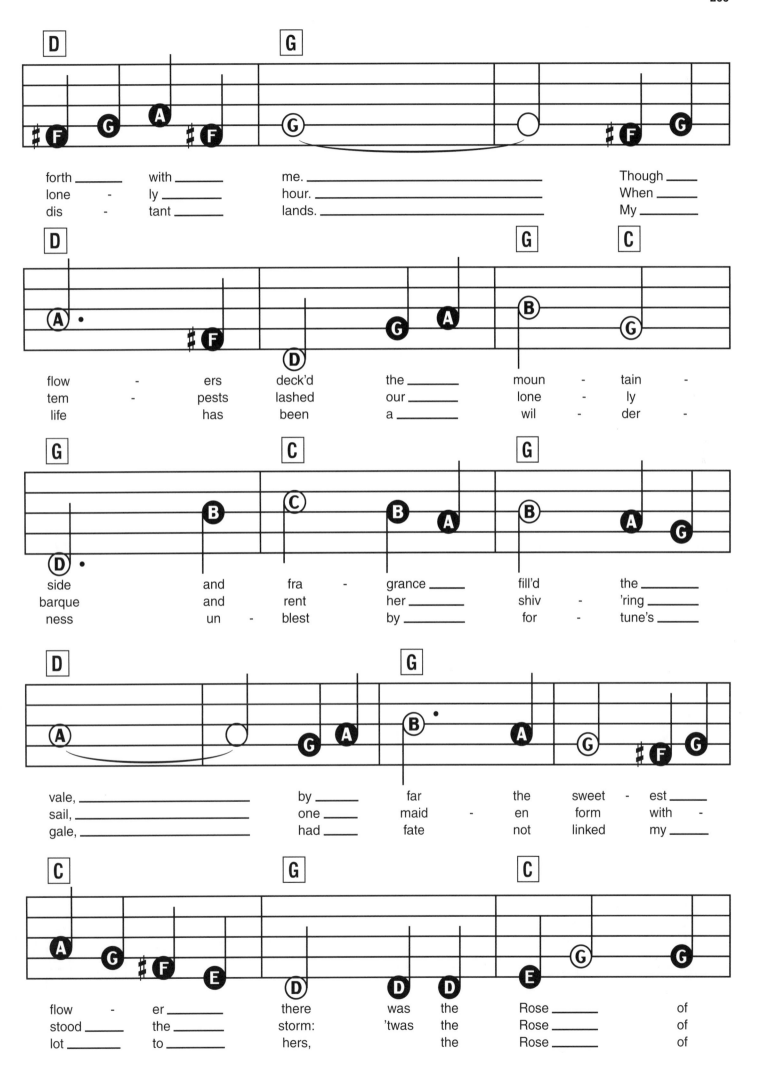

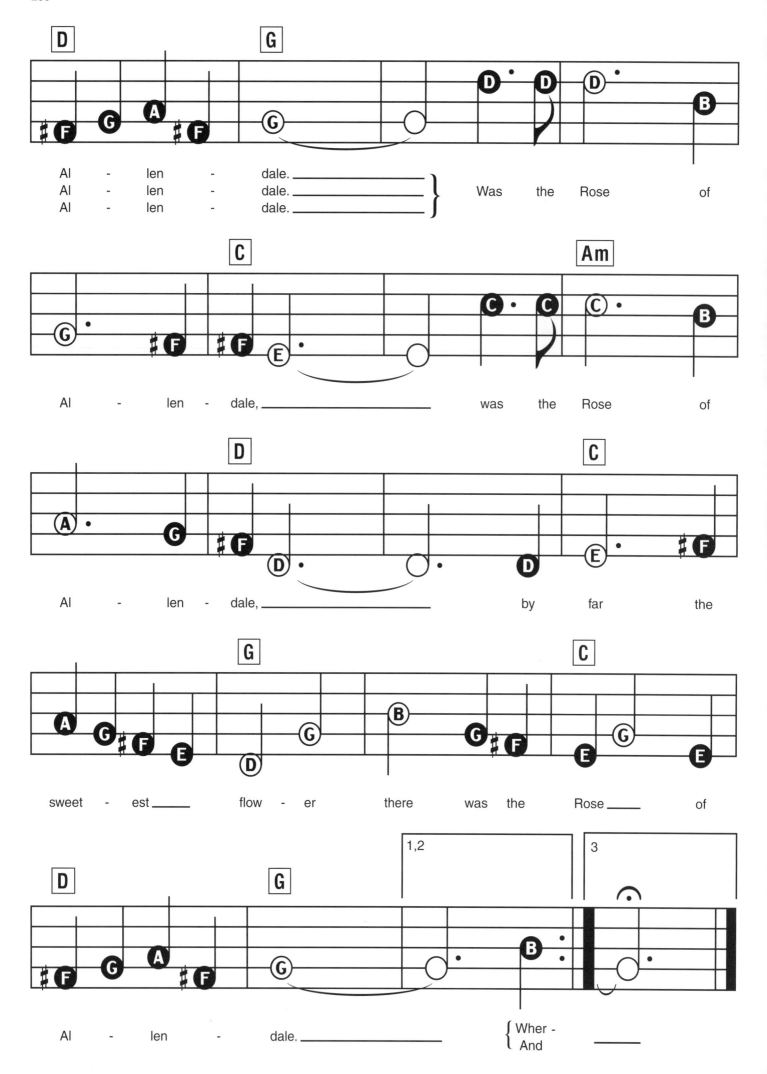

The Rose of Mooncoin

Registration 1
Rhythm: Waltz

Traditional Irish Folk Song

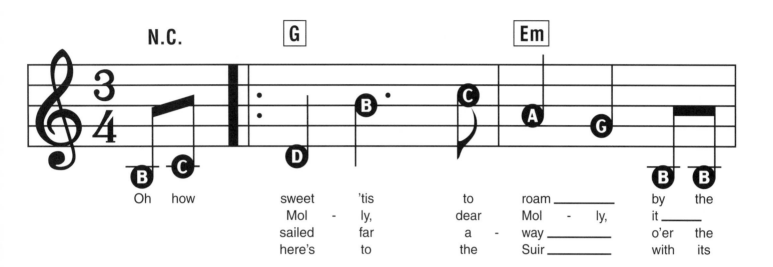

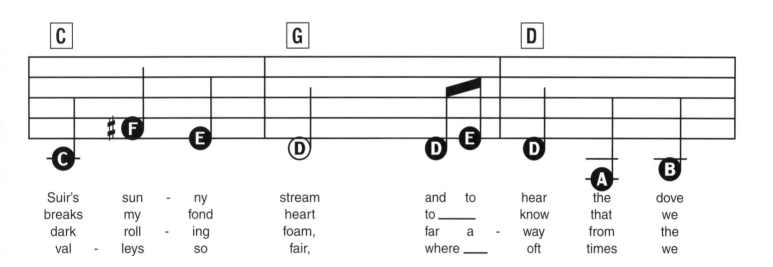

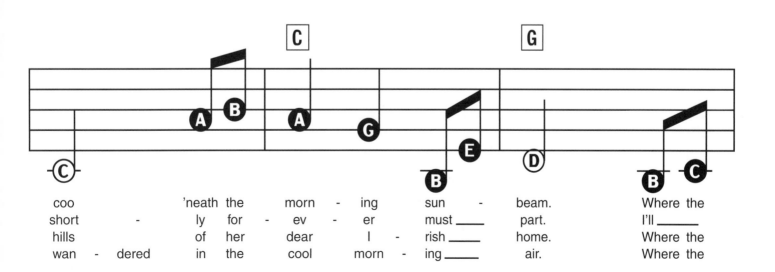

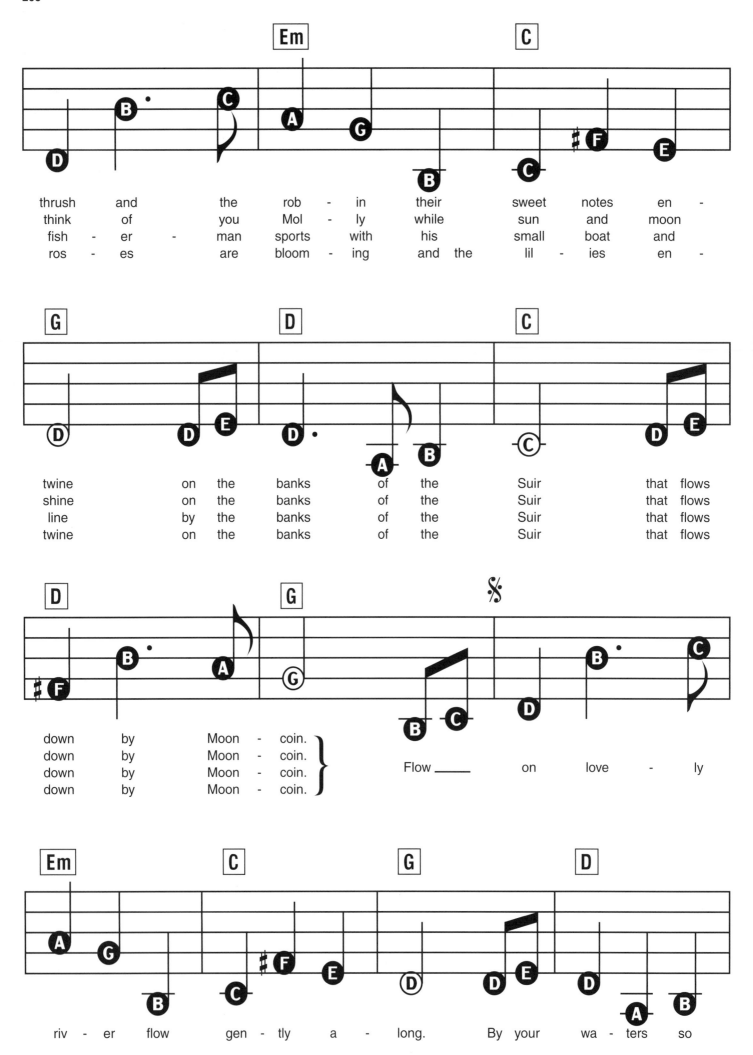

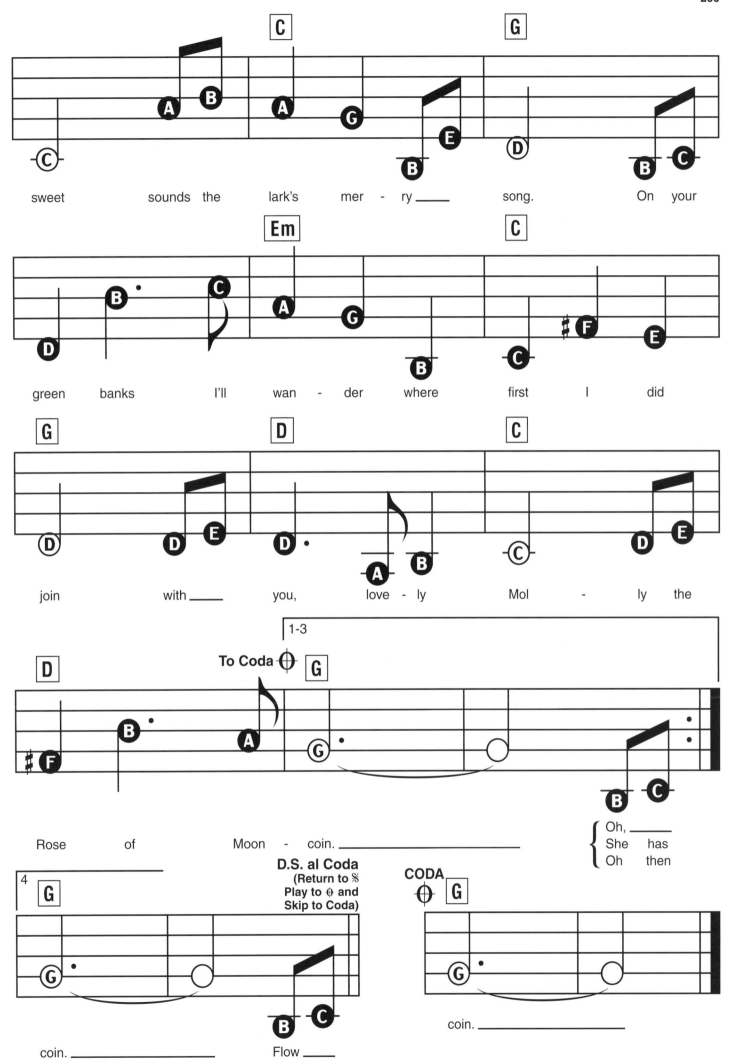

The Rose of Tralee

Registration 3
Rhythm: Waltz

Words by C. Mordaunt Spencer
Music by Charles W. Glover

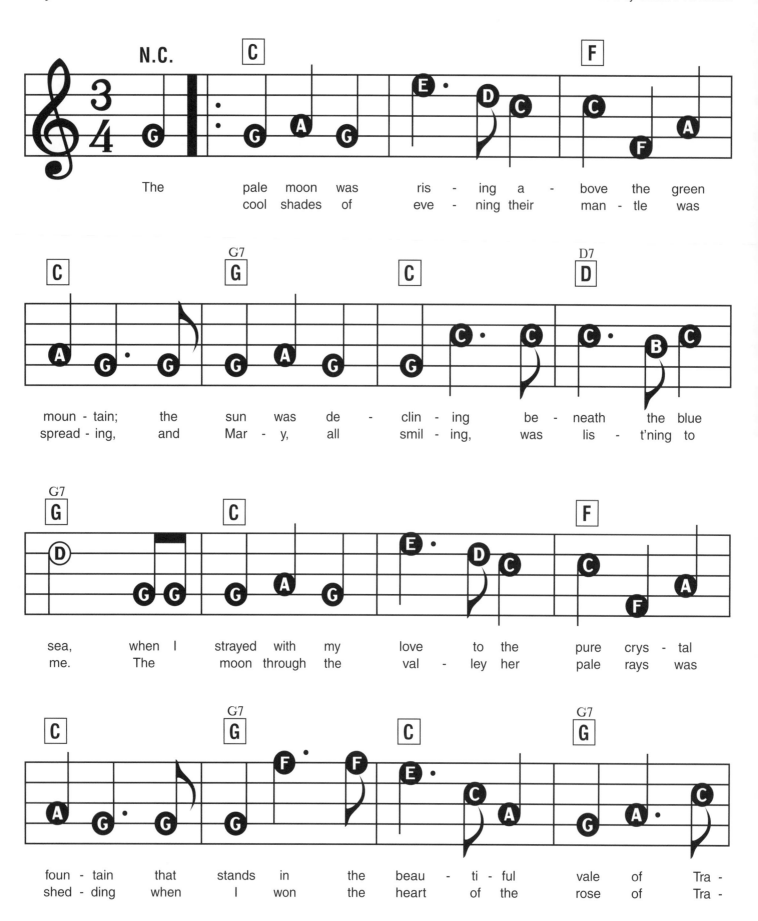

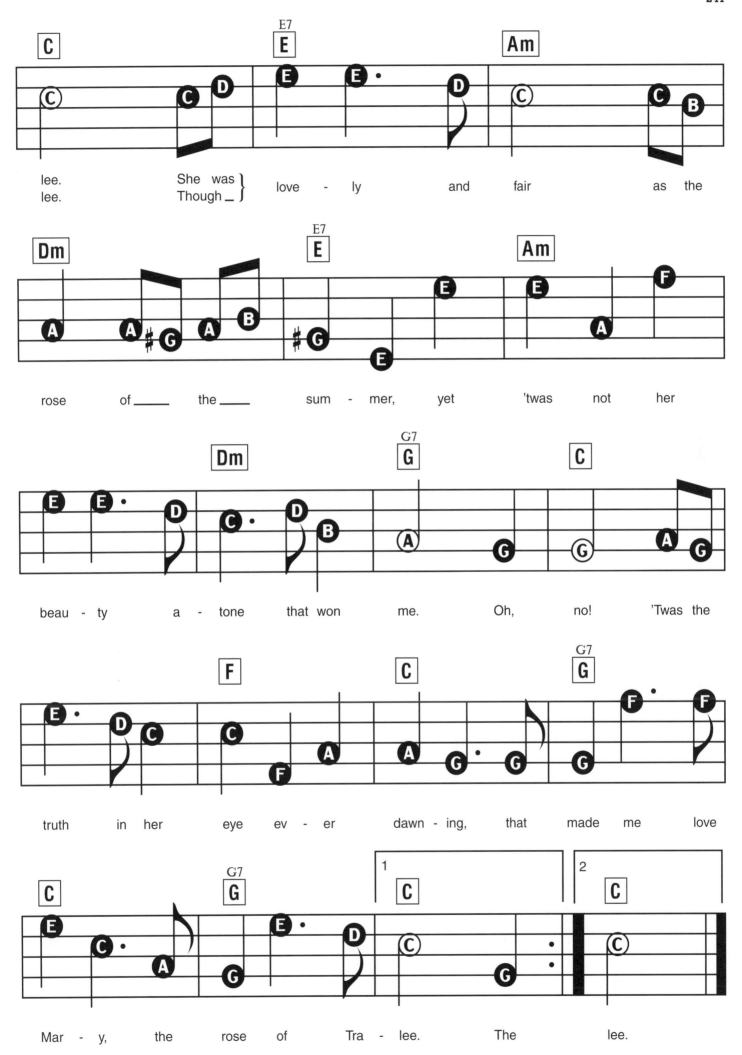

Rosin the Bow

Registration 1
Rhythm: Waltz

Traditional

1. I've ... trav - elled this world _____ all o - ver _____ and now to an - oth - er must go. _____ Say - ing know that good quar - ters are wait - ing

2. dead and laid out on the count - er; _____ a voice you will hear from be - low. _____ "Send down a hogs - head of whis - key

3. get a half doz - en stout fel - lows; _____ and stack them all up in a row. _____ Let them drink out of half gal - lon bot - tles;

4.- 6. *(See additional lyrics)*

243

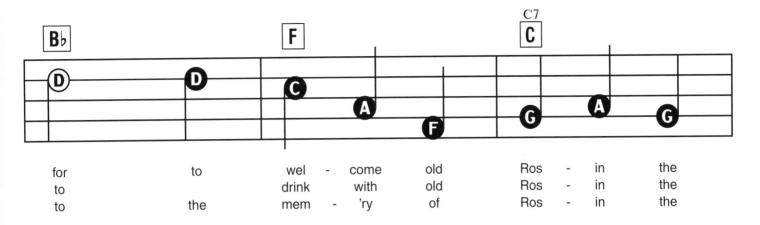

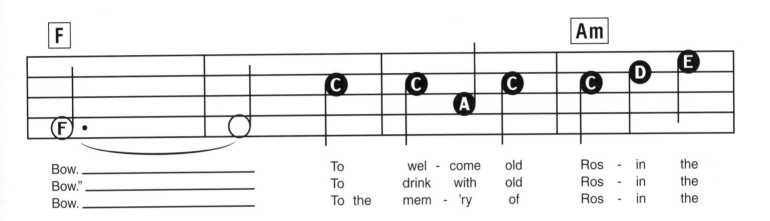

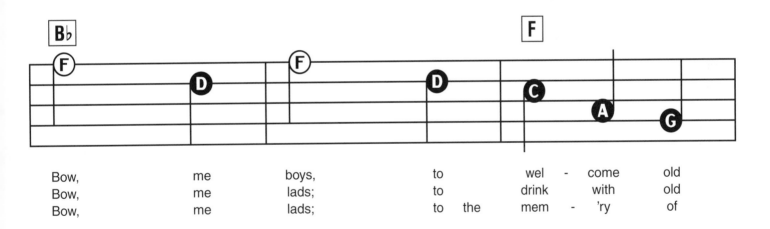

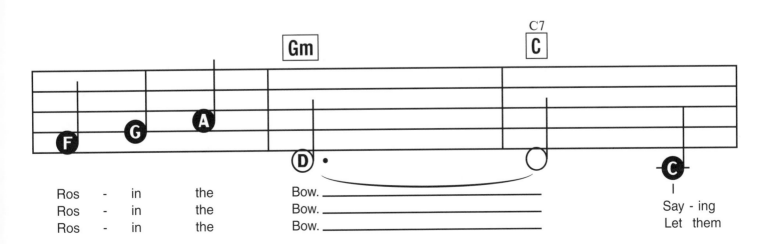

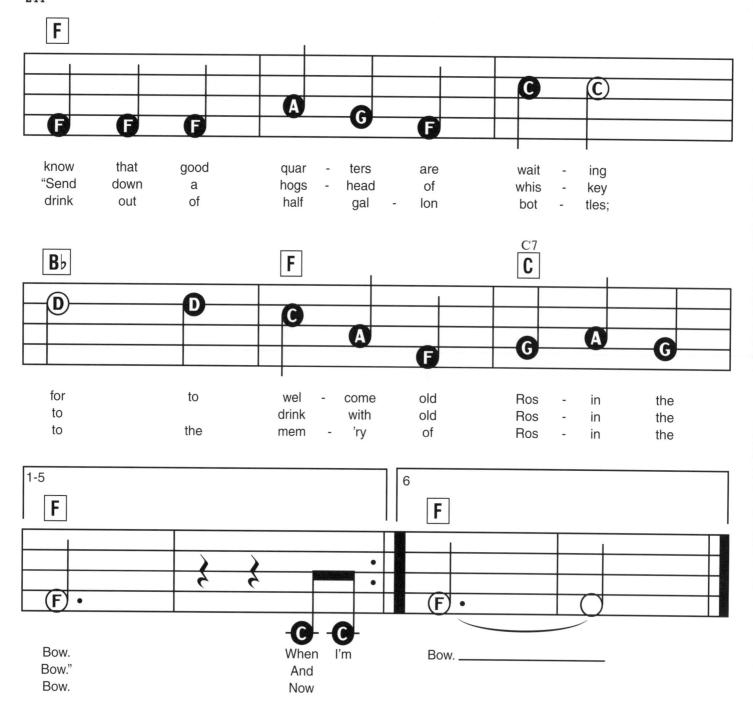

know	that	good	quar	- ters	are	wait	- ing
"Send	down	a	hogs	- head	of	whis	- key
drink	out	of	half	gal	- lon	bot	- tles;

for	to	wel	- come	old	Ros	- in	the
to		drink	with	old	Ros	- in	the
to	the	mem	- 'ry	of	Ros	- in	the

1-5		6	
Bow.	When I'm	Bow. _____	
Bow."	And		
Bow.	Now		

Additional Lyrics

4. Now get this half dozen stout fellows; and let them all stagger and go,
And dig a great hole in the meadow; and in it put Rosin the Bow.
And in it put Rosin the Bow, me lads; and in it put Rosin the Bow.
And dig a great hole in the meadow; and in it put Rosin the Bow.

5. Now get ye a couple of bottles; put one at me head and me toe.
With a diamond ring scratch out upon them; the name of old Rosin the Bow.
The name of old Rosin the Bow, me lads; the name of old Rosin the Bow.
With a diamond ring scratch out upon them; the name of old Rosin the Bow.

6. I feel that old Tyrant approaching; that cruel remorseless old foe.
Let me lift up my glass in his honour; take a drink with old Rosin the Bow.
Take a drink with old Rosin the Bow, me lads; take a drink with old Rosin the Bow.
Let me lift up my glass in his honour; take a drink with old Rosin the Bow.

Sally Brown

Registration 7
Rhythm: March

Traditional Irish Folk Song

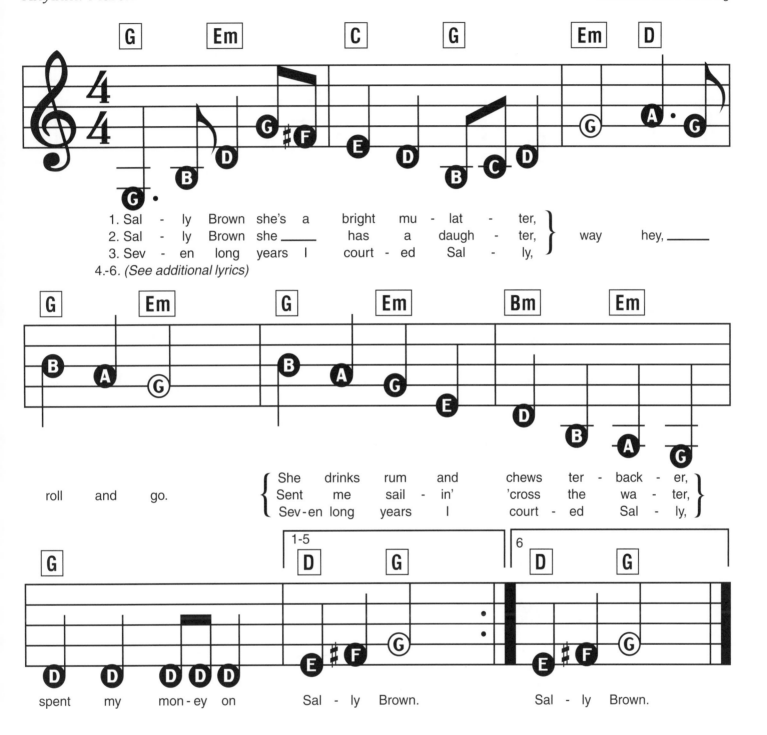

Additional Lyrics

4. Sally Brown, I'm bound to leave you,
   Way hey, roll and go.
   Sally Brown, I'll not deceive you,
   Spent my money on Sally Brown.

5. Sally she's a "Badian" beauty,
   Way hey, roll and go.
   Sally she's a "Badian" beauty,
   Spent my money on Sally Brown.

6. Sally lives on the old plantation,
   Way hey, roll and go.
   She belongs to the Wild Goose Nation,
   Spent my money on Sally Brown.

Sam Hall

Registration 2
Rhythm: Fox Trot

Traditional Irish Folk Song

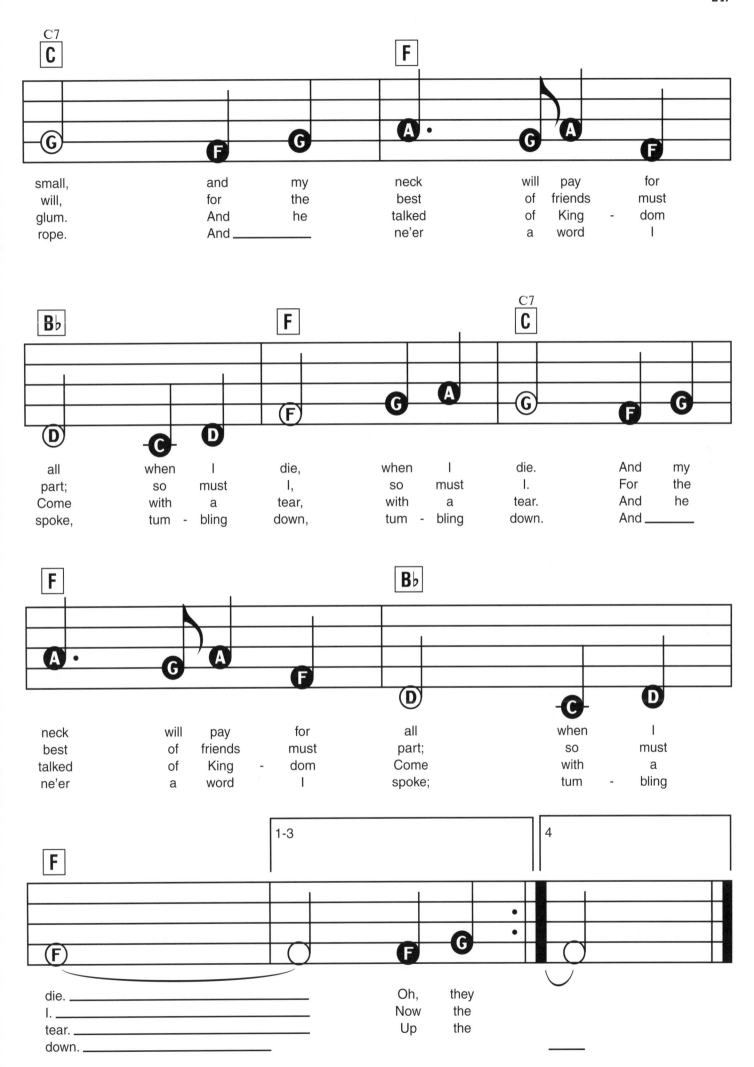

Skibbereen

Registration 8
Rhythm: Fox Trot

Traditional Irish Folk Song

249

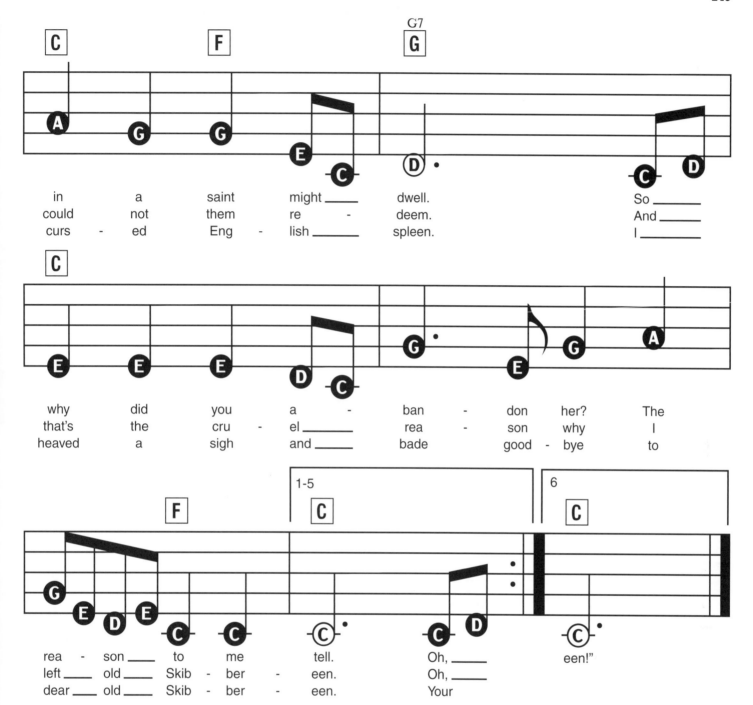

Additional Lyrics

4. Your mother too, God rest her soul, fell on the stony ground.
She fainted in her anguish, seeing desolation 'round.
She never rose, but passed away from life to immortal dream.
She found a quiet grave, me boy, in dear old Skibbereen.

5. And you were only two years old and feeble was your frame;
I could not leave you with my friends, for you bore your father's name.
I wrapped you in my cota mor in the dead of night unseen.
I heaved a sigh and said goodbye to dear old Skibbereen.

6. Oh, father dear, the day will come when, in answer to the call,
All Irish men of freedom stern will rally one and all.
I'll be the man to lead the band beneath the flag of green,
And loud and clear we'll raise the cheer: "Revenge for Skibbereen!"

Slievenamon

Registration 4
Rhythm: 6/8 March or Jig/Gigue

Traditional Irish Folk Song

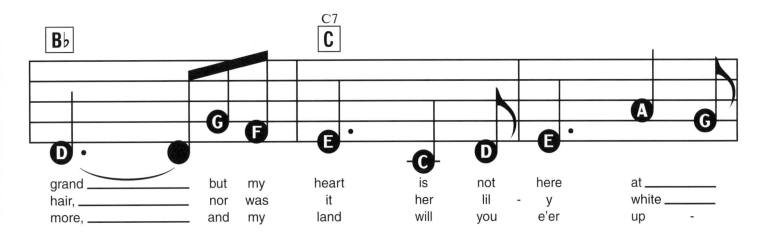

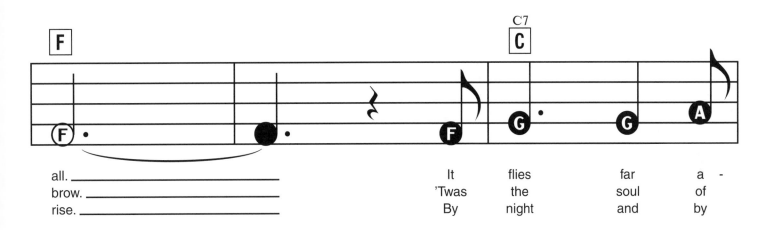

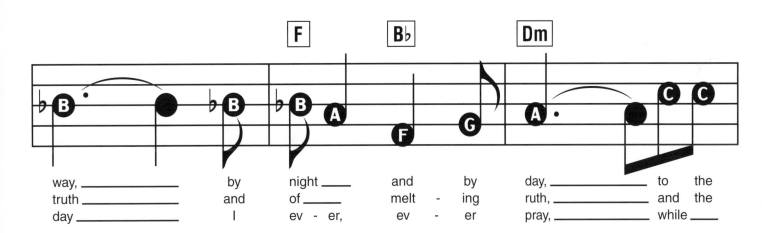

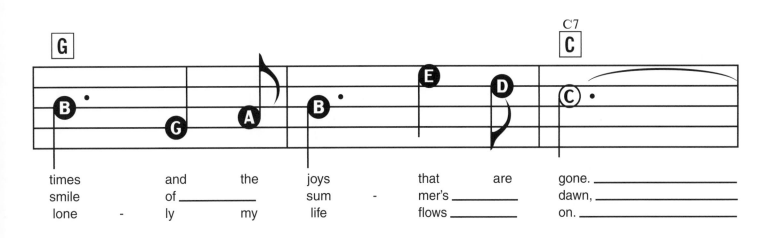

252

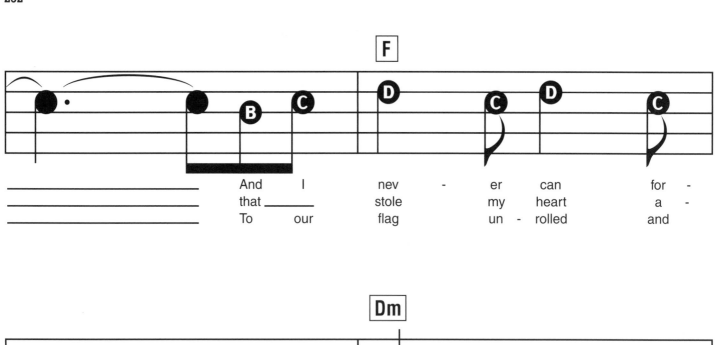

And   I   nev - er   can   for -
that _____ stole   my   heart   a -
To   our   flag   un - rolled   and

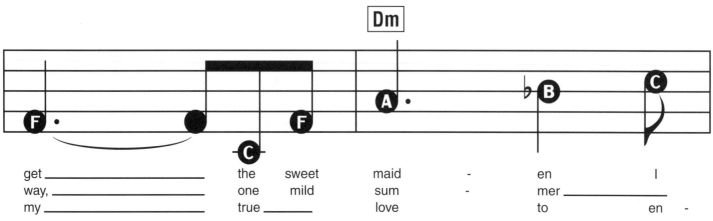

get _____ the sweet maid - en   I
way, _____ one mild sum - mer _____
my _____ true _____ love   to   en -

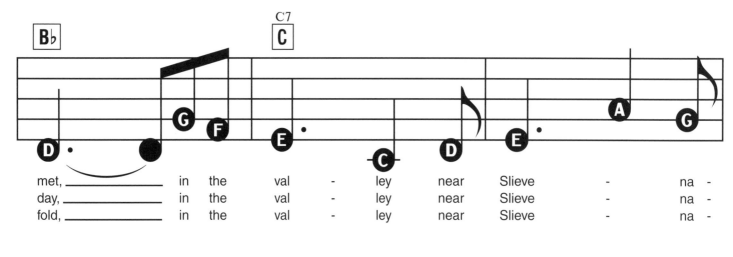

met, _____ in the val - ley near Slieve - na -
day, _____ in the val - ley near Slieve - na -
fold, _____ in the val - ley near Slieve - na -

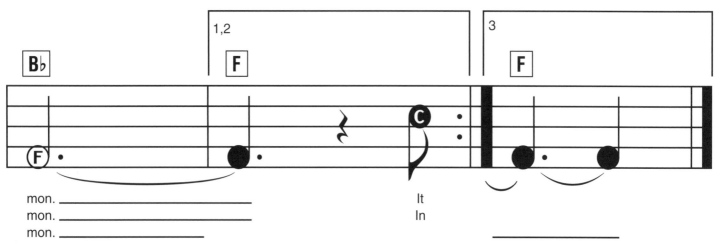

mon. _____
mon. _____   It
mon. _____   In

Three Score and Ten

Registration 1
Rhythm: Ballad or Fox Trot

Traditional Irish Folk Song

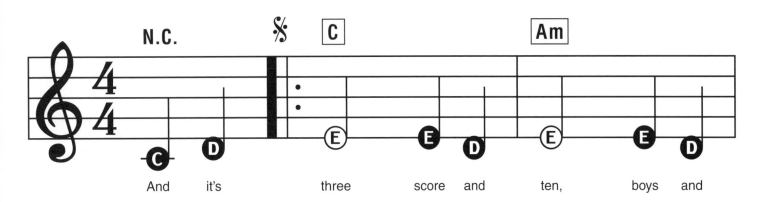

And it's three score and ten, boys and

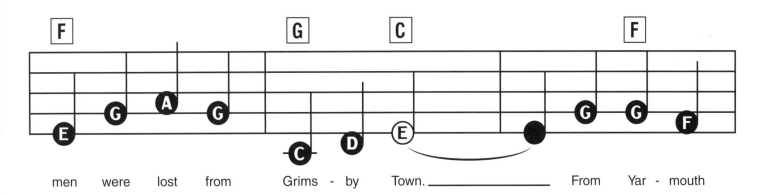

men were lost from Grims - by Town. _____ From Yar - mouth

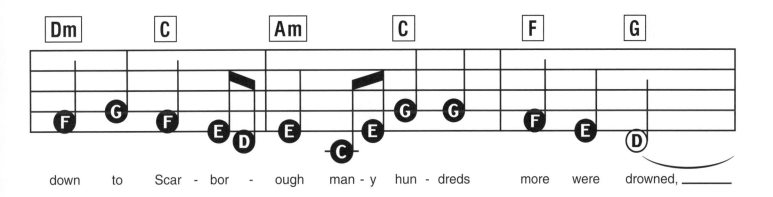

down to Scar - bor - ough man - y hun - dreds more were drowned, _____

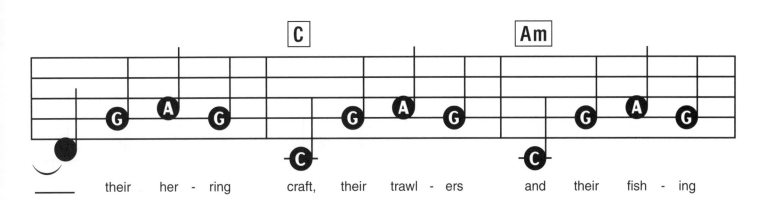

_____ their her - ring craft, their trawl - ers and their fish - ing

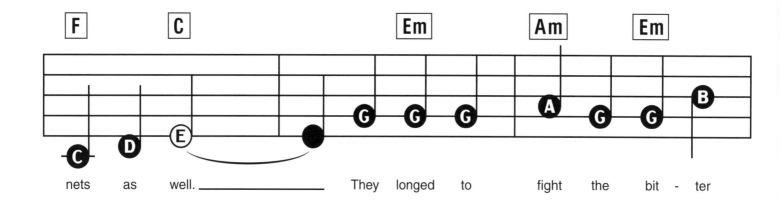

nets as well. _____ They longed to fight the bit - ter

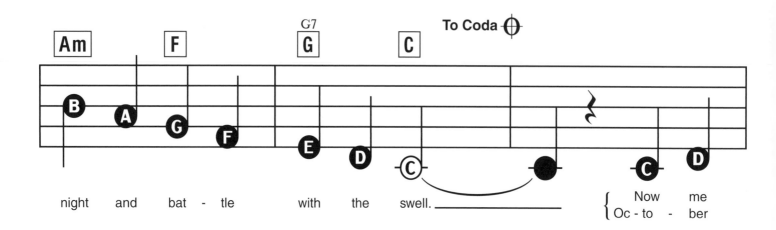

night and bat - tle with the swell. _____ { Now me / Oc - to - ber

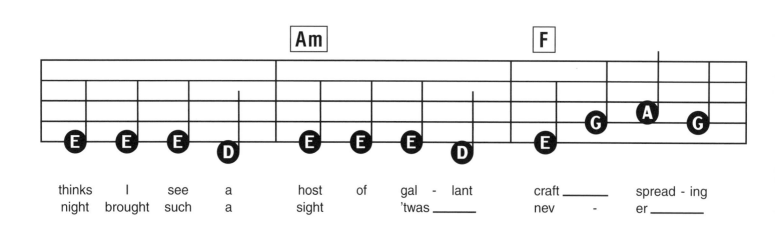

thinks I see a host of gal - lant craft _____ spread - ing
night brought such a sight 'twas _____ nev - er _____

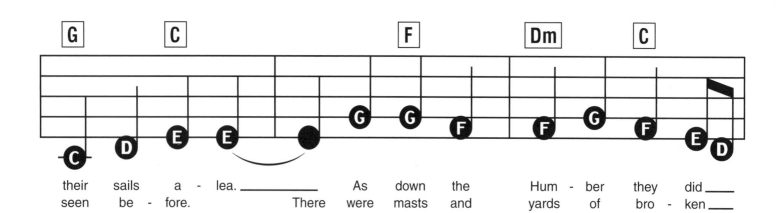

their sails a - lea. _____ As down the Hum - ber they did _____
seen be - fore. _____ There were masts and yards of bro - ken _____

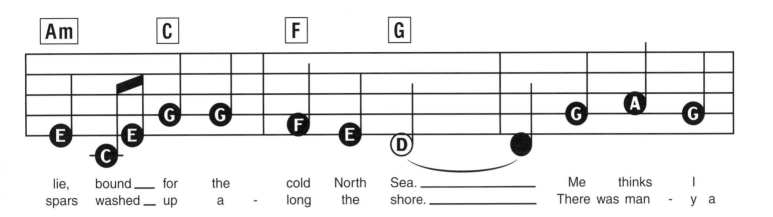

lie, bound ___ for the cold North Sea. _____ Me thinks I
spars washed __ up a - long the shore. _____ There was man - y a

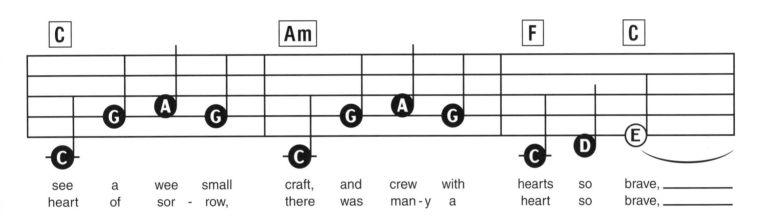

see a wee small craft, and crew with hearts so brave, _____
heart of sor - row, there was man - y a heart so brave, _____

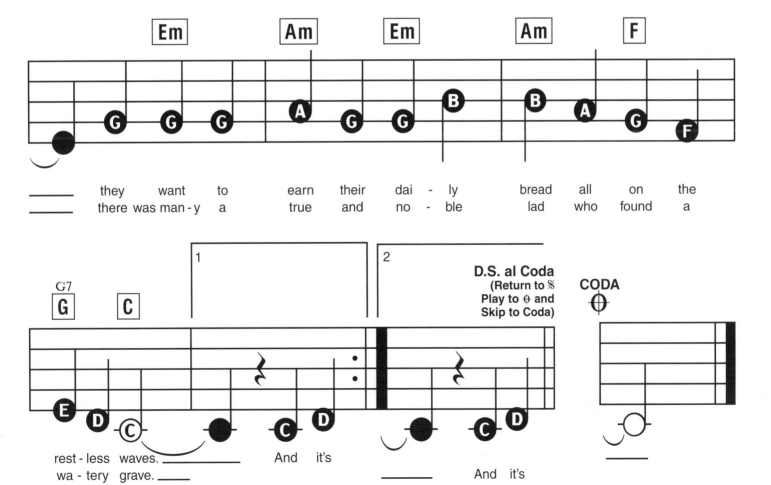

_____ they want to earn their dai - ly bread all on the
_____ there was man - y a true and no - ble lad who found a

rest - less waves. _____ And it's
wa - tery grave. _____ _____ And it's

1

2

D.S. al Coda
(Return to %
Play to ⊕ and
Skip to Coda)

CODA

The Snowy-Breasted Pearl

Registration 4
Rhythm: Fox Trot

Traditional Irish Folk Song

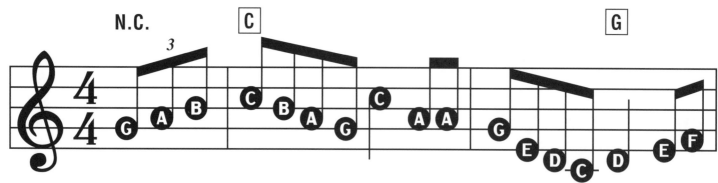

1. There's a _____ col - leen fair as May. For a year and for a day, I have
2. Oh, thou _____ bloom-ing milk white dove, to whom I've giv-en true love, do not
1. Tá _____ cail - in deas am chrá le _____ bliain ag - us le lá, ´S ní
2. (See additional lyrics)

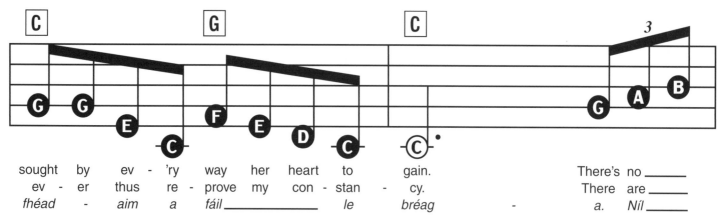

sought by ev - 'ry way her heart to gain. There's no _____
ev - er thus re - prove my con - stan - cy. There are _____
fhéad - aim a fáil _____ le bréag - a. Níl _____

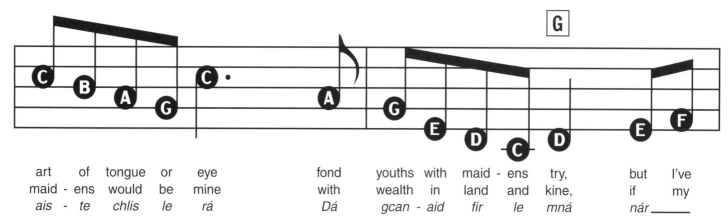

art of tongue or eye fond youths with maid - ens try, but I've
maid - ens would be mine with wealth in land and kine, if my
ais - te chlis le rá Dá gcan - aid fir le mná nár _____

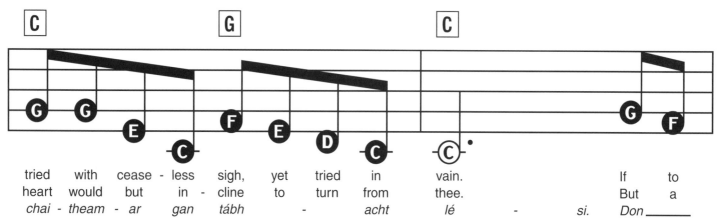

tried with cease - less sigh, yet tried in vain. If to
heart would but in - cline to turn from thee. But a
chai - theam - ar gan tábh - acht lé - si. Don _____

far off France or Spain she'd cross the wa - ter - y main, to
kiss with wel - come bland and touch of thy fair ____ hand, are
Fhrainnc nó don ____ Spáinn dá dtéadh _____ mo ghrá, go

see her face a - gain the seas I'd brave. And _____
all that I de - mand, wouldst thou not spurn. For _____
raghainn - se gach lá _____ dá féach - ain. Is mar an

if 'tis heav - en's de - cree that mine she may not be, may the
if not mine, dear girl, oh snow - y - breast - ed pearl, may I
dúinn a - tá ____ i ndán an ainn - ir chiúin seo d'fháil, Och! Mac

Son of Mar - y me in mer - cy save!
nev - er from the fair with life re - turn!
Muir - e na ngrás _____ dár saor - a!

Additional Lyrics

2. *Póg is míle fáilte*   *Is a chailín chailcee bhláith,*
  Is barra geal do lámh'   *Dá dtugas searc is grá,*
  Sé 'n-iarrfainn-se go bráth mar spré leat;   *Ná túir-se gach tráth dhom éara;*
  'S maran domh-sa taoi tú i ndán,   *'S a liacht ainnir mhín im dheádh*
  A phéarla an bhrollaigh bháin,   *Le buaibh is maoin 'n-a láimh,*
  Nár thí mise slán ón aonach!   *Dá ngabhaimís it áit-se céile.*

Spancil Hill

Registration 3
Rhythm: 6/8 March or Jig/Gigue

Traditional Irish Folk Song

1. Last night as I lay
2. light - ed with the
3. be - ing the twen - ty
4.-6. *(See additional lyrics)*

dream - ing of _____ pleas - ant days gone by, _____ me
nov - el - ty, en - chant - ed with the scene, _____ where
third of June, the _____ day _____ be - fore the fair, _____ when

mind bein' bent on ram - bling to Ire - land I _____ did
in my ear - ly boy - hood where of - ten I _____ had
Ire - land's sons and daugh - ters where in crowds as - sem - bled

fly. _____ I stepped a - board a vi - sion and
been. _____ I thought I heard a mur - mur and I
there. _____ The young, the old, the brave and the bold, they

259

Additional Lyrics

4. I went to see my neighbors, to hear what they might say,
   The old ones were all dead and gone, the others turning grey.
   I met with tailor Quigley, he's as bold as ever still,
   Sure he used to make my britches when I lived in Spancil Hill.

5. I paid a flying visit to my first and only love,
   She's white as any lily and gentle as a dove.
   She threw her arms around me, saying, "Johnny, I love you still."
   She's Mag, the farmer's daughter and the pride of Spancil Hill.

6. I dreamt I stooped and kissed her as in the days of yore.
   She said, "Johnny, you're only joking, as many's the time before."
   The cock crew in the morning, he crew both loud and shrill,
   And I woke in California, many miles from Spancil Hill.

The Spanish Lady

Registration 4
Rhythm: Fox Trot

Traditional Irish Folk Song

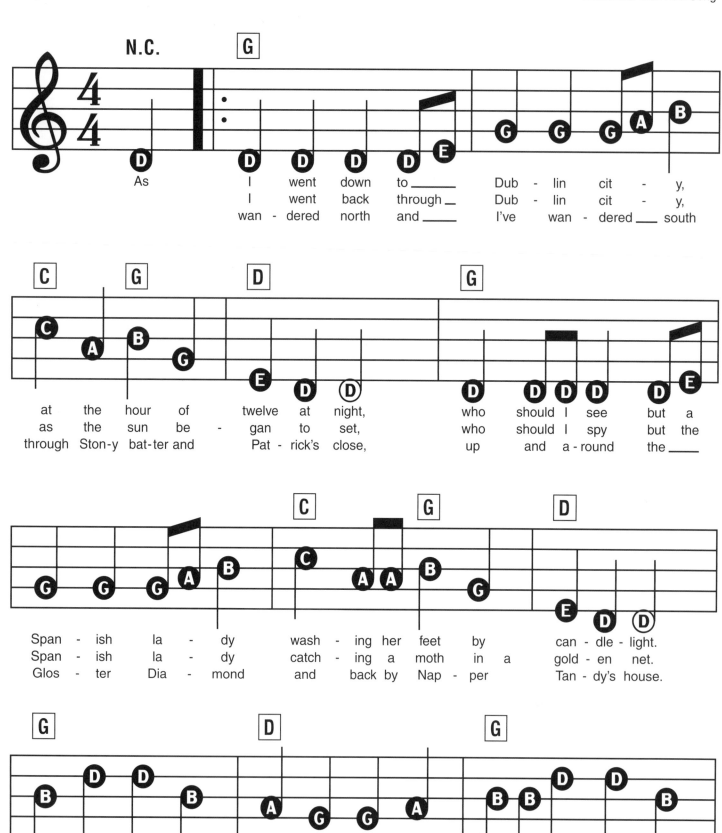

As I went down to _____ Dub - lin cit - y,
I went back through _ Dub - lin cit - y,
wan - dered north and _____ I've wan - dered _ south

at the hour of twelve at night, who should I see but a
as the sun be - gan to set, who should I spy but the
through Ston-y bat-ter and Pat - rick's close, up and a-round the _____

Span - ish la - dy wash - ing her feet by can - dle - light.
Span - ish la - dy catch - ing a moth in a gold - en net.
Glos - ter Dia - mond and back by Nap - per Tan - dy's house.

First she washed them, then she dried them o - ver a fire of
When she saw me, then she fled me, lift - ing her pet - ti - coat
Old age has laid her hand on me, cold as a fire of

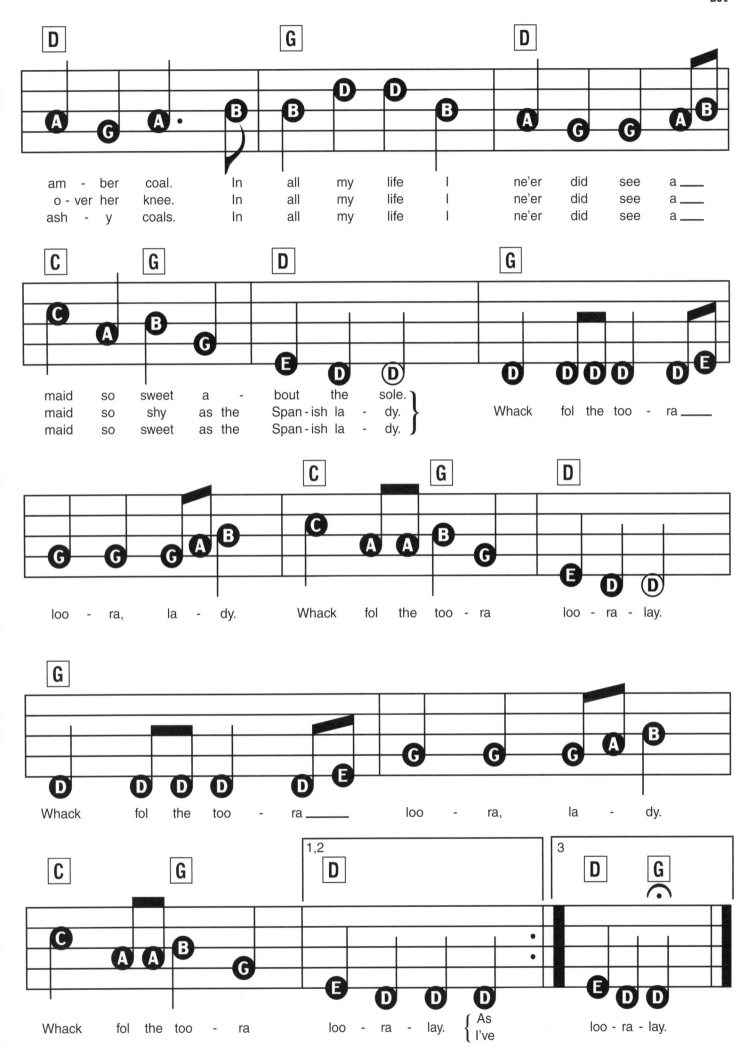

Star of County Down

Registration 3
Rhythm: March

Traditional Irish Folk Song

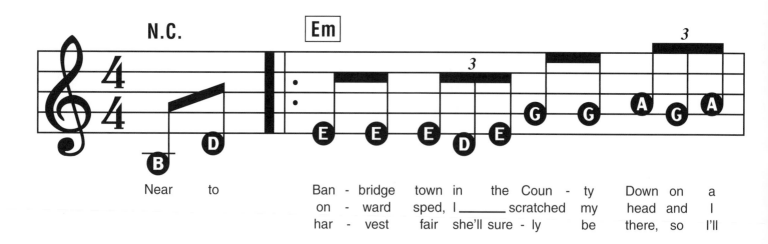

Near to Ban - bridge town in the Coun - ty Down on a
on - ward sped, I scratched my head and I
har - vest fair she'll sure - ly be there, so I'll

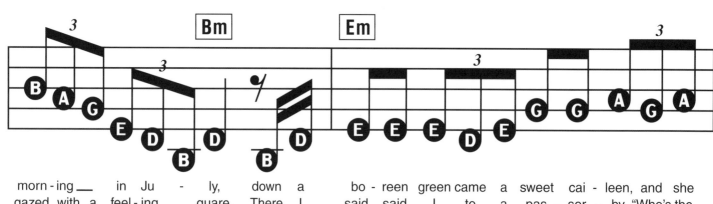

morn - ing in Ju - ly, down a bo - reen green came a sweet cai - leen, and she
gazed with a feel - ing quare. There I said, said I to a pas - ser - by, "Who's the
dress in my Sun - day clothes. And I'll try sheep's eyes and de - lud - th'rin lies on the

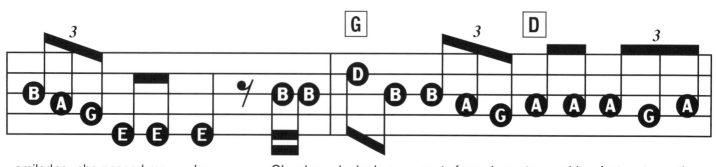

smiled as she passed me by. Oh, she looked so neat from her two white feet to the
maid with the nut - brown hair?" Oh, he smiled at me, and with pride says he, "That's the
heart of the nut - brown Rose. No pipe I'll smoke, no horse I'll yoke, though my

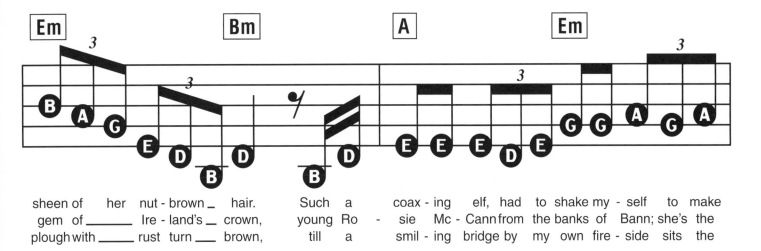

sheen of her nut - brown＿ hair. Such a coax - ing elf, had to shake my - self to make
gem of ＿＿＿ Ire - land's ＿ crown, young Ro - sie Mc - Cann from the banks of Bann; she's the
plough with ＿＿＿ rust turn ＿ brown, till a smil - ing bridge by my own fire - side sits the

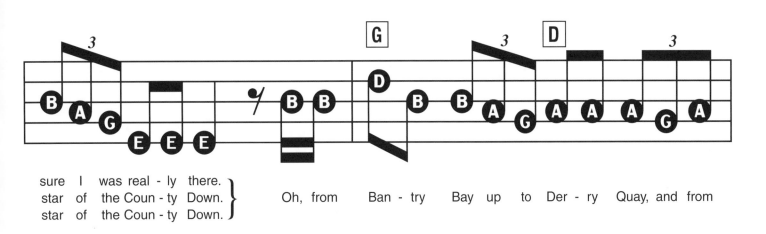

sure I was real - ly there.
star of the Coun - ty Down.
star of the Coun - ty Down.

Oh, from Ban - try Bay up to Der - ry Quay, and from

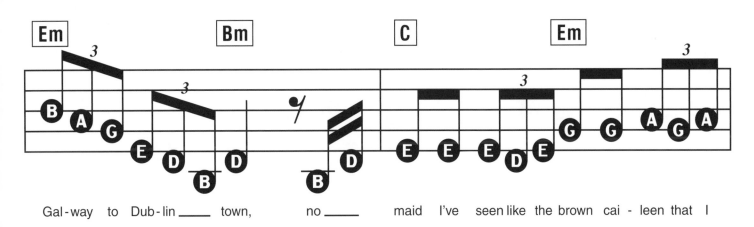

Gal - way to Dub - lin ＿＿＿ town, no ＿＿＿ maid I've seen like the brown cai - leen that I

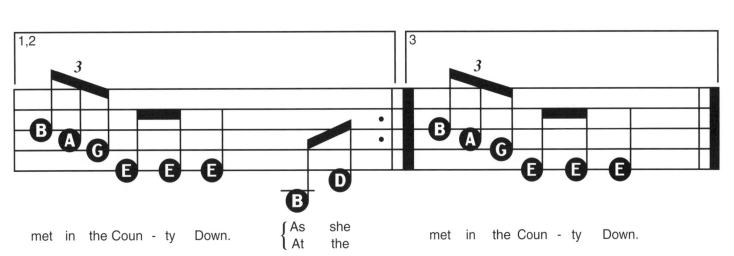

met in the Coun - ty Down.
As she
At the

met in the Coun - ty Down.

Sweet Carnlough Bay

Registration 8
Rhythm: Waltz

Traditional Irish Folk Song

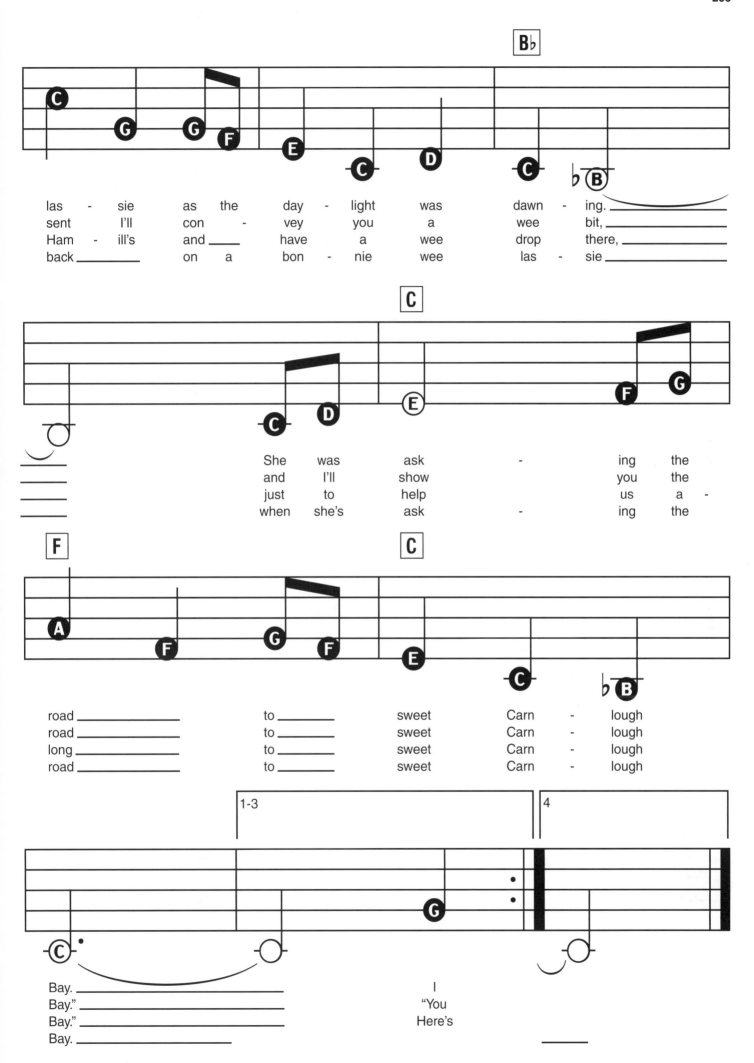

'Tis the Last Rose of Summer

Registration 2
Rhythm: Waltz

Traditional Irish Folk Song

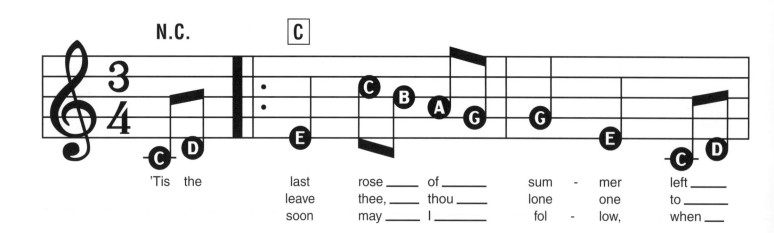

'Tis the   last   rose ____ of ____   sum - mer   left ____
leave   thee, ____ thou ____   lone   one   to ____
soon   may ____ I ____   fol - low,   when ____

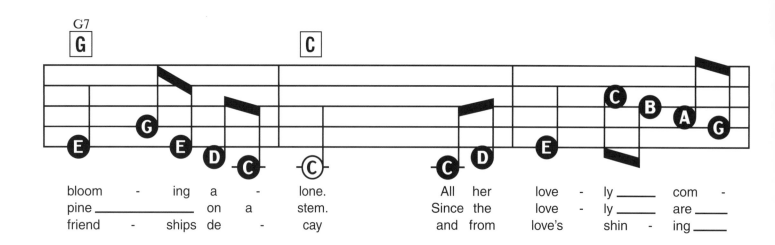

bloom - ing a -   lone.   All her   love - ly ____ com -
pine ____ on a   stem.   Since the   love - ly ____ are ____
friend - ships de -   cay   and from   love's shin - ing ____

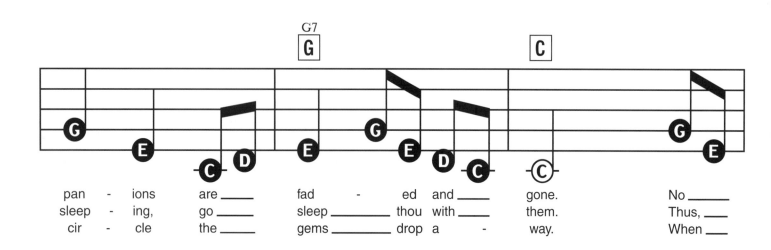

pan - ions are ____   fad - ed and ____   gone.   No ____
sleep - ing,   go ____   sleep ____ thou with ____   them.   Thus, ____
cir - cle   the ____   gems ____ drop a -   way.   When ____

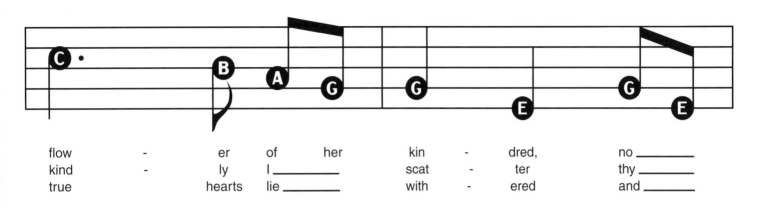

flower — er of her kin - dred, no _____
kind — ly I _____ scat - ter thy _____
true — hearts lie _____ with - ered and _____

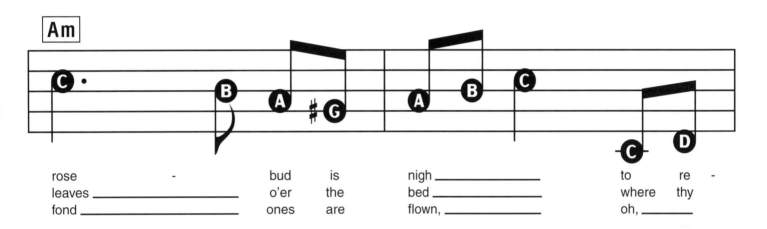

rose — bud is nigh _____ to re -
leaves _____ o'er the bed _____ where thy
fond _____ ones are flown, _____ oh, _____

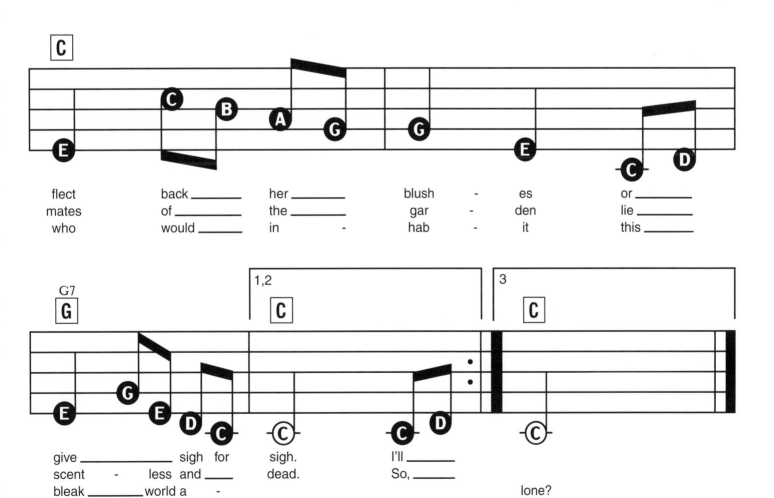

flect back _____ her _____ blush - es or _____
mates of _____ the _____ gar - den lie _____
who would _____ in - hab - it this _____

give _____ sigh for sigh. I'll _____
scent - less and _____ dead. So, _____
bleak _____ world a - lone?

Too-Ra-Loo-Ra-Loo-Ral
(That's an Irish Lullaby)
from GOING MY WAY

Registration 1
Rhythm: Waltz

Words and Music by
James R. Shannon

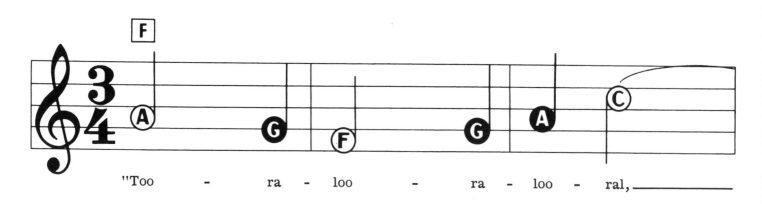

"Too - ra - loo - ra - loo - ral, ____

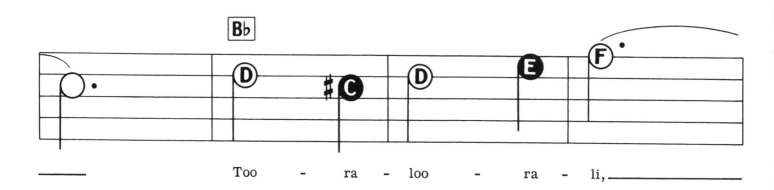

____ Too - ra - loo - ra - li, ____

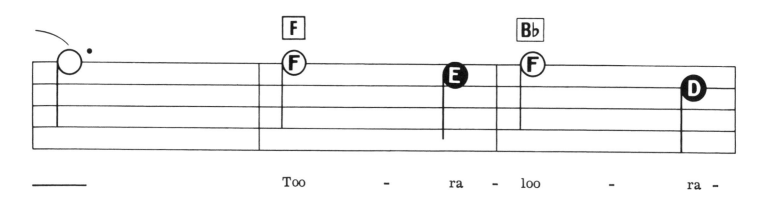

____ Too - ra - loo - ra -

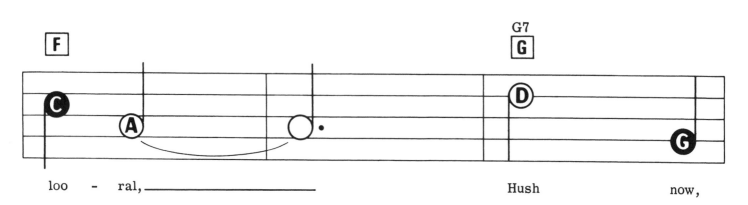

loo - ral, ____ Hush now,

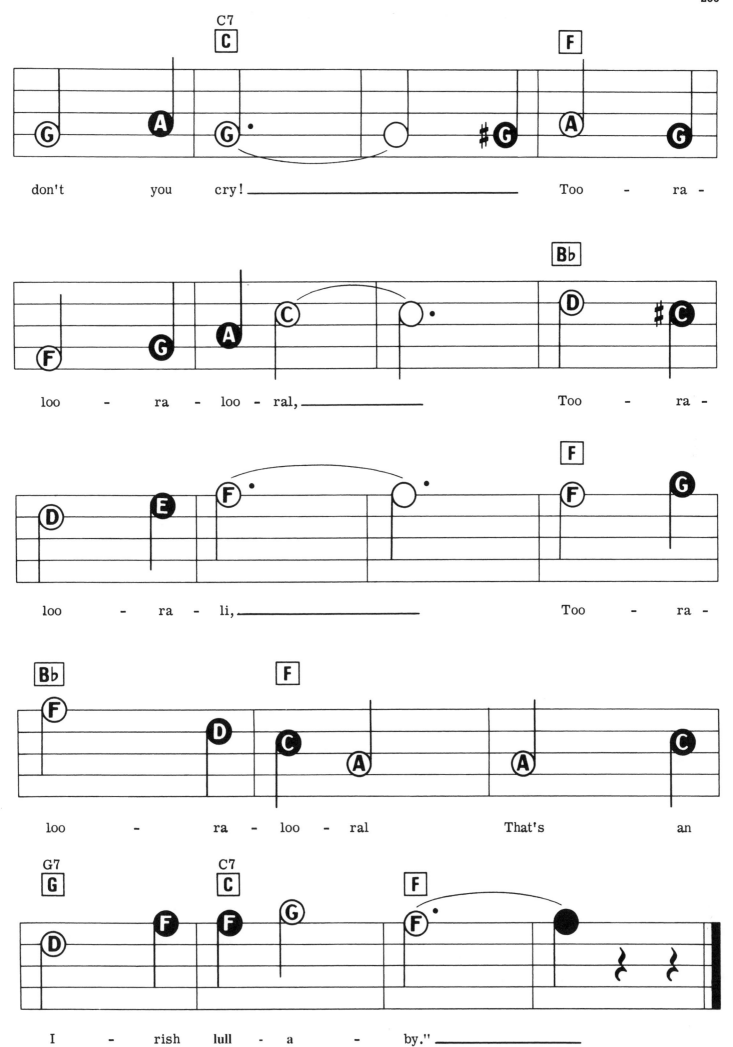

The Town of Ballybay

Registration 3
Rhythm: 6/8 March or Jig/Gigue

Traditional Irish Folk Song

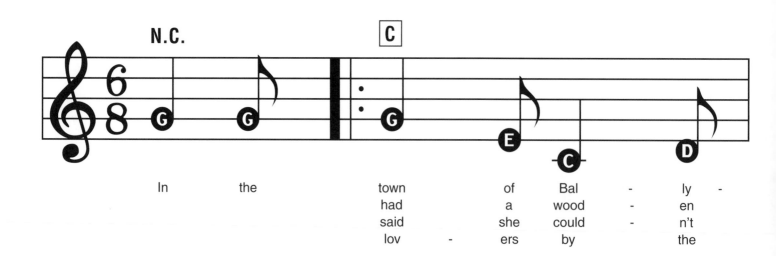

In the town of Bal - ly -
had a wood - en
said she could - n't
lov - ers by the

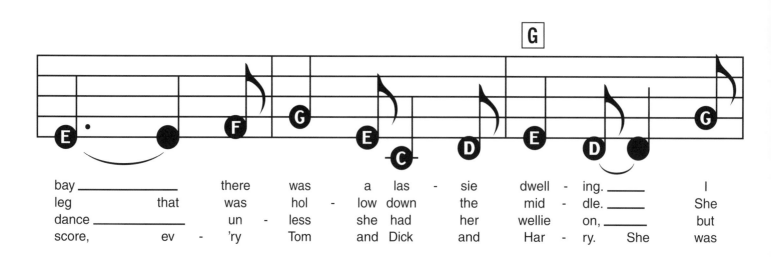

bay there was a las - sie dwell - ing. I
leg that was hol - low down the mid - dle. She
dance un - less she had her wellie on, but
score, ev - 'ry Tom and Dick and Har - ry. She was

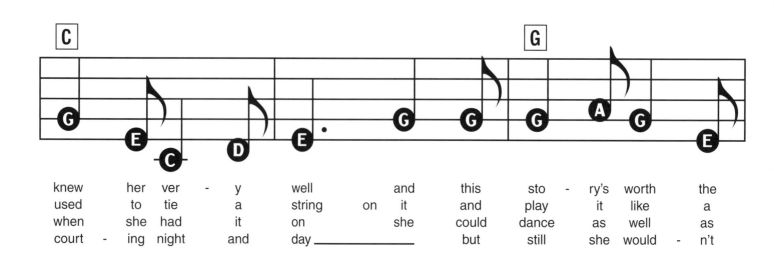

knew her ver - y well and this sto - ry's worth the
used to tie a string on it and play it like a
when she had it on she could dance as well as
court - ing night and day but still she would - n't

271

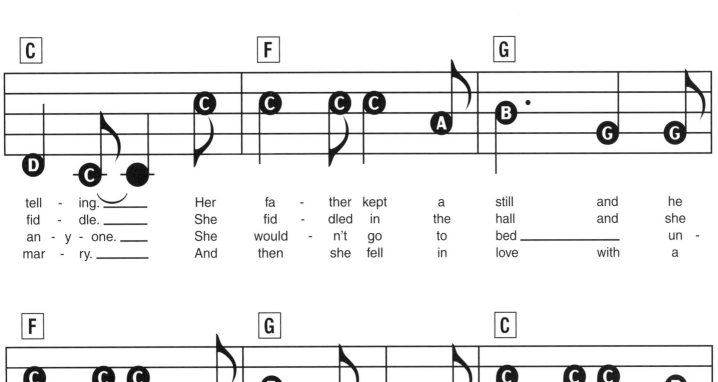

tell - ing. _____ Her fa - ther kept a still and he
fid - dle. _____ She fid - dled in the hall and she
an - y-one. _____ She would - n't go to bed _____ un -
mar - ry. _____ And then she fell in love with a

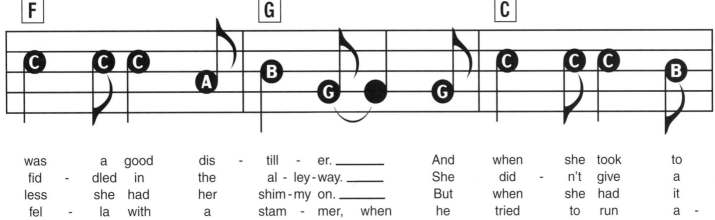

was a good dis - till - er. _____ And when she took to
fid - dled in the al - ley-way. _____ She did - n't give a
less she had her shim-my on. _____ But when she had it
fel - la with a stam - mer, when he tried to run a -

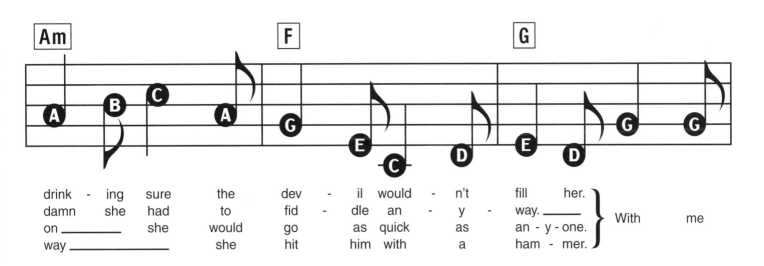

drink - ing sure the dev - il would - n't fill her.
damn she had to fid - dle an - y - way. _____ } With me
on _____ she would go as quick as an - y-one.
way _____ she hit him with a ham - mer. }

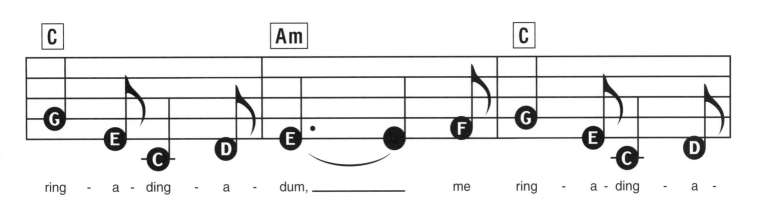

ring - a - ding - a - dum, _____ me ring - a - ding - a -

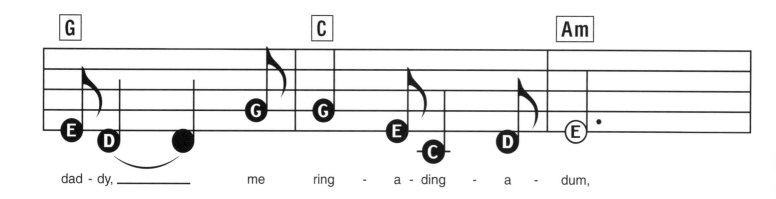

dad - dy, _____ me ring - a - ding - a - dum,

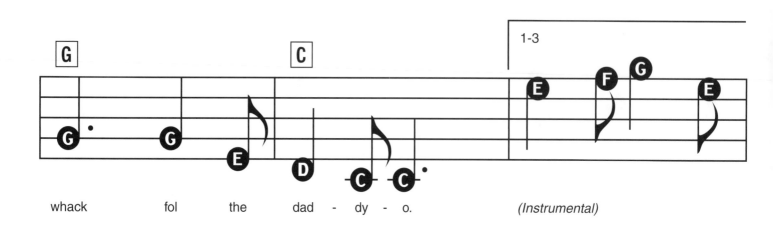

whack   fol   the   dad - dy - o.   *(Instrumental)*

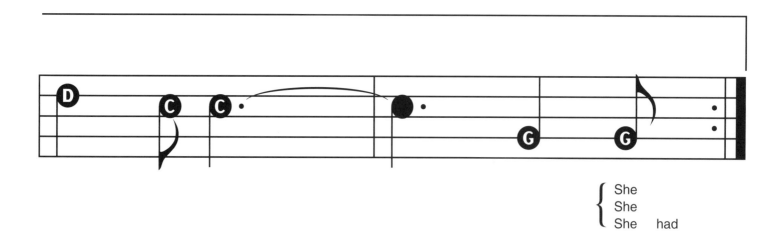

She
She
She had

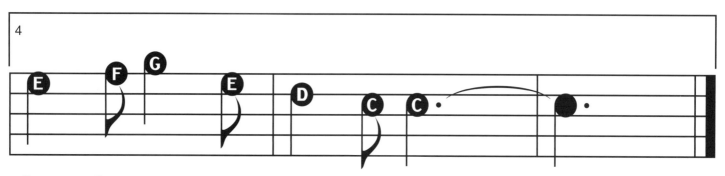

(Instrumental)

Whiskey in the Jar

Registration 7
Rhythm: Fox Trot

Traditional Irish Folk Song

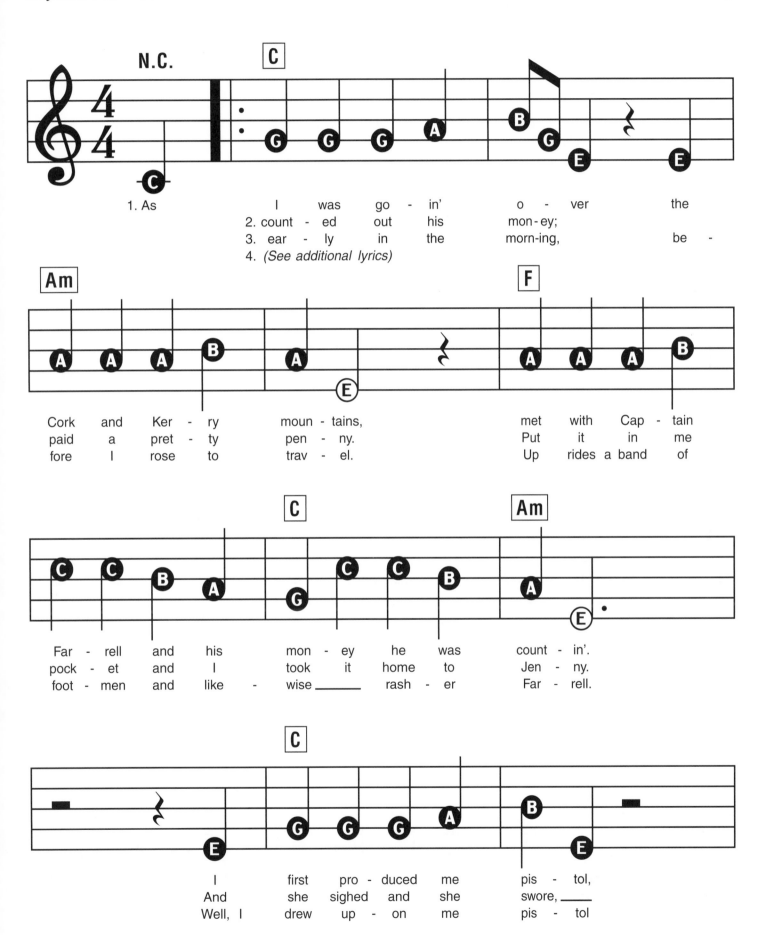

274

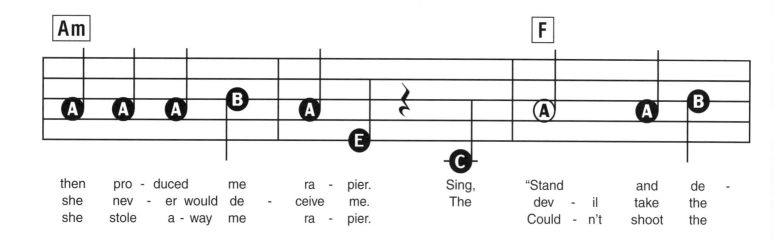

then pro - duced me ra - pier.
she nev - er would de - ceive me.
she stole a - way me ra - pier.

Sing, "Stand and de -
The dev - il take the
Could - n't shoot the

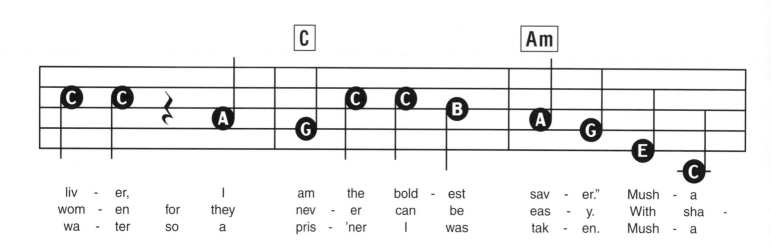

liv - er, I am the bold - est sav - er." Mush - a
wom - en for they nev - er can be eas - y. With sha -
wa - ter so a pris - 'ner I was tak - en. Mush - a

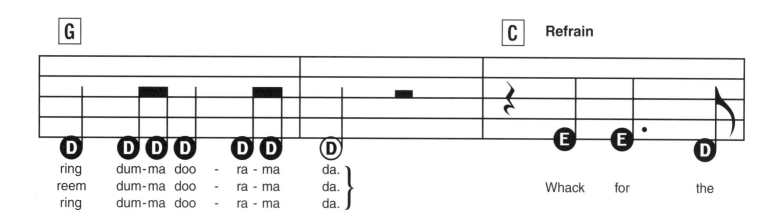

ring dum-ma doo - ra - ma da.
reem dum-ma doo - ra - ma da.
ring dum-ma doo - ra - ma da.

Whack for the

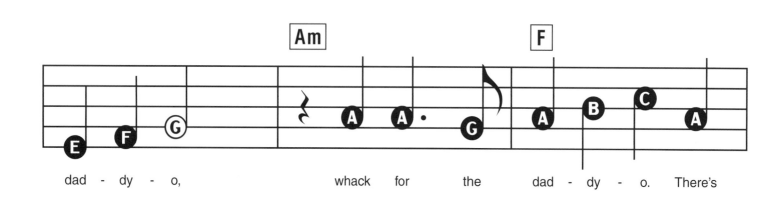

dad - dy - o, whack for the dad - dy - o. There's

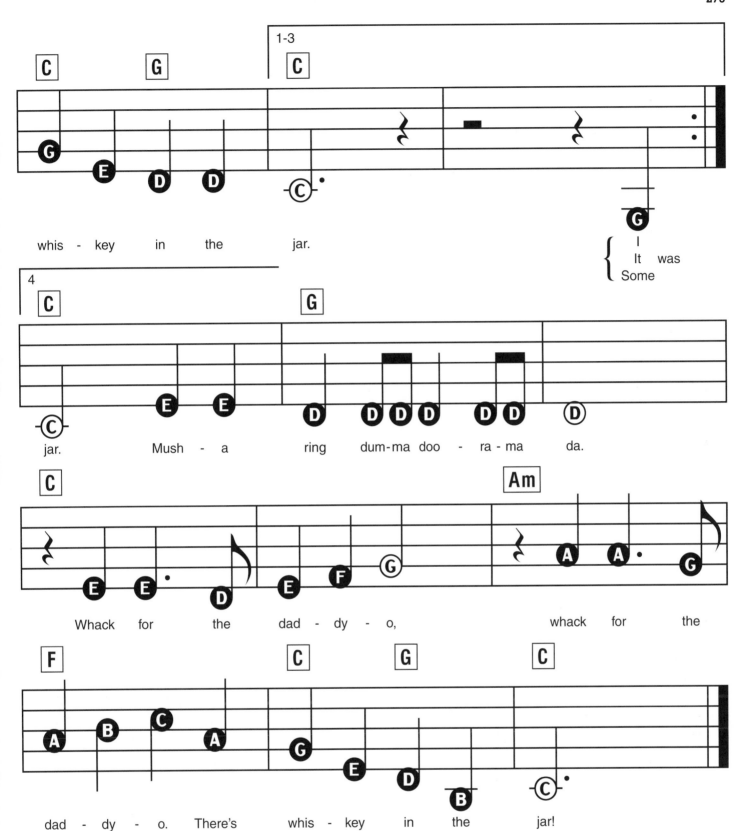

Additional Lyrics

4. Some take delight in the fishin' and the fowlin'.
   Others take delight in the carriage gently rollin'.
   Ah, but I take delight in the juice of the barley;
   Courtin' pretty women in the mountains of Killarney.
   Musha ring dumma doo-rama da.
   Refrain

The Wearing of the Green

Registration 8
Rhythm: Fox Trot

18th Century Irish Folksong

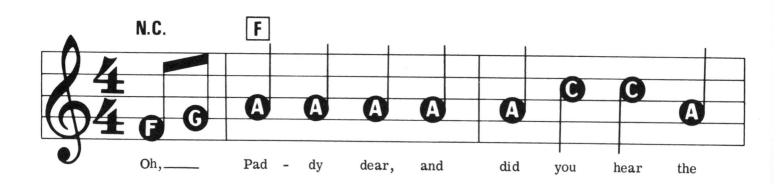

Oh,___ Pad - dy dear, and did you hear the

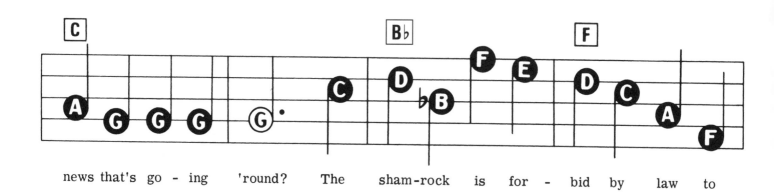

news that's go - ing 'round? The sham-rock is for - bid by law to

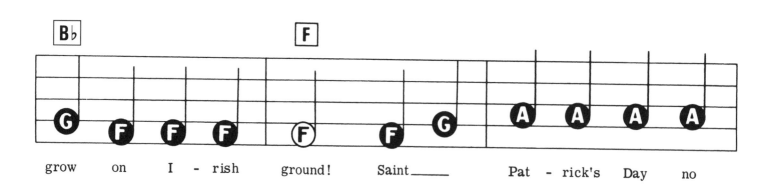

grow on I - rish ground! Saint___ Pat - rick's Day no

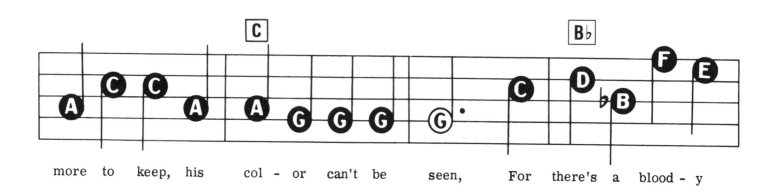

more to keep, his col - or can't be seen, For there's a blood - y

277

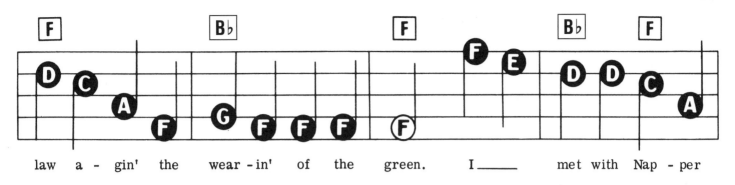

law a - gin' the wear - in' of the green. I ____ met with Nap - per

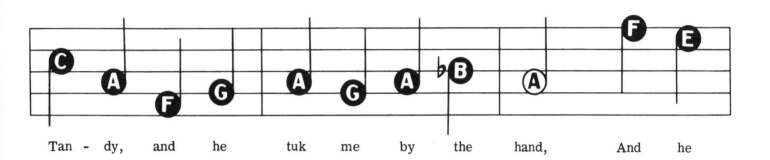

Tan - dy, and he tuk me by the hand, And he

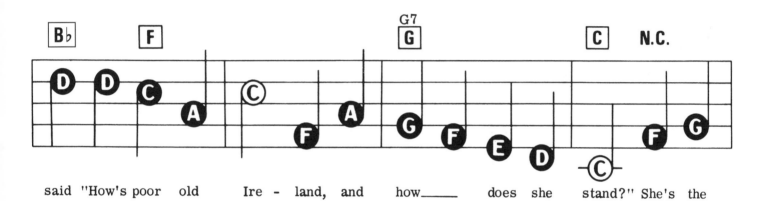

said "How's poor old Ire - land, and how____ does she stand?" She's the

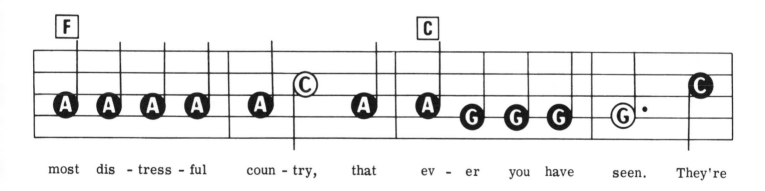

most dis - tress - ful coun - try, that ev - er you have seen. They're

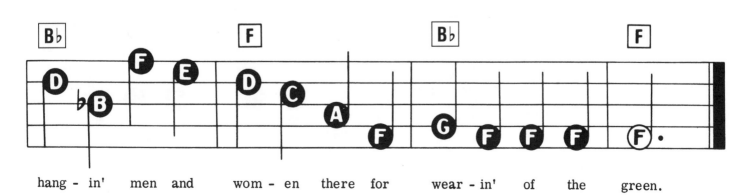

hang - in' men and wom - en there for wear - in' of the green.

Weile Walia

Registration 4
Rhythm: March

Traditional Irish Folk Song

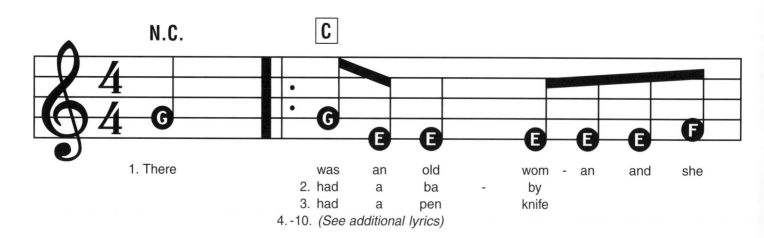

1. There was an old wom-an and she
2. had a ba - by
3. had a pen knife
4.-10. *(See additional lyrics)*

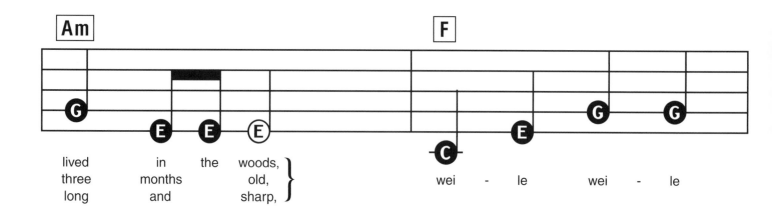

lived in the woods,
three months old,
long and sharp,

wei - le wei - le

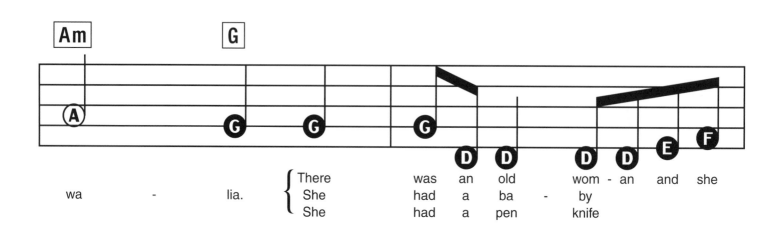

wa - lia.

There was an old wom-an and she
She had a ba - by
She had a pen knife

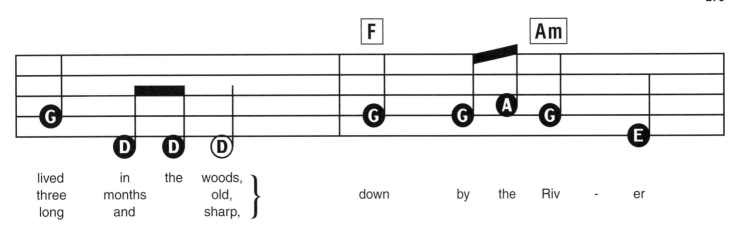

lived   in   the   woods,
three   months   old,
long   and   sharp,

down   by   the   Riv   -   er

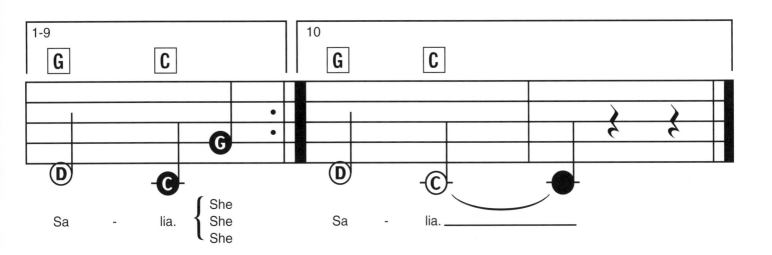

Sa   -   lia. { She / She / She }   Sa   -   lia. _____

Additional Lyrics

4. She stuck the pen knife in the baby's heart, weile, weile, walia.
She stuck the pen knife in the baby's heart, down by the River Salia.

5. Three loud knocks came a-knocking on the door, weile, weile, walia.
Three loud knocks came a-knocking on the door, down by the River Salia.

6. Two policemen and a man, weile, weile, walia.
Two policemen and a man, down by the River Salia.

7. "Are you the woman that killed the child?" weile, weile, walia.
"Are you the woman that killed the child?" down by the River Salia.

8. They tied her hands behind her back, weile, weile, walia.
They tied her hands behind her back, down by the River Salia.

9. The rope was pulled and she got hung, weile, weile, walia.
The rope was pulled and she got hung, down by the River Salia.

10. And that was the end of the woman in the woods, weile, weile, walia.
And that was the end of the baby too, down by the River Salia.

The West's Awake

Registration 10
Rhythm: Waltz

Traditional Irish Folk Song

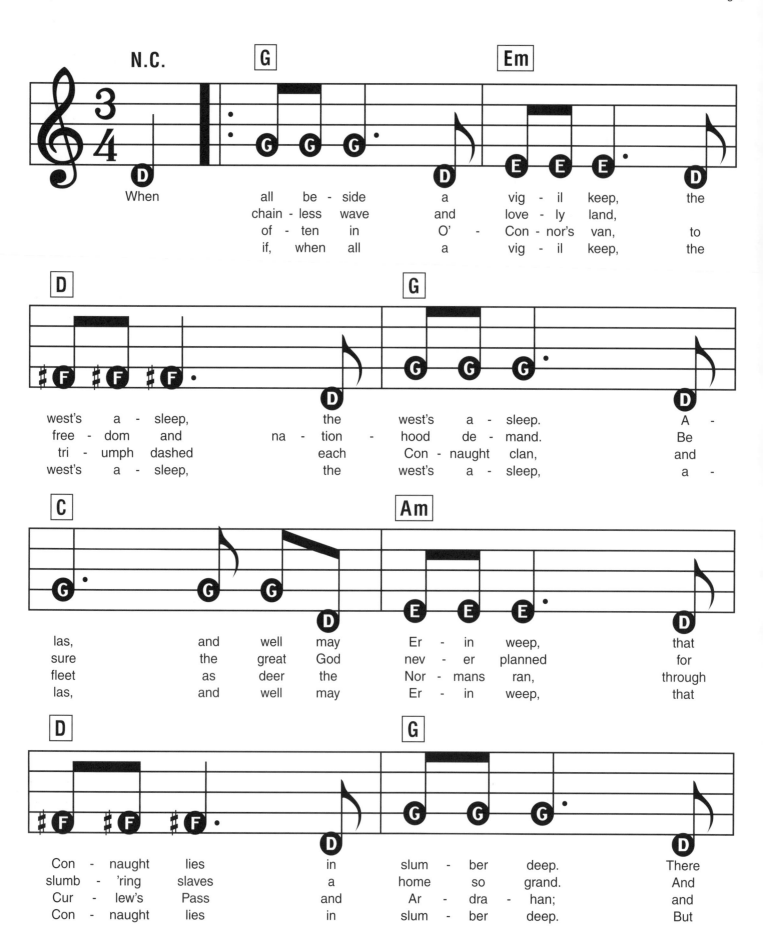

When Irish Eyes Are Smiling

Registration 3
Rhythm: Waltz

Words by Chauncey Olcott and George Graff, Jr.
Music by Ernest R. Ball

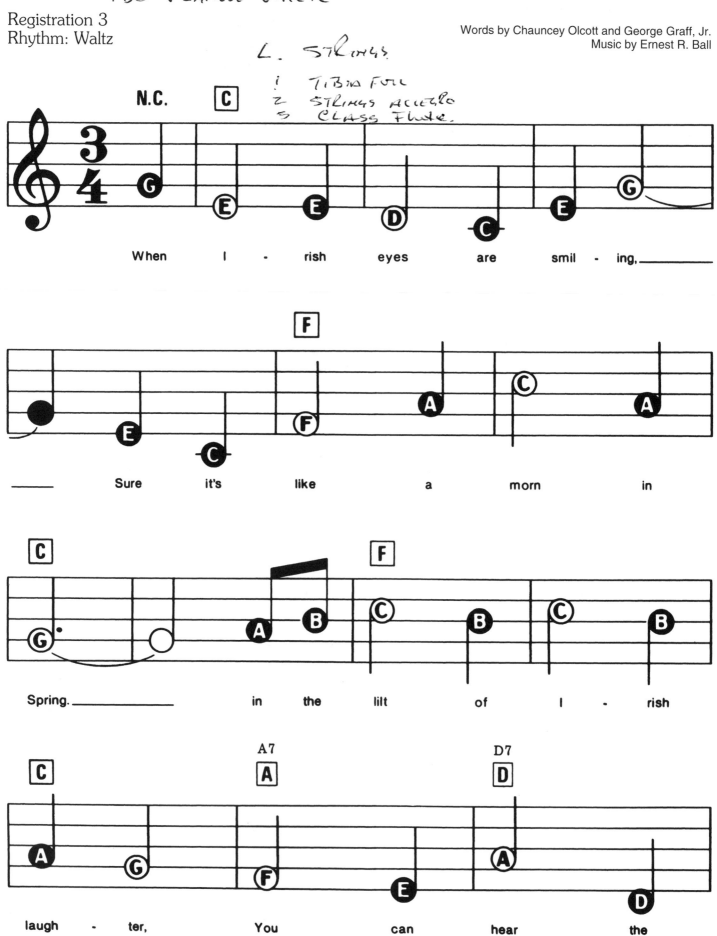

283

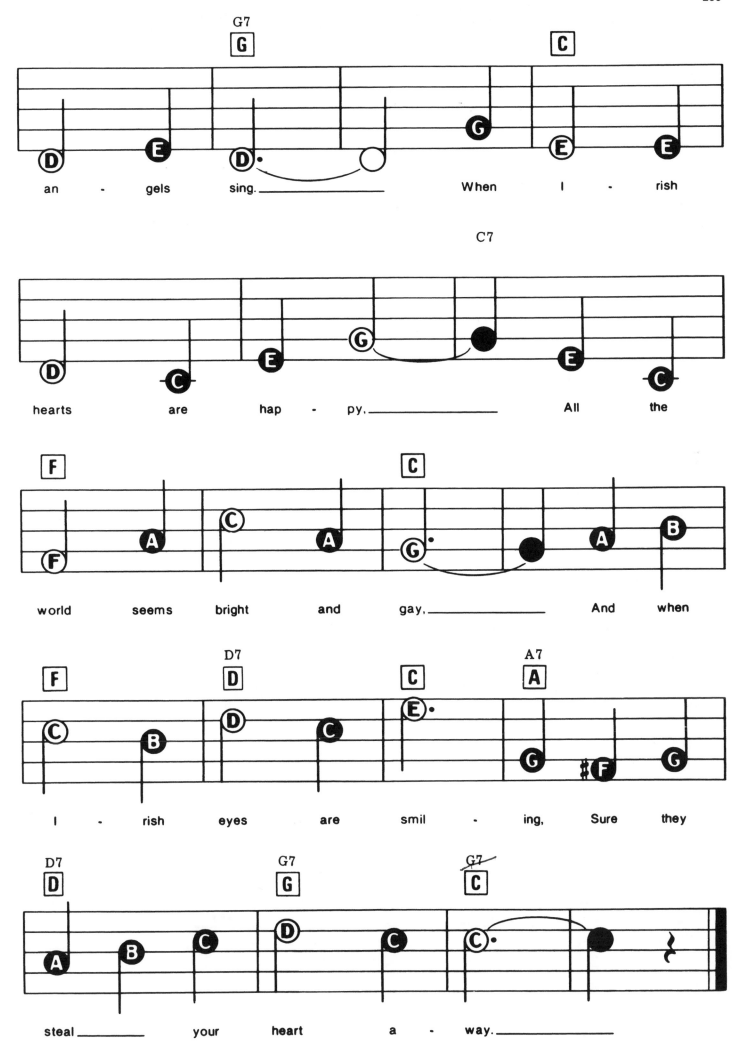

The Rocky Road to Dublin

Registration 1
Rhythm: Waltz

Traditional Irish Folk Song

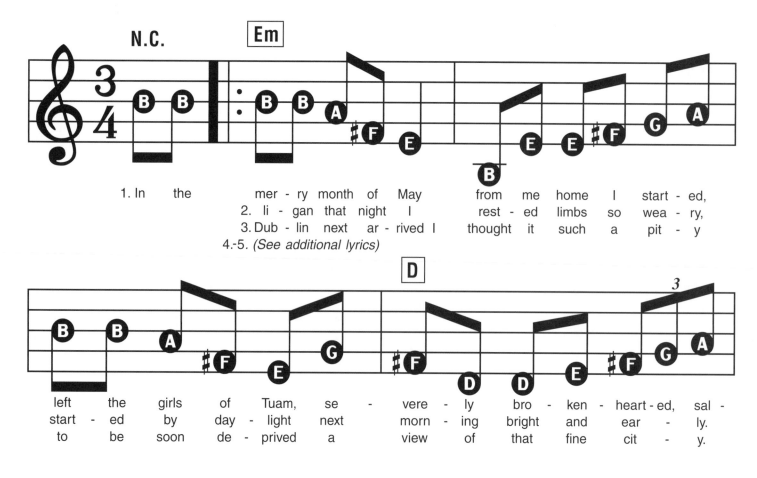

1. In the mer - ry month of May from me home I start - ed,
2. li - gan that night I rest - ed limbs so wea - ry,
3. Dub - lin next ar - rived I thought it such a pit - y
4.-5. *(See additional lyrics)*

left the girls of Tuam, se - vere - ly bro - ken - heart - ed, sal -
start - ed by day - light next morn - ing bright and ear - ly.
to be soon de - prived a view of that fine cit - y.

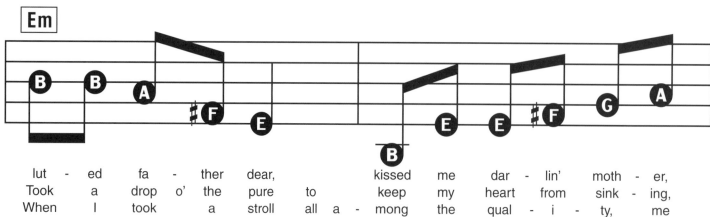

lut - ed fa - ther dear, kissed me dar - lin' moth - er,
Took a drop o' the pure to keep my heart from sink - ing,
When I took a stroll all a - mong the qual - i - ty, me

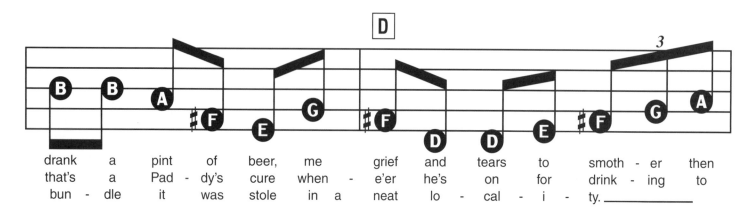

drank a pint of beer, me grief and tears to smoth - er then
that's a Pad - dy's cure when - e'er he's on for drink - ing to
bun - dle it was stole in a neat lo - cal - i - ty. _____

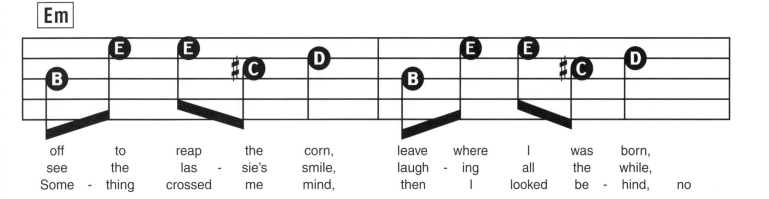

Em

off to reap the corn, leave where I was born,
see the las - sie's smile, laugh - ing all the while,
Some - thing crossed me mind, then I looked be - hind, no

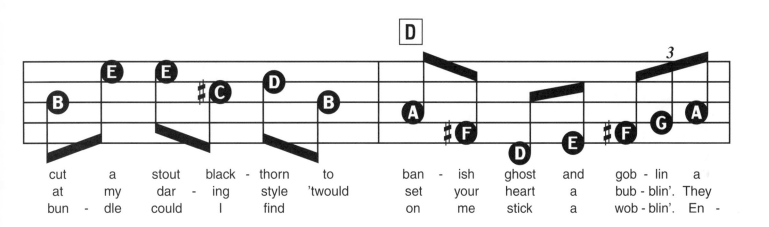

D

cut a stout black - thorn to ban - ish ghost and gob - lin a
at my dar - ing style 'twould set your heart a bub - blin'. They
bun - dle could I find on me stick a wob - blin'. En -

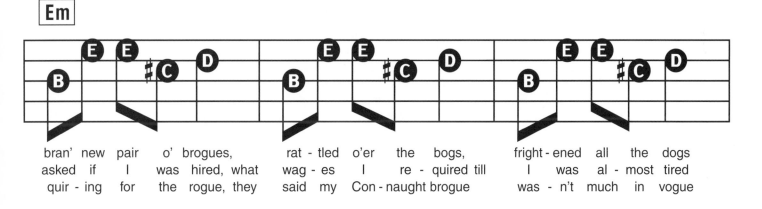

Em

bran' new pair o' brogues, rat - tled o'er the bogs, fright - ened all the dogs
asked if I was hired, what wag - es I re - quired till I was al - most tired
quir - ing for the rogue, they said my Con - naught brogue was - n't much in vogue

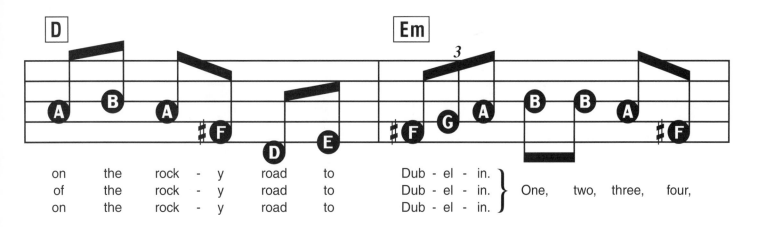

D   Em

on the rock - y road to Dub - el - in.
of the rock - y road to Dub - el - in. } One, two, three, four,
on the rock - y road to Dub - el - in.

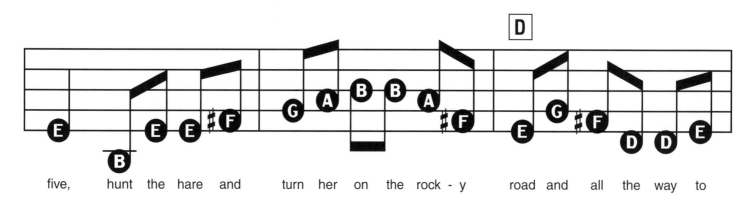

five, hunt the hare and turn her on the rock-y road and all the way to

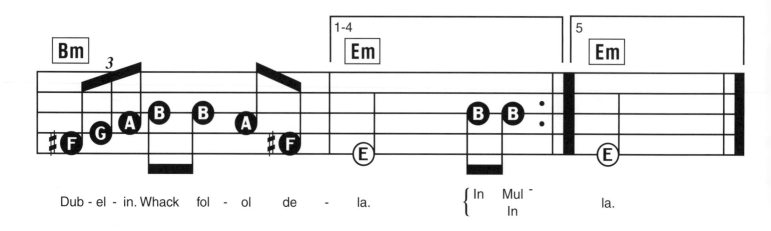

Dub-el-in. Whack fol - ol de - la. { In Mul - la.
  In

Additional Lyrics

4. From there I got away, me spirits never failing,
   Landed on the quay as the ship was sailing.
   Captain at me roared, said that no room had he.
   When I jumped aboard, a cabin for Paddy
   Down among the pigs I played some funny rigs
   Danced some hearty jigs, the water 'round me bubblin'
   When off Holyhead I wished meself was dead
   Or better far instead, on the rocky road to Dublin.

5. The boys of Liverpool when we safely landed
   Called meself a fool, I could no longer stand it.
   Blood began to boil, temper I was losing.
   Poor old Erin's Isle they began abusing.
   "Hurrah, me boys," says I, shillelagh I let fly
   Some Galway boys were by and saw I was a-hobblin'.
   Then with loud "Hurray!" they joined in the affray
   And quickly paved the way for the rocky road to Dublin.

The Wild Colonial Boy

Registration 5
Rhythm: Waltz

Australian Folk Song

288

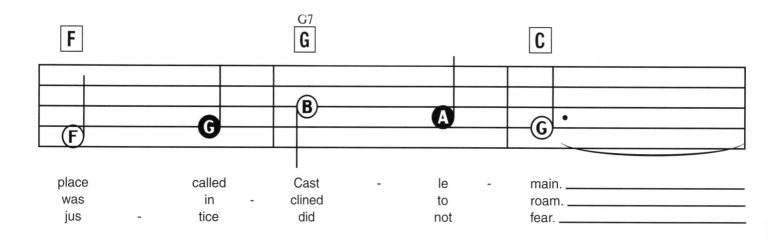

place   called   Cast - le - main._____
was   in - clined   to   roam._____
jus - tice   did   not   fear._____

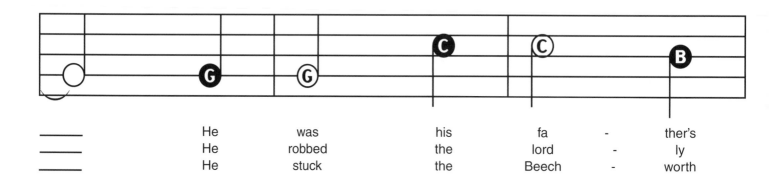

_____   He   was   his   fa - ther's
_____   He   robbed   the   lord - ly
_____   He   stuck   the   Beech - worth

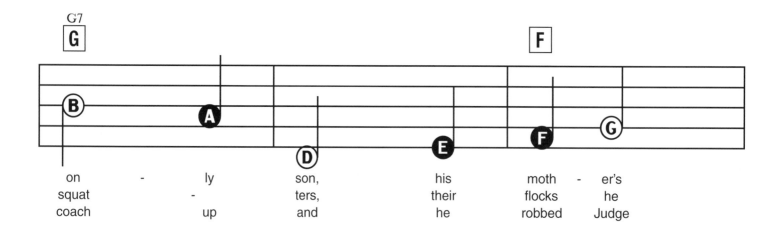

on - ly   son,   his   moth - er's
squat - ters,   their flocks he
coach   up   and   he   robbed Judge

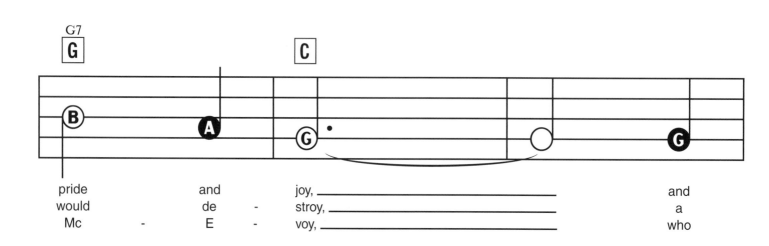

pride   and   joy,_____   and
would   de - stroy,_____   a
Mc - E - voy,_____   who

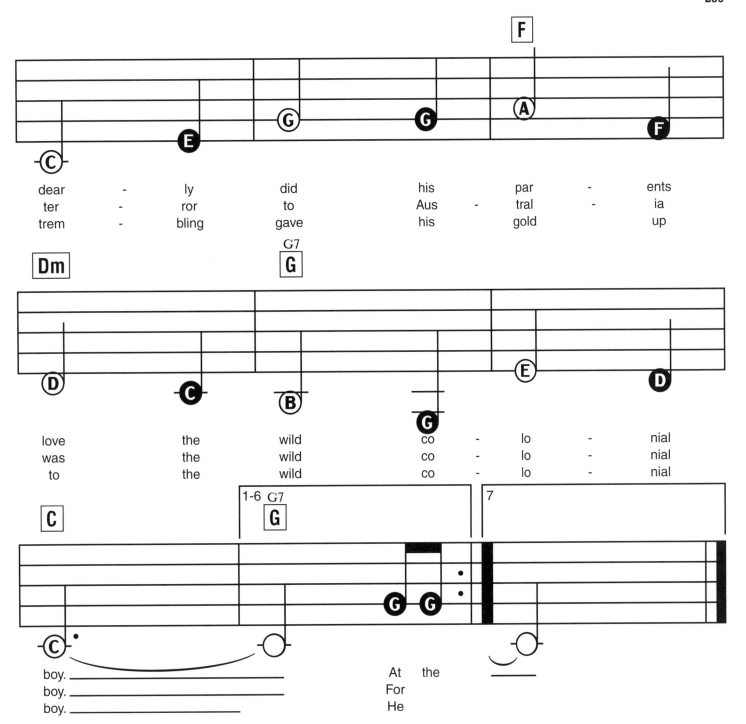

dear	-	ly	did	his	par	-	ents
ter	-	ror	to	Aus	-	tral	-	ia
trem	-	bling	gave	his	gold		up

love	the	wild	co	-	lo	-	nial
was	the	wild	co	-	lo	-	nial
to	the	wild	co	-	lo	-	nial

boy. _____		At the _____
boy. _____		For
boy. _____		He

Additional Lyrics

4. He bade the judge "Good morning" and he told him to beware,
   For he never robbed an honest judge what acted "on the square."
   Yet you would rob a mother of her son and only joy,
   And breed a race of outlaws like the wild colonial boy.

5. One morning on the prairie Wild Jack Duggan rode along,
   While listening to the mockingbirds singing a cheerful song.
   Out jumped three troopers fierce and grim, Kelly, Davis and FitzRoy,
   They all set out to capture him, the wild colonial boy.

6. "Surrender now, Jack Duggan, you can see there's three to one,
   Surrender in the Queen's name, sir, you are a plundering son."
   Jack drew two pistols from his side and glared upon FitzRoy,
   "I'll fight, but not surrender," cried the wild colonial boy.

7. He fired point-blank at Kelly and brought him to the ground.
   He fired a shot at Davis, too, who fell dead at the sound.
   But a bullet pierced his brave your heart from the pistol of FitzRoy,
   And that was how they captured him, the wild colonial boy.

The Zoological Gardens

Registration 1
Rhythm: Waltz

Traditional Irish Folk Song

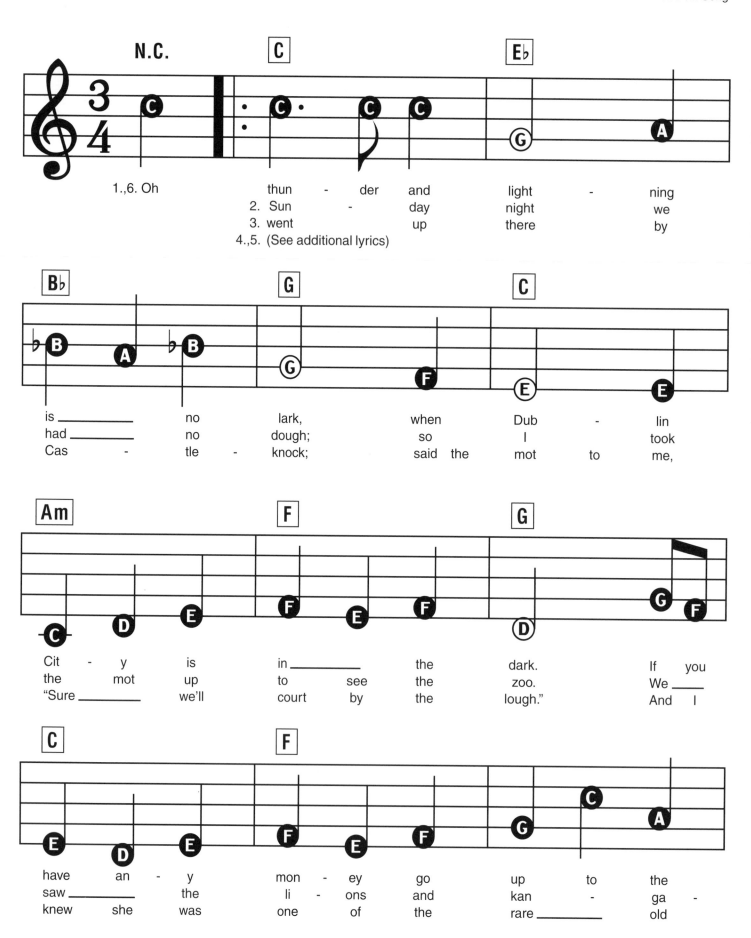

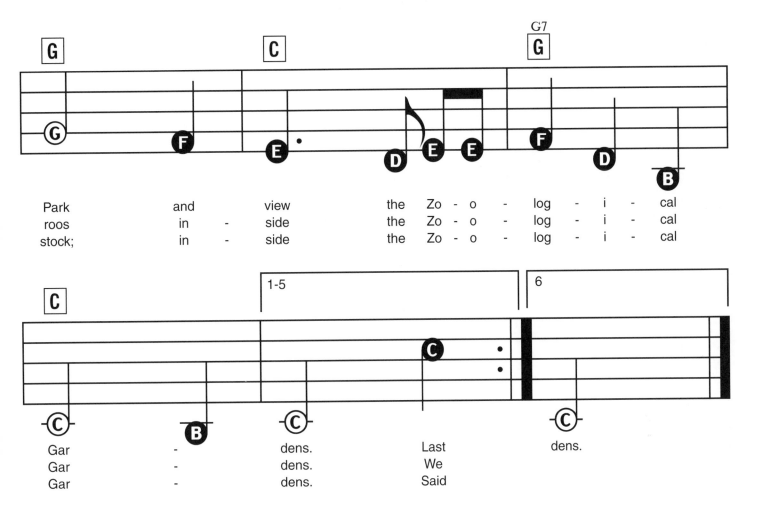

Park	and	view	the	Zo	-	o	-	log	-	i	-	cal
roos	in	- side	the	Zo	-	o	-	log	-	i	-	cal
stock;	in	- side	the	Zo	-	o	-	log	-	i	-	cal

Gar	-	dens.	Last	dens.
Gar	-	dens.	We	
Gar	-	dens.	Said	

Additional Lyrics

4. Said the mot to me, "My dear friend Jack;
Would you like a ride on the elephant's back?"
If you don't get outta that I'll give you such a crack;
Inside the Zoological Gardens.

5. We went up there on our honeymoon;
Says she to me, "If you don't come soon
Sure I'll have to jump in with the hairy baboon;
Inside the Zoological Gardens.

6. *(Repeat 1st verse)*

MORE CELTIC & IRISH SONGBOOKS

The popularity of Celtic music has soared over the last decade
due to the resurgence of folk instruments, Celtic dancing, and Irish culture overall.

Learn how to play these beloved songs with these great songbooks!

THE BEST OF IRISH MUSIC

80 of the best Irish songs ever written in one comprehensive collection. Includes: Danny Boy • If I Knock the "L" out of Kelly • Macnamara's Band • Molly Malone • My Wild Irish Rose • Peg o' My Heart • Too-Ra-Loo-Ra-Loo-Ral (That's an Irish Lullaby) • Wearin' of the Green • When Irish Eyes Are Smiling • and more.
00315064 P/V/G $16.95

THE BIG BOOK OF IRISH SONGS

A great collection of 75 beloved Irish tunes, from folk songs to Tin Pan Alley favorites! Includes: Erin! Oh Erin! • Father O'Flynn • Finnegan's Wake • I'll Take You Home Again, Kathleen • The Irish Rover • The Irish Washerwoman • Jug of Punch • Kerry Dance • Who Threw the Overalls in Mrs. Murphy's Chowder • Wild Rover • and more.
00310981 P/V/G $19.95

THE CELTIC COLLECTION

The Phillip Keveren Series

Features 15 traditional Irish folk tunes masterfully arranged in Celtic style by the incomparable Phillip Keveren. Songs include: Be Thou My Vision • The Galway Piper • Kitty of Coleraine • The Lark in the Clear Air • Molly Malone (Cockles & Mussels) • and more.
00310549 Piano Solo $12.95

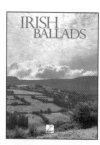

THE GRAND IRISH SONGBOOK

125 cherished folk songs, including: Believe Me, If All Those Endearing Young Charms • The Croppy Boy • Danny Boy • The Galway Races • Johnny, I Hardly Knew You • Jug of Punch • My Wild Irish Rose • Too-Ra-Loo-Ra-Loo-Ral (That's an Irish Lullaby) • The Wearing of the Green • When Irish Eyes Are Smiling • and more.
00311320 P/V/G $19.95

IRISH BALLADS

Nearly 60 traditional Irish ballads, including: Black Velvet Band • Brennan on the Moor • Cliffs of Doneen • Down by the Sally Gardens • I Know My Love • I Never Will Marry • Johnny, I Hardly Knew You • Leaving of Liverpool • Minstrel Boy • Red Is the Rose • When You Were Sweet Sixteen • Wild Rover • and more.
00311322 P/V/G $14.95

IRISH FAVORITES

From sentimental favorites to happy-go-lucky singalongs, this songbook celebrates the Irish cultural heritage of music. 30 songs, including: Danny Boy (Londonderry Air) • The Girl I Left Behind Me • Killarney • My Wild Irish Rose • Tourelay • Who Threw the Overalls in Mistress Murphy's Chowder • and more!
00311615..$10.95

IRISH PUB SONGS

Grab a pint and this songbook for an evening of Irish fun! 40 songs, including: All for Me Grog • The Fields of Athenry • I Never Will Marry • I'm a Rover and Seldom Sober • The Irish Rover • Jug of Punch • Leaving of Liverpool • A Nation Once Again • The Rare Ould Times • Whiskey in the Jar • Whiskey, You're the Devil • and more.
00311321 P/V/G $12.95

IRISH SONGS

25 traditional favorites, including: At the Ball of Kirriemuir • At the End of the Rainbow • Dear Old Donegal • Galway Bay • Hannigan's Hooley • The Isle of Innisfree • It's the Same Old Shillelagh • The Moonshiner • The Spinning Wheel • The Whistling Gypsy • Will Ye Go, Lassie, Go • and more.
00311323 P/V/G $12.95

THE CELTIC FAKE BOOK

This amazing collection assembles over 400 songs from Ireland, Scotland and Wales – complete with Gaelic lyrics where applicable – and a pronunciation guide. Titles include: Across the Western Ocean • Along with My Love I'll Go • Altar Isle o' the Sea • Auld Lang Syne • Avondale • The Band Played On • Barbara Allen • Blessing of the Road • The Blue Bells of Scotland • The Bonniest Lass • A Bunch of Thyme • The Chanty That Beguiled the Witch • Columbus Was an Irishman • Danny Boy • Duffy's Blunders • Erin! Oh Erin! • Father Murphy • Finnegan's Wake • The Galway Piper • The Girl I Left Behind Me • Has Anybody Here Seen Kelly • I Know Where I'm Goin' • Irish Rover • Loch Lomond • My Bonnie Lies over the Ocean • The Shores of Amerikay • The Sons of Liberty • Who Threw the Overalls in Mistress Murphy's Chowder • and hundreds more. Also includes many Irish popular songs as a bonus.
00240153 Melody/Lyrics/Chords $19.95

1006

HAL•LEONARD ESSENTIAL SONGS

FOR ORGANS, PIANOS & ELECTRONIC KEYBOARDS

E-Z PLAY® TODAY

Play the best songs from the Roaring '20s to today! Each collection features dozens of the most memorable songs of each decade, arranged in our world-famous, patented E-Z Play® Today notation.

The notation features easy-to-read, easy-to-play music with the notes in the note head and oversized notation. Books also include a registration guide and guitar chord chart.

ESSENTIAL SONGS – THE 1920s

Over 100 songs that shaped the decade, including: Ain't We Got Fun? • All by Myself • April Showers • Basin Street Blues • Bill • The Birth of the Blues • Blue Skies • Bye Bye Blackbird • California, Here I Come • Can't Help Lovin' Dat Man • Chicago (That Toddlin' Town) • Five Foot Two, Eyes of Blue (Has Anybody Seen My Girl?) • I Can't Give You Anything but Love • I Wanna Be Loved by You • I'm Looking Over a Four Leaf Clover • If You Knew Susie (Like I Know Susie) • Indian Love Call • Let a Smile Be Your Umbrella • Look for the Silver Lining • Makin' Whoopee! • Manhattan • Moonlight and Roses (Bring Mem'ries of You) • My Blue Heaven • Ol' Man River • Puttin' On the Ritz • St. Louis Blues • Second Hand Rose • Stardust • Thou Swell • Toot, Toot, Tootsie! (Good-bye!) • 'Way down Yonder in New Orleans • Who's Sorry Now • Yes Sir, That's My Baby • and more.
00100214 E-Z Play Today #23 ....$16.95

ESSENTIAL SONGS – THE 1930s

101 essential songs from the 1930s, including: All the Things You Are • April in Paris • Autumn in New York • Body and Soul • Cheek to Cheek • Cherokee (Indian Love Song) • Easy to Love (You'd Be So Easy to Love) • Falling in Love with Love • Georgia on My Mind • Heart and Soul • How Deep Is the Ocean (How High Is the Sky) • I'll Be Seeing You • I've Got My Love to Keep Me Warm • In a Sentimental Mood • In the Mood • Isn't It Romantic? • The Lady Is a Tramp • Mood Indigo • My Funny Valentine • Pennies from Heaven • September Song • You Are My Sunshine • and more.
00100206 E-Z Play Today #24 ....$16.95

ESSENTIAL SONGS – THE 1940s

An amazing collection of over 100 songs that came out of the 1940s, including: Ac-cent-tchu-ate the Positive • Anniversary Song • Be Careful, It's My Heart • Bewitched • Boogie Woogie Bugle Boy • Don't Get Around Much Anymore • Have I Told You Lately That I Love You • I'll Remember April • Is You Is, or Is You Ain't (Ma' Baby) • It Could Happen to You • It Might As Well Be Spring • Route 66 • Sentimental Journey • Stella by Starlight • The Surrey with the Fringe on Top • Take the "A" Train • They Say It's Wonderful • This Nearly Was Mine • You'd Be So Nice to Come Home To • You're Nobody 'til Somebody Loves You • and more.
00100207 E-Z Play Today #25 ....$16.95

ESSENTIAL SONGS – THE 1950s

Over 100 pivotal songs from the 1950s, including: All Shook Up • At the Hop • Blueberry Hill • Bye Bye Love • Chantilly Lace • Don't Be Cruel (To a Heart That's True) • Fever • Great Balls of Fire • Kansas City • Love and Marriage • Mister Sandman • Mona Lisa • (You've Got) Personality • Rock Around the Clock • Sea of Love • Sixteen Tons • Smoke Gets in Your Eyes • Tennessee Waltz • Tom Dooley • Twilight Time • Wear My Ring Around Your Neck • Wonderful! Wonderful! • and more.
00100208 E-Z Play Today #51 ....$17.95

FOR MORE INFORMATION, SEE YOUR LOCAL MUSIC DEALER, OR WRITE TO:

HAL•LEONARD® CORPORATION
7777 W. BLUEMOUND RD. P.O. BOX 13819 MILWAUKEE, WI 53213

ESSENTIAL SONGS – THE 1960s

104 '60s essentials, including: Baby Love • Barbara Ann • Born to Be Wild • California Girls • Can't Buy Me Love • Dancing in the Street • Downtown • Good Vibrations • Hang on Sloopy • Hey Jude • I Heard It Through the Grapevine • It's Not Unusual • My Guy • Respect • Something • Spooky • Stand by Me • Stop! in the Name of Love • Suspicious Minds • A Time for Us (Love Theme) • Twist and Shout • Will You Love Me Tomorrow (Will You Still Love Me Tomorrow) • Yesterday • You Keep Me Hangin' On • and more.
00100209 E-Z Play Today #52..............................$17.95

ESSENTIAL SONGS – THE 1970s

A fantastic collection of 98 of the best songs from the '70s, including: ABC • After-noon Delight • American Pie • At Seventeen • Baker Street • Band on the Run • The Boys Are Back in Town • Come Sail Away • Da Ya Think I'm Sexy • Do You Know Where You're Going To? • Dust in the Wind • Feelings (¿Dime?) • I Feel the Earth Move • Knock Three Times • Let It Be • Morning Has Broken • Smoke on the Water • Take a Chance on Me • The Way We Were • What's Going On • You Are the Sunshine of My Life • You Light Up My Life • You're So Vain • Your Song • and more.
00100210 E-Z Play Today #53..............................$19.95

ESSENTIAL SONGS – THE 1980s

Over 70 classics from the age of new wave, power pop, and hair metal, including: Abracadabra • Against All Odds (Take a Look at Me Now) • Axel F • Call Me • Centerfold • Don't You (Forget About Me) • Ebony and Ivory • The Heat Is On • Higher Love • Hurts So Good • Jump • Man in the Mirror • Manic Monday • Material Girl • Sister Christian • Somewhere Out There • Take My Breath Away (Love Theme) • Time After Time • Up Where We Belong • We Are the World • What's Love Got to Do with It • and more.
00100211 E-Z Play Today #54..............................$19.95

Complete contents listings are available online at **www.halleonard.com**

Prices, contents, and availability subject to change without notice.

FOR ORGANS, PIANOS & ELECTRONIC KEYBOARDS

E-Z PLAY® TODAY PUBLICATIONS

The E-Z Play® Today songbook series is the shortest distance between beginning music and playing fun! It features full-size 9" x 12" books with patented easy-to-read, easy-to-play notation. The accurate arrangements are simple enough for the beginner, but with authentic-sounding chord and melody lines. The books also include a registration guide for choosing appropriate keyboard sounds.

FOR MORE INFORMATION, SEE YOUR LOCAL MUSIC DEALER, OR WRITE TO:

HAL•LEONARD® CORPORATION

7777 W. BLUEMOUND RD. P.O. BOX 13819 MILWAUKEE, WI 53213

Songlists and more titles available at **www.halleonard.com**

Prices, contents, and availability subject to change without notice.